THE GLOBALIZATION OF POVERTY
AND THE NEW WORLD ORDER

Second Edition

Also by Michel Chossudovsky

War and Globalisation
The Truth Behind September 11

The Globalization of Poverty
and the New World Order

Second Edition

Michel Chossudovsky

Global Research

The Globalization of Poverty and the New World Order — Second Edition. Copyright © 2003 by Michel Chossudovsky. All rights reserved — Global Research, Center for Research on Globalization (CRG).

Global Research is a division of the Centre for Research on Globalization (CRG) 101, boul. Cardinal-Léger, P.O. Box 51004, Pincourt (Québec) J7V 9T3 Canada

For more information contact the publisher at the above address or by email at our website at www.globalresearch.ca

SECOND EDITION
Cover Artwork by Paul Marcus, © 2003
Cover Graphics by Richard Corey and Blaine Machan

Printed and bound in Canada
Printed on acid free paper
ISBN 0-9737147-0-0

Library of Congress Cataloging-in-Publication Data

Chossudovsky, Michel

The Globalization of Poverty and the New World Order / Michel Chossudovsky / 2nd ed.
Includes bibliographical references and index
ISBN 0-9737147-0-0 (paperback)
First ed. published under the title: The Globalisation of Poverty: Impacts of IMF and World Bank Reforms

1. International Monetary Fund – Developing countries. 2. International Monetary Fund – Europe, Eastern. 3. World Bank – Developing countries. 4. World Bank – Europe, Eastern. 5. Poverty – Developing countries. 6. Poverty – Europe, Eastern. I. International Monetary Fund. II. World Bank. III. Title.

HG3881.5 I58 C47 2003   339.4'6 – dc20   2003-22287

National Library of Canada Cataloguing in Publication

Chossudovsky, Michel

The Globalization of Poverty and the New World Order / Michel Chossudovsky / 2nd ed.
Includes bibliographical references and index
ISBN 0-9737147-0-0
First ed. published under the title: The Globalisation of Poverty: Impacts of IMF and World Bank Reforms

1. International Monetary Fund – Developing countries. 2. International Monetary Fund – Europe, Eastern. 3. World Bank – Developing countries. 4. World Bank – Europe, Eastern. 5. Poverty – Developing countries. 6. Poverty – Europe, Eastern. I. Title.

HG3881.5 I58 C47 2003   339.4'6   C2003-902648-5

To my daughters Maya and Natacha

Content

Preface to the Second Edition   xxi

Introduction   1
    The Post Cold War Recession   1
    Demise of the "Asian Tigers"   2
    Poverty and Economic Dislocation in the West   3
    A Thriving Criminal Economy   4
    Wall Street Bankers behind the Scenes   5
    The Cheap Labor Economy   5
    Accumulation of Wealth,
    Distortion of Production   7
    Overproduction: Increased
    Supply, Reduced Demand   8
    Global Integration, Local Disintegration   8
    Destroying the Local Economy   9
    War and Globalization   10
    Disarming the New World Order   11

PART I
GLOBAL POVERTY AND MACRO-ECONOMIC REFORM

Chapter 1
The Globalization of Poverty   17
    Global Geopolitics   17
    Social Polarization and the
    Concentration of Wealth   18
    IMF Economic Medicine   18
    Economic Genocide
    Destroying the National Economy   20
    The Dollarization of Prices   20
    The "Thirdworldization" of the
    Former Eastern Bloc   21
    The Role of Global Institutions   22
    Entrenched Rights for Banks and
    Multinational Corporations   22

Chapter 2

Global Falsehoods   27

   Manipulating the Figures on Global Poverty   28

   Defining Poverty at "a Dollar a Day"   29

   The United Nations' Poverty Figures   29

   Double Standards in the "Scientific"

   Measurement of Poverty   30

   Concealing Country-level Realities   32

Chapter 3

Policing Countries Through Loan "Conditionalities"   35

   The Global Debt   35

   A Marshall Plan for the Rich Countries   42

   Policy-based Lending   42

   Enlarging the Debt   43

   The IMF "Shadow Program"   44

   The Policy Framework Paper   45

   The IFIs' Lending Facilities   47

   International Monetary Fund   47

   World Bank   47

   Phase One: "Economic Stabilization"   47

   Destroying A Nation's Currency   47

   The Social Consequences of Devaluation   48

   The "Dollarization" of Domestic Prices   49

   The Deindexation of Wages   49

   Analyzing the Impact of Devaluation   49

   Taking Control of the Central Bank   50

   Destabilizing a Nation's Public Finances   51

   The Budget Deficit: A Moving Target   51

   Engineering the Collapse of–

   State Investment   52

   Price Liberalization   52

   The Pricing of Petroleum

   Products and Public Utilities   53

   Phase Two: "Structural Reform"   54

   Trade Liberalization   54

Divestiture and Privatization of
State Enterprises 55
Tax Reform 55
Land Tenure and the Privatization of
Agricultural Land 55
Deregulation of the Banking System 56
Liberalizing Capital Movements 57
Recycling Dirty Money towards
Debt Servicing 57
"Poverty Alleviation" and the
"Social Safety Net" 58
"Good Governance": Promoting
Bogus Parliamentary Institutions 58
The Consequences of Structural Adjustment 59
The IMF Tacitly Acknowledges Policy Failure 60
The Counterfactual Argument 60
The Social Impact of Macro-economic Reform 61
The Restructuring of the Health Sector 62
The Resurgence of Communicable Diseases 62

Chapter 4
The World Bank and Women's Rights 65
The World Bank's Gender Perspective 65
Derogating Women's Educational Rights 66
Cost Recovery in Health 67
Hidden Agenda 67

Chapter 5
The Global Cheap-Labor Economy 69
Introduction 69
Macro-economic Reform Supports the
Relocation of Industry 70
Industrial Export Promotion 71
Global Adjustment 71
"Decomposition" of National Economies 72
World Unemployment 73
Declining Wages 74

Plant Closures and Industrial Delocation
in the Developed Countries   74
The Worldwide Compression
of Consumer Spending   75
Relocation within Trading Blocs   76
The Dynamic Development
of Luxury Consumption   77
The Rentier Economy   78
The Globalization of Manufacturing   79
Import-led Growth in the Rich Countries   79
The Appropriation of Surplus
by non-Producers   80
An Example: the Garment Industry   81
Wages and Labor Costs
in the Developed Countries   82
Mobile and Immobile Sectors   90
The Immobility of Labor   90
The Sectors of non-Material Production   90
The Impact of the Scientific Revolution   91
The Delocation of the Services Economy   91

PART II
SUB-SAHARAN AFRICA

Chapter 6
Somalia: the Real Causes of Famine   95
The IMF Intervention in the Early 1980s   95
Towards the Destruction of Food Agriculture   96
Collapse of the Livestock Economy   96
Destroying the State   97
Famine Formation in sub-Saharan Africa:
The Lessons of Somalia   99
Concluding Remarks   100

Chapter 7

Economic Genocide in Rwanda   103

Part A

The IMF and the World Bank set the Stage   103

The Legacy of Colonialism   104
The Economy since Independence   106
The Fragility of the State   107
The IMF-World Bank Intervention   107

Part B

Installing a US Protectorate in Central Africa   111

Militarization of Uganda   112
Militarization and the Ugandan External Debt   112
Financing both Sides in the Civil War   113
Postwar Cover-up   115
In the Wake of the Civil War:
Reinstating the IMF's Deadly Economic Reforms   115
Post War "Reconstruction and Reconciliation"   116
Civil War in the Congo   117
American Mining Interests   118
Concluding Remarks   118

Chapter 8

"Exporting Apartheid" to sub-Saharan Africa   125

The Expropriation of Peasant Lands   126
Derogating Customary Land Rights   128
Afrikaner Farms in Mozambique   128
Creating "Rural Townships"   130
Foreign Aid Supports the
Establishments of White Farms   131
Fostering Ecotourism   132
Carving up the National Territory   133

Chapter 9

Wreaking Ethiopia's Peasant Economy,
Destroying Biodiversity   137

Crisis in the Horn   137
The Promise of the "Free Market"   138
Wrecking the Peasant Economy   139
Laundering America's GM Grain Surpluses   141
Biodiversity up for Sale   142
Impacts of Famine   143

PART III
SOUTH AND SOUTHEAST ASIA

Chapter 10

India: The IMF's "Indirect Rule"   149

Introduction   149
Crushing the Rural and Urban Poor   151
"Eliminating the Poor" through
Starvation Deaths   152
The IMF Supports Caste Exploitation   154
Poverty Supports Exports
to the Rich Countries   154
Towards Political Collapse   155
The IMF's Indirect Rule   155

Chapter 11

Bangladesh: Under the Tutelage of the "Aid" Consortium   159

The 1975 Military Coup   159
The Establishment of a Parallel Government   160
Establishing a Bogus Democracy   160
Supervising the Allocation of State Funds   161
Undermining the Rural Economy   161
Dumping US Grain Surpluses   162
Undermining Food Self-Sufficiency   163
The Fate of Local Industry   163
The Recycling of Aid Money   164
"The Social Dimensions of Adjustment"   164

Chapter 12

The Post-War Economic Destruction of Vietnam   167

Rewriting the History of the War   168

The New Vietnam War   169

Reimbursing the "Bad Debts"
of the Saigon Regime   170

Destroying the National Economy   171

Excluding Domestic Producers
from their Own Market   173

Thwarting the Channels of Internal Trade   173

The Disintegration of the
State's Public Finances   174

Collapse of State Capital Formation   175

Reintegrating the Japanese Empire   176

The Outbreak of Famine   177

Child Malnutrition   179

Into the Net of International Agri-business   180

Vietnam as a Major Exporter of Rice   180

The Concentration of Land   181

The Destruction of Education   183

Collapse of the Health System   185

The Resurgence of Infectious Diseases   186

PART IV
LATIN AMERICA

Chapter 13

Debt and "Democracy" in Brazil   191

Brazil's Debt Saga: Act I: Plan Collor   193

Act II: Conforming to
"The Washington Consensus"   194

Act III: In the Aftermath
of Collor's Impeachment   196

Act IV: A Marxist Sociologist
as Finance Minister   197

Act V: Rescheduling the Commercial Debt   198

Act VI, Epilogue: The Management
of Poverty at Minimal Cost to the Creditors   200
Consolidating a Parallel Government   203

Chapter 14
IMF Shock Treatment in Peru   207
Historical Background   208
The APRA's Non Orthodox
Economic Policy (1985-87)   211
The APRA's Debt-Negotiating Strategy   212
The Economic Program Enters a Deadlock   213
De Facto "Shock Treatment" (1988-90)   214
Failure of the APRA's Non-orthodox
Economic Package   215
The Restoration of IMF Rule   215
The August 1990 IMF-Fujishock   216
The IMF-World Bank Tutelage   218
The Granting of Fictitious Money   219
The Role of the Military   219
The Collapse of the State   220
The Plight of the Rural Economy   221
The Concentration of Land   221
The Illegal Narco-economy   222
The Anti-Drug Agreement with Washington   223
US Military and Security Objectives   225

Chapter 15
Debt and the Illegal Drug Economy: The Case of Bolivia   229
Bolivia's New Economic Policy   229
Economic and Social Impact   230
Programmed Economic Stagnation   231
The Impact on the Rural Economy   231
The Laundering of Dirty Money   232
"Eradication" of Coca Production   231
The Narco-State   231

PART V
THE FORMER SOVIET UNION AND THE BALKANS

Chapter 16
The "Thirdworldization" of the Russian Federation   239
    Macro-Economic Reform
    in the Russian Federation   239
    Phase I: The January 1992
    Shock Treatment   239
    The Legacy of Perestroika   241
    Developing a Bazaar Bourgeoisie   242
    Distorting Social Relations   242
    Pillage of the Russian Economy   243
    Undermining Russian Capitalism   243
    Acquiring State Property "at a Good Price"   244
    Weakening Russia's High-Tech Economy   245
    Taking Over Russia's Banking System   246
    Undermining the Ruble Zone   247
    Phase II: The IMF Reforms Enter an Impasse   247
    Abolishing the Parliament
    in the Name of "Governance"   248
    "Western Aid" to Boris Yeltsin   250
    Into the Strait-Jacket of Debt-Servicing   251
    The Collapse of Civil Society   251

Chapter 17
Dismantling Former Yugoslavia,
Recolonizing Bosnia-Herzegovina   257
    Neocolonial Bosnia   258
    Historical background   259
    Mr. Markovic goes to Washington   261
    Crushed by the Invisible Hand   262
    Overhauling the Legal Framework   262
    The Bankruptcy Program   263
    "Shedding Surplus Workers"   264
    The Political Economy of Disintegration   265

"Western Help" 266
Post War Reconstruction
and the "Free Market" 267
Reconstruction Colonial Style 269
From Bosnia to Kosovo 270
Taking over Kosovo's Mineral Wealth 272
The Installation of a Mafia State 273
Neoliberalism, the Only Possible World? 273

Chapter 18
Albania's IMF Sponsored Financial Disaster 279
Historical Background of the Crisis 279
The IMF-World Bank Sponsored Reforms 280
An "Economic Success Story" 281
The Bankruptcy Programme 282
Financial Deregulation 283
The Scramble for State Property 286
Selling Off Strategic Industries 286
Foreign Control over Infrastructure 287
The Grey Economy 287
Rural Collapse 288
Macro-economic Chaos 290
The Outbreak of Endemic Diseases 291
Criminalization of the State 291
"Guns and Ammo for Greater Albania" 292
Organized Crime Invests in Legal Business 293
Recycling Dirty Money Towards
Western Creditors 294
What Prospects under the Socialists? 295

PART VI
THE NEW WORLD ORDER

Chapter 19
Structural Adjustment in the Developed Countries 301
Dismantling the Welfare State 301
The Conversion of Private Debts 302

Towards a Narrowing of the Tax Base   303
Under the Political Trusteeship
of Finance Capital   304
The Illusory "Independence"
of the Central Bank   304
Crisis of the State   305

Chapter 20
Global Financial Meltdown   309
The 1987 Wall Street Crash   309
The Institutional Speculator   310
The 1997 Financial Meltdown   311
The Asian Crisis   314
"Economic Contagion"   314
The 1998 Stock Market Meltdown   315
Financial Deregulation   315
The Merger Frenzy   316
Financial Deregulation at a Global Level   317

Chapter 21
Economic Warfare   321
Manipulating the "Free Market"   321
The Demise of Central Banking   322
Creditors and Speculators   323
Who Funds the IMF Bailouts?   324
Strong Economic Medicine   325
Deregulating Capital Movements   326
Speculators Call the Shots
on Crisis Management   326
The Concentration of Wealth   327

Chapter 22
The Recolonization of Korea   331
The IMF Mission Arrives in Seoul   331
Shuttling back to Washington   333
"Arm Twisting" in the wake
of the Presidential Race   334

Enforcing "Enabling Legislation"
through Financial Blackmail 334
Wall Street Bankers meet on Christmas Eve. 337
No Capital Inflows under the Bailout 337
The Macro-Economic Agenda 337
Dismantling the Chaebols 338
Wall Street on a Shopping Spree 339
Taking over Korea's Commercial Banks 340
California and Texas Tycoons to the Rescue 340
US and German Capitalists share the Spoils 342
Instating a System of Direct Colonial Rule 343
Reunification and the "Free Market" 343
Colonizing North Korea 344

Chapter 23
The Brazilian Financial Scam 347
Squeezing Credit 348
Background of the IMF Agreement 348
Enticing Speculators 349
"A Marshall Plan for Creditors and Speculators" 350
Wall Street in Charge of Brazil's Central Bank 351
"Dollarization" of Latin America 351
SELECTED BIBLIOGRAPHY 355
INDEX 369

Preface to the Second Edition

Barely a few weeks after the military coup in Chile on September 11, 1973, overthrowing the elected government of President Salvador Allende, the military Junta headed by General Augusto Pinochet ordered a hike in the price of bread from 11 to 40 escudos, a hefty overnight increase of 264%. This *economic shock treatment* had been designed by a group of economists called the "Chicago Boys".

At the time of the military coup, I was teaching at the Institute of Economics of the Catholic University of Chile, which was a nest of Chicago trained economists, disciples of Milton Friedman. On that September 11, in the hours following the bombing of the Presidential Palace of La Moneda, the new military rulers imposed a 72-hour curfew. When the university reopened several days later, the "Chicago Boys" were rejoicing. Barely a week later, several of my colleagues at the Institute of Economics were appointed to key positions in the military government.

While food prices had skyrocketed, wages had been frozen to ensure "economic stability and stave off inflationary pressures." From one day to the next, an entire country was precipitated into abysmal poverty: in less than a year the price of bread in Chile increased thirty-six times and eighty-five percent of the Chilean population had been driven below the poverty line.

These events affected me profoundly in my work as an economist. Through the tampering of prices, wages and interest rates, people's lives had been destroyed; an entire national economy had been destabilized. I started to understand that macro-economic reform was neither "neutral" – as claimed by the academic mainstream – nor separate from the broader process of social and political transformation. In my earlier writings on the Chilean military Junta, I looked upon the so-called "free market" as a well-organized instrument of "economic repression".

Two years later in 1976, I returned to Latin America as a visiting professor at the National University of Cordoba in the northern industrial heartland of Argentina. My stay coincided with another military coup d'Jtat. Tens of thousands of people were arrested and the *Desaparecidos* were assassinated. The military takeover in Argentina was a "carbon copy" of the CIA-led coup in Chile. Behind the massacres and human rights violations, "free market" reforms had also been prescribed – this time under the supervision of Argentina's New York creditors.

The International Monetary Fund's (IMF's) deadly economic prescriptions applied under the guise of the "structural adjustment program" had not yet been officially launched. The experience of Chile and Argentina under the "Chicago Boys" was a dress rehearsal of things to come. In due course, the economic bullets of the free market system were hitting country after country. Since the onslaught of the debt crisis of the 1980s, the same IMF economic medicine has routinely been applied in more than 150 developing countries. From my earlier work in Chile, Argentina and Peru, I started to investigate the global impacts of these reforms. Relentlessly feeding on poverty and economic dislocation, a New World Order was taking shape.

Meanwhile, most of the military regimes in Latin America had been replaced by parliamentary "democracies", entrusted with the gruesome task of putting the national economy on the auction block under the World Bank sponsored privatization programs. In 1990, I returned to the Catholic University of Peru where I had taught after leaving Chile in the months following the 1973 military coup.

I had arrived in Lima at the height of the 1990 election campaign. The country's economy was in crisis. The outgoing populist government of President Alan Garcia had been placed on the IMF "black list". President Alberto Fujimori became the new president on the 28th of July 1990. And barely a few days later, "economic shock therapy" struck – this time with a vengeance. Peru had been punished for not conforming to IMF diktats: the price of fuel was hiked up by 31 times and the price of bread increased more than twelve times in a single day. The IMF – in close consultation with the US Treasury – had been operating behind the scenes. These reforms – carried out in the name of "democracy" – were far more devastating than those applied in Chile and Argentina under the fist of military rule.

In the 1980s and 1990s I traveled extensively in Africa. The field-research for the first edition was, in fact, initiated in Rwanda which, despite high levels of poverty, had achieved self-sufficiency in food production. From the early 1990s, Rwanda had been destroyed as a functioning national economy; its once vibrant agricultural system was destabilized. The IMF had demanded the "opening up" of the domestic market to the dumping of US and European grain surpluses. The objective was to "encourage Rwandan farmers to be more competitive". (See Chapter 7.)

From 1992 to 1995, I undertook field research in India, Bangladesh and Vietnam and returned to Latin America to complete my study on Brazil. In all the countries I visited, including Kenya, Nigeria, Egypt, Morocco and The Philippines, I observed the same pattern of economic manipulation and political interference by the Washington-based institutions. In India, directly resulting from the IMF reforms, millions of people had been driven into starvation. In Vietnam – which constitutes among the world's most prosperous rice producing economies – local-level famines had erupted resulting directly from the lifting of price controls and the deregulation of the grain market.

Coinciding with the end of the Cold War, at the height of the economic crisis, I traveled to several cities and rural areas in Russia. The IMF-sponsored reforms had entered a new phase – extending their deadly grip to the countries of the former Eastern bloc. Starting in 1992, vast areas of the former Soviet Union, from the Baltic states to Eastern Siberia, were pushed into abysmal poverty.

Work on the first edition was completed in early 1996, with the inclusion of a detailed study on the economic disintegration of Yugoslavia. (See Chapter 17.) Devised by World Bank economists, a "bankruptcy program" had been set in motion. In 1989-90, some 1100 industrial firms were wiped out and more than 614,000 industrial workers were laid off. And that was only the beginning of a much deeper economic fracturing of the Yugoslav Federation.

Since the publication of the first edition in 1997, the World has changed dramatically; the "globalization of poverty" has extended its grip to all major regions of the World including Western Europe and North America.

A New World Order has been installed destroying national sovereignty and the rights of citizens. Under the new rules of the World Trade Organization (WTO) established in 1995, "entrenched rights" were granted to the world's largest banks and multinational conglomerates. Public debts have spiraled, state institutions have collapsed, and the accumulation of private wealth has progressed relentlessly.

The US-led wars on Afghanistan (2001) and Iraq (2003), mark an important turning point in this evolving New World Order. As the second edition goes to print, American and British forces have invaded Iraq, destroying its public infrastructure and killing thousands of civilians. After 13 years of economic sanctions, the war on Iraq plunged an entire population into poverty.

War and globalizaton go hand in hand. Supported by America's war machine, a new deadly phase of corporate-led globalization has unfolded. In the largest display of military might since the Second World War, the United States has embarked upon a military adventure, which threatens the future of humanity.

The decision to invade Iraq had nothing to do with "Saddam's weapons of mass destruction" or his alleged links to Al Qaeda. Iraq possesses 11 percent of the World's oil reserves, i.e. more than five times those of the US. The broader Middle East-Central Asian region (extending from the tip of the Arabian peninsula to the Caspian sea basin) encompasses approximately 70% of the World's reserves of oil and natural gas.

This war, which has been in the planning stage for several years, threatens to engulf a much broader region. A 1995 US Central Command document confirms that "the purpose of US engagement. . . is to protect US vital interest in the region - uninterrupted, secure US/Allied access to Gulf oil" .

In the wake of the invasion, Iraq's economy has been put under the jurisidiction of the US military occupation government led by retired General Jay Gardner, a former CEO of one of America's largest weapons producers.

In liaison with the US administration and the Paris Club of official creditors, the IMF and World Bank are slated to play a key role in Iraq`s post-war "reconstruction". The hidden agenda is to impose the US dollar as Iraq's proxy currency, in a currency board arrangement, similar to that imposed on Bosnia-Herzegovina under the 1995 Dayton Accord. (See Chapter 17.) In turn, Iraq's extensive oil reserves are slated to be taken over by the Anglo-American oil giants.

Iraq's spiralling external debt will be used as an instrument of economic plunder. Conditionalities will be set. The entire national economy will be put on the auction block. The IMF and the World Bank will be called in to provide legitimacy to the plunder of Iraq's oil wealth.

The deployment of America's war machine purports to enlarge America's economic sphere of influence in an area extending from the

Mediterranean to China's Western frontier. The US has established a permanent military presence not only in Iraq and Afghanistan, but it has military bases in several of the former Soviet republics as well. In other words, militarization supports the conquest of new economic frontiers and the worldwide imposition of the "free market" system.

Global Depression

The onslaught of the US-led war is occurring at the height of a global economic depression, which has its historical roots in the debt crisis of the early 1980s. America's war of conquest has a direct bearing on the economic crisis. State resources in the US have been redirected towards financing the military-industrial complex and beefing up domestic security at the expense of funding much needed social programs which have been slashed to the bone.

In the wake of September 11, 2001, through a massive propaganda campaign, the shaky legitimacy of the "global free market system" has been reinforced, opening the door to a renewed wave of deregulation and privatization, resulting in corporate take-overs of most, if not all, public services and state infrastructure (including health care, electricity, water and transportation).

Morcover, in the US, Great Britain and most countries of the European Union, the legal fabric of society has been overhauled. Based on the repeal of the Rule of Law, the foundations of an authoritarian state apparatus have emerged with little or no organized opposition from the mainstay of civil society.

The new chapters added to this second edition address some of the key issues of the 21st century : the merger boom and the concentration of corporate power, the collapse of national and local level economies, the meltdown of financial markets, the outbreak of famine and civil war and the dismantling of the Welfare State in most Western countries.

In Part 1, a new Introduction and a chapter entitled "Global Falsehoods" have been added. Also in Part 1, the impacts of "free markets" on women's rights are examined. In Part II, on sub-Saharan Africa, the chapter on Rwanda has been expanded and updated following fieldwork conducted in 1996 and 1997. Two new chapters, respectively, on the 1999-2000 famine in Ethiopia and on Southern Africa in the post-Apartheid era have been added. The chapter on Albania in Part 5, focuses on the role of the IMF in destroying the real economy and precipitating the breakdown of the country's banking system.

A new Part 6 entitled "The New World Order" includes five chapters. Chapter 18 centers on the "structural adjustment program" applied in Western countries under the surveillance of the World's largest commercial and merchant banks. The ongoing economic and financial crisis is reviewed in Chapters 19 and 20. Chapters 21 and 22 examine, respectively, the fate of South Korea and Brazil in the wake of the 1997-1998 financial meltdown, as well as the complicity of the IMF in furthering the interests of currency and stock market speculators.

I am indebted to many people in many countries who provided me with insights on the economic reforms and assisted me in carrying out the country-level research, which was conducted (since the beginning of my work on the first edition) over a period of more than ten years. In the course of my fieldwork, I came in contact with members of peasant communities, industrial workers, teachers, health workers, civil servants, students, members of research institutes, university professors and members of non-governmental organizations, with whom I developed ties of friendship and solidarity. This book is dedicated to their struggle.

I am also indebted to Paul Marcus, Richard Corey and Blaine Machan for the design and artwork, which went into the front cover, to Lea Gilboe who assisted in the editing of the manuscript and to Johanne Dionne and Donna Kurtz for the layout and final editing of the book.

The support of the Social Sciences and Humanities' Research Council of Canada (SSHRC) and the University of Ottawa, Faculty of Social Sciences' Research Committee is gratefully acknowledged. The views expressed in this book are those of the author.

Introduction

Humanity is undergoing, in the post-Cold War era, an economic and social crisis of unprecedented scale leading to the rapid impoverishment of large sectors of the world population. National economies are collapsing and unemployment is rampant. Local level famines have erupted in sub-Saharan Africa, South Asia and parts of Latin America. This "globalization of poverty" – which has largely reversed the achievements of post-war de-colonization – was initiated in the Third World coinciding with the debt crisis of the early 1980s and the imposition of the IMF's deadly economic reforms.

The New World Order feeds on human poverty and the destruction of the natural environment. It generates social apartheid, encourages racism and ethnic strife, undermines the rights of women and often precipitates countries into destructive confrontations between nationalities. Since the 1990s, it has extended its grip to all major regions of the World including North America, Western Europe, the countries of the former Soviet Bloc and the "Newly Industrialized Countries" (NICs) of South East Asia and the Far East.

This worldwide crisis is more devastating than the Great Depression of the 1930s. It has far-reaching geo-political implications; economic disloca-tion has also been accompanied by the outbreak of regional wars, the frac-turing of national societies and, in some cases, the destruction of entire countries. By far, this is the most serious economic crisis in modern history.

The Post Cold War Recession

In the former Soviet Union, directly resulting from the IMF's deadly "eco-nomic medicine" initiated in 1992, economic decline has surpassed the plunge in production experienced at the height of the Second World War, following the German occupation of Belarus and parts of the Ukraine in

1941 and the extensive bombing of Soviet industrial infrastructure. From a situation of full employment and relative price stability in the 1970s and 1980s, inflation has skyrocketed, real earnings and employment have collapsed and health programmes have been phased out. In turn, cholera and tuberculosis have spread at an alarming speed across a vast area of the former Soviet Union.[1]

The pattern in the former Soviet Union has been replicated throughout Eastern Europe and the Balkans. National economies have collapsed one after the other. In the Baltic states (Lithuania, Latvia and Estonia), as well as in the Caucasian republics of Armenia and Azerbaijan, industrial output declined by as much as 65 percent. In Bulgaria, old age pensions had, by 1997, collapsed to two dollars a month.[2] The World Bank conceded that 90 percent of Bulgarians are living below the World Bank defined poverty threshold of $ 4 a day.[3] Unable to pay for electricity, water and transportation, population groups throughout Eastern Europe and the Balkans have been brutally marginalized from the modern era.

Demise of the "Asian Tigers"

In East Asia, the 1997 financial crisis – marked by speculative assaults against national currencies – has largely contributed to the demise of the so-called "Asian Tigers" (Indonesia, Thailand and Korea). The IMF bailout agreements, imposed in the immediate wake of the financial meltdown, were conducive – virtually overnight – to abrupt declines in the standard of living. In Korea, following the IMF's "mediation" – reached after high-level consultations with the World's largest commercial and merchant banks – "an average of more than 200 companies [were] shut down per day (. . .) 4,000 workers every day were driven out onto streets as unemployed"[4]. (See Chapter 22.) Meanwhile, in Indonesia, – amidst violent street riots – wages in the cheap labor sweat shops in the export processing zones had plummeted from 40 to 20 dollars a month, and the IMF had insisted on the deindexation of wages as a means of mitigating inflationary pressures.

In China, under the privatization or forced bankruptcy of thousands of state enterprises, 35 million workers are slated to be laid off.[5] According to a recent estimate, there are some 130 million surplus workers in China's rural areas.[6] In a bitter irony, the World Bank had predicted that, with the adoption of "free market" reforms, poverty in China would fall to 2.7 percent in 2000.[7]

Poverty and Economic Dislocation in the West

During the Reagan-Thatcher era, harsh austerity measures resulted in the gradual disintegration of the Welfare State. The *economic stabilization measures* (in principle adopted *to alleviate the evils of inflation*) contributed to depressing the earnings of working people and weakening the role of the state. Since the 1990s, the economic therapy applied in the developed countries contains many of the essential ingredients of the structural adjustment programmes imposed by the IMF and the World Bank in the Third World and Eastern Europe.

In contrast to the developing countries, however, policy reforms in Europe and North America are imposed without the intermediation of the IMF. The accumulation of large public debts in Western countries has provided the financial elites with political leverage as well as the power to dictate government economic and social policy. Under the sway of neoliberalism, public expenditures are trimmed and social welfare programs are undone. State policies promote the deregulation of the labor market: deindexation of earnings, part-time employment, early retirement and the imposition of so-called "voluntary" wage cuts. . .

In turn, the practice of attrition – which shifts the social burden of unemployment onto the younger age groups – has contributed to barring an entire generation from the job market.[8] The rules of personnel management in the United States are: "bust the unions, pit older workers against younger, call in the scabs, slash wages and cut company paid medical insurance".[9]

Since the 1980s, a large share of the labor force in the United States has been driven out of high pay unionized jobs into low pay *minimum wage jobs*. *Thirdworldization* of Western cities. . .poverty in America's ghettoes is, in many respects, comparable to that of the Third World. While the "recorded" rate of unemployment in the US declined in the 1990s, the number of people on low wage part-time jobs has spiralled. With further declines in minimum wage employment, large sectors of the working population are pushed out of the labor market altogether:

> The real savage edge of the recession cuts basically through the communities and new immigrants in Los Angeles, where unemployment rates have tripled and where there is no social safety net. People are in free fall, their lives are literally falling apart as they lose their minimum wage jobs.[10]

In turn, economic restructuring has created profound divisions between social classes and ethnic groups. The environment of major metropolitan areas is marked by *social apartheid:* the urban landscape is compartmentalized along social and ethnic lines. In turn, the state has become increasingly repressive in managing social dissent and curbing civil unrest.

With the wave of corporate mergers, downsizing and plant closures, all categories of the labor force are affected. The recession hits middle class households and the upper echelons of the labor force. Research budgets are curtailed; scientists, engineers and professionals are fired; highly paid civil servants and middle managers are ordered to retire.

Meanwhile, the achievements of the early post-war period have largely been reversed through the derogation of unemployment insurance schemes and the privatization of pension funds. Schools and hospitals are being closed down creating conditions for the outright privatization of social services.

A Thriving Criminal Economy

The "free market" reforms favor the growth of illicit activities as well as the concurrent "internationalization" of the criminal economy. In Latin America and Eastern Europe, criminal syndicates have invested in the acquisition of state assets under the IMF-World Bank sponsored privatization programmes. According to the United Nations, total worldwide revenues of the "transnational criminal organizations" (TCOs) are of the order of one trillion dollars, representing an amount equivalent to the combined GDP of the group of low income countries (with a population of 3 billion people).[11] The United Nations estimate includes the trade in narcotics, arms sales, smuggling of nuclear materials, etc. as well as the earnings derived from the Mafia-controlled services economy (e.g. prostitution, gambling, exchange banks, etc.). What these figures do not adequately convey is the magnitude of routine investments by criminal organizations in "legitimate" business undertakings, as well as their significant command over productive resources in many areas of the legal economy.

Criminal groups routinely collaborate with legal business enterprises investing in a variety of "legitimate" activities, which provide not only a cover for the laundering of dirty money but also a convenient procedure for accumulating wealth outside the realm of the criminal economy. According to one observer, "organized crime groups outperform most Fortune 500 companies. . .with organizations that resemble General Motors more than they resemble the traditional Sicilian Mafia".[12] According to the testimony of FBI director Jim Moody to a US Congressional Sub-committee, criminal organizations in Russia are "cooperating with other foreign criminal groups, including those based in Italy and Colombia (. . .) the transition to capitalism [in the former Soviet Union] provided new opportunities quickly exploited by criminal organizations".[13]

Wall Street Bankers behind the Scenes

A political consensus has developed; governments throughout the world have unequivocally embraced the neoliberal policy agenda. The same economic prescriptions are applied worldwide. Under the jurisdiction of the IMF, the World Bank and the WTO, the reforms create an "enabling environment" for global banks and multinational corporations. This is not, however, a "free" market system: while supported by neoliberal rhetoric, the so-called *structural adjustment program*, sponsored by the Bretton Woods institutions, constitutes a new interventionist framework.

The IMF, the World Bank and the WTO, however, are mere bureaucracies. They are *regulatory bodies* operating under an intergovernmental umbrella and acting on behalf of powerful economic and financial interests. Wall Street bankers and the heads of the world's largest business conglomerates are indelibly behind these global institutions. They interface regularly with IMF, World Bank and WTO officials in closed sessions, as well as in numerous international venues. Moreover, participating in these meetings and consultations are the representatives of powerful global business lobbies, including the International Chamber of Commerce (ICC), The Trans Atlantic Business Dialogue (TABD) (which brings together in its annual venues the leaders of the largest Western business conglomerates with politicians and WTO officials), the United States Council for International Business (USCIB), the Davos World Economic Forum, the Washington based Institute of International Finance (IIF) representing the world's largest banks and financial institutions, etc. Other "semi-secret" organizations – which play an important role in shaping the institutions of the New World Order – include the Trilateral Commission, the Bildebergers and the Council on Foreign Relations.

The Cheap Labor Economy

The globalization of poverty is occurring during a period of rapid technological and scientific advance. While the latter has contributed to vastly increasing the *potential capacity* of the economic system to produce necessary goods and services, expanded levels of productivity have not translated into a corresponding reduction in levels of global poverty. At the dawn of a new millennium, this global decline in living standards is not the result of a scarcity of productive resources.

On the contrary, downsizing, corporate restructuring and relocation of production to cheap labor havens in the Third World have been conducive to increased levels of unemployment and significantly lower earnings to urban workers and farmers. *This new international economic order feeds on human poverty* and cheap labor: high levels of national unemployment in both developed and developing countries have contributed to depressing real wages. Unemployment has been internationalized, with capital migrating from one country to another in a perpetual search for cheaper supplies of labor. According to the International Labor Organization (ILO), worldwide unemployment affects one billion people or nearly one third of the global workforce.[14] National labor markets are no longer segregated: workers in different countries are brought into overt competition with one another. Workers rights are derogated as labor markets are deregulated.

World unemployment operates as a lever which regulates labor costs at a world level: the abundant supplies of cheap labor in the Third World and the former Eastern Bloc contribute to depressing wages in the developed countries. Virtually all categories of the labor force (including the highly qualified, professional and scientific workers) are affected, even as competition for jobs encourages social divisions based on class, ethnicity, gender and age.

Micro-Efficiency, Macro-Insufficiency

The global corporation minimizes labor costs on a world level. Real wages in the Third World and Eastern Europe are as much as seventy times lower than in the US, Western Europe or Japan: the possibilities of production are immense given the mass of cheap impoverished workers throughout the world.

While mainstream economics stresses the "efficient allocation" of society's "scarce resources", harsh social realities call into question the consequences of this means of allocation. Industrial plants are closed down, small and medium sized enterprises are driven into bankruptcy, professional workers and civil servants are laid off and human and physical capital stand idle in the name of "efficiency". The relentless drive towards the "efficient" use of society's resources at the micro-economic level leads to exactly the opposite situation at the macro-economic level. Resources are not used efficiently when there remain large amounts of unused industrial capacity and millions of unemployed workers. Modern capitalism appears totally incapable of mobilizing these untapped human and resources.

Accumulation of Wealth, Distortion of Production

This global economic restructuring promotes stagnation in the supply of necessary goods and services, while redirecting resources towards lucrative investments in the luxury goods economy. Moreover, with the drying up of capital formation in productive activities, profit is sought in increasingly speculative and fraudulent transactions, which, in turn, tends to promote disruptions on the world's major financial markets.

A privileged social minority has accumulated vast amounts of wealth at the expense of the large majority of the population. The number of billionaires in the US alone increased from 13 in 1982 to 149 in 1996 to more than 300 in 2000. The *Global Billionaires Club* (with some 450 members) has a total worldwide wealth well in excess of the combined GDP of the group of low income countries with 59 percent of the world's population. (See Table 1.1.)[15] The private wealth of the Northwest Arkansas Walton family, owners of the retail chain Wal-Mart ($ 85 billion) – including heiress Alice Walton, brothers Robson, John and Jim and mother Helen – is more than twice the GDP of Bangladesh ($ 33.4 billion) with a population of 127 million people and a per capita income of $ 260 per annum.[16]

Moreover, the process of wealth accumulation is increasingly taking place outside the real economy divorced from bona fide productive and commercial activities: "Successes on the Wall Street stock market [meaning speculative trade] produced most of last year's [1996] surge in billionaires."[17] In turn, billions of dollars accumulated from speculative transactions are funneled towards confidential numbered accounts in the more than 50 offshore banking havens around the world. The US investment bank, Merrill Lynch, conservatively estimates the wealth of private individuals managed through private banking accounts in offshore tax havens at $ 3.3 trillion.[18] The IMF puts the offshore assets of corporations and individuals at $ 5.5 trillion, a sum equivalent to 25 percent of total world income.[19] The largely ill-gotten loot of Third World elites in numbered accounts was estimated in the 1990s at $ 600 billion, with one third of that held in Switzerland.[20]

Overproduction: Increased Supply, Reduced Demand

The expansion of output in the global capitalist system takes place by "minimizing employment" and compressing workers' wages. This process in turn backlashes on the levels of consumer demand for necessary goods and services: unlimited capacity to produce, limited capacity to consume. In a global cheap labor economy, the very process of expanding output (through downsizing, lay-offs and low wages) contributes to compressing society's capacity to consume.

The tendency is, therefore, towards overproduction on an unprecedented scale. Corporate expansion in this system can only take place through the concurrent disengagement of idle productive capacity, namely through the bankruptcy and liquidation of "surplus enterprises". The latter are closed down in favor of the most advanced mechanized production: entire branches of industry stand idle, the economy of entire regions is affected, and only a part of the world's agricultural potential is utilized.

This global oversupply of commodities is a direct consequence of the decline in purchasing power and rising levels of poverty. The latter is also the result of the *minimization of labor costs* and employment at a world level under the brunt of the IMF-World Bank-WTO reforms.

Oversupply contributes in turn to further depressing the earnings of the direct producers through the closure of excess productive capacity. Contrary to Say's law of markets, heralded by mainstream economics, *supply doesn't create its own demand*. Since the early 1980s, overproduction of commodities leading to plummeting (real) commodity prices has wreaked havoc particularly among Third World primary producers, but also in the area of manufacturing.

Global Integration, Local Disintegration

In developing countries, entire branches of industry producing for the internal market are driven into bankruptcy on the orders of the World Bank and the IMF. The informal urban sector – which historically has played an important role as a source of employment creation – has been undermined as a result of currency devaluations, the liberalization of imports and commodity dumping. In sub-Saharan Africa, for instance, the informal sector garment industry has been wiped out and replaced by the market for used garments (imported from the West at 80 dollars a ton).[21]

Against a background of economic stagnation (including negative growth rates recorded in Eastern Europe, the former Soviet Union and sub-Saharan Africa), the world's largest corporations have experienced unprecedented growth and expansion of their share of the global market. This process, however, has largely taken place through the displacement of pre-existing productive systems – i.e. at the expense of local-level, regional and national producers. Expansion and "profitability" for the world's largest corporations is predicated on a global contraction of purchasing power and the impoverishment of large sectors of the world population. In turn, "free market" reforms have contributed ruthlessly to opening up new economic frontiers, while ensuring "profitability" through the imposition of abysmally low wages and the deregulation of the labor market. In this process, *poverty is an input on the supply side*. The gamut of IMF-World Bank-WTO reforms imposed worldwide plays a decisive role in regulating labor costs on behalf of corporate capital.

Survival of the fittest: the enterprises with the most advanced technologies or those with command over the lowest wages survive in a world economy marked by overproduction. While the spirit of Anglo-Saxon liberalism is committed to "fostering competition", G-7 macro-economic policy (through tight fiscal and monetary controls), has, in practice, supported a wave of corporate mergers and acquisitions, as well as the bankruptcy of small and medium-sized enterprises.

Destroying the Local Economy

At the local level, small and medium sized enterprises are pushed into bankruptcy or obliged to produce for a global distributor. In turn, large multinational companies have taken control of local-level markets through the system of corporate franchising. This process enables large corporate capital (the franchiser) to gain control over human resources, cheap labor and entrepreneurship. A large share of the earnings of small local level firms and/or retailers is thereby appropriated by the global corporation, while the bulk of investment outlays is assumed by the independent producer (the franchisee).

A parallel process can be observed in Western Europe. Under the Maastricht treaty, the process of political restructuring in the European Union increasingly heeds to dominant financial interests at the expense of the unity of European societies. In this system, state power has deliberately sanctioned the progress of private monopolies: large capital destroys small capital in all its forms. With the drive towards the formation of economic blocks both in Europe and North America, the regional and local-level entrepreneur is uprooted, city life is transformed and individual small-scale ownership is wiped out. "Free trade" and economic integration provide greater mobility to the global enterprise while, at the same time, suppressing (through non-tariff and institutional barriers) the movement of small, local-level capital.[22] "Economic integration" (under the dominion of the global enterprise), while displaying a semblance of political unity, often promotes factionalism and social strife between and within national societies.

War and Globalization

The imposition of macro-economic and trade reforms under the supervision of the IMF, World Bank and World Trade Organization (WTO) purports to "peacefully" recolonize countries through the deliberate manipulation of market forces. While not explicitly requiring the use of force, the ruthless enforcement of the economic reforms nonetheless constitutes a form of warfare. More generally, the dangers of war must be understood. War and globalization are not separate issues.

What happens to countries that refuse to "open up" to Western banks and MNCs, as demanded by the World Trade Organization ? The Western military-intelligence apparatus and its various bureaucracies routinely interface with the financial establishment. The IMF, the World Bank and the WTO – which police country level economic reforms – also collaborate with NATO in its various "peacekeeping" endeavors, not to mention the financing of "post-conflict" reconstruction under the auspices of the Bretton Woods institutions. . .

At the dawn of the third millennium, war and the "free market" go hand in hand. War does not require the WTO or a multilateral investment treaty (i.e. a MAI) entrenched in international law: *War is the MAI of last resort.* War physically destroys what has not been dismantled through deregulation, privatization and the imposition of "free market" reforms. Outright colonization through war and the installation of Western protectorates is tantamount to providing "national treatment" to Western banks and MNCs (as stipulated by the WTO) in all sectors of activity. "Missile diplomacy" replicates the "gunboat diplomacy" used to enforce "free trade" in the 19th century. The US Cushing Mission to China in 1844 (in the wake of the Opium Wars) had forewarned the Chinese imperial government "that refusal to grant American demands might be regarded as an invitation to war."[23]

Disarming the New World Order

The ideology of the "free" market upholds a novel and brutal form of state interventionism predicated on the deliberate tampering of market forces. Derogating the rights of citizens, "free trade" under the World Trade Organization (WTO) grants "entrenched rights" to the world's largest banks and global corporations. The process of enforcing international agreements by the World Trade Organization at national and international levels invariably bypasses the democratic process. The WTO articles threaten to lead to the disempowerment of national societies as it hands over extensive powers to the financial establishment. (See Chapter 1.) Beneath the rhetoric on so-called "governance" and the "free market", neoliberalism provides a shaky legitimacy to those in the seat of political power.

The New World Order is based on the "false consensus" of Washington and Wall Street, which ordains the "free market system" as the only possible choice on the fated road to a "global prosperity". All political parties including Greens, Social Democrats and former Communists now share this consensus.

The insidious links of politicians and international officials to powerful financial interests must be unveiled. To bring about meaningful changes, State institutions and intergovernmental organizations must eventually be removed from the clutch of the financial establishment. In turn, we must democratize the economic system and its management and ownership structures, resolutely challenge the blatant concentration of ownership and private wealth, disarm financial markets, freeze speculative trade, arrest the laundering of dirty money, dismantle the system of offshore banking, redistribute income and wealth, restore the rights of direct producers and rebuild the Welfare State.

It should, however, be understood that the Western military and security apparatus endorses and supports dominant economic and financial interests – i.e. the build-up, as well as the exercise, of military might enforces "free trade". The Pentagon is an arm of Wall Street; NATO coordinates its military operations with the World Bank and the IMF's policy interventions, and vice versa. Consistently, the security and defense bodies of the Western military alliance, together with the various civilian governmental and intergovernmental bureaucracies (e.g. IMF, World Bank, WTO) share a common understanding, ideological consensus and commitment to the New World Order. The international campaign against "globalization" must be integrated within a broader coalition of social forces geared towards dismantling the military-industrial complex, NATO and the defense establishment including its intelligence, security and police apparatus.

The global media fabricates the news and overtly distorts the course of world events. This "false consciousness" which pervades our societies, prevents critical debate and masks the truth. Ultimately, this false consciousness precludes a collective understanding of the workings of an economic system, which destroys people's lives. The only promise of the "free market" is a world of landless farmers, shuttered factories, jobless workers and gutted social programs with "bitter economic medicine" under the WTO and the IMF constituting the only prescription. We must restore the truth, disarm the controlled corporate media, reinstate sovereignty to our countries and to the people of our countries and disarm and abolish global capitalism.

The struggle must be broad-based and democratic encompassing all sectors of society at all levels, in all countries, uniting in a major thrust: workers, farmers, independent producers, small businesses, professionals, artists, civil servants, members of the clergy, students and intellectuals. People must be united across sectors, "single issue" groups must join hands in a common and collective understanding on how this economic system destroys and impoverishes. The globalization of this struggle is fundamental, requiring a degree of solidarity and internationalism unprecedented in world history. This global economic system feeds on social divisiveness between and within countries. Unity of purpose and worldwide coordination among diverse groups and social movements is crucial. A major thrust is required which brings together social movements in all major regions of the world in a common pursuit and commitment to the elimination of poverty and a lasting world peace.

Endnotes

1.   Associated Press, 14 August 1993.

2.   The Wind in the Balkans, *The Economist*, London, February 8, 1997, p. 12.

3.   Jonathan C. Randal, "Reform Coalition Wins, Bulgarian Parliament", *The Washington Post*, April 20 1997, p. A21.

4.   Korean Federation of Trade Unions, "*Unbridled Freedom to Sack Workers Is No Solution At All*", Communiqué, Seoul, 13 January 1998.

5.   Eric Ekholm, "On the Road to Capitalism, China Hits a Nasty Curve: Joblessness", *New York Times*, January 20, 1998.

6. *Ibid.*

7. See World Bank, *1990 World Development Report*, Washington DC, 1990.

8. In the United States, the majority of jobs created in the 1980s were part-time and/or temporary contracts. See Serge Halimi, "Mais qui donc finance la création de millions d'emplois aux Etats-Unis", *Le Monde diplomatique*, March 1989.

9. See Earl Silber and Steven Ashby, "UAW and the 'Cat' Defeat", *Against the Current*, July/August 1992.

10. Mike Davis, "Realities of the Rebellion", *Against the Current*, July/August 1991, p. 17.

11. See the proceedings on the United Nations Conference on Crime Prevention, Cairo, May 1995. See also Jean Hervé Deiller, "Gains annuels de 1000 milliards pour l'Internationale du crime", *La Presse*, Montreal, 30 April 1996

12. Daniel Brandt, "Organized Crime Threatens the NewWorld Order", *Namebase Newsline*, Ohio, no 8, January-March 1995.

13. Reuters News Dispatch, January 25, 1995.

14. International Labor Organization, *Second World Employment Report*, Geneva, 1996.

15. International Billionaires, the World's Richest People, *Forbes Magazine*, New York, annual. List at http://www.forbes.com/.

16. *Ibid.*

17. Charles Laurence, "Wall Street Warriors force their way into the Billionaires Club", *Daily Telegraph*, London, 30 September 1997.

18. "Increased Demand Transforms Markets," *Financial Times*, London, June 21, 1995, p. II.

19. *Financial Times*, London, 7 June 1996, p. III.

20. Peter Bosshard, "Cracking the Swiss Banks," *The Multinational Monitor*, November 1992

21. Based on author's interviews in Tunisia and Kenya, December 1992.

22. While the large multinational enterprises move freely within the North-American free trade area, non-tariff restrictions prevent small-scale local capital in one Canadian province to extend its activities to another Canadian province.

23. Quoted in Michel Chossudovsky, *Towards Capitalist Restoration, Chinese socialism after Mao*, Macmillan, London, 1986, p. 134.

PART I

GLOBAL POVERTY AND
MACRO-ECONOMIC REFORM

Chapter 1

The Globalization of Poverty

Since the early 1980s, the "macro-economic stabilization" and structural adjustment programs imposed by the IMF and the World Bank on developing countries (as a condition for the renegotiation of their external debt) have led to the impoverishment of hundreds of millions of people. Contrary to the spirit of the Bretton Woods agreement, which was predicated on "economic reconstruction", and the stability of major exchange rates, the structural adjustment program has contributed largely to destabilizing national currencies and ruining the economies of developing countries.

Internal purchasing power has collapsed, famines have erupted, health clinics and schools have been closed down and hundreds of millions of children have been denied the right to primary education. In several regions of the developing world, the reforms have been conducive to a resurgence of infectious diseases including tuberculosis, malaria and cholera. While the World Bank's mandate consists of "combating poverty" and protecting the environment, its support for large-scale hydroelectric and agro-industrial projects has also speeded up the process of deforestation and the destruction of the natural environment, leading to the forced displacement and eviction of several million people.

Global Geopolitics

In the wake of the Cold War, macro-economic restructuring has supported global geopolitical interests including US foreign policy. Structural adjustment has been used to undermine the economies of the former Soviet Bloc and dismantle its system of state enterprises. Since the late 1980s, the IMF-World Bank "economic medicine" has been imposed on Eastern Europe, Yugoslavia and the former Soviet Union with devastating economic and social consequences. (See Chapters 16 and 17.)

While the mechanism of enforcement is distinct, the structural adjustment program has, since the 1990s, been applied also in the developed countries. Whereas the macro-economic therapies (under the jurisdiction of national governments) tend to be less brutal than those imposed on the South and the East, the theoretical and ideological underpinnings are broadly similar. The same global financial interests are served. Monetarism is applied on a world scale and the process of global economic restructuring strikes also at the very heart of the rich countries. The consequences are unemployment, low wages and the marginalization of large sectors of the population. Social expenditures are curtailed and many of the achievements of the welfare state are repealed. State policies have encouraged the destruction of small and medium-sized enterprises. Low levels of food consumption and malnutrition are also hitting the urban poor in the rich countries. According to a recent study, 30 million people in the United States are classified as "hungry".[1]

The impacts of structural adjustment, including the derogation of the social rights of women and the detrimental environmental consequences of economic reform, have been amply documented. While the Bretton Woods institutions have acknowledged "the social impact of adjustment", no shift in policy direction is in sight. In fact, since the early 1990s, coinciding with the collapse of the Eastern bloc, the IMF-World Bank policy prescriptions (now imposed in the name of "poverty alleviation") have become increasingly harsh and unyielding.

Social Polarization and the Concentration of Wealth

In the South, the East and the North, a privileged social minority has accumulated vast amounts of wealth at the expense of the large majority of the population. This new international financial order feeds on human poverty and the destruction of the natural environment. It generates social apartheid, encourages racism and ethnic strife, undermines the rights of women and often precipitates countries into destructive confrontations between nationalities. Moreover, these reforms – when applied simultaneously in more than 150 countries – are conducive to a "globalization of poverty", a process which undermines human livelihood and destroys civil society in the South, East and the North.

IMF Economic Medicine

Under IMF jurisdiction, the same "menu" of budgetary austerity, devaluation, trade liberalization and privatization is applied simultaneously in more than 150 indebted countries. Debtor nations forego economic sovereignty and control over fiscal and monetary policy, the Central Bank and the Ministry of Finance are reorganized (often with the complicity of the local bureaucracies), state institutions are undone and an "economic tutelage" is installed. A "parallel government", which bypasses civil society, is established by the international financial institutions (IFIs). Countries which do not conform to the IMF's "performance targets" are blacklisted.

While adopted in the name of "democracy" and so-called "good governance", the structural adjustment program requires the strengthening of the internal security apparatus and the military intelligence apparatus: political repression – with the collusion of the Third World élites – supports a parallel process of "economic repression".

"Good governance" and the holding of multi-party elections are added conditions imposed by donors and creditors, yet the very nature of the economic reforms precludes a genuine democratization – i.e. their implementation invariably requires (contrary to the "spirit of Anglo-Saxon liberalism") the backing of the military and the authoritarian state. Structural adjustment promotes bogus institutions and a fake parliamentary democracy which, in turn, supports the process of economic restructuring.

Throughout the Third World, the situation is one of social desperation and the hopelessness of a population impoverished by the interplay of market forces. Anti-SAP riots and popular uprisings are brutally repressed: **Caracas, 1989**: President Carlos Andres Perez, after having rhetorically denounced the IMF of practicing "an economic totalitarianism which kills not with bullets but with famine", declares a stateof emergency and sends regular units of the infantry and the marines into the slum areas (*barrios de ranchos*) on the hills overlooking the capital. The Caracas anti-IMF riots had been sparked off as a result of a 200 percent increase in the price of bread. Men, women and children were fired upon indiscriminately. "The Caracas morgue was reported to have up to 200 bodies of people killed in the first three days (. . .) and warned that it was running out of coffins." [2] Unofficially, more than a thousand people were killed; **Tunis, January 1984**: the bread riots instigated largely by unemployed youth protesting the rise of food prices; **Nigeria, 1989**: the anti-SAP student riots leading to the closing of six of the country's universities by the Armed Forces Ruling Council; **Morocco, 1990**: a general strike and a popular uprising against the government's IMF-sponsored reforms; **Mexico, 1993**: the insurrection of the Zapatista Liberation Army in the Chiapas region of southern Mexico; protest movements against the IMF reforms in the Russian Federation and the storming of the Russian parliament in 1993; mass protest movement of the people of Ecuador against the adoption of the US dollar as their national currency in January 2000 leading to the resignation of the President; **Cochabamba, Bolivia, April 2000**: thousands of peasants protest against the privatization of the country's water resources and the imposition of user fees.

The list is long.

Economic Genocide

Structural adjustment is conducive to a form of "economic genocide" which is carried out through the conscious and deliberate manipulation of market forces. When compared to previous periods of colonial history (e.g. forced labor and slavery), its social impact is devastating. Structural adjustment programs affect directly the livelihood of more than four billion people. The application of the structural adjustment program in a large number of individual debtor countries favors the internationalization of macro-economic policy under the direct control of the IMF and the World Bank acting on behalf of powerful financial and political interests (e.g. the Paris and London Clubs, the G7). This new form of economic and political domination – a form of "market colonialism" – subordinates people and governments through the seemingly "neutral" interplay of market forces. The Washington-based international bureaucracy has been entrusted by international creditors and multinational corporations with the execution of a global economic design, which affects the livelihood of more than 80 percent of the world's population. At no time in history has the "free" market – operating in the world through the instruments of macro-economics – played such an important role in shaping the destiny of sovereign nations.

Destroying the National Economy

The restructuring of the world economy, under the guidance of the Washington-based financial institutions, increasingly denies individual developing countries the possibility of building a national economy: the internationalization of macro-economic policy transforms countries into open economic territories and national economies into "reserves" of cheap labor and natural resources. The application of the IMF's "economic medicine" tends to further depress world commodity prices because it forces individual countries to simultaneously gear their national economies towards a shrinking world market.

At the heart of the global economic system lies an unequal structure of trade, production and credit which defines the role and position of developing countries in the global economy. What is the nature of this unfolding world economic system; on what structure of global poverty and income inequality is it based ? By the turn of the century, the world population will be over six billion, of which five billion will be living in poor countries. While the rich countries (with some 15 percent of the world population) control close to 80 percent of total world income, approximately 60 percent of the world population representing the group of "low-income countries" (including India and China) – with a population in excess of 3.5 billion people – receives 6.3 percent of total world income (less than the GDP of France and its overseas territories). With a population of more than 600 million people, the gross domestic product of the entire sub-Saharan African region is approximately half that of the state of Texas.3 Together, the lower and middle-income countries (including the former "socialist" countries and the former Soviet Union), representing some 85 percent of world population, receive approximately 20 percent of total world income. (See Table 1.1.)

In many indebted Third World countries, real salaried earnings in the modern sector had, by the early 1990s, already declined by more than 60 percent. The situation of the informal sector and the unemployed was even more critical. In Nigeria, under the military government of General Ibrahim Babangida, for instance, the minimum wage declined by 85 percent in the course of the 1980s. Wages in Vietnam were below US$ 10 a month, while the domestic price of rice had risen to the world level as a result of the IMF program carried out by the Hanoi government: a Hanoi secondary school teacher, for instance, with a university degree, received in 1991 a monthly salary of less than US$ 15.[2] (See Chapter 12.) In Peru – in the aftermath of the IMF-World Bank sponsored Fujishock implemented by President Alberto *Fujimori* in August 1990 – fuel prices increased 31 times overnight, whereas the price of bread increased 12 times. The real minimum wage had declined by more than 90 percent (in relation to its level in the mid-1970s). (See Chapter 14.)

Table 1.1
The Distribution of World Population and Income (1998)

	Population (Millions)	Share of World Population (%)	Per Capita Income (in US$)	Total Income (US$ billions)	Share of World Income (%)
Low Income Countries	3 515	59.6	520	1 828	6.3
Middle Income Countries	1 496	25.4	2 950	4 413	15.3
Total Poor Countries	5 011	85.0	1 250	6 264	21.7
Sub-Saharan Africa	628	10.6	480	301	1.0
South Asia	1 305	22.1	430	561	1.9
China	1 239	21.0	750	929	3.2
Former USSR & Eastern Europe	395	6.7	1 965	776	2.7
Total Third World	4 616	78.3	1 180	5 447	18.9
Total Rich Countries *	885	15.0	25 510	22 576	78.3
OECD **	932	15.8	20 853	19 435	67.4
World Total	5 897	100.0	4 890	28 836	100.0

Source: Estimated from World Bank data in *World Development Report*, 1999/2000, Washington DC, 2000, pp. 230-231

* Rich countries are high income countries.

** Turkey and Mexico are included.

Technical Note: Total poor countries is the sum of low income countries and middle income countries.
Total third world countries is total poor countries less former USSR & Eastern Europe.

The Dollarization of Prices

While there are sizeable variations in the cost of living between developing and developed countries, devaluation, combined with trade liberalization and the deregulation of domestic commodity markets (under the structural adjustment program), is conducive to the "dollarization" of domestic prices. Increasingly, the domestic prices of basic food staples are brought up to their world market levels. This New World Economic Order, while based on the internationalization of commodity prices and a fully integrated world commodity market, functions increasingly in terms of a watertight separation between two distinct labor markets. This global market system is characterized by a duality in the structure of wages and labor costs between rich and poor countries. Whereas prices are unified and brought up to world levels, wages (and labor costs) in the Third World and Eastern Europe are as much as 70 times lower than in the OECD countries.

Income disparities between nations are superimposed on extremely wide income disparities between social-income groups within nations. In many Third World countries, more than 60 percent of national income accrues to the upper 20 percent of the population. In many low and middle-income developing countries, 70 percent of rural households have a per capita income between 10 and 20 percent of the national average. These vast disparities in income between and within countries are the consequence of the structure of commodity trade and the unequal international division of labor which imparts to the Third World and, more recently, to the countries of the former Soviet bloc, a subordinate status in the global economic system. The disparities have widened in the course of the 1990s as a result of the remolding of national economies under the structural adjustment programme.[3]

The "Thirdworldization" of the Former Eastern Bloc

The end of the Cold War has had a profound impact on the global distribution of income. Until the early 1990s, Eastern Europe and the Soviet Union were considered as part of the developed "North" – i.e. with levels of material consumption, education, health, scientific development, etc. broadly comparable to those prevailing in the OECD countries. Whereas average incomes were on the whole lower, Western scholars, nonetheless, acknowledged the achievements of the Eastern Bloc countries, particularly in the areas of health and education.

Impoverished as a result of the IMF-sponsored reforms, the countries of the former socialist Bloc are now categorized by the World Bank as "developing economies", alongside the "low" and "middle-income countries" of the Third World. The Central Asian republics of Kazakhstan and Turkmenistan appear next to Syria, Jordan and Tunisia in the "lower middle-income" category, whereas the Russian Federation is next to Brazil with a per capita income of the order of US$ 3,000. This shift in categories reflects the outcome of the Cold War and the underlying process of "third-worldization" of Eastern Europe and the former Soviet Union.

The Role of Global Institutions

The inauguration of the World Trade Organization (WTO) in 1995 marked a new phase in the evolution of the post war economic system. A new triangular division of authority among the IMF, the World Bank and the WTO has unfolded. The IMF had called for more effective "surveillance" of developing countries' economic policies and increased coordination between the three international bodies signifying a further infringement on the sovereignty of national governments.

Under the new trade order (which emerged from the completion of the Uruguay Round at Marrakech in 1994), the relationship of the Washington based institutions to national governments is to be redefined. Enforcement of IMF-World Bank policy prescriptions will no longer hinge upon ad hoc country-level loan agreements (which are not legally binding documents). Henceforth, many of the mainstays of the structural adjustment program (e.g. trade liberalization, privatization and the foreign investment regime) have been permanently entrenched in the articles of agreement of the new WTO. These articles set the foundations for policing countries (and enforcing "conditionalities") according to international law.

The deregulation of trade under WTO rules, combined with new clauses pertaining to intellectual property rights, enable multinational corporations to penetrate local markets and extend their control over virtually all areas of national manufacturing, agriculture and the service economy.

Entrenched Rights for Banks and Multinational Corporations

In this new economic environment, international agreements negotiated by bureaucrats under intergovernmental auspices have come to play a crucial role in the remoulding of national economies. The Articles of Agreement of the WTO provide what some observers have entitled a *"charter of rights for multinational corporations"* derogating the ability of national societies to regulate their national economies threatening national level social programs, job creation policies, affirmative action and community based initiatives. The WTO articles threaten to lead to the disempowerment of national societies as it hands over extensive powers to global corporations.

The WTO was put in place following the signing of a "technical agreement" negotiated behind closed doors by bureaucrats. Even the heads of country-level delegations to Marrakech in 1994 were not informed regarding the statutes of the WTO, which were drafted in separate closed sessions by technocrats. The WTO framework ensures a "single undertaking approach" to the results of the Uruguay Round – thus, "membership in the WTO entails accepting all the results of the Round without exception."[5]

Following the Marrakech meeting, the 550-page Agreement (plus its numerous appendices) was either rubber-stamped in a hurry, or never formally ratified by national parliaments. The articles of agreement of the WTO resulting from this "technical agreement" – including Dispute Settlement procedures – were casually entrenched in international law. The 1994 Marrakech Agreement – which instates the WTO as a multilateral body – bypasses the democratic process in each of the member countries. It blatantly derogates national laws and constitutions, while providing extensive powers to global banks and multinational corporations. These powers have, in fact, become entrenched in the articles of agreement of the WTO.

The process of actual creation of the WTO following the Final Act of Uruguay Round is blatantly illegal. Namely, a totalitarian intergovernmental body has been casually installed in Geneva, empowered under international law with the mandate to police country-level economic and social policies, derogating the sovereign rights of national governments. Similarly, the WTO almost neutralizes "with the stroke of a pen" the authority and activities of several agencies of the United Nations including the United Nations Conference on Trade and Development (UNCTAD) and the International Labor Organization (ILO). The articles of the WTO are not only in contradiction with pre-existing national and international laws; they are also at variance with "The Universal Declaration of Human Rights". Acceptance of the WTO as a legitimate organization is tantamount to an "indefinite moratorium" or repeal of the Universal Declaration of Human Rights.

In addition to the blatant violation of international law, WTO rules provide legitimacy to trade practices which border on criminality, including: "intellectual piracy" by multinational corporations; the derogation of plant breeders rights – not to mention genetic manipulation by the biotechno-logy giants, and the patenting of life forms including plants, animals, micro-organisms, genetic material and human life forms under the TRIPs agreement. (See Chapter 9, which illustrates the role of the biotech con-glomerates in Ethiopia.)

In the sphere of financial services, the provisions of the General Agreement on Trade and Services (GATS) provide legitimacy to large-scale financial and speculative manipulations directed against developing countries, which are often conducive to the demise of country-level mon-etary policy.

Under WTO rules, the banks and multinational corporations (MNCs) can legitimately manipulate market forces to their advantage leading to the outright re-colonization of national economies. The WTO articles provide legitimacy to global banks and MNCs in their quest to destabilize institu-tions, drive national producers into bankruptcy and ultimately take control of entire countries.

Endnotes

1. According to the Tufts University Centre on Hunger, Poverty and Nutrition Policy.

2. *Financial Times*, 3 March 1989.

3. It is worth noting that the share of the Third World in total world income has declined steadily since the onslaught of the debt crisis. Whereas the group of low-income countries increased its share of world population by more than 2 percent in the three-year period between 1988 and 1991, its share of world income declined from 5.4 to 4.9 percent. Similarly, sub-Saharan Africa's share of world income declined in the same period from 0.9 to 0.7 percent. In 1993, the World Bank redefined the basis of measuring and comparing per capita income. The figures contained in Table 1.1 are based on a new World Bank methodology which indicates a higher share for the low income countries than during the 1980s.

4. Interviews conducted by author in Hanoi and Ho Chi Minh City in January 1991.

5. For details see the text of *The Final Act Establishing the World Trade Organization* at the WTO webpage at http://www.wto.org/

Chapter 2
Global Falsehoods

G7 governments and global institutions, including the IMF, the World Bank and the World Trade Organization casually deny the increasing levels of global poverty; social realities are concealed, official statistics are manipulated, and economic concepts are turned upside down. In turn, public opinion is bombarded in the media with glowing images of global growth and prosperity. The world economy is said to be booming under the impetus of "free market" reforms: "Happy days are here again . . .a wonderful opportunity for sustained and increasingly global economic growth is waiting to be seized."[1] Without debate or discussion, so-called "sound macro-economic policies" (meaning the gamut of austerity measures, deregulation, downsizing and privatization) are heralded as the key to economic success.

The dominant economic discourse has also reinforced its hold in academic and research institutions throughout the world. Critical analysis is strongly discouraged; social and economic reality is to be seen through a single set of fictitious economic relations, which serve the purpose of concealing the workings of the global economic system. Mainstream economic scholarship produces theory without facts ("pure theory") and facts without theory ("applied economics"). The dominant economic dogma admits neither dissent from nor discussion of its main theoretical paradigm: the universities' main function is to produce a generation of loyal and dependable economists who are incapable of unveiling the social foundations of the global market economy. Similarly, Third World intellectuals are increasingly enlisted in support of the neoliberal paradigm; the internationalization of economic "science" unreservedly supports the process of global economic restructuring.

This "official" neoliberal dogma also creates its own "counter-paradigm" embodying a highly moral and ethical discourse. The latter focuses on "sustainable development" and "poverty alleviation" while often distorting and stylizing the policy issues pertaining to poverty, the protection of the environment and the social rights of women. This "counter-ideology" rarely challenges neoliberal policy prescriptions. It develops alongside and in harmony rather than in opposition to the official neoliberal dogma.

Within this counter-ideology (which is generously funded by the research establishment), development scholars (not to mention numerous nongovernmental organizations) find a comfortable niche. Their role is to generate (within this counter-discourse) a semblance of critical debate without addressing the social foundations of the global market system. The World Bank plays, in this regard, a key role in promoting research on "poverty alleviation" and the so-called "social dimensions of adjustment". This ethical focus and the underlying categories (e.g. poverty alleviation, gender issues, equity, etc.) provide a "human face" for the Bretton Woods institutions and a semblance of commitment to social change. However, inasmuch as this analysis is functionally divorced from an understanding of the main macro-economic reforms, it rarely constitutes a threat to the neoliberal economic agenda.

Manipulating the Figures on Global Poverty

The legitimacy of the "free market" reforms rests on the illusion that globalization is conducive to long-term prosperity. This illusion is sustained through the blatant manipulation of economic and social data including the figures on poverty. The World Bank "estimates" that 18 percent of the Third World is "extremely poor" and 33 percent is "poor". In the World Bank's authoritative study on global poverty, the "upper poverty line" is arbitrarily set at a per capita income of US$ 1 a day corresponding to an annual per capita income of US$ 370 per annum.[2] Population groups in individual countries with per capita incomes in excess of US$ 1 a day are arbitrarily identified as "non-poor". Through the gross manipulation of income statistics, the World Bank figures serve the useful purpose of representing the poor in developing countries as a minority group.

The World Bank arbitrarily sets a "poverty threshold" at one dollar a day, labelling population groups with a per capita income above one dollar a day as "non-poor". The World Bank, for instance, "estimates" that in Latin America and the Caribbean only 19 percent of the population is "poor" – a gross distortion when we know for a fact that in the United States (with an annual per capita income of more than US$ 25,000) one American in seven is defined (by the Bureau of the Census) to be below the poverty line. (See Table 2.2.) [3]

This subjective and biased assessment is carried out irrespective of actual conditions at the country level.[6] With the liberalization of commodity markets, the domestic prices of basic food staples in developing countries have risen to world market levels. The one dollar a day standard has no rational basis; population groups in developing countries with per capita incomes of 2, 3 or even 5 dollars a day remain poverty stricken (i.e. unable to meet basic expenditures on food, clothing, shelter, health and education).

Defining Poverty at "a Dollar a Day"

Once the "one dollar a day" poverty threshold has been set, the estimation of national and global poverty levels becomes an arithmetical exercise. Poverty indicators are computed in a mechanical fashion from the initial one dollar a day assumption. The data is then tabulated in glossy tables with forecasts of declining levels of global poverty into the 21st century.

These forecasts of poverty are based on an assumed rate of growth of per capita income; growth of the latter implies pari passu a corresponding lowering of the levels of poverty. For instance, according to the World Bank's calculations, the incidence of poverty in China was to decline from 20 percent in 1985 to 2.9 percent in 2000.[4] Similarly, in the case of India (where according to official data more than 80 percent of the population have a per capita income below one dollar a day), a World Bank "simulation" (which contradicts its own "one dollar a day" methodology) indicates a lowering of poverty levels from 55 percent in 1985 to 25 percent in the year 2000.[5]

The entire "one dollar a day" framework is totally removed from an examination of real life situations. No need to analyse household expenditures on food, shelter and social services; no need to observe concrete conditions in impoverished villages or urban slums. In the World Bank framework, the "estimation" of poverty indicators has become a numerical exercise, which usefully serves to conceal the globalization of poverty.

The United Nations' Poverty Figures

The United Nations echoes World Bank falsehoods. The United Nations Development Programme (UNDP) Human Development Group claims without supporting evidence that "the progress in reducing poverty over the 20th century is remarkable and unprecedented. . . . The key indicators of human development [in the late 20th century] have advanced strongly."[7] The UNDP had devised a "human poverty index" (HPI) based on "the most basic dimensions of deprivation: a short life span, lack of basic education and lack of access to public and private resources."[8] Based on these criteria, the UNDP Human Development Group comes up with "estimates" of human poverty which are totally inconsistent with country-level realities. The human poverty index (HPI) for Colombia, Mexico and Thailand, for instance, is around 10-11 percent. (See Table 2.1.) Country-level social realties are fabricated: the UNDP measurements point to achievements in poverty reduction in sub-Saharan Africa, the Middle East and India which are totally at odds with country-level data and poverty estimates.

In fact, the human poverty estimates put forth by the UNDP portray an even more distorted and misleading pattern than those of the World Bank. For instance, only 10.9 percent of Mexico's population are categorized by the UNDP as "poor". Yet this estimate contradicts the situation observed in Mexico in the course of the last twenty years: mass unemployment, collapse in social services, impoverishment of small farmers and a dramatic decline in real earnings triggered by successive currency devaluations.

Double Standards in the "Scientific" Measurement of Poverty

Double standards prevail in the measurement of poverty. The World Bank's one dollar a day criterion applies only to "developing countries". Both the Bank and the UNDP fail to acknowledge the existence of poverty in Western Europe and North America. Moreover, the "one dollar a day" standard contradicts established methodologies used by Western governments to define and measure poverty in their own countries.

In the West, methods for measuring poverty have been based on minimum levels of household spending required to meet essential expenditures on food, clothing, shelter, health and education. In the United States, for instance, the Social Security Administration (SSA) in the 1960s set a "poverty threshold" which consisted of "the cost of a minimum adequate diet multiplied by three to allow for other expenses." This measurement was based on a broad consensus within the US Administration.[9] The US "poverty threshold" for a family of four (two adults and two children) in 1996 was $ 16,036. This figure translates into a per capita income of eleven dollars a day (compared to the one dollar a day criterion of the World Bank used for developing countries). In the US, 13.7 percent of the

US population and 19.6 percent of the population in central cities of metropolitan areas were below the poverty threshold.[10]

Neither the UNDP nor the World Bank undertakes comparisons in poverty levels between "developed" and "developing" countries. Comparisons of this nature would no doubt be the source of "scientific embarrassment", as the poverty indicators presented by both organizations for Third World countries are in some cases *lower* than the official poverty levels in the US, Canada and the European Union. In Canada – which occupies the first rank among all nations according to the UNDP Human Development Index – 17.4 percent of the population are below the national poverty threshold compared to 10.9 percent for Mexico and 4.1 percent for Trinidad and Tobago, according to the UNDP's HPI.[11]

Conversely, if the US Bureau of Census methodology (based on the cost of meeting a minimum diet) were applied to the developing countries, the overwhelming majority of the population would be categorized as "poor". The World Bank would no doubt argue that the use of "Western standards" and definitions of poverty is not applicable in developing countries. Yet recent evidence confirms that retail prices of essential consumer goods are not appreciably lower than in the US or Western Europe. In fact, with deregulation and "free trade" the cost of living in many Third World cities is now higher than in the United States.

Moreover, household budget surveys for several Latin American countries suggest that at least sixty percent of the population of the region does not meet minimum calorie and protein requirements. In Peru, for instance, – resulting from the IMF reforms – 83 percent of the Peruvian population, according to household census data, was unable to meet minimum daily calorie and protein requirements. (See Chapter 14) The prevailing situation in sub-Saharan Africa and South Asia is more serious, where a majority of the population suffer from chronic undernourishment.

Poverty assessments by the World Bank and the United Nations are largely office-based exercises conducted in Washington and New York with insufficient awareness of local realities. For example, the UNDP Poverty Report points to a decline of one third to one half in child mortality in sub-Saharan Africa where poverty has, in fact, increased and public health programmes have collapsed. What the Report fails to mention is that closing down health clinics and massive lay-offs of health professionals (often replaced by semi-illiterate health volunteers) – responsible for compiling mortality data – resulted in a de facto decline in *recorded* mortality, i.e. the breakdown of reliable data systems on mortality and morbidity.

Concealing Country-level Realities

These are the realities, which have been deliberately concealed by the World Bank and UNDP poverty studies. Their poverty indicators blatantly misrepresent country-level situations, as well as the seriousness of global poverty. They serve the purpose of portraying the poor as a minority group representing some 20 percent of world population.

Declining levels of poverty, including forecasts of future trends, are derived with a view to vindicating "free market" policies and upholding the "Washington Consensus" on macro-economic reform. The "free market" system is presented as the most effective means of achieving poverty alleviation, while the impacts of macro-economic reform are denied. Both institutions point to the benefits of the technological revolution and the contribution of foreign investment and trade liberalization, without identifying how these global trends foster increased poverty levels.

Table 2.1
The UNDP's Human Poverty Index
Selected Developing Countries

Country	Poverty Level (percent of the population below the poverty line)
Trinidad and Tobago	4.1
Mexico	10.9
Thailand	11.7
Colombia	10.7
Philippines	17.7
Jordan	10.9
Nicaragua	27.2
Jamaica	12.1
Iraq	30.7
Rwanda	37.9
Papua New Guinea	32.0
Nigeria	41.6
Zimbabwe	17.3

Source: United Nations Development Programme (UNDP), *Human Development Report 1997*, table 1.1, p. 21

Table 2.2
Poverty in Selected G7 Countries by National Standards

Country	Poverty Level (percent of the population below the poverty line)
United States (1996)*	13.7
Canada (1995)**	17.8
United Kingdom (1993)***	20.0
Italy (1993)***	17.0
Germany (1993)***	13.0
France (1993)***	17.0

Source: *US Bureau of Census.
        **Center for International Statistics, Canadian Council on
            Social Development.
        ***European Information Service.

Endnotes

1. "Let Good Times Roll", *Financial Times*, editorial commenting the OECD economic forecasts, December 31, 1994- January 1st, 1995, p. 6.

2. See World Bank, *World Development Report 1990, Poverty*,Washington, DC., 1990.

3. Broadly corresponding to the period of the 1990 World Bank report on Poverty, the US Bureau of the Census estimates the level of poverty in the US at 18.2 percent in 1986; see Bruce E. Kaufman, *The Economics of Labor and Labor Markets*, second edition, Orlando, 1989, p. 649.

4. See World Bank, *World Development Report, 1990, Poverty*, Washington DC, 1990

5. See World Bank, *World Development Report, 1997*, table 9.2, chapter 9.

6. *Ibid*, chapter 9, table 9.2.

7. United Nations Development Program, *Human Development Report, 1997*, New York, 1997, p. 2.

8. *Ibid*, p. 5.

9. See US Bureau of the Census, Current Population Reports, Series P60-198, *Poverty in the United States: 1996*, Washington, 1997.

10. US Bureau of the Census, *Poverty in the United States: 1996*, Washington, 1997.

11. According to the official definition of Statistics Canada. Ottawa, 1995. For country ranks based on the UNDP's Human Development index, see Table 6, *Human Development Report, 1997*, p. 161.

Chapter 3
Policing Countries Through
Loan "Conditionalities"

The Global Debt

How were sovereign countries brought under the tutelage of the international financial institutions ? Because countries were indebted, the Bretton Woods institutions were able to oblige them through the so-called "conditionalities" attached to the loan agreements to appropriately redirect their macro-economic policy in accordance with the interests of the official and commercial creditors.

The debt burden of developing countries has increased steadily since the early 1980s despite the various rescheduling, restructuring and debt-conversion schemes put forward by the creditors. In fact, these procedures, when combined with IMF-World Bank policy-based lending (under the structural adjustment program), were conducive to enlarging the outstanding debt of developing countries, while ensuring prompt reimbursement of interest payments.

The total outstanding long-term debt of developing countries (from official and private sources) stood at approximately US$ 62 billion in 1970. It increased sevenfold in the course of the 1970s to reach $ 481 billion in 1980. The total debt of developing countries stood at close to $ 2 trillion (1998) – a 32-fold increase in relation to 1970. (See Table 3.1.)

Table 3.1
Developing Countries' External Debt
(in US $ billions)

Year	Total external debt	Long-term debt	Short-term debt	Use of IMF Credit
1980	658	481	164	12
1981	672	498	159	14
1982	745	557	168	20
1983	807	633	140	33
1984	843	675	132	36
1985	990	809	141	40
1986	1218	996	179	43
1987	1369	1128	198	43
1988	1334	1092	207	35
1989	1403	1134	237	32
1990	1510	1206	269	35
1991	1594	1265	291	38
1992	1667	1305	324	38
1993	1776	1391	345	40
1994	1921	1523	355	44
1995	2066	1626	378	61
1996	2095	1650	385	60
1997	2317	1783	463	71
1998	2465	1958	412	96
2000	2500	2048	N.A	64

Source: World Bank, *World Debt Tables*, Several Issues, Washington D.C.

Technical Note: The pre-1985 data are based on all countries reporting to the World Bank and are not directly comparable to the post-1985 data. The data for 2000 are estimates based on the 2001 *World Debt Tables* which are not fully comparable with the 1990-98 figures.

Table 3.2
Share of Exports Allocated to Debt Servicing (%)
by Geographical Region

Year	East Asia & Pacific	Europe & Central Asia	Latin America & the Caribbean	Middle East & North Africa	South Asia	Sub-Saharan Africa
1980	13.6	18.1	36.9	20.3	11.6	11.0
1981	7.1	12.8	21.6	20.5	10.2	9.9
1982	18.0	20.4	47.6	21.3	14.5	19.3
1983	18.6	20.2	42.1	23.0	17.7	22.4
1984	18.3	22.4	38.9	22.3	18.2	25.5
1985	25.1	25.5	42.7	23.8	22.6	30.8
1986	26.0	26.6	46.9	30.9	28.7	31.3
1987	25.0	19.4	37.4	15.9	27.5	23.4
1988	19.1	18.7	39.6	17.5	26.2	27.2
1989	16.8	17.1	32.1	16.9	26.8	17.9
1990	15.3	16.8	26.3	14.7	27.6	17.8
1991	13.4	20.5	26.2	16.8	25.0	16.4
1992	13.1	12.8	28.9	16.2	24.7	15.7
1993	14.7	12.4	30.0	15.5	23.7	14.9
1994	12.0	14.6	27.5	15.4	25.6	14.0
1995	12.8	13.8	26.1	14.9	24.6	14.5
1996	13.0	11.4	32.3	11.4	22.0	14.2
1997	11.3	11.5	35.5	13.2	20.3	12.8
1998	12.0	13.3	33.8	13.5	17.9	14.9

Source: World Bank. *World Debt Tables*. Several Issues, Washington D.C.

Note: The share of exports allocated to debt servicing is the ratio of debt service payments (interest and principal) to exports of goods and services.

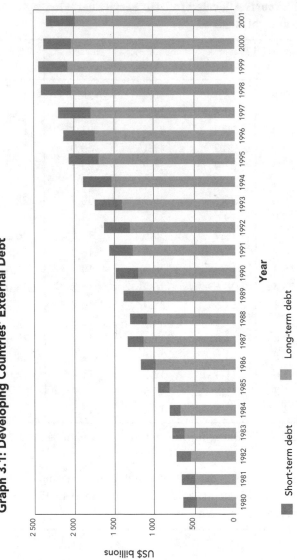

Graph 3.1: Developing Countries' External Debt

■ Short-term debt   ■ Long-term debt

Source: World Bank, *World Debt Tables*, Several Issues, Washington D.C.

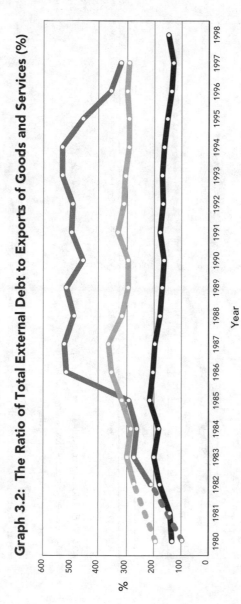

Graph 3.2: The Ratio of Total External Debt to Exports of Goods and Services (%)

All developing countries

Severely indebted low-income countries

Severely indebted middle-income countries

Source: World Bank, *World Debt Tables*, Several Issues, Washington D.C.

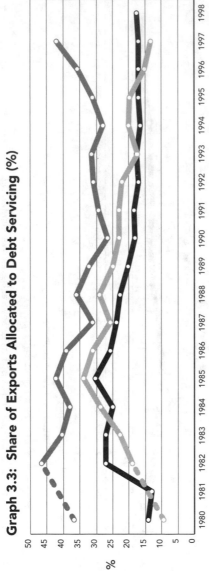

Graph 3.3: Share of Exports Allocated to Debt Servicing (%)

All developing countries
Severely indebted low-income countries
Severely indebted middle-income countries

Source: World Bank, *World Debt Tables*, Several Issues, Washington D.C.
Note: The share of exports allocated to debt servicing is the ratio of debt service payments (interest and principal) to exports of goods and services.

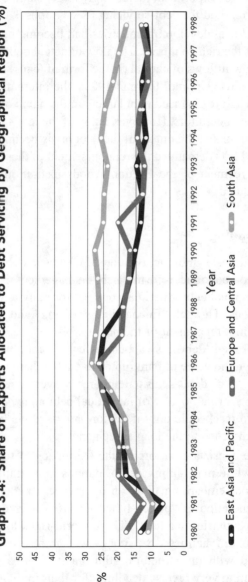

Graph 3.4: Share of Exports Allocated to Debt Servicing by Geographical Region (%)

East Asia and Pacific   Europe and Central Asia   South Asia

Source: World Bank, *World Debt Tables*, Several Issues, Washington D.C.
Note: The share of exports allocated to debt servicing is the ratio of debt service payments (interest and principal) to exports of goods and services.

A Marshall Plan for the Rich Countries

While commodity prices tumbled leading, since the early 1980s, to a decline in the value of exports, an increasingly larger share of export earnings had been earmarked for debt-servicing (See Graphs 3.1 – 3.4.).

By the mid-1980s, developing countries had become net exporters of capital in favor of the rich countries. The flow of actual debt servicing was in excess of the new inflows of capital (in the form of loans, foreign investment and foreign aid).[1] Up until the mid-1980s, the international financial institutions (IFIs) had re-financed debt largely in the name of the commercial bank and official creditors. However, many of the loans granted by the multilateral institutions at the outset of the debt crisis became due and the Washington-based IFIs demanded the reimbursement of these loans. Under the articles of agreement of the Bretton Woods institutions, these loans cannot be rescheduled.

Policy-based Lending

There is a close, almost symbiotic, relationship between debt-management policy and macro-economic reform. Debt management is confined to ensuring that individual debtor nations continue formally to abide by their financial obligations. Through "financial engineering" and the careful art of debt rescheduling, repayment of the principal is deferred while interest payments are enforced; debt is swapped for equity and "new" money is "lent" to nations on the verge of bankruptcy to enable them to pay off their interest arrears on "old" debts so as to temporarily avert default, and so on. In this process, the formal loyalty of individual debtors is paramount. The creditors accept to reschedule only if debtor nations abide by the "policy conditionalities" attached to the loan agreements.

The objective consists in enforcing the legitimacy of the debt-servicing relationship while maintaining debtor nations in a straitjacket, which prevents them from embarking upon an independent national economic policy. A new generation of "policy-based loans" was ized. Money was provided "to help countries to adjust". These World-Bank loan agreements included tight "conditionalities": the money was granted only if the government complied with the structural adjustment reforms while, at the same time, respecting very precise deadlines for their implementation.

In turn, the adoption of the IMF's policy prescriptions under the structural adjustment program was not only conditional for obtaining new loans from multilateral institutions, it also provided "the green light" to the Paris and London Clubs, foreign investors, commercial banking institutions and bilateral donors. Countries which refused to accept the Fund's corrective policy measures faced serious difficulties in rescheduling their debt and/or obtaining new development loans and international assistance. The IMF also had the means of seriously disrupting a national economy by blocking short-term credit in support of commodity trade.

So-called "conditionalities" were attached to "the quick disbursing policy-based loans". These loans by the IFIs were granted subject to the adoption of a comprehensive program of macro-economic stabilization and structural economic reform – i.e. the loan agreements were not in any way related to an investment program as in conventional project lending. The loans were intended to support policy changes; the latter were tightly monitored by the Bretton Woods institutions, their evaluation being based on "policy performance". Once the loan agreement had been signed, disbursements could be interrupted if the government did not conform with the danger that the country would be blacklisted by the so-called "aid coordination group" of bilateral and multilateral donors.[2]

The nature of these loan agreements did not favor the real economy, since none of the money was channeled into investment. Another important objective was served, however: the adjustment loans diverted resources away from the domestic economy and encouraged countries to keep on importing large quantities of consumer goods, including food staples, from the rich countries. The money granted in support of the "adjustment" of agriculture, for instance, was not meant for investment in agricultural projects. The loans could be spent freely on commodity imports including consumer durables and luxury goods.[3] The result of this process was stagnation of the domestic economy, enlargement of the balance of payments crisis and growth of the debt burden.

Enlarging the Debt

The new "quick disbursing loans" (theoretically earmarked for commodity imports) represented "fictitious money" because the amounts granted to debtor nations were invariably lower than the amounts reimbursed in the form of debt servicing. Envisage, for instance, a developing country, which has a total debt stock of US$ 10 billion and owes $ 1 billion in (annual) debt-servicing obligations to the Paris and London Clubs. With depressed export earnings, however, the country is unable to meet these obligations.

And unless new loans "to pay back old debts" are forthcoming, arrears will accumulate and the country will be placed on an international blacklist.

In our example, a quick disbursing loan of US$ 500 million is granted in the form of balance of payments support earmarked for the purchase of commodity imports. The loan acts as *a catalyzer*: it allows the country's foreign exchange earnings from exports to be redirected towards interest payments, thereby enabling the government to meet the deadlines of commercial and official creditors. A billion dollars of debt-servicing is collected through a new loan of US$ 500 million.

The net outflow of resources is US$ 500 million. The loan is "fictitious" because the money, which had been advanced (i.e. by the IMF or the World Bank), is immediately reappropriated by the official and/or commercial creditors. Moreover, this process has resulted in a $ 500 million increase in the debt stock because the new loan was used to pay back the interest portion of debt servicing and not the principal.

The IMF "Shadow Program"

Invariably, substantial reforms will be required prior to the holding of actual loan negotiations. The government has to provide evidence to the IMF that it is "seriously committed to economic reform". This process often takes the form of a so-called "Letter of Intent" submitted to the IMF identifying the government's major orientations in macro-economic policy and debt management. This process was also carried out in the context of the so-called "IMF Shadow Program" in which the IMF provided policy guidelines and technical advice to the government without formal loan support. The Shadow Program applies to countries whose economic reforms are (according to the IMF) *not on track* (e.g. Brazil under presidents Fernando Collor de Mello and Itamar Franco (1990-94)). The Shadow Program was also implemented in countries of the former Soviet Bloc as well as Vietnam in the form of IMF-World Bank technical assistance prior to their formal membership of the Bretton Woods institutions and/or the signing of loan agreements.

"Satisfactory performance" under the Shadow Program is a prerequisite (i.e. a prior condition) to formal loan negotiations. Once the loan has been granted, policy performance is tightly monitored on a quarterly basis by the Washington institutions. The disbursements granted in several "tranches" can be interrupted if the reforms are "not on track" in which case the country is back "on the blacklist" with the danger of reprisals in the area of trade and capital flows. The disbursements can also be interrupted if the country falls behind in its current debt-servicing obligations. The country may, nonetheless, continue to receive IMF-World Bank technical assistance – i.e. a new Shadow Program (as in the case of Kenya in 1991) is set up leading to a new round of policy negotiations.

The Policy Framework Paper

In many indebted countries, the government is obliged, under its agreement with the Washington-based institutions, to outline its priorities in a so-called "Policy Framework Paper" (PFP). The latter is often accompanied by a "Letter of Intent" submitted to the IMF together with a "Memorandum of Economic and Financial Policies." (See Box 3.1.)

Although officially a government document determined by the national authorities, the PFP is written under the close supervision of the IMF and the World Bank according to a standard pre-set format. There is, in this context, a clear division of tasks between the two sister organizations. The IMF is involved in key policy negotiations with regard to the exchange rate and the budget deficit, whereas the World Bank is far more involved in the actual reform process through its country-level representative office and its numerous technical missions.

The IMF monitors a country's economic performance in the context of "Article IV Consultations" (regular review of a member country's economy) on an annual basis. This review provides – in addition to the more stringent quarterly monitoring of performance targets under loan agreements – the basis of so-called "IMF surveillance activities" of members' economic policies.

The World Bank is present in many of the ministries: the reforms in health, education, industry, agriculture, transportation, the environment, etc. are under its jurisdiction. Moreover, since the late 1980s, the World Bank supervises the privatization of state enterprises, the structure of public investment and the composition of public expenditure through the so-called Public Expenditure Review (PER).

Box 3.1 The Letter Of Intent

Mr. Michel Camdessus Managing Director
International Monetary Fund
Washington, D.C. 20431

Dear Mr. Camdessus:

1. The objectives of Guinea's program of economic and financial adjustment for the three-year period 1999-2001 are set out in the updated policy framework paper prepared in close collaboration with the staffs of the Fund and the World Bank, which is being transmitted to you under separate cover.

2. The attached memorandum of economic and financial policies, based on the policy framework paper referred to above, sets out the objectives and policies that the government of Guinea intends to pursue during 1999-2000. In support of these objectives and policies, the government hereby requests the third annual arrangement under the Enhanced Structural Adjustment Facility (ESAF) in an amount equivalent to SDR 23.6 million (30 percent of quota). In this context, Guinea also requests an extension of the original three-year ESAF commitment period to January 12, 2001.

3. The government of Guinea will provide the Fund with such information as the Fund requests in connection with the progress made in implementing the economic and financial policies and achieving the objectives of the program.

4. The government of Guinea believes that the policies and measures set out in the attached memorandum are adequate to achieve the objectives of its program; it will take any further measures that may become appropriate for this purpose. During the period of the third annual ESAF arrangement, the government will consult with the Managing Director on the adoption of any measures that could be appropriate, at the initiative of the government or whenever the Managing Director requests such a consultation. Moreover, after the period of the third annual ESAF arrangement and while Guinea has outstanding financial obligations to the Fund arising from loans under the arrangement, the government will consult with the Fund from time to time, at the initiative of the government or whenever the Managing Director requests consultation on Guinea's economic and financial policies.

5. The government of Guinea will conduct with the Fund the first review of its program supported by the third annual arrangement not later than June 30, 2000 and the second review not later than December 31, 2000.

Sincerely,

Ibrahima Kassory Fofana
Minister of Economy and Finance

Chérif Bah
Governor of the Central Bank of Guinea

The IFIs' Lending Facilities

Various "lending facilities" were used by the Bretton Woods institutions in support of policy-based loans:

International Monetary Fund

Stand-by arrangements, the Compensatory and Contingency Financing Facility (CCFF), the Extended Fund Facility (EFF), IMF structural adjustment and enhanced structural adjustment facilities (SAF and ESAF), the Systemic Transformation Facility (STF), Emergency Lending Facility for Post-Conflict countries.

World Bank

Structural adjustment loans (SAL) and sector adjustment loans (SECAL).

The Systemic Transformation Facility (STF), applied in the former Eastern Bloc countries, operates broadly with the same conditionalities as the structural adjustment loans.

Phase One: "Economic Stabilization"

Structural adjustment is viewed by the IFIs as consisting of two distinct phases: "Short-term" macro-economic stabilization (implying devaluation, price liberalization and budgetary austerity) to be followed by the implementation of a number of more fundamental (and so-called "necessary") structural reforms. More often, however, these "structural" reforms are carried out concurrently with the "economic stabilization" process. The IMF-World Bank stabilization exercise addresses both the budget deficit and the balance of payments. According to the World Bank, this requires: "Getting macro-economic policy right. . . Keeping budget deficits small helps in controlling inflation and avoiding balance of payments problems. Keeping a realistic exchange rate pays off in greater international competitiveness and in supporting convertible currencies."[4]

Destroying A Nation's Currency

The exchange rate is by far the most important instrument of macro-economic reform: currency devaluation (including the unification of the exchange rate and the elimination of exchange controls) affects fundamental supply and demand relations within the national economy. The IMF plays a key political role in decisions to devalue. The rate of exchange regulates the real prices paid to the direct producers as well as the real value of wages.

The IMF invariably argues that the exchange rate is "overvalued". Currency devaluation is often demanded (as a pre-condition) prior to the negotiation of a structural adjustment loan: the destabilization of the national currency is a key objective of the IMF-World Bank's "hidden agenda". A "maxi-devaluation" – resulting in immediate and abrupt price hikes – is conducive to a dramatic compression of real earnings while, at the same time, reducing the value of labor costs expressed in hard currency. The devaluation also reduces the dollar value of government expenditure thereby facilitating the release of state revenues towards the servicing of the external debt.

The IMF imposes the unification of the exchange rate in the context of the clauses of Article VIII of the IMF Articles of Agreement. Countries accepting Article VIII are prevented from adopting multiple exchange-rate practices or foreign exchange controls without IMF approval. More than one hundred member countries of the IMF have accepted the clauses of Article VIII.

The Social Consequences of Devaluation

The social impact of the IMF-sponsored devaluation is brutal and immediate: the domestic prices of food staples, essential drugs, fuel and public services increase overnight. While the devaluation invariably triggers inflation and the "dollarization" of domestic prices, the IMF obliges the government (as part of the economic package) to adopt a so-called "anti-inflationary program". The latter has little to do with the real causes of inflation (i.e. the devaluation). It is predicated on a contraction of demand, requiring the dismissal of public employees, drastic cuts in social-sector programs and the deindexation of wages. In sub-Saharan Africa, for instance, the devaluation of the Central and West African (CFA) franc imposed by the IMF and the French Treasury in 1994 compressed (with the stroke of a pen) the real value of wages and government expenditure (expressed in hard currency) by 50 percent while massively redirecting state revenues towards debt-servicing.

In some cases, currency devaluation has provided the basis for a short-term reactivation of commercial agriculture geared towards the export market. More often, however, the underlying benefits accrue to the large commercial plantations and agro-industrial exporters (in the form of lower real wages to agricultural workers). The "short-term gains" from devaluation are invariably wiped out when competing Third World countries are forced to devalue (in similar agreements with the IMF).

The "Dollarization" of Domestic Prices

The devaluation leads to a "realignment of domestic prices" at the levels prevailing in the world market. This process of "dollarization" of domestic prices leads to abrupt price hikes in most commodities, including food staples, consumer durables and gasoline and fuel, as well as most inputs and raw materials used in production (e.g. farm inputs, equipment, etc.). In this regard, domestic prices will adjust to their world market levels irrespective of the direction of monetary policy.

The devaluation – rather than an expansion in the supply of money – constitutes the main factor which triggers the inflationary spiral. The IMF denies the inflationary impact of currency devaluation: tight restrictions on money supply are imposed in the aftermath of the devaluation once the price hikes have already taken place with a view to "combating inflationary pressures". This freeze on money creation obliges the government to curtail real expenditures, reduce real wages and lay off civil servants.

The Deindexation of Wages

Needless to say, pressures build up within society to increase nominal wages to compensate for the dramatic decline in real earnings, yet the agreement with the IMF formally disallows the indexation of real earnings (and social expenditures). The IMF requires "the liberalization of the labor market", the elimination of cost of living adjustment clauses in collective agreements and the phasing out of minimum- wage legislation. The argument in favor of deindexation is based on the "inflationary impact of wage demands".

Analyzing the Impact of Devaluation

The impact of the devaluation must be analyzed in relation to the following variables:

- the level of domestic prices (P),
- nominal wages (W),
- real wages (W/P),

- nominal government expenditure (G),
- real government expenditure (G/P),
- the nominal money supply (M),
- the real money supply (M/P).

The dollarization of domestic prices leads to a contraction in:

- real wages (W/P),
- the real value of government expenditure (G/P).

The nominal supply of money (M) may increase but the real value of the supply of money (M/P) declines dramatically. The devaluation implies a process of monetary contraction (M/P) and a massive compression of the real value of government expenditure (G/P) and wages (W/P). The real prices paid to direct producers also decline as a result of the devaluation.

Taking Control of the Central Bank

The IMF tightly monitors and provides resources for the restructuring of the Central Bank. The IMF requires so-called "Central Bank independence from political power as a remedy against the inflationary bias of governments".[5] In practice, this means that the IMF, rather than the government, controls money creation. The agreement signed between the government and the IMF prevents the funding of government expenditure and the provision of credit by the Central Bank through money creation, – i.e. the IMF, on behalf of the creditors, is in a position virtually to paralyze the financing of real economic development. Incapable of using domestic monetary policy to mobilize its internal resources, the country becomes increasingly dependent on international sources of funding which has the added consequence of increasing the level of external indebtedness.

Another important condition put forth by the IMF is that "Central Bank independence holds also with respect to parliament"[6] Namely, once the senior officials of the Central Bank have been appointed, they are neither accountable to the government nor to parliament. Increasingly, their allegiance is to the IFIs. In many developing countries, senior officials of the Central Bank are former staff members of the IFIs and of the regional development banks. Moreover, Central Bank officials often receive "salary supplements" in hard currency financed from multilateral and bilateral sources.

Destabilizing a Nation's Public Finances

The dismissal of public employees and drastic cuts in social-sector programs are imposed by the Bretton Woods institutions. These austerity measures hit all categories of public expenditure. At the outset of the debt crisis, the IFIs would limit their intervention to setting an overall target for the budget deficit in view of releasing state revenues for debt servicing. Since the late 1980s, the World Bank has closely monitored the structure of public expenditure through the so-called Public Expenditure Review (PER). In this context, the composition of expenditure in each of the ministries is under the supervision of the Bretton Woods institutions. The World Bank recommends "a cost effective" transfer from regular expenditure categories to "targeted expenditures". According to the World Bank, the PER is to "promote the reduction of poverty in a cost effective and efficient fashion".

With regard to the social sectors, the IFIs insist on the principle of cost recovery and the gradual withdrawal of the state from basic health and educational services. The concept of targeting in the social sectors pertains to the identification of so-called "vulnerable groups". The austerity measures in the social sectors – requiring a shift from regular to targeted programs – has largely been responsible for the collapse of schools, health clinics and hospitals, while providing a semblance of legitimacy to the Washington-based institutions.

The Budget Deficit: A Moving Target

Initial targets are set in the loan agreements for the budget deficit. However, since the early 1990s, the IMF has applied the concept of a "moving target" for the budget deficit: a target of 5 percent of GDP is first set, the government meets the IMF target; in subsequent loan negotiations or within the same loan agreement, the IMF lowers the target to 3.5 percent on the grounds that government expenditure patterns are "inflationary". Once the 3.5 percent target has been met, the IMF will insist on reducing the budget deficit to 1.5 percent of GDP, and so on. This exercise ultimately exacerbates the fiscal crisis of the State leading to the collapse of state programs while releasing state revenue (in the short-run) for the payment of interest on the external debt.

Engineering the Collapse of State Investment

The budget targets imposed by the Bretton Woods institutions, combined with the effects of the devaluation, trigger the collapse of public investment. New rules pertaining to both recurrent and development expenditures are established: precise "ceilings" are placed on all categories of expenditure; the state is no longer permitted to mobilize its own resources for the building of public infrastructure, roads or hospitals, etc. – i.e. the creditors not only become the "brokers" of all major public investment projects, they also decide in the context of the "Public Investment Program" (PIP) (established under the technical auspices of the World Bank) on what type of public infrastructure should or should not be funded by the "donor community". The concept of targeted investment is put forth and capital formation in necessary economic and social infrastructure is dramatically curtailed.

Under the PIP, all project loans require a system of procurement and international tender ("competitive bidding") which allocates the entire execution of public works projects to international construction and engineering firms. The latter, in turn, skim off large amounts of money into a variety of consulting and management fees. Local construction companies (whether public or private) tend to be excluded from the tendering process although local companies (using local labor at very low wages) will undertake much of the actual construction work in separate sub-contracting deals reached with the transnationals. In other words, loan money earmarked for infrastructural projects is largely "recycled" in favor of multinational contractors.

While project financing is granted in the form of "soft loans" at concessional interest rates, with extended repayment periods, the actual costs (and the imputed interest rate which underlies these costs) to the country are exceedingly high. The PIP, under the supervision of the World Bank, is predicated on enlarging the external debt while contributing to the demobilization of domestic resources.

Price Liberalization

The IMF-World Bank claims that it is necessary to eliminate so-called price distortions. "Getting Prices Right" consists in the elimination of all subsidies and price controls. The impact on levels of real earnings (in both the formal and informal sectors) is immediate.

The deregulation of domestic grain prices, as well as the liberalization of staple food imports, is an essential feature of this program. The liberalization program also pertains to the prices of inputs and raw materials. Combined with the devaluation, the underlying measures lead to substantial hikes in the domestic prices of fertilizer, farm inputs, equipment, etc., which have an immediate impact on the cost structure in most areas of economic activity.

The Pricing of Petroleum Products and Public Utilities

The price of petroleum products is regulated by the state under the supervision of the World Bank. The price hikes, both in fuel and public utilities (often of several hundred percent), invariably contribute to destabilizing domestic production, – i.e. the high domestic price of gasoline (substantially above world market levels) backlashes on the cost structure of domestic industry and agriculture. The production costs are often artificially pushed up above the domestic sale price of the commodity thereby precipitating a large number of small and medium-sized producers into bankruptcy.

Moreover, the periodic price hikes of petroleum products imposed by the World Bank (adopted concurrently with the liberalization of commodity imports) operate as an "internal transit duty" which serves the purpose of cutting domestic producers off from their own market. The high price of gasoline contributes to the disruption of internal freight. Exceedingly high petrol and diesel prices (i.e. in relation to very low wages), combined with the numerous user fees and tolls for bridges, roads, inland waterways, etc. affect the entire cost structure of domestically produced goods largely to the advantage of imported commodities. In sub-Saharan Africa, the high cost of transportation imposed by the IFIs is one of the key factors which prevent farmers from selling their produce in the urban market in direct competition with heavily subsidized agricultural commodities imported from Europe and North America.

Although the modalities differ, the tariff on fuel and public utilities has similar consequences to the internal transit duty imposed in India by the British East India Company in the late 18th century.

Phase Two: "Structural Reform"

The application of macro-economic "stabilization" (which is a condition for the granting of bridge financing by the IMF and the rescheduling of the external debt with the Paris and London Clubs) are followed by the implementation of so-called "necessary" structural reforms. There is a division of tasks between the IMF and the World Bank. These "necessary" economic reforms are supported by World Bank SALs and sectoral adjustment loans (SECALs). The package of structural reforms discussed below consists of measures pertaining to trade liberalization, the deregulation of the banking sector, the privatization of state enterprises, tax reform, the privatization of agricultural land, "poverty alleviation" and "good governance".

Trade Liberalization

The Bretton Woods institutions argue that the tariff structure constitutes a so-called "anti-export bias" which discourages the development of the export economy – i.e. it favors the development of the domestic market at the expense of the export sector leading to a misallocation of resources. There is little evidence to suggest, however, that the elimination of tariffs has facilitated "the switch of resources" in favor of exports.

The trade liberalization program invariably consists of the elimination of import quotas and the reduction and unification of tariffs. The consequent decline in customs' revenues also has a significant impact on the state's public finances. Not only do these measures backfire on the budget deficit, thus exacerbating fiscal imbalances, they also prevent the authorities from selectively rationing (through tariffs and quotas) the use of scarce foreign exchange.

While the elimination of quotas and the reduction of protective tariff barriers are intended "to make domestic industry more competitive", the liberalization of trade invariably leads to the collapse of domestic manufacturing (geared towards the internal market). The measures also fuel the influx of luxury goods, while the tax burden of the upper income groups is reduced as a result of the lowering of import tariffs on automobiles and consumer durables. Imported consumer goods not only replace domestic production, this consumer frenzy, sustained on borrowed money (through the various quick disbursing loans), ultimately contributes to swelling the external debt.

Divestiture and Privatization of State Enterprises

Structural adjustment constitutes a means for taking over the real assets of indebted countries through the privatization program, as well as collecting debt-servicing obligations. The privatization of state enterprises is invariably tied to the renegotiation of the country's external debt. The most profitable parastatals are taken over by foreign capital or joint ventures often in exchange for debt. The proceeds of these sales deposited in the Treasury are channeled towards the London and Paris Clubs. International capital gains control and/or ownership over the most profitable state enterprises at a very low cost. Moreover, with a large number of indebted countries selling (or trading) their public enterprises at the same time, the price of state assets tumbles.

In some countries, state ownership over "strategic sectors" (e.g. oil, gas, telecommunications) and public utilities is entrenched in the constitution. Privatization of these sectors may require, as in the case of Brazil, the prior amendment of the constitution. (See Chapter 13.)

Tax Reform

Under the guidance of the World Bank, a number of fundamental changes are implemented in the fiscal structure. These changes tend to undermine domestic production both on the demand and supply sides. The introduction of a value-added or sales tax and changes in the structure of direct taxation invariably imply a greater tax burden for the lower- and middle-income groups. Included in the World Bank framework is the registration, for tax purposes, of small agricultural producers and units of the informal urban sector. While domestic producers are subjected to government taxes, joint ventures and foreign capital invariably enjoy generous tax holidays as a means of "attracting foreign investment".

Land Tenure and the Privatization of Agricultural Land

The reforms are conducted in the context of the World Bank's sectoral adjustment loans. The relevant legislation on the ownership of land is often developed with technical support provided by the World Bank's Legal Department. The reforms consist in issuing land titles to farmers while, at the same time encouraging, the concentration of farm land in fewer hands. Customary land rights are also affected. The tendency is towards the forfeiture and/or mortgaging of land by small farmers, the growth of the agri-business sector and the formation of a class of landless seasonal agricultural workers.

Moreover, the measures often contribute – under the disguise of modernity – to the restoration of the rights of the "old-time" landlord class. Ironically, the latter is often the champion of economic "liberalization".

The privatization of land also serves the objective of debt servicing since the proceeds of public land sales, under advice from the World Bank, are used to generate state revenues, which are channeled by the national Treasury to the international creditors.

Deregulation of the Banking System

The Central Bank loses control over monetary policy: interest rates are determined in the "free market" by the commercial banks. Concessional credit to agriculture and industry is phased out. The underlying measures are usually conducive to significant hikes in both real and nominal interest rates. The movement of interest rates interacts with that of domestic prices. Nominal interest rates are pushed up to abnormally high levels as a result of periodic devaluations and the resulting "dollarization" of domestic prices. The deregulation of the banking system also leads to the influx of "hot money" attracted by artificially high interest rates. The commercial banks are no longer in a position to provide credit to the real economy at reasonable rates. This policy – combined with the phasing out of the state development banks – leads to the collapse of credit to both agriculture and domestic industry. Whereas short-term credit to merchants involved in the export trade is maintained, the domestic banking sector is no longer geared towards providing credit to local producers.

The international financial institutions will also require the privatization of state development banks and the deregulation of the commercial banking system. It is worth noting that under the Uruguay Round Agreement, conducted under the umbrella of the GATT and signed in 1994, foreign commercial banks are allowed free entry into the domestic banking sector.

The movement is towards the divestiture of state banking institutions (under the privatization program), as well as the displacement of private domestic banks. The restructuring of the banking sector is implemented in the context of a Financial Sector Adjustment program (FSAP). The latter includes the divestiture and sale of all state banks under the supervision of the IFIs with key state banking institutions taken over by foreign financial interests.

The process of divestiture is related directly to the collection of debt servicing obligations. The restructuring of the commercial debt under the Brady Plan, for instance, was often conditional upon the prior privatization of state banking institutions under the clauses of the FSAP, with the proceeds of these sales channeled into the servicing of the commercial debt.

Liberalizing Capital Movements

The IMF insists on the "transparency" and "free movement" of foreign exchange in and out of the country (through electronic transfers). This process enables foreign companies freely to repatriate their profits in foreign exchange.

Recycling Dirty Money towards Debt Servicing

Another important objective, however, is served: the liberalization of capital movements encourages the "repatriation of capital flight", namely, the return of "black" and "dirty money" which had been deposited by the Third World élites since the 1960s in offshore bank accounts. "Dirty money" constitutes the proceeds of illegal trade and/or criminal activity whereas "black money" is money which has escaped taxation.

The crisis of the legal economy under the brunt of the macro-economic reforms is related directly to the rapid growth of illicit trade. Moreover, the convenience and speed at which dirty money transactions can be undertaken (through electronic transfers) tend to facilitate the development of illicit trade at the expense of the legal economy.

The liberalization of capital movements serves the interests of the creditors. It constitutes a means for channeling "dirty" and "black money" deposited offshore towards the servicing of the external debt, while providing the privileged social classes with a convenient mechanism for laundering large amounts of money which were obtained illegally.

This process works as follows: hard currency is transferred from an offshore bank account into the interbank market of a developing country ("no questions asked"). The foreign exchange is then converted into local currency and used to purchase state assets and/or public land put on the auction block by the government in the context of the World Bank-sponsored privatization program. In turn, the foreign exchange proceeds of these sales are channeled towards the national Treasury where they are earmarked for debt-servicing.

"Poverty Alleviation" and the "Social Safety Net"

Since the late 1980s, "poverty alleviation" has become a "conditionality" of World Bank loan agreements. "Poverty alleviation" supports the objective of debt-servicing: "sustainable poverty reduction", under the dominion of the Bretton Woods institutions, is predicated on slashing social-sector budgets and redirecting expenditure on a selective and token basis "in favor of the poor". The "Social Emergency Fund" (established on the Bolivia-Ghana model) is intent on providing "a flexible mechanism" for "managing poverty" while, at the same time, dismantling the state's public finances. The poor are defined in this framework as "target groups".

The Social Emergency Fund (SEF) requires a social engineering approach, a policy framework for "managing poverty" and attenuating social unrest at minimal cost to the creditors. So-called "targeted programs" earmarked "to help the poor" combined with "cost recovery" and the "privatization" of health and educational services are said to constitute "a more efficient" way of delivering social programs. The state withdraws and many programs under the jurisdiction of line ministries will henceforth be managed by the organizations of civil society under the umbrella of the SEF. The latter also finances, under the "social safety net", severance payments and/or minimum-employment projects earmarked for public-sector workers laid off as a result of the adjustment program.

The SEF officially sanctions the withdrawal of the state from the social sectors and "the management of poverty" (at the micro-social level) by separate and parallel organizational structures. Various non-governmental organizations (NGOs), funded by international "aid programs", have gradually taken over many of the functions of local-level governments. Small-scale production and handicraft projects, sub-contracting for export processing firms, community-based training and employment programs, etc. are set up under the umbrella of the "social safety net". A meager survival to local-level communities is ensured while, at the same time, the risk of social upheaval is contained.

"Good Governance": Promoting Bogus Parliamentary Institutions

"Democratization" has become the motto of the free market. So-called "governance" and the holding of multi-party elections are added as conditionalities to the loan agreements. The nature of the economic reforms, however, prevents a genuine democratization.

The Consequences of Structural Adjustment

The solution to the debt crisis becomes the cause of further indebtedness. The IMF's economic stabilization package is, in theory, intended to assist countries in restructuring their economies with a view to generating a surplus on their balance of trade so as to pay back the debt and initiate a process of economic recovery. Exactly the opposite occurs. The very process of "belt-tightening" imposed by the creditors undermines economic recovery and the ability of countries to repay their debt.

The underlying measures contribute to enlarging the external debt:

1) The new policy-based loans granted to pay back old debt contribute to increasing the debt stock.

2) Trade liberalization tends to exacerbate the balance of payments crisis. Domestic production is replaced by imports (in a wide range of commodities) and new quick-disbursing loans are granted to enable countries to continue importing goods from the world market.

3) With the completion of the Uruguay Round and the formation of the World Trade Organization, a much larger share of the import bill is made up of "services", including the payment of intellectual property rights. The import bill will increase without a corresponding influx of ("produced") commodities.

4) The structural adjustment program has implied a significant shift out of project lending and a consequent freeze on capital formation in all areas which do not directly serve the interests of the export economy.

The economic stabilization package destroys the possibility of an "endogenous national economic development process" controlled by national policy makers. The IMF-World Bank reforms brutally dismantle the social sectors of developing countries, undoing the efforts and struggles of the post-colonial period and reversing "with the stroke of a pen" the fulfillment of past progress. Throughout the developing world, there is a consistent and coherent pattern: the IMF-World Bank reform package constitutes a coherent program of economic and social collapse. The austerity measures lead to the disintegration of the state, the national economy is remolded, production for the domestic market is destroyed through the compression of real earnings and domestic production is redirected towards the world market. These measures go far beyond the phasing out of import-substituting industries. They destroy the entire fabric of the domestic economy.

The IMF Tacitly Acknowledges Policy Failure

Ironically, the IMF and the World Bank have tacitly acknowledged policy failure. In the words of a Senior IMF official:

> Although there have been a number of studies on the subject over the past decade, one cannot say with certainty whether programs have "worked" or not (. . .). On the basis of existing studies, one certainly cannot say whether the adoption of programs supported by the Fund led to an improvement in inflation and growth performance. In fact it is often found that programs are associated with a rise in inflation and a fall in the growth rate.[7]

While calling for the development of "improved methods of evaluation" of fund-supported programs, the empirical tests proposed by the IMF Research Department are not able to refute the evidence.

The Counterfactual Argument

The measures are justified by the Bretton Woods institutions on the grounds of micro-economic efficiency. According to the IFIs, the "social costs" must be balanced against the "economic benefits" of macro-economic stabilization. The IMF-World Bank motto is "short- term pain for long-term gain".

While recognizing the "social dimensions of adjustment", the Bretton Woods institutions have also underscored the so-called "counterfactual argument": "the situation is bad, but it would have been far worse had the structural adjustment measures not been adopted". According to a recent World Bank report:

> Africa's disappointing economic performance in the aggregate represents a failure to adjust [rather than] a failure of adjustment (. . .). More Adjustment – Not Less – Would Help the Poor and the Environment. (. . .) Adjustment is the necessary first step on the road to sustainable poverty reduction.[8]

Whereas the economic policy package is, in principle, intended to promote efficiency and a more rational allocation of productive resources based on the market mechanism, this objective is brought about through a massive disengagement of human and material resources. The counterpart of "micro-economic efficiency" is programmed austerity at the macro-economic level. It is, consequently, difficult to justify these measures on the grounds of efficiency and resource allocation.

The Social Impact of Macro-economic Reform

The social implications of these reforms (including their impact on health, education, the social rights of women and the environment) have been amply documented.[9] Educational establishments are closed down and teachers are laid off due to lack of funds; in the health sector, there is a general breakdown in curative and preventive care as a result of the lack of medical equipment and supplies, poor working conditions and the low pay of medical personnel. The lack of operating funds is, in part, compensated by the exaction of registration and user fees – e.g. the "drug cost recovery scheme" under the Bamako Proposal and the Parent Teachers' Associations (PTA) levies exacted by local communities to cover expenses previously incurred by the Ministry of Education.

This process, however, implies the partial privatization of essential government social services and the de facto exclusion of large sectors of the population (particularly in rural areas) which are unable to pay the various fees attached to health and educational services.[10]

It should be emphasized that the structural adjustment program not only results in increased levels of urban and rural poverty. It also implies a reduced capacity of people (including middle-class households) to pay for health and educational services associated with the cost recovery scheme.

Freezing the number of graduates of the teacher training colleges and increasing the number of pupils per teacher are explicit conditions of World Bank social-sector adjustment loans. The educational budget is curtailed, the number of contact-hours spent by children in school is cut down and a double shift system is installed: one teacher now does the work of two, the remaining teachers are laid off and the resulting savings to the Treasury are funneled towards the external creditors.

These "cost effective" initiatives, however, are still considered to be incomplete: in sub-Saharan Africa, the donor community has recently proposed a new imaginative ("cost-effective") formula which consists in eliminating the teachers' meager salary altogether (in some countries as low as US$ 15-20 a month) while granting small loans to enable unemployed teachers to set up their own informal "private schools" in rural backyards and urban slums. Under this scheme, the Ministry of Education would, nonetheless, still be responsible for monitoring "the quality" of teaching.

The Restructuring of the Health Sector

A similar approach prevails in the area of health: state subsidies to health are said to create undesirable "market distortions", which "benefit the rich". Moreover, according to the World Bank, an expenditure of US$ 8 per person per annum is amply sufficient to meet acceptable standards of clinical services.[11] Moreover, user fees for primary health care to impoverished rural communities should be exacted both on the grounds of "greater equity" and "efficiency". These communities should also participate in the running of the primary health care units by substituting the qualified nurse or medical auxiliary (hitherto paid by the Ministry of Health) by an untrained and semi-illiterate health volunteer.

The results: with the exception of a small number of externally funded showpieces, health establishments in sub-Saharan Africa have de facto become a source of disease and infection. The shortage of funds allocated to medical supplies (including disposable syringes), as well as the price hikes (recommended by the World Bank) in electricity, water and fuel (e.g. required to sterilize needles) increase the incidence of infection (including HIV transmission). In sub-Saharan Africa, for instance, the inability to pay for prescription drugs tends to reduce the levels of attendance and utilization in government health centers to the extent that health infrastructure and personnel are no longer utilized in a cost-effective fashion.[12]

While the cost recovery scheme may ensure the limited operational viability of a select number of health centers, the tendency is towards a) increased social polarization in the health-care delivery system and b) a reduction in health coverage and an increase in the already large percentage of the population which has no access to health. Macro-economic policy is conducive to a major disengagement of human and material resources in the social sectors.

The Resurgence of Communicable Diseases

In sub-Saharan Africa there has been a resurgence of a number of communicable diseases which were believed to be under control. These include cholera, yellow fever and malaria. Similarly, in Latin America the prevalence of malaria and dengue has worsened dramatically since the mid-1980s in terms of parasite incidence. Control and prevention activities (directly associated with the contraction of public expenditure under the structural adjustment program) have declined dramatically. The outbreak of bubonic and pneumonic plague in India in 1994 has been recognized as "the direct consequence of a worsening urban sanitation and public health infrastructure which accompanied the compression of national and municipal budgets under the 1991 IMF/World Bank-sponsored structural adjustment program".[13]

The social consequences of structural adjustment are fully acknowledged by the IFIs. The IMF-World Bank methodology considers, however, the "social sectors" and "the social dimensions of adjustment" as something "separate" – i.e. according to the dominant economic dogma, these "undesired side effects" are not part of the workings of an economic model. They belong to a separate "sector": the social sector.

Endnotes

1. See World Bank, *World Debt Tables*, several issues.
2. The loan disbursements are normally granted in several tranches. The release of each tranche is conditional upon the implementation of precise economic reforms.
3. These loans constitute so-called "balance of payments aid".
4. World Bank, *Adjustment in Africa*, Oxford University Press, Washington, 1994, p. 9.
5. Carlo Cottarelli, *Limiting Central Bank Credit to the Government*, IMF, Washington DC, 1993, p. 3.
6. *Ibid.*, p. 26.
7. Mohsin Khan, "The Macroeconomic Effects of Fund Supported Adjustment Programs", *IMF Staff Papers*, Vol. 37, No. 2, 1990, p. 196, p. 222.
8. World Bank, *Adjustment in Africa*, Oxford University Press, Washington 1994, p. 17.
9. Various studies including a major study by UNICEF entitled "Structural Adjustment with a Human Face" have examined the impact of macro-economic policy on a number of social indicators including morbidity and the frequency of infectious diseases, infant mortality, levels of child nutrition, levels of education.
10. It is worth noting that under a scheme of cost recovery proposed by the international financial institutions to indebted countries, the Ministry

of Health would reduce its disbursements and transfer the cost of running the health centers to impoverished rural and urban communities. Under the cost-recovery scheme, there would be "decentralization of decision-making" and "community involvement and control": what this means is that impoverished rural and urban communities – while ecoming formally "self-reliant" – would bear the burden of subsidizing the Ministry of Health.

11. See World Bank, *World Development Report, 1993: Investing in Health*, Washington DC, 1993, p. 106.

12. On the issue of cost recovery see UNICEF, "Revitalising Primary Health Care/Maternal and Child Health, the Bamako Initiative", report by the Executive Director, February 1989, p. 16.

13. See *Madrid Declaration of Alternative Forum, The Other Voices of the Planet*, Madrid, October 1994.

Chapter 4

The World Bank and Women's Rights

The World Bank has become the defender of women's rights urging national governments to "invest more in women in order to reduce gender inequality and boost economic development".[1] Through its Women In Development Program (WID) adopted throughout the developing world, the World Bank dictates the ground rules on gender policy. A "market-oriented" approach to gender is prescribed; a monetary value is attached to gender equality. Women's programs are to be framed in relation to the "opportunity cost" and "efficiency" of women's rights.

While recognizing the possibility of "market failure" (and consequently the need for state intervention to protect women's rights), the World Bank contends that "free markets" broadly support the "empowerment of women" and the achievement of gender equality:

> It is critical that governments take the lead where markets fail to capture the full benefits to society of investment in women. (…) Investments in women are vital in achieving economic efficiency and growth. [T]he Bank is to promote gender equality as a matter of social justice and enhance women's participation in economic development.[2]

Policies that "deepen markets" and "stimulate more competitive market structures" are said to contribute to greater gender equality. The World Bank asserts that the structural adjustment program (SAP) improves women's economic status in the labor market, while acknowledging that there are also "risks" to women associated with the cuts in social spending and the downsizing of state programs.

The World Bank's Gender Perspective

The World Bank acts as a custodian: it determines the concepts, methodological categories and data base used to analyze gender issues. The "donor community" controls the institutional framework (at the country level), including the Women's Bureau and the Ministry of Women's Affairs. Because the World Bank constitutes the main source of funding, national women's organizations – associated with the seat of political power – will often endorse the WB gender perspective. The main objective of the latter is not to enhance women's rights, but to impose a free market gender perspective and to demobilize the women's movement.

Under the trusteeship of the international financial institutions, the "empowerment of women" is to be achieved through the usual macro-economic recipes: devaluation, budget austerity, the application of user fees in health and education, the phasing out of state-supported credit, trade liberalization, the deregulation of grain markets, the elimination of minimum wage legislation, and so on. In other words, donor support to Women's programs – via Women in Development (WID) funded projects – is conditional upon the prior derogation of women's rights through "satisfactory compliance" with IMF-World Bank conditionalities.

For instance, the implementation of token credit schemes earmarked for rural women under the World Bank's micro-level credit programs invariably requires the prior divestiture of the state-supported development banks, dramatic hikes in interest rates and the phasing out of the rural credit cooperatives. The same applies to the "anti-poverty programs". The latter are conditional upon the prior adoption of macro-economic measures, which generate mass poverty. The anti-poverty programs, implemented under the "social safety net", are geared towards so-called "vulnerable groups": "disadvantaged women, indigenous women, female heads of households, refugees and migrant women and women with disabilities". The structural causes of poverty and the role of macro-economic reform are denied.

Derogating Women's Educational Rights

Another area of World Bank intervention has been the implementation of token scholarships and/or subsidies to girls *(Letting Girls Learn)* to finance the costs of primary and secondary school tuition including books and school materials.[3] World Bank support in this area, however, is conditional upon the prior laying off of teachers and the adoption of double-shift and multi-grade teaching. (See Chapter 3.)

The World Bank Education Sector loan agreements specifically require the Ministry of Education to cut its budget, lay-off teachers and increase the student-teacher ratio. The implementation of "book rental fees" and tuition fees – also under World Bank guidance – has been conducive to a dramatic decline in both female and male school enrolment. The WB focus is to implement cost-effective "targeted programs" for girls while, at the same time, prescribing the withdrawal of the state from the financing of primary and secondary education.

Cost Recovery in Health

Cost recovery and the application of user fees in health, under World Bank supervision, contribute to the derogation of women's rights to reproductive health. In this regard, the structural adjustment programs have been conducive in many parts of the world to the phasing out of maternal-child health programs (MCH). The evidence confirms a resurgence of maternal and infant mortality.

In sub-Saharan Africa, the tendency is towards the "de-professionalization" of health services, ultimately leading to the collapse of primary health care. Village Health Volunteers (VHV) and traditional healers have replaced community health nurses. The savings to the Treasury are applied to servicing the country's external debt. According to the World Bank, "informal health care" is not only "cost effective", it is more "democratic" because it "empowers'" women in local communities in the running of village-based health centers.

Hidden Agenda

The WB framework portrays a 'free' market society composed of individuals of both sexes. Women are identified as belonging to a separate social category distinct from men (as if men and women belonged to different social classes). The confrontation between men and women (i.e. as individuals) is viewed as the main source of social conflict. Under the World Bank gender framework, the social status of women hinges upon the relationship of men and women within the household. How globalization affects women is not an issue. According to the World Bank, the concentration of wealth and the structures of corporate economic power have no bearing on women's rights.

Modernity and "the empowerment of women" through the "free market" are the means to achieving gender equality. The system of global trade and finance is never in doubt; the role of global institutions (including the World Trade Organization and the Bretton Woods institutions) is not a matter for serious debate. Yet this global economic system (based on 'cheap labor' and the private accumulation of wealth) ultimately constitutes one of the main barriers to the achievement of gender equality. In turn, the neoliberal gender perspective (under the trusteeship of the 'donors') is largely intent upon creating divisions within national societies, demobilizing the women's movement and breaking the solidarity between women and men in their struggle against the New World Order.

Endnotes

1.   World Bank, *'Toward Gender Equality: The Role of Public Policy*, United Nations Fourth Conference on Women, Beijing, 1995). See also World Bank 'Advanced Gender Equality: From Concept to Action:' United Nations Fourth Conference on Women, Beijing, 1995).

2.   World Bank, *The Gender Issue as Key to Development*, Washington, Document HCO, 95/01, 1995, p. 1.

3.   World Bank, *Letting Girls Learn*, World Bank Discussion Paper Series, Washington, 1995.

Chapter 5
The Global Cheap-Labor Economy

Introduction

The globalization of poverty is accompanied by the reshaping of national economies of developing countries and the redefinition of their role in the New World Economic Order. The national level macro-economic reforms (discussed in the previous Chapter) applied simultaneously in a large number of individual countries play a key role in regulating wages and labor costs at a world level. Global poverty is "an input" on the supply side; the global economic system feeds on cheap labor.

The world economy is marked by the relocation of a substantial share of the industrial base of the advanced capitalist countries to cheap-labor locations in developing countries. The development of the cheap-labor export economy was launched in SouthEast Asia in the 1960s and 1970s largely in "labor-intensive manufacturing". Initially limited to a few export enclaves (e.g. Hong Kong, Singapore, Taiwan and South Korea), the development of offshore cheap-labor production gained impetus in the 1970s and 1980s.

Since the late 1970s, a "new generation" of free trade areas has developed with major growth poles in SouthEast Asia and the Far East, China, Brazil, Mexico and Eastern Europe. This globalization of industrial production affects a wide range of manufactured goods. Third World industry encompasses most areas of manufacturing (automobiles, ship-building, aircraft assembly, arms production, etc.).[1]

Whereas the Third World continues to play a role as a major primary producer, the contemporary world economy is no longer structured along traditional divisions between "industry" and "primary production" (e.g. the debate on the terms of trade between primary and industrial producers). An increasingly large share of world manufacturing is undertaken in SouthEast Asia, China, Latin America and Eastern Europe.

This worldwide development of cheap-labor industries (in increasingly sophisticated and heavier areas of manufacturing) is predicated on the compression of internal demand in individual Third World economies and the consolidation of a cheap, stable and disciplined industrial labor force in a "secure" political environment. This process is based on the destruction of national manufacturing for the internal market (i.e. import-substituting industries) in individual Third World countries and the consolidation of a cheap-labor export economy. With the completion of the Uruguay Round at Marrakech and the establishment of the World Trade Organization (WTO) in 1995, the frontiers of these cheap labor "free trade zones" have been extended to the entire national territory of developing countries.

Macro-economic Reform Supports the Relocation of Industry

The restructuring of individual national economies, under the auspices of the Bretton Woods institutions, contributes to the weakening of the state. Industry for the internal market is undermined and national enterprises are pushed into bankruptcy. The compression of internal consumption resulting from the structural adjustment program (SAP) implies a corresponding reduction in labor costs; therein lies the "hidden agenda" of the SAP: the compression of wages in the Third World and Eastern Europe supports the relocation of economic activity from the rich countries to the poor countries.

The globalization of poverty endorses the development of a worldwide cheap-labor export economy; the possibilities of production are immense given the mass of cheap impoverished workers throughout the world. In contrast, poor countries do not trade among themselves: poor people do not constitute a market for the goods they produce.

Consumer demand is limited to approximately 15 percent of the world population, confined largely to the rich countries together with small pockets of wealth in the Third World and the countries of the former Soviet bloc. (See Table 1.1.) In this system and contrary to the famous dictum of the French economist Jean Baptiste Say (Say's Law), supply does not create its own demand. On the contrary, poverty means "low costs of production": poverty is "an input" into the cheap-labor economy ("on the supply side").

Industrial Export Promotion

"Die or Export" is the motto, import substitution and production for the internal market are obsolete concepts. "Countries should specialize according to their comparative advantage", which lies in the abundance and low price of their labor; the secret of "economic success" is export promotion. Under the close watch of the World Bank and the IMF, the same "non-traditional" exports are promoted simultaneously in a large number of developing countries. The latter now joined by cheap-labor producers in Eastern Europe are forced into cutthroat competition. Everybody wants to export to the same European and North American markets: oversupply obliges Third World producers to cut their prices; the factory prices of industrial goods tumble on world markets in much the same way as those of primary commodities. Competition between and within developing countries contributes to depressing wages and prices. Export promotion (when applied simultaneously in a large number of individual countries) leads to overproduction and the contraction of export revenues. Ironically, the promotion of exports leads ultimately to lower commodity prices and less export revenue from which to repay the external debt. In a bitter irony, the most successful exporting economies are also the World's largest debtor nations.

Moreover, the economic stabilization measures imposed on the South and the East backfire on the economies of the rich countries: poverty in the Third World contributes to a global contraction in import demand which in turn affects economic growth and employment in the OECD countries.

Structural adjustment transforms national economies into open economic spaces and countries into territories. The latter are "reserves" of cheap labor and natural resources. But because this process is based on the globalization of poverty and the worldwide compression of consumer demand, export promotion in the developing countries can succeed only in a limited number of cheap-labor locations. In other words, the simultaneous development of new export activities in a large number of locations is conducive to greater competition between developing countries in both primary production and manufacturing. In as much as world demand is not expanding, the creation of new productive capacity in some countries will be matched by economic decline (and disengagement) in competing Third World locations.

Global Adjustment

What happens when macro-economic reform is applied simultaneously in a large number of countries ? In an interdependent world economy, the "summation" of national-level SAPs is conducive to a "global adjustment" in the structures of world trade and economic growth.

The impact of "global adjustment" on the terms of trade is fairly well understood: the simultaneous application of export promotion policies in individual Third World countries is conducive to oversupply – in particular, commodity markets coupled with further declines in world commodity prices. In many countries subjected to structural adjustment, the volume of exports has gone up substantially, but the value of export revenues has deteriorated. In other words, this "global structural adjustment" (predicated on the internationalization of macro-economic policy) further depresses commodity prices and promotes a negative transfer of economic resources between debtor and creditor nations.

"Decomposition" of National Economies

Saps play a key role in the "decomposition" of the national economy of an indebted country and in the "recomposition" of a "new relationship" to the global economy. In other words, the economic reforms imply the "decomposition/recomposition" of the structures of national production and consumption. Compression of real earnings is conducive to a lowering of labor costs and a decline in the levels of necessary mass consumption (basic human needs) by the large majority of the population. On the other hand, the "recomposition" of consumption is characterized by the enlargement of "high-income consumption" through the liberalization of trade and the dynamic influx of imported consumer durables and luxury goods for a small segment of society. This "decomposition/recomposition" of the national economy and its insertion into the global cheap-labor economy is predicated on the compression of internal demand (and of the levels of social livelihood): poverty, low wages and an abundant supply of cheap labor are "inputs" on the supply side. Poverty and the reduction of production costs constitute the instrumental basis (on the supply side) for reactivating production geared towards the external market.

The simultaneous application of SAPs in debtor countries accelerates the relocation of manufacturing industry to cheap-labor locations in Third World countries and Eastern Europe from existing production sites in the developed countries. Yet the new (export oriented) productive capacity which results is developed against a general background of slow and/or depressed growth of world demand. This positive "engagement" in the creation of new productive capacity (for export) in one or more individual Third World countries is matched by a process of "disengagement of productive resources" and decline elsewhere in the world economic system.

Decomposition does not ensure "successful" recomposition. In other words, the phasing out of domestic industry for the internal market does not ensure the development of a new "viable" and stable relationship to the world market – i.e. the compression of labor costs (in support of supply) does not in itself ensure the growth of the export sector and the insertion of the national Third World economy into the international market (nor docs it, for that matter, ensure the development of industrial exports). Complex economic, geo-political and historical factors will determine the geographical location of these new poles of cheap-labor production geared towards the world market.

"Recomposition" tends to take place in specific functional regions of the global economy. The formation of new dynamic poles of the cheap-labor economy in Mexico, Eastern Europe and SouthEast Asia is in marked contrast to the situation prevailing in most of sub-Saharan Africa and parts of Latin America and the Middle East.

World Unemployment

Many regions of the world – although not actively inserted into the global cheap-labor economy – nonetheless contain important "reserves of cheap labor" which play an important role in regulating the costs of labor at a world level. If labor unrest, including social pressures on wages, occurs in one Third World location, transnational capital can switch its production site or subcontract (through out-sourcing) to alternative cheap-labor locations. In other words, the existence of "reserve countries" with abundant supplies of cheap labor tends to dampen the movement of wages and labor costs prevailing in the more active (cheap-labor) export economies (e.g. South East Asia, Mexico, China and Eastern Europe).

In other words, the determination of national wage levels in individual developing countries not only depends on the structure of the national labor market, but also on the level of wages prevailing in competing cheap-labor locations. The level of labor costs is therefore conditioned by the existence of a "global reserve pool of cheap labor" made up of the "reserve armies" of labor in different countries. This "world surplus population" conditions the international migration of productive capital in the same branch of industry from one country to another: international capital (the direct or indirect purchaser of labor power) moves from one national labor market to another. From the point of view of capital, the "national reserves of labor" are integrated into a single international reserve pool where workers in different countries are brought into overt competition with one another.

World unemployment becomes "a lever" of global capital accumulation which "regulates" the cost of labor in each of the national economies. Mass poverty regulates the international cost of labor. Wages are also conditioned, at the level of each national economy, by the urban-rural relationship. Namely, rural poverty and the existence of a large mass of unemployed and landless farm-workers tend to promote low wages in the urban-manufacturing economy.

Declining Wages

In many cheap-labor exporting economies, the share of wages in GDP has declined dramatically. In Latin America, for instance, the adjustment programs were conducive to a marked contraction of wages both as a share of GDP and as a percentage of value added in manufacturing. While employee earnings in the developed countries constitute approximately 40 percent of value added in manufacturing, the corresponding percentage in Latin America and SouthEast Asia is of the order of 15 percent.

Plant Closures and Industrial Delocation in the Developed Countries

The development of cheap-labor export factories in the Third World is matched by plant closures in the industrial cities of the advanced countries. The earlier wave of plant closures affected largely the (labor-intensive) areas of light manufacturing. Since the 1980s, however, all sectors of the Western economy (and all categories of the labor force) have been affected: corporate restructuring of the aerospace and engineering industries, relocation of automobile production to Eastern Europe and the Third World, closure of the steel industry, etc.

The development of manufacturing in the *maquilas* and export processing zones, located to the immediate south of the Rio Grande on the US-Mexican border, was matched throughout the 1980s by industrial lay-offs and unemployment in industrial centers in the US and Canada. Under the North American Free Trade Agreement (NAFTA), this process of relocation has been extended to the entire Mexican economy. Similarly, Japanese transnationals are relocating a significant part of their manufacturing industry to production sites in Thailand or the Philippines where industrial workers can be hired for US$ 3 or $ 4 a day.[2] German capitalism is expanding beyond the Oder-Neisse back into its pre-war Lebensraum. In assembly plants in Poland, Hungary and the Czech and Slovak republics, the cost of labor (of the order of US$ 120 a month) is substantially lower than in the European Union. In contrast, workers in German automobile plants have wages of the order of US$ 28 an hour.

In this context, the former "socialist" countries are integrated into the global cheap-labor economy. Despite idle factories and high levels of unemployment in the former German Democratic Republic, it was more profitable for German capitalism to expand its manufacturing base in Eastern Europe.

For every job lost in the developed countries and transferred to the Third World, there is a corresponding decline of consumption in the developed countries. While plant closures and lay-offs are usually presented in the press as isolated and unrelated cases of corporate restructuring, their combined impact on real earnings and employment is devastating. Consumer markets collapse because a large number of enterprises (in several countries) simultaneously reduce their workforce. In turn, sagging sales backlash on production, contributing to a further string of plant closures and bankruptcies, and so on.

The Worldwide Compression of Consumer Spending

In the North, the compression in levels of spending is further exacerbated by the deregulation of the labor market: deindexation of earnings, part-time employment, early retirement and the imposition of so-called "voluntary" wage cuts. In turn, the practice of attrition (which shifts the social burden of unemployment onto the younger age groups) bars an entire generation from the job-market.

In other words, the process of phasing-out industry in the developed countries contributes to a contraction of market demand, which in turn undermines the efforts of developing countries to sell manufactured goods to a (shrinking) Western market.

It's a vicious circle: the relocation of industry to the South and the East leads to economic dislocation and unemployment in the developed countries which, in turn, tends to push the world economy into global recession. This system is characterized by an unlimited capacity to produce. Yet the very act of expanding production – through relocation of material production from the "high wage" to the "low wage" economies – contributes to a contraction of spending (e.g. by those who have been laid off) which leads the world economy ultimately to the path of global stagnation.

Relocation within Trading Blocs

The delocation of economic activity is increasingly taking place within the continental shelf of each trading block. Both Western Europe and North America are respectively developing "cheap-labor hinterlands" on their immediate geographic borders. In the European context, the "Oder-Neisse line" is to Poland what the Rio Grande is to Mexico. The former "iron curtain" performs the same role as the Rio Grande. It separates the high-wage economy of Western Europe from the low-wage economy of the former Soviet bloc.

NAFTA, however, is distinct from the Maastricht Treaty, which allows for the "free movement" of labor within the countries of the European Union. Within NAFTA, the Rio Grande separates two distinct labor markets: production units are closed down in the US and Canada and moved to Mexico where wages are at least ten times lower. "The immobility of labor", rather than "free trade", and the removal of tariff barriers, is the central feature of NAFTA.

Under NAFTA, American corporations can reduce their labor costs by more than 80 percent by relocating to or subcontracting in Mexico. This mechanism is not limited to manufacturing or to activities using unqualified labor: nothing prevents the movement of America's high-tech industries to Mexico where engineers and scientists can be hired for a few hundred dollars a month. Delocation potentially affects a large share of the US and Canadian economies, including the services sector.

NAFTA has, from the outset, been predicated on a contraction of employment and real wages. Industrial relocation to Mexico destroys jobs and depresses real earnings in the US and Canada. NAFTA exacerbates this economic recession: workers laid off in the US and Canada are not redeployed elsewhere in the economy and no new avenues of economic growth are created as a result of the delocation of industry. The contraction of consumer spending which results from the lay-offs and plant closures leads to a general contraction in sales and employment and to further industrial lay-offs.

Moreover, while NAFTA enables American and Canadian corporations to penetrate the Mexican market, this process is undertaken largely by displacing existing Mexican enterprises. The tendency is towards increased industrial concentration, the elimination of small and medium-sized enterprises, as well as the taking over of part of Mexico's service economy through corporate franchising. The US "exports its recession" to Mexico. With the exception of a small market of privileged consumption, poverty and low wages in Mexico do not favor the expansion of consumer demand. In Canada, the free trade agreement signed with the US in 1989 has led to the phasing out of the branch-plant economy. Canadian subsidiaries are closed down and replaced by a regional sales office.

The formation of NAFTA has contributed to exacerbating the economic recession: the tendency is towards the reduction of wages and employment in all three countries. The potential to produce is enhanced, yet the very act of expanding production (through relocation of production from the US and Canada to Mexico) contributes to a contraction of spending.

The Dynamic Development of Luxury Consumption

The increased concentration of income and wealth in the hands of a social minority (in the advanced countries as well as in small pockets of affluence in the Third World and Eastern Europe) has led to the dynamic growth of the luxury-goods economy: travel and leisure, the automobile, the electronics and telecommunications revolution, etc. The "drive-in" and "duty free" cultures built around the axes of the automobile and air transport are the focal points of the modern "high-income" consumption and leisure economy, towards which massive amounts of financial resources are channeled.

Whereas the range of consumer goods available in support of upper-income lifestyles has expanded almost beyond limit, there has been (since the debt crisis of the early 1980s) a corresponding contraction in the levels of consumption of the large majority of the world population. In contrast to the large diversity of goods available to a social minority, basic consumption (for some 85 percent of the world population) is confined to a small number of food staples and essential commodities.

This dynamic growth of luxury consumption, nonetheless, provides a temporary "breathing space" to a global economy beset by recession.[3]

Rapid growth of luxury consumption, however, contrasts increasingly with the stagnation of the sectors producing necessary goods and services. In the Third World and Eastern Europe, stagnation of food production, housing and essential social services contrasts with the development of small pockets of social privilege and luxury consumption. The élites of indebted countries, including the former *apparatchiks* and the new business tycoons of Eastern Europe and the former Soviet Union, are both the protagonists and beneficiaries of this process. Social and income disparities in Hungary and Poland are now comparable to those prevailing in Latin America. (For instance, a Porsche-Carrera can now be purchased at Porsche-Hungaria in downtown Budapest for the modest sum of 9,720,000 forints, more than an average Hungarian worker earns in a lifetime – i.e. 70 years earnings at the average (annual) industrial wage).[4]

The low wage structure in the Third World, coupled with the effects of economic restructuring and recession in the advanced countries, does not favor the development of mass consumption and an overall improvement of purchasing power. The global productive system is thus increasingly geared towards supplying limited markets – i.e. upper-income consumer markets in the North plus small pockets of luxury consumption in the South and the East.

In the foregoing context, low wages and low costs of production are conducive to low purchasing power and deficient demand. This contradictory relationship is an essential feature of the global cheap- labor economy: those who produce are not those who consume.

The Rentier Economy

With the phasing out of manufacturing, a "rentier economy" (which virtually does not produce anything) has developed in the rich countries. This rentier economy – centered in the services sector – siphons off the profits of Third World manufacturing. The high-technology economy based on the ownership of industrial know-how, product designs, research and development, etc. subordinates the sectors of "material production". "Non-material production" subordinates "material production"; the services sector appropriates the value added of manufacturing. Moreover, in addition to the payment of royalties and licensing fees for the use of Western and Japanese technology, the earnings of Third World producers are invariably appropriated by distributors, wholesalers and retailers in the developed countries. Industrial production remains subordinate to corporate monopoly capital.

The development of so-called "industry" in the Third World is the consequence of a process of global restructuring of production. The growth poles in the advanced countries are in the "non-material sectors" (high technology including: product design and innovation, services economy, real estate, commercial and financial infrastructure, communications and transportation) rather than in material manufacturing production *per se*.

This apparent "deindustrialization" of the industrialized countries should be understood: the meaning of the term "industry" has changed profoundly. The high-technology growth poles are experiencing rapid development at the expense of the old traditional industries which developed historically in the advanced countries from the inception of the industrial revolution.

The Globalization of Manufacturing

We are dealing with a world economy in which a large number of national economies produce manufactured goods for export to the market of the OECD countries. With some important exceptions (e.g. Korea, Brazil, Mexico), these countries, however, cannot be considered as "newly industrialized": the process of "industrialization" is largely the consequence of the relocation of production to cheap- labor areas in the Third World. It is conditioned by the reshaping of the global economy.

The decentralization and relocation of material production to the Third World were motivated largely by the sizeable differentials in wages between rich and poor countries. The latter have become producers of "industrial staples". In this context, overproduction of industrial commodities takes place on a world level, depressing the prices of manufactured goods much in the same way as the process of oversupply, which characterizes primary-commodity markets. The entry of China into the international division of labor in the late 1970s has, in this regard, exacerbated the structures of oversupply.

Import-led Growth in the Rich Countries

The rentier economy appropriates the earnings of the direct producers. Material production takes place offshore in a Third World cheap-labor economy, yet the largest increases in GDP are recorded in the importing country. GDP growth in the rich countries is, in this regard, "import led": cheap-labor imports (in primary commodities and manufacturing) generate a corresponding increase in income in the services economy of the rich countries.

The application of the IMF-sponsored SAP in a large number of individual countries also contributes to the consolidation of this rentier-type economy: each country is obliged to produce (in competition with other developing countries) the same range of staple primary and industrial commodities for the world market. While competition characterizes material commodity production in the developing countries, the channels of international trade, as well as the wholesale and retail trade markets in the advanced countries, are controlled by corporate monopolies. This duality between competition and monopoly is a fundamental feature of the system of global exchange. Cutthroat competition between the "direct producers", often located in different countries under a structure of global oversupply, is in contrast to a structure of monopoly control over international trade, industrial patents, wholesale and retail trade, etc. by a small number of global corporations.

The Appropriation of Surplus by non-Producers

Because goods produced in developing countries are imported at very low international (fob) prices, the recorded "value" of OECD imports from developing countries is relatively small (i.e. in comparison to total trade as well as in relation to the value of domestic production). Yet as soon as these commodities enter into the wholesale and retail channels of the rich countries, their prices are multiplied several-fold. The retail price of goods produced in the Third World is often up to 10 times higher than the price at which the commodity was imported. A corresponding "value added" is thus artificially created within the services economy of the rich countries without any material production taking place. This "value" is added to the Gross Domestic Product of the rich country. For instance, the retail price of coffee is seven to 10 times higher than the fob price and approximately 20 times the price paid to the farmer in the Third World. (See Table 5.1.)

In other words, the bulk of the earnings of primary producers is appropriated by merchants, intermediaries, wholesalers and retailers. A similar process of appropriation exists with regard to most industrial commodities produced in offshore cheap-labor locations. For instance, 60 percent of the shoes sold in the US are produced in industrial sweatshops in China. The revenues resulting from the sale of shoes in the US does not accrue to Chinese workers who receive exceedingly low wages, but to US corporate capital leading to an expansion of the US Gross Domestic Product. (See Box 5.1.)

Box 5.1

Wages in Chinese Factories Producing for US Retailers

"Women working in the production of Timberland shoes at Pou Yuen Factory V, Zhongshan City in Guangdong Province, work 14-hour days. The factory employs 16 and 17-year-old girls at 22 cents an hour ($16 for a 70-hour workweek). At a factory producing Kathie Lee [Gifford] handbags for Wal-Mart, the highest wages were $7 a week or 8 cents an hour. Pay for the top 14 percent of workers at Qin Shi was $18 per month." (Jon E. Dougherty, "Brutal Chinese Working Conditions benefit Wal-Mart", WorldNetDaily.com, September 2000)

At another factory producing car stereos, young women were paid 31 cents an hour and "sit hunched over, staring into microscopes for nine [product] hours a day, six days a week, soldering the fine pieces of the stereo." *(Ibid)*

"The companies [operating in China] only hire single women 17 to 25 years of age, after which they are replaced with another crop of young women" when they finally "wear out," the researchers noted. ... "No one lasts long working under these conditions, so the women either leave or are pushed out after they reach 26 years of age. At any rate, they are replaced with another batch of young women, and the work goes on. (...) "And if a woman happens to become pregnant, the "unwritten rule" is that "she will be fired". *(Ibid)*

An Example: the Garment Industry

In the international garment trade, for instance, an international fashion designer will purchase a Paris-designed shirt for US$3 to $4 in Bangladesh, Vietnam or Thailand.[5] The product will then be resold in the European market at five to 10 times its price: the GDP of the importing Western country increases without any material production taking place.

Data collected at the factory level in Bangladesh enable us roughly to identify the structure of costs and the distribution of earnings in the garment export industry: the factory price of one dozen shirts is US$36 to $40 (fob).[6] All the equipment and raw materials are imported. The shirts are retailed at approximately US$22 a piece or US$266 a dozen in the United States. (See Table 5.2.) Female and child labor in Bangladeshi garment factories is paid approximately US$20 a month, at least 50 times less than the wages paid to garment workers in North America. Less than two percent of the total value of the commodity accrues to the direct producers (the garment workers) in the form of wages. Another one percent accrues as industrial profit to the "competitive" independent Third World producer.

The gross mark-up between the factory price and the retail price (US$ 266 – $38 = $228) is essentially divided into three components:

1) Merchant profit to international distributors, wholesalers and retailers including the owners of shopping centers, etc. (i.e. the largest share of the gross mark-up).

2) The real costs of circulation (transport, storage, etc.).

3) Customs duties exacted on the commodity upon entry into the developed countries' markets and indirect (value-added) taxes exacted at the point of retail sale of the commodity.

While the retail price is seven times the factory price, profit does not necessarily accrue to small retailers in the developed countries. A large share of the surplus generated at the levels of wholesale and retail trade is appropriated in the form of rent and interest payments by powerful commercial, real estate and banking interests.

It is worth noting that the flow of imports from the Third World also constitutes a means of generating fiscal revenues for the state in the rich countries in the form of sales and/or value-added taxes. In Western Europe, the VAT is well in excess of 10 percent of the retail price. The process of tax collection is, therefore, dependent on the structure of unequal commodity exchange. In the case of the garment trade example, the Treasury of the rich countries appropriates almost as much as the producing country and approximately four times the amount accruing to garment workers in the producing country. (See Table 5.3.)

Wages and Labor Costs in the Developed Countries

In the global economy, the services of labor are purchased by capital in several separate and distinct national labor markets, – i.e. a part of the labor costs associated with transport, storage, wholesale and retail trade are incurred in the "high-wage" labor market of the rich countries. For instance, retail salesmen in the developed countries receive a daily wage, which is at least 40 times higher than that of the Bangladeshi factory worker. A comparatively much larger share of the total (dollar) labor costs of producing

Table 5.1
Coffee - Hierarchy of Prices
(US dollars)

	Price	Cumulative Share of Value Added (%)
Farmgate	0.25 - 0.50	4.00
International FOB	1.00	10.00
Final Retail	10.00	100.00

Source: Illustration based on approximate fob prices (early 1990s) and retail prices in the North American market (early 1990s). Farmgate prices vary considerably from one country to another.

Table 5.2
Cost Structure
Third World Garment Exporter
(US dollars)

Materials and accessories (imported)	27
Depreciation on equipment	3
Wages	5
Net industrial profit	3
Factory price (one dozen shirts)	38
Gross mark-up	228
Retail price (per dozen) in the advanced countries	266
Retail price including sales tax (10 per cent)	292.60

Source: Based on cost structure and sale prices of Bangladesh garment factory, 1992.

and distributing the commodity will accrue, therefore, to service-sector workers in the high-wage countries.

There is, however, no relationship of "unequal exchange" between factory workers in Bangladesh and retail personnel in the US: the available evidence confirms that service workers in the rich countries are heavily underpaid. Moreover, their wages (which constitute a bona fide value-added – i.e. a "real cost") constitute a relatively small percentage of total sales.

In our example, the labor costs associated with the production of one dozen shirts in Bangladesh is US$5 which corresponds to 25 to 30 hours of labor (at 15-20 cents an hour). Assuming a retail worker in the US is paid US$5 an hour and sells half a dozen shirts per hour, the labor costs of producing a dozen shirts (US$5) is half the cost of retailing (US$10). The latter, however, still represents a relatively small percentage of the total price (US$292.60 including sales tax); i.e. the bulk of the surplus is appropriated in the form of merchant profit and rent by non-producers in the rich countries. (See Table 5.2.)

Whereas Third World enterprises operate under conditions which approximate "perfect competition", the buyers of their products are trading companies and multinational firms. The net industrial profit accruing to the "competitive" Third World entrepreneur (US$3) is of the order of one percent of the total value of the commodity. Because Third World factories operate in a global economy marked by oversupply, the factory price tends to decline, pushing industrial profit margins to a bare minimum. This process facilitates the collection and appropriation of surplus by powerful international traders and distributors.

Table 5.3

Third World Manufacturing, the Distribution of Earnings

The distribution of earnings: one dozen shirts produced in a Third World cheap-labor factory	Amount in US dollars	Percentage of sale price
1. Earnings accruing to Third World country	8.00	2.7
1.1 Wages	5.00	1.7
1.2 Net industrial Profit	3.00	1.0
2. Earnings accruing to developed country	284.60	97.3
2.1 Materials, accessories and equipment imported from the rich countries	30.00	10.2
2.2 Freight and commissions	4.00	1.4
2.3 Customs duty on FOB price	4.00	1.4
2.4 Wages to wholesale and retail personnel	10.00	3.4
2.5 Gross commercial profit, rent and other income of distributors	210.00	71.8
2.6. Sales taxes (10% of retail price), accruing to developed country state Treasury	26.60	9.1
3. Total retail price (including sales taxes)	292.60	100.0

Note: For the purposes of this illustration, the margins for freight and commissions, customs duty and sales taxes have been set at realistic levels (in accordance with available information). No information, however, is available on the wholesale and retail labor costs. In this illustration, the costs of retailing one dozen shirts have been assumed at approximately 25 percent of the fob price (US$10).

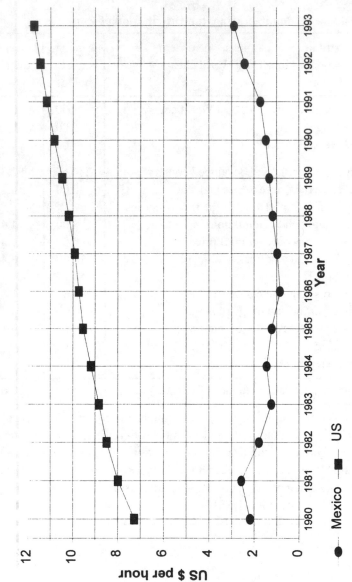

Graph 5.1 : The Comparative Cost of Labour in Manufacturing (nomimal wage in US dollars)

Sources : International Labour Office, Yearbook of Labour Statistics, Geneva, 1980-1994. International Monetary Fund, International Financial Statistics, Washington, DC, 1995.

Graph 5.2: The Comparative Cost of Labour in Manufacturing (nominal wage in US dollars)

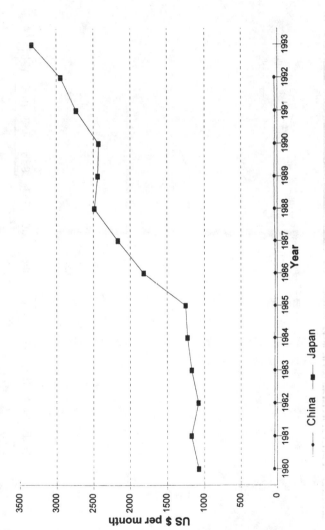

Sources: International Labour Office, Yearbook of Labour Statistics, Geneva, 1980-1994. International Monetary Fund, International Financial Statistics, Washington, DC, 1995.

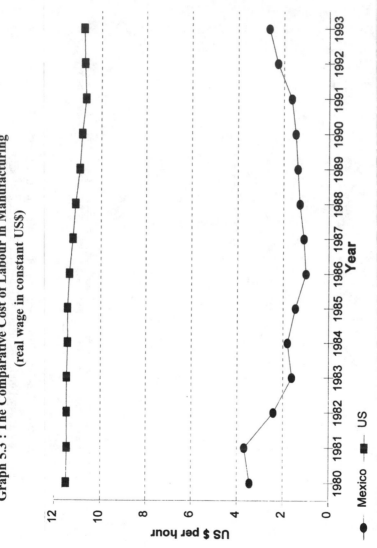

Graph 5.3 : The Comparative Cost of Labour in Manufacturing
(real wage in constant US$)

Sources: International Labour Office, Yearbook of Labour Statistics, Geneva, 1980-1994.
International Monetary Fund, International Financial Statistics, Washington, DC, 1995.

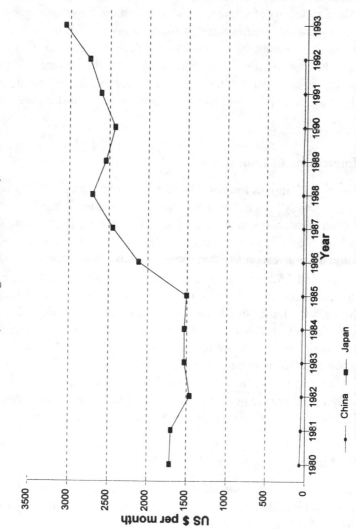

Graph 5.4 : The Comparative Cost of Labour in Manufacturing (real wage in constant US$)

China — Japan

Sources: International Labour Office, Yearbook of Labour Statistics, Geneva, 1980-1994. International Monetary Fund, International Financial Statistics, Washington, DC, 1995.

Mobile and Immobile Sectors

The relocation of material production to cheap-labor locations is not limited to a few areas of light manufacturing. It encompasses all areas of material production, which are "mobile" internationally. The "mobile sectors" are defined as sectors of activity, which can be moved from one geographic location to another – either through offshore investment in a cheap-labor country, or by subcontracting production with an independent Third World producer. In contrast, the "immobile sectors" of the advanced countries include activities, which by their very nature, cannot be relocated internationally: construction, public works, agriculture and most of the services economy.

The Immobility of Labor

"Mobile capital" moves towards "immobile labor reserves". Whereas capital moves "freely" from one labor market to another, labor is prevented from crossing international boundaries. National labor markets are closed compartments with heavily guarded borders. The system is based on keeping national labor reserves within their respective borders.

Under NAFTA, for instance, the movement of Mexicans across the US-Mexican frontier will be tightly restricted so as to retain Mexico's labor force "within the boundaries of the cheap-labor economy". However, in economic activities such as construction, public works and agriculture, which by their very nature are not internationally "mobile", the agreement allows for the selective movement of a contractual seasonal labor force. Manpower exports, (to these "immobile" activities) from both Mexico and the Caribbean, serve the purpose of depressing the wages paid to American and Canadian workers, as well as undermining the role of trade unions.

The Sectors of Non-material Production

With delocation, the structure of industry in the advanced countries is fundamentally modified. With the phasing out of material production, the new industries in information systems, telecommunications, etc. become the new growth poles. The old red-brick industrial centers are phased out: the "factory system" is closed down. Material production in manufacturing (which constitutes a "mobile" sector) is relocated to the low-wage economies. A sizeable sector of the labor force in the developed countries is now associated with the services economy and "the non-material sectors" of economic activity. In contrast, the percentage of the labor force in the production of material commodities has declined dramatically.

The duality respectively between "material" and "non-material production" and between "mobile" and "immobile" sectors is central to an understanding of the changing structure of the global economy. Global recession is not incompatible with the dynamic growth of the new high-technology sectors. The designs, technology and know-how are owned and controlled by international corporate capital. "Non-material production" and the control over intellectual property rights subordinate "material production". The surplus from material industrial production is appropriated by the non-material sectors.

The Impact of the Scientific Revolution

The late 20th century has witnessed far-reaching progress in telecommunications, computer technology and production engineering. The latter constitute a vital lever in the process of industrial relocation: the centers of corporate decision-making are in instant contact with manufacturing sites and assembly plants around the world. The high-tech innovations of the 1980s and 1990s represent, under global capitalism, a powerful instrument of worldwide corporate control and supervision. The global enterprise minimizes labor costs at a world level through its ability to link-up (or subcontract) with cheap-labor production sites around the world. Workers are laid off in one (high-wage) country, production is transferred to another (low-wage) country and a smaller number of workers toil for longer hours and receive substantially lower wages.

Moreover, the technological revolution, while opening up new areas of professional work in the advanced countries, significantly reduces the overall labor requirements of industry. New robotized assembly lines are opened while workers in existing production facilities are fired. Technological change – combined with delocation and enterprise restructuring tends – thereby favors a new wave of mergers and corporate acquisitions in key industries.

The Delocation of the Services Economy

With the revolution in global telecommunications and information technology, certain service activities of the advanced capitalist countries are being transferred to cheap-labor locations in the Third World and Eastern

Europe. In other words, part of the services economy is no longer an "immobile activity". Commercial and financial establishments can reduce their personnel in a variety of office activities. The accounting systems of large firms, for instance, can now be delocated and managed at considerable savings by computer link-up and electronic mail in developing countries, where qualified accountants and computer specialists can be hired for less than US$ 100 a month. Similarly, data and word processing can be rapidly subcontracted (e.g. by electronic mail) to office personnel working in sweat labor conditions for US$ 2 or $ 3 a day in the Philippines, and so on. With more than 70 percent of the labor force of the advanced capitalist countries in the services sector, the potential impact of delocation on wages and employment (not to mention the social repercussions) is far-reaching.

Endnotes

1. The international relocation of manufacturing was initiated in the 1960s with the four Asian dragons: Hong Kong, Taiwan, Singapore and South Korea. At the outset, it was confined to the "softer" areas of export processing and assembly (such as the garment industry and electronics assembly).

2. The minimum industrial wage in Bangkok of US$ 4 a day (1991) is not enforced in modern factories.

3. In the face of low civilian spending, military expenditure also plays an important role in reactivating demand.

4. "In zwei Jahren über den Berg", *Der Spiegel*, No. 19, 1991, p. 194.

5. The export-processing fee in Ho Chi Minh City is US $ 0.80 cents per shirt (January 1991).

6. Interviews by author conducted in the Bangladesh garment industry, 1992.

PART II

SUB-SAHARAN AFRICA

Chapter 6

Somalia: the Real Causes of Famine

In 1993, the US military launched "Operation Restore Hope" under the auspices of the United Nations. The objective was to come to the rescue of an impoverished population. Drought, desertification and civil war were the "official" causes of famine. The deadly economic reforms imposed by Somalia's external creditors in the years leading up to the civil war were never mentioned.

The IMF Intervention in the Early 1980s

Somalia was a pastoral economy based on "exchange" between nomadic herdsmen and small agriculturalists.[1] Nomadic pastoralists accounted for 50 percent of the population. In the 1970s, resettlement programs led to the development of a sizeable sector of commercial pastoralism. Livestock contributed to 80 percent of export earnings until 1983.[2] Despite recurrent droughts, Somalia remained virtually self-sufficient in food until the 1970s.[3]

The IMF-World Bank intervention in the early 1980s contributed to exacerbating the crisis of Somali agriculture. The economic reforms undermined the fragile exchange relationship between the "nomadic economy" and the "sedentary economy" – i.e. between pastoralists and small farmers characterized by money transactions as well as traditional barter. A very tight austerity program was imposed on the government largely to release the funds required to service Somalia's debt with the Paris Club. In fact, a large share of the external debt was held by the Washington-based financial institutions.[4] According to an ILO mission report:

> [T]he Fund alone among Somalia's major recipients of debt service payments, refuses to reschedule. (…) De facto it is helping to finance an adjustment program, one of whose major goals is to repay the IMF itself.[5]

Towards the Destruction of Food Agriculture

The structural adjustment program reinforced Somalia's dependency on imported grain. From the mid-1970s to the mid-1980s, food aid increased fifteen-fold, at the rate of 31 percent per annum.[6] Combined with increased commercial imports, this influx of cheap surplus wheat and rice sold in the domestic market led to the displacement of local producers, as well as to a major shift in food consumption patterns to the detriment of traditional crops (maize and sorghum). The devaluation of the Somali shilling, imposed by the IMF in June 1981, was followed by periodic devaluations, leading to hikes in the prices of fuel, fertilizer and farm inputs. The impact on agricultural producers was immediate particularly in rain-fed agriculture, as well as in the areas of irrigated farming. Urban purchasing power declined dramatically, government extension programs were curtailed, infrastructure collapsed, the deregulation of the grain market and the influx of "food aid" led to the impoverishment of farming communities.[7]

Also, during this period, much of the best agricultural land was appropriated by bureaucrats, army officers and merchants with connections to the government.[8] Rather than promoting food production for the domestic market, the donors were encouraging the development of so-called "high value-added" fruits, vegetables, oilseeds and cotton for export on the best irrigated farmland.

Collapse of the Livestock Economy

As of the early 1980s, prices for imported livestock drugs increased as a result of the depreciation of the currency. The World Bank encouraged the exaction of user fees for veterinarian services to the nomadic herdsmen, including the vaccination of animals. A private market for veterinary drugs was promoted. The functions performed by the Ministry of Livestock were phased out, with the Veterinary Laboratory Services of the ministry to be fully financed on a cost-recovery basis. According to the World Bank:

> Veterinarian services are essential for livestock development in all areas, and they can be provided mainly by the private sector. (. . .) Since few private veterinarians will choose to practice in the remote pastoral areas, improved livestock care will also depend on "para vets" paid from drug sales.[9]

The privatization of animal health was combined with the absence of emergency animal feed during periods of drought, the commercialization of water and the neglect of water and rangeland conservation. The results were predictable: the herds were decimated and so were the pastoralists, who represent 50 percent of the country's population. The "hidden objective" of this program was to eliminate the nomadic herdsmen involved in the traditional exchange economy. According to the World Bank, "adjustments" in the size of the herds are, in any event, beneficial because nomadic pastoralists in sub-Saharan Africa are narrowly viewed as a cause of environmental degradation.[10]

The collapse in veterinarian services also indirectly served the interests of the rich countries: in 1984, Somalian cattle exports to Saudi Arabia and the Gulf countries plummeted as Saudi beef imports were redirected to suppliers from Australia and the European Community. The ban on Somali livestock imposed by Saudi Arabia was not, however, removed once the rinderpest disease epidemic had been eliminated.

Destroying the State

The restructuring of government expenditure under the supervision of the Bretton Woods institutions also played a crucial role in destroying food agriculture. Agricultural infrastructure collapsed and recurrent expenditure in agriculture declined by about 85 percent in relation to the mid-1970s.[11] The Somali government was prevented by the IMF from mobilizing domestic resources. Tight targets for the budget deficit were set. Moreover, the donors increasingly provided "aid", not in the form of imports of capital and equipment, but in the form of "food aid". The latter would in turn be sold by the government on the local market and the proceeds of these sales (i.e. the so-called "counterpart funds") would be used to cover the domestic costs of development projects. As of the early 1980s, "the sale of food aid" became the principal source of revenue for the state, thereby enabling donors to take control of the entire budgetary process.[12]

The economic reforms were marked by the disintegration of health and educational programmes.[13] By 1989, expenditure on health had declined by 78 percent in relation to its 1975 level. According to World Bank figures, the level of recurrent expenditure on education in 1989 was about US$ 4 per annum per primary school student down from about $ 82 in 1982. From 1981 to 1989, school enrolment declined by 41 percent (despite a sizeable increase in the population of school age), textbooks and school materials disappeared from the class-rooms, school buildings deteriorated and nearly a quarter of the primary schools closed down. Teachers' salaries declined to abysmally low levels.

The IMF-World Bank program has led the Somali economy into a vicious circle: the decimation of the herds pushed the nomadic pastoralists into starvation which in turn backlashes on grain producers who sold or bartered their grain for cattle. The entire social fabric of the pastoralist economy was undone. The collapse in foreign exchange earnings from declining cattle exports and remittances (from Somali workers in the Gulf countries) backlashed on the balance of payments and the state's public finances leading to the breakdown of the government's economic and social programs.

Small farmers were displaced as a result of the dumping of subsidized US grain on the domestic market combined with the hike in the price of farm inputs. The impoverishment of the urban population also led to a contraction of food consumption. In turn, state support in the irrigated areas was frozen and production in the state farms declined. The latter were slated to be closed down or privatized under World Bank supervision.

According to World Bank estimates, real public-sector wages in 1989 had declined by 90 percent in relation to the mid-1970s. Average wages in the public sector had fallen to US$ 3 a month, leading to the inevitable disintegration of the civil administration.[14] A program to rehabilitate civil service wages was proposed by the World Bank (in the context of a reform of the civil service), but this objective was to be achieved within the same budgetary envelope by dismissing some 40 percent of public-sector employees and eliminating salary supplements.[15] Under this plan, the civil service would have been reduced to a mere 25,000 employees by 1995 (in a country of six million people). Several donors indicated keen interest in funding the cost associated with the retrenchment of civil servants.[16]

In the face of impending disaster, no attempt was made by the international donor community to rehabilitate the country's economic and social infrastructure, to restore levels of purchasing power and to rebuild the civil service: the macro-economic adjustment measures proposed by the creditors in the year prior to the collapse of the government of General Siyad Barre in January 1991 (at the height of the civil war) called for a further tightening over public spending, the restructuring of the Central Bank, the liberalization of credit (which virtually thwarted the private sector) and the liquidation and divestiture of most of the state enterprises.

In 1989, debt-servicing obligations represented 194.6 percent of export earnings. The IMF's loan was cancelled because of Somalia's outstanding arrears. The World Bank had approved a structural adjustment loan for US$ 70 million in June 1989 which was frozen a few months later due to Somalia's poor macro-economic performance.[17] Arrears with creditors had to be settled before the granting of new loans and the negotiation of debt rescheduling. Somalia was tangled in the straightjacket of debt servicing and structural adjustment.

Famine Formation in sub-Saharan Africa: The Lessons of Somalia

Somalia's experience shows how a country can be devastated by the simultaneous application of food "aid" and macro-economic policy. There are many Somalias in the developing world and the economic reform package implemented in Somalia is similar to that applied in more than 100 developing countries. But there is another significant dimension: Somalia is a pastoralist economy, and throughout Africa both nomadic and commercial livestock are being destroyed by the IMF-World Bank program in much the same way as in Somalia. In this context, subsidized beef and dairy products imported (duty free) from the European Union have led to the demise of Africa's pastoral economy. European beef imports to West Africa have increased seven-fold since 1984: "the low quality EC beef sells at half the price of locally produced meat. Sahelian farmers are finding that no-one is prepared to buy their herds".[18]

The experience of Somalia shows that famine in the late 20th century is not a consequence of a shortage of food. On the contrary, famines are spurred on as a result of a global oversupply of grain staples. Since the 1980s, grain markets have been deregulated under the supervision of the World Bank and US grain surpluses are used systematically (as in the case of Somalia) to destroy the peasantry and destabilize national food agriculture. The latter becomes, under these circumstances, far more vulnerable to the vagaries of drought and environmental degradation.

Throughout the continent, the pattern of "sectoral adjustment" in agriculture under the custody of the Bretton Woods institutions has been unequivocally towards the destruction of food security. Dependency vis-à-vis the world market has been reinforced, "food aid" to sub-Saharan Africa increased by more than seven times since 1974 and commercial grain imports more than doubled. Grain imports for sub-Saharan Africa expanded from 3.72 million tons in 1974 to 8.47 million tons in 1993. Food aid increased from 910,000 tons in 1974 to 6.64 million tons in 1993.[19]

"Food aid", however, was no longer earmarked for the drought-stricken countries of the Sahelian belt; it was also channeled into countries which were, until recently, more or less self-sufficient in food. Zimbabwe (once considered the bread basket of Southern Africa) was severely affected by the famine and drought which swept Southern Africa in 1992. The country experienced a drop of 90 percent in its maize crop, located largely in less productive lands.[20] Yet, ironically, at the height of the drought, tobacco for export (supported by modern irrigation, credit, research, etc.) registered a bumper harvest.[21] While "the famine forces the population to eat termites", much of the export earnings from Zimbabwe's tobacco harvest were used to service the external debt.

Under the structural adjustment program, farmers have increasingly abandoned traditional food crops; in Malawi, which was once a net food exporter, maize production declined by 40 percent in 1992 while tobacco output doubled between 1986 and 1993. One hundred and fifty thousand hectares of the best land was allocated to tobacco.[22] Throughout the 1980s, severe austerity measures were imposed on African governments and expenditures on rural development drastically curtailed, leading to the collapse of agricultural infrastructure. Under the World Bank program, water was to become a commodity to be sold on a cost-recovery basis to impoverished farmers. Due to lack of funds, the state was obliged to withdraw from the management and conservation of water resources. Water points and boreholes dried up due to lack of maintenance, or were privatized by local merchants and rich farmers. In the semi-arid regions, this commercialization of water and irrigation leads to the collapse of food security and famine.[23]

Concluding Remarks

While "external" climatic variables play a role in triggering off a famine and heightening the social impact of drought, famines in the age of globalization are man-made. They are not the consequence of a scarcity of food but of a structure of global oversupply which undermines food security and destroys national food agriculture. Tightly regulated and controlled by international agri-business, this oversupply is ultimately conducive to the stagnation of both production and consumption of essential food staples and the impoverishment of farmers throughout the world. Moreover, in the era of globalization, the IMF-World Bank structural adjustment program bears a direct relationship to the process of famine formation because it systematically undermines all categories of economic activity, whether urban or rural, which do not directly serve the interests of the global market system.

Endnotes

1. The 1970s witnessed the impoverishment of the nomadic pastoralists, while the privatization of boreholes and rangelands supported the enrichment of commercial livestock interests. As in other developing countries, cash crops for export occupied the best land thereby weakening food agriculture and the small peasantry.

2. From the mid-1970s, there was also a surge of cash remittances from Somali workers in the Gulf states bolstered by the oil boom.

3. There was almost no food aid in the early 1970s.

4. The World Bank and the IMF held 20 percent of the Somali debt during the 1983-85 period. See International Labor Organization, *Generating Employment and Incomes in Somalia*, Jobs and Skills Program for Africa, Addis Ababa, 1989, p. 5.

5. International Labor Organization, *op. cit.*, p. 16.

6. By the mid-1980s it was in excess of 35 percent of food consumption. See Hossein Farzin, "Food Aid: Positive and Negative Effects in Somalia?", *The Journal of Developing Areas*, January 1991, p. 265.

7. According to the ILO, the State Agricultural Development Corporation (ADC) had historically played an important role in supporting high farmgate prices for agriculturalists: "the ADC was encouraging too much production of maize and sorghum, not too little". International Labor Organization, *op. cit.*, p. 9. World Bank data, on the other hand, suggests an increase in maize and sorghum production after the deregulation of the grain prices in 1983.

8. See African Rights, *Somalia, Operation Restore Hope: A Preliminary Assessment*, London, May 1993, p. 18.

9. World Bank, *Sub-Saharan Africa, From Crisis to Sustainable Growth*, Washington DC, 1989, p. 98.

10. *Ibid*, pp. 98-101. Overgrazing is detrimental to the environment but the problem cannot be solved by curtailing the livelihood of the pastoralists.

11. From 1975 to 1989.

12. Counterpart funds from the various commodity assistance programs were the sole source of funding of development projects. Most recurrent expenditures were also dependent on the donors.

13. The allocation to defense spending remained high in percentage terms but declined in real terms.

14. Public-sector wages constituted a mere 0.5 percent of GNP in 1989.

15. Retrenchment of civil servants over a period of five-years (1991-95).

16. A 40 percent decrease in public-sector employment over a five-year period (1991-95).

17. The first tranche of this IDA credit (ASAP II) was disbursed, the second tranche was frozen in 1990. The credit was cancelled in January 1991 after the collapse of the Syiad Barre government.

18. Leslie Crawford, "West Africans Hurt by EC Beef Policy", *Financial Times*, 21 May 1993.

19. The figures for 1970 are from World Bank, *World Development Report*, 1992. The 1993 figures are from *Food and Agricultural Organization, Food Supply Situation and Crop Prospects in Sub-Saharan Africa*, Special Report, No. 1, Rome, April 1993, p. 10.

20. See Haut Commissariat des Nations Unies pour les refugiés, *"Afrique australe, la sécheresse du siècle,"* Geneva, July 1992.

21. *Ibid*, p. 5.

22. See "Tobacco, the Golden Leaf", *Southern African Economist*, May 1993, pp. 49-51.

23. See World Bank, *World Development Report*, 1992, chapter 5.

Chapter 7
Economic Genocide in Rwanda

Part A

The IMF and the World Bank set the Stage

The Rwandan crisis, which led up to the 1994 ethnic massacres, has been presented by the Western media as a profuse narrative of human suffering, while the underlying social and economic causes have been carefully ignored by reporters. As in other "countries in transition", ethnic strife and the outbreak of civil war are increasingly depicted as something which is almost "inevitable" and "innate to these societies", constituting "a painful stage in their evolution from a one-party state towards democracy and the free market." The brutality of the massacres shocked the world community, but what the international media failed to mention was that the civil war was preceded by the flare-up of a deep-seated economic crisis. It was the restructuring of the agricultural system under IMF-World Bank supervision which precipitated the population into abject poverty and destitution.

This deterioration of the economic environment, which immediately followed the collapse of the international coffee market and the imposition of sweeping macro-economic reforms by the Bretton Woods institutions exacerbated simmering ethnic tensions and accelerated the process of political collapse. In 1987, the system of quotas established under the International Coffee Agreement (ICA) started to fall apart, world prices plummeted and the *Fonds d'égalisation* (the state coffee-stabilization fund), which purchased coffee from Rwandan farmers at a fixed price, started to accumulate a sizeable debt. A lethal blow to Rwanda's economy came in June 1989 when the ICA reached a deadlock as a result of political pressures from Washington on behalf of the large US coffee traders. At the conclusion of a historic meeting of producers held in Florida, coffee prices plunged in a matter of months by more than 50 percent.[1] For

Rwanda and several other African countries, the drop in prices wreaked havoc. The farmgate price had fallen to less than 5 percent of the US retail price of coffee. Resulting from the trade of coffee at depressed international prices, a tremendous amount of wealth was being appropriated in the rich countries to the detriment of the direct producers. (See Chapter 5.)

The Legacy of Colonialism

What is the responsibility of the West in this tragedy ? First it is important to stress that the conflict between the Hutu and Tutsi was largely the product of the colonial system, many features of which still prevail today. From the late 19th century, the early German colonial occupation had used the *mwami* (King) of the *nyiginya* (monarchy) installed at Nyanza as a means of establishing its military posts. However, it was largely the administrative reforms initiated in 1926 by the Belgians which were decisive in shaping socio-ethnic relations. The Belgians used dynastic conflicts explicitly to reinforce their territorial control. The traditional chiefs in each hill *(colline)* were used by the colonial administration to requisition forced labor. Routine beatings and corporal punishment were administered on behalf of the colonial masters by the traditional chiefs. The latter were under the direct supervision of a Belgian colonial administrator responsible for a particular portion of territory. A climate of fear and distrust was installed, communal solidarity broke down and traditional client relations were transformed to serve the interests of the colonizer. The objective was to fuel inter-ethnic rivalries as a means of achieving political control, as well as preventing the development of solidarity between the two ethnic groups which would inevitably have been directed against the colonial regime. The Tutsi dynastic aristocracy was also made responsible for the collection of taxes and the administration of justice. The communal economy was undermined and the peasantry forced to shift out of food agriculture into cash crops for export. Communal lands were transformed into individual plots geared solely towards cash-crop cultivation (the so-called *cultures obligatoires*).[2]

Colonial historiographers were entrusted with the task of "transcribing" as well as distorting Rwanda-Urundi's oral history. The historical record was falsified: the *mwami* monarchy was identified exclusively with the Tutsi aristocratic dynasty. The Hutus were represented as a dominated caste.[3] Identity cards were issued indicating "ethnic origin". The latter had been defined arbitrarily on the ownership of heads of cattle, with the Tutsi as "cattle owners" and the Hutus as "farmers".

From imposed socio-ethnic divisions, the Belgian colonialists developed a new social class, the so-called *"nègres évolués"* recruited from among the Tutsi aristocracy, and the school system was put in place to educate the sons of the chiefs and to provide the African personnel required by the Belgians. In turn, the various apostolic missions and vicariates received under Belgian colonial rule an almost political mandate. The clergy, for example, was often used to oblige the peasants to integrate the cash crop economy. These socio-ethnic divisions – which have unfolded since the 1920s – have left a profound mark on contemporary Rwandan society.

Since independence in 1962, relations with the former colonial powers and donors became exceedingly more complex. Inherited from the Belgian colonial period, however, the same objective of pushing one ethnic group against the other ("divide and rule") largely prevailed in the various "military", "human rights" and "macro economic" interventions undertaken from the outset of the civil war in 1990. The Rwandan crisis became encapsulated in a continuous agenda of donor roundtables (held in Paris), cease-fire agreements and peace talks. These various initiatives were closely monitored and coordinated by the donor community in a tangled circuit of "conditionalities" (and cross-conditionalities). The release of multilateral and bilateral loans since the outbreak of the civil war was made conditional upon implementing a process of so-called "democratization" under the tight surveillance of the donor community. In turn, Western aid in support of multiparty democracy was made conditional (in an almost symbiotic relationship) upon the government reaching an agreement with the IMF, and so on. These attempts were all the more illusive because since the collapse of the coffee market in 1989, actual political power in Rwanda rested largely, in any event, in the hands of the donors. A communiqué of the US State Department issued in early 1993 illustrates this situation vividly: the continuation of US bilateral aid was made conditional on good behavior in policy reform as well as progress in the pursuit of democracy.

"Democratization" – based on an abstract model of inter-ethnic solidarity envisaged by the Arusha peace agreement signed in August 1993 – was an impossibility from the outset and the donors knew it. The brutal impoverishment of the population which resulted both from the war and the IMF reforms precluded a genuine process of democratization. The objective was to meet the conditions of "good governance" (a new term in the donors' glossary) and oversee the installation of a bogus multiparty coalition government under the trusteeship of Rwanda's external creditors.

In fact, multipartyism – as narrowly conceived by the donors – contributed to fuelling the various political factions of the regime. Not surprisingly, as soon as the peace negotiations entered a stalemate, the World Bank announced that it was interrupting the disbursements under its loan agreement.[4]

The Economy since Independence

The evolution of the post-colonial economic system played a decisive role in the development of the Rwandan crisis. While progress since independence in diversifying the national economy was indeed recorded, the colonial-style export economy based on coffee *(les cultures obligatoires)* established under the Belgian administration was largely maintained, providing Rwanda with more than 80 percent of its foreign exchange earnings. A rentier class with interests in coffee trade and with close ties to the seat of political power had developed. Levels of poverty remained high, yet during the 1970s and the first part of the 1980s, economic and social progress was nonetheless realized: real GDP growth was of the order of 4.9 percent per annum (1965-89), school enrolment increased markedly and recorded inflation was among the lowest in sub-Saharan Africa – less than 4 percent per annum.[5]

While the Rwandan rural economy remained fragile, marked by acute demographic pressures (3.2 percent per annum population growth), land fragmentation and soil erosion, local-level food self-sufficiency had, to some extent, been achieved alongside the development of the export economy. Coffee was cultivated by approximately 70 percent of rural households, yet it constituted only a fraction of total monetary income. A variety of other commercial activities had been developed including the sale of traditional food staples and banana beer in regional and urban markets.[6] Until the late 1980s, imports of cereals, including food aid, were minimal compared to the patterns observed in other countries of the region. The food situation started to deteriorate in the early 1980s with a marked decline in the per capita availability of food. In overt contradiction to the usual trade reforms adopted under the auspices of the World Bank, protection to local producers had been provided up to that time through restrictions on the import of food commodities.[7] These were lifted with the adoption of the 1990 structural adjustment program.

The Fragility of the State

The economic foundations of the post-independence Rwandan state remained extremely fragile. A large share of government revenues depended on coffee, with the risk that a collapse in commodity prices would precipitate a crisis in the state's public finances. The rural economy was the main source of funding for the state. As the debt crisis unfolded, a larger share of coffee and tea earnings had been earmarked for debt servicing, putting further pressure on small-scale farmers.

Export earnings declined by 50 percent between 1987 and 1991. The demise of state institutions unfolded thereafter. When coffee prices plummeted, famines erupted throughout the Rwandan countryside. According to World Bank data, the growth of GDP per capita declined from 0.4 percent in 1981-86 to -5.5 percent in the period immediately following the slump of the coffee market (1987-91).

The IMF-World Bank Intervention

A World Bank mission traveled to Rwanda in November 1988 to review Rwanda's public expenditure program. A series of recommendations had been established with a view to putting Rwanda back on the track of sustained economic growth. The World Bank mission presented the country's policy options to the government, as consisting of two "scenarios". Scenario I entitled "No Strategy Change" contemplated the option of remaining with the "old system of state planning", whereas Scenario II labeled "With Strategy Change" was that of macro-economic reform and "transition to the free market". After careful economic "simulations" of likely policy outcomes, the World Bank concluded, with some grain of optimism, that if Rwanda adopted Scenario II, levels of consumption would increase markedly over 1989-93 alongside a recovery of investment and an improved balance of trade. The "simulations" also pointed to added export performance and substantially lower levels of external indebtedness.[8] These outcomes depended on the speedy implementation of the usual recipe of trade liberalization and currency devaluation, alongside the lifting of all subsidies to agriculture, the phasing out of the *Fonds d' égalisation* (the State coffee Stabilization Fund), the privatization of state enterprises and the dismissal of civil servants.

The "With Strategy Change" (Scenario II) was adopted. The government had no choice.[9] A 50 percent devaluation of the Rwandan franc was carried out in November 1990 – barely six weeks after the incursion from

Uganda of the rebel army of the Rwandan Patriotic Front (RPF).

The devaluation was intended to boost coffee exports. It was presented to public opinion as a means of rehabilitating a war-ravaged economy. Not surprisingly, exactly the opposite results were achieved, exacerbating the plight of the civil war. From a situation of relative price stability, the plunge of the Rwandan franc contributed to triggering inflation and the collapse of real earnings. A few days after the devaluation, sizeable increases in the prices of fuel and consumer essentials were announced. The consumer price index increased from 1.0 percent in 1989 to 19.2 percent in 1991. The balance of payments situation deteriorated dramatically and the outstanding external debt, which had already doubled since 1985, increased by 34 percent between 1989 and 1992. The state administrative apparatus was in disarray, state enterprises were pushed into bankruptcy and public services collapsed.[10] Health and education disintegrated under the brunt of the IMF-imposed austerity measures: despite the establishment of "a social safety net" (earmarked by the donors for programs in the social sectors), the incidence of severe child malnutrition increased dramatically; the number of recorded cases of malaria increased by 21 percent in the year following the adoption of the IMF program, largely as a result of the absence of anti-malarial drugs in the public health centers; and the imposition of school fees at the primary-school level led to a massive decline in school enrolment.[11]

The economic crisis reached its climax in 1992 when Rwandan farmers, in desperation, uprooted some 300,000 coffee trees.[12] Despite soaring domestic prices, the government had frozen the farmgate price of coffee at its 1989 level (RwF 125/kg), under the terms of its agreement with the Bretton Woods institutions. The government was not allowed (under the World Bank loan) to transfer state resources to the *Fonds d'égalisation*. It should also be mentioned that a significant profit was appropriated by local coffee traders and intermediaries serving to put further pressure on the peasantry.

In June 1992, a second devaluation was ordered by the IMF, leading – at the height of the civil war – to a further escalation of the prices of fuel and consumer essentials. Coffee production tumbled by another 25 percent in a single year.[13] Because of over-cropping of coffee trees, there was increasingly less land available to produce food, but the peasantry was not able easily to switch back into food crops. The meager cash income derived from coffee had been erased, yet there was nothing to fall back on. Not only were cash revenues from coffee insufficient to buy food, the prices of farm inputs had soared and money earnings from coffee were grossly insufficient. The crisis of the coffee economy backlashed on the production of traditional food staples leading to a substantial drop in the production of cassava, beans and sorghum. The system of savings and loan cooperatives, which provided credit to small farmers, had also disintegrated. Moreover, with the liberalization of trade and the deregulation of grain markets – as recommended by the Bretton Woods institutions – (heavily-subsidized) cheap food imports and food aid from the rich countries were entering Rwanda with the effect of destabilizing local markets.

Under "the free market" system imposed on Rwanda, neither cash crops nor food crops were economically viable. The entire agricultural system was pushed into crisis. The state administrative apparatus was in disarray due not only to the civil war, but also as a result of the austerity measures and sinking civil service salaries – a situation which contributed inevitably to exacerbating the climate of generalized insecurity which had unfolded in 1992.

The seriousness of the agricultural situation had been amply documented by the FAO which had warned of the existence of widespread famine in the southern provinces.[14] A report released in early 1994 also pointed to the total collapse of coffee production as a result of both the war and the failure of the state marketing system which was being phased out with the support of the World Bank. Rwandex, the mixed enterprise responsible for the processing and export of coffee, had become largely inoperative.

The decision to devalue (and "the IMF stamp of approval") had already been reached on 17 September 1990, prior to the outbreak of hostilities, in high-level meetings held in Washington between the IMF and a mission headed by Rwandan Minister of Finance Mr. Ntigurirwa. The "green light" had been granted: as of early October, at the very moment when the fighting started, millions of dollars of so-called "balance of payments aid" (from multilateral and bilateral sources) came pouring into the coffers of the Central Bank. These funds, administered by the Central Bank, had been earmarked (by the donors) for commodity imports, yet it appears likely that a sizeable portion of these "quick disbursing loans" had been diverted by the regime (and its various political factions) towards the acquisition of military hardware (from South Africa, Egypt and Eastern Europe).[15] The purchases of Kalashnikov guns, heavy artillery and mortar were undertaken in addition to the bilateral military aid package provided by France which included, inter alia, Milan and Apila missiles (not to mention a Mystère Falcon jet for President Habyarimana's personal use).[16] Moreover, since October 1990, the armed forces had expanded virtually overnight from 5,000 to 40,000 men requiring inevitably (under conditions of budgetary austerity) a sizeable influx of outside money. The new recruits were largely enlisted from the ranks of the urban unemployed of which the numbers had dramatically swelled since the collapse of the coffee market in 1989. Thousands of delinquent and idle youths from a drifting population were also drafted into the civilian militia responsible for the massacres. And part of the arms' purchases enabled the armed forces to organize and equip the militiamen.

In all, from the outset of the hostilities (which coincided chronologically with the devaluation and the initial "gush of fresh money" in October 1990), a total envelope of some US$ 260 million had been approved for disbursal (with sizeable bilateral contributions from France, Germany, Belgium, the European Community and the US). While the new loans contributed to releasing money for the payment of debt servicing as well as equipping the armed forces, the evidence would suggest that a large part of this donor assistance was neither used productively nor was it channeled into providing relief in areas affected by famine.

It is also worth noting that the World Bank (through its soft-lending affiliate, the International Development Association (IDA) had ordered, in 1992, the privatization of Rwanda's state enterprise Electrogaz. The proceeds of the privatization were to be channeled towards debt servicing. In a loan agreement, co-financed with the European Investment Bank (EIB) and the Caisse française de développement (CFD), the Rwandan authorities were to receive in return (after meeting the "conditionalities") the modest sum of US$ 39 million which could be spent freely on commodity imports.[17] The privatization carried out at the height of the civil war also included dismissals of personnel and an immediate hike in the price of electricity which further contributed to paralyzing urban public services. A similar privatization of Rwandatel, the state telecommunications company under the Ministry of Transport and Communications, was implemented in September 1993.[18]

The World Bank had carefully reviewed Rwanda's public investment program. The *fiches de projet* having been examined, the World Bank recommended scrapping more than half the country's public investment projects. In agriculture, the World Bank had also demanded a significant down-sizing of state investment including the abandonment of the inland swamp reclamation program which had been initiated by the government in response to the severe shortages of arable land (and which the World Bank considered "unprofitable"). In the social sectors, the World Bank proposed a so-called "priority program" (under "the social safety net") predicated on maximizing efficiency and "reducing the financial burden of the government" through the exaction of user fees, lay-offs of teachers and health workers and the partial privatization of health and education.

The World Bank would no doubt contend that things would have been much worse had Scenario II not been adopted. This is the so-called "counterfactual argument". (See Chapter 3.) Such reasoning, however, sounds absurd particularly in the case of Rwanda. No sensitivity or concern was expressed as to the likely political and social repercussions of economic shock therapy applied to a country on the brink of civil war. The World Bank team consciously excluded the "non-economic variables" from their "simulations"...

Part B

Installing a US Protectorate in Central Africa[19]

From the outset of the Rwandan civil war in 1990, Washington's hidden agenda consisted in establishing an American sphere of influence in a region historically dominated by France and Belgium. America's design was to displace France by supporting the Rwandan Patriotic Front and by arming and equipping its military arm, the Rwandan Patriotic Army (RPA).

From the mid-1980s, the Kampala government, under President Yoweri Musaveni, had become Washington's African showpiece of "democracy". Uganda had also become a launchpad for US-sponsored guerilla movements into the Sudan, Rwanda and the Congo. Major General Paul Kagame had been head of military intelligence in the Ugandan Armed Forces; he had been trained at the US Army Command and Staff College (CGSC) in Leavenworth, Kansas which focuses on warfighting and military strategy. Kagame returned from Leavenworth to lead the RPA, shortly after the 1990 invasion.

Prior to the outbreak of the Rwandan civil war, the RPA was part of the Ugandan Armed Forces. Shortly prior to the October 1990 invasion of Rwanda, military labels were switched. From one day to the next, large numbers of Ugandan soldiers joined the ranks of the Rwandan Patriotic Army (RPA). Throughout the civil war, the RPA was supplied from United People's Defense Forces (UPDF) military bases inside Uganda. The Tutsi commissioned officers in the Ugandan army took over positions in the RPA. The October 1990 invasion by Ugandan forces was presented to public opinion as a war of liberation by a Tutsi led guerilla army.

Militarization of Uganda

The militarization of Uganda was an integral part of US foreign policy. The build-up of the Ugandan UPDF Forces and of the Rwandan Patriotic Army (RPA) had been supported by the US and Britain. The British had provided military training at the Jinja military base:

> From 1989 onwards, America supported joint RPF [Rwandan Patriotic Front]-Ugandan attacks upon Rwanda. . . There were at least 56 'situation reports' in [US] State Department files in 1991... As American and British relations with Uganda and the RPF strengthened, so hostilities between Uganda and Rwanda escalated... By August 1990 the RPF had begun preparing an invasion with the full knowledge and approval of British intelligence.[20]

Troops from Rwanda's RPA and Uganda's UPDF had also supported John Garang's People's Liberation Army in its secessionist war in southern Sudan. Washington was firmly behind these initiatives with covert support provided by the CIA.[21]

Moreover, under the Africa Crisis Reaction Initiative (ACRI), Ugandan officers were also being trained by US Special Forces in collaboration with a mercenary outfit, Military Professional Resources Inc. (MPRI) which was on contract with the US Department of State. MPRI had provided similar training to the Kosovo Liberation Army (KLA) and the Croatian Armed Forces during the Yugoslav civil war and more recently to the Colombian military in the context of Plan Colombia.

Militarization and the Ugandan External Debt

The buildup of the Ugandan external debt under President Musaveni coincided chronologically with the Rwandan and Congolese civil wars. With the accession of Musaveni to the presidency in 1986, the Ugandan external debt stood at 1.3 billion dollars. With the gush of fresh money, the external debt spiraled overnight, increasing almost threefold to 3.7 billion by 1997. In fact, Uganda had no outstanding debt to the World Bank at the outset of its "economic recovery program". By 1997, it owed almost 2 billion dollars solely to the World Bank.[22]

Where did the money go ? The foreign loans to the Musaveni government had been tagged to support the country's economic and social reconstruction. In the wake of a protracted civil war, the IMF-sponsored "economic stabilization program" required massive budget cuts of all civilian programs.

The World Bank was responsible for monitoring the Ugandan budget on behalf of the creditors. Under the "public expenditure review" (PER), the government was obliged to fully reveal the precise allocation of its budget. In other words, *every single category of expenditure* – including the budget of the Ministry of Defense – was open to scrutiny by the World Bank. Despite the austerity measures (imposed solely on "civilian" expenditures), the donors had allowed defense spending to increase without impediment.

Part of the money tagged for civilian programs had been diverted into funding the United People's Defense Force (UPDF) which, in turn, was involved in military operations in Rwanda and the Congo. The Ugandan external debt was being used to finance these military operations on behalf of Washington with the country and its people ultimately footing the bill. In fact by curbing social expenditures, the austerity measures had facilitated the reallocation of state of revenue in favor of the Ugandan military.

Financing both Sides in the Civil War

A similar process of *financing military expenditure from the external debt* had occurred in Rwanda under the Habyarimana government. In a cruel irony, both sides in the civil *war were financed by the same donor institutions* with the World Bank acting as watchdog.

The Habyarimana regime had at its disposal an arsenal of military equipment, including 83mm missile launchers, French made Blindicide, Belgian and German made light weaponry, and automatic weapons such as kalachnikovs made in Egypt, China and South Africa [as well as] (. . .) armored AML-60 and M3 armored vehicles.[23] While part of these purchases had been financed by direct military aid from France, the influx of development loans from the World Bank's soft lending affiliate the International Development Association (IDA), the African Development Fund (AFD), the European Development Fund (EDF) as well as from Germany, the United States, Belgium and Canada had been diverted into funding the military and Interhamwe militia.

A detailed investigation of government files, accounts and correspondence conducted in Rwanda in 1996-97 by the author – together with Belgian economist Pierre Galand – confirmed that many of the arms purchases had been negotiated outside the framework of government to government military aid agreements through various intermediaries and private arms dealers. These transactions – recorded as bona fide government expenditures – had, nonetheless, been included in the state budget which was under the supervision of the World Bank. Large quantities of machetes and other items used in the 1994 ethnic massacres – routinely classified as "civilian commodities" – had been imported through regular trading channels.[24]

According to the files of the National Bank of Rwanda (NBR), some of these imports had been financed in violation of agreements signed with the donors. According to NBR records of import invoices, *approximately one million machetes had been imported through various channels including Radio Mille Collines, an organization linked to the Interhamwe militia and used to foment ethnic hatred.*[25]

The money had been earmarked by the donors to support Rwanda's economic and social development. It was clearly stipulated that funds could not be used to import: *"military expenditures on arms, ammunition and other military material"*.[26] In fact, the loan agreement with the World Bank's IDA was even more stringent. The money could not be used to import civilian commodities such as fuel, foodstuffs, medicine, clothing and footwear *"destined for military or paramilitary use"*. The records of the NBR, nonetheless, confirm that the Habyarimana government used World Bank money to finance the import of machetes which had been routinely classified as imports of "civilian commodities".[27]

An army of consultants and auditors had been sent in by the World Bank to assess the Habyarimana government's "policy performance" under the loan agreement.[28] The use of donor funds to import machetes and other material used in the massacres of civilians did not show up in the independent audit commissioned by the government and the World Bank – under the IDA loan agreement (IDA Credit Agreement. 2271-RW).[29] In 1993, the World Bank decided to suspend the disbursement of the second installment of its IDA loan. There had been, according to the World Bank mission, unfortunate "slip-ups" and "delays" in policy implementation. The free market reforms were no longer "on track"; the conditionalities – including the privatization of state assets – had not been met. The fact that the country was involved in a civil war was not even mentioned. *How the money was spent was never an issue.*[30]

Whereas the World Bank had frozen the second installment (tranche) of the IDA loan, the money granted in 1991 had been deposited in a Special Account at the Banque Bruxelles Lambert in Brussels. This account remained open and accessible to the former regime (in exile), two months after the April 1994 ethnic massacres.[31]

Postwar Cover-up

In the wake of the civil war, the World Bank sent a mission to Kigali with a view to drafting a so-called loan "Completion Report".[32] This was a routine exercise, largely focussing on macro-economic rather than political issues. The report acknowledged that "the war effort prompted the [former] government to increase spending substantially, well beyond the fiscal targets agreed under the SAP.[33] The misappropriation of World Bank money was not mentioned. Instead, the Habyarimana government was praised for having *"made genuine major efforts – especially in 1991 – to reduce domestic and external financial imbalances, eliminate distortions hampering export growth and diversification and introduce market based mechanisms for resource allocation. . ."*[34] The massacres of civilians were not mentioned; from the point of view of the donors, "nothing had happened". In fact, the World Bank completion report failed to even acknowledge the existence of a civil war prior to April 1994.

In the Wake of the Civil War:
Reinstating the IMF's Deadly Economic Reforms

In 1995, barely a year after the 1994 ethnic massacres, Rwanda's external creditors entered into discussions with the Tutsi-led RPF government regarding the debts of the former regime which had been used to finance the massacres. The RPF decided to fully recognize the legitimacy of the "odious debts" of 1990-94. RPF strongman Vice-President Paul Kagame instructed the Cabinet not to pursue the matter nor to approach the World Bank. Under pressure from Washington, the RPF was not to enter into any form of negotiations, let alone an informal dialogue with the donors.

The legitimacy of the wartime debts was never questioned. Instead, the creditors had carefully set up procedures to ensure their prompt reimbursement. In 1998 at a special donors' meeting in Stockholm, a Multilateral Trust Fund of 55.2 million dollars was set up under the banner of postwar reconstruction.35 In fact, none of this money was destined for Rwanda. It had been earmarked to service Rwanda's "odious debts" with the World Bank (i.e. IDA debt), the African Development Bank and the International Fund for Agricultural Development (IFAD).

In other words, "fresh money" – which Rwanda will eventually have to reimburse – was lent to enable Rwanda to service the debts used to finance the massacres. Old loans had been swapped for new debts under the banner of post-war reconstruction.[36] The "odious debts" had been whitewashed; they had disappeared from the books. The creditor's responsibility had been erased. Moreover, the scam was also conditional upon the acceptance of a new wave of IMF-World Bank reforms.

Post War "Reconstruction and Reconciliation"

Bitter economic medicine was imposed under the banner of "reconstruction and reconciliation". In fact, the IMF post-conflict reform package was far more stringent than that imposed at the outset of the civil war in 1990. While wages and employment had fallen to abysmally low levels, the IMF had demanded a freeze on civil service wages alongside a massive retrenchment of teachers and health workers. The objective was to "restore macro-economic stability". A downsizing of the civil service was launched.[37] Civil service wages were not to exceed 4.5 percent of GDP, so-called "unqualified civil servants" (mainly teachers) were to be removed from the state payroll.[38]

Meanwhile, the country's per capita income had collapsed from $ 360 (prior to the war) to $ 140 in 1995. State revenues had been tagged to service the external debt. Kigali's Paris Club debts were rescheduled in exchange for "free market" reforms. Remaining state assets were sold off to foreign capital at bargain prices.

The Tutsi-led RPF government, rather than demanding the cancellation of Rwanda's odious debts, had welcomed the Bretton Woods institutions with open arms. They needed the IMF "greenlight" to boost the development of the military.

Despite the austerity measures, defense expenditures continued to grow. The 1990-94 pattern had been reinstated. The development loans granted since 1995 were not used to finance the country's economic and social development. Outside money had again been diverted into financing a military buildup, this time of the Rwandan Patriotic Army (RPA). And this build-up of the RPA occurred in the period immediately preceding the outbreak of civil war in former Zaire.

Civil War in the Congo

Following the installation of a US client regime in Rwanda in 1994, US trained Rwandan and Ugandan forces intervened in former Zaire – a stronghold of French and Belgian influence under President Mobutu Sese Seko. Amply documented, US special operations troops – mainly Green Berets from the 3rd Special Forces Group based at Fort Bragg, N.C – had been actively training the RPA. This program was a continuation of the covert support and military aid provided to the RPA prior to 1994. In turn, the tragic outcome of the Rwandan civil war, including the refugee crisis, had set the stage for the participation of Ugandan and Rwandan RPA in the civil war in the Congo:

> Washington pumped military aid into Kagame's army, and U.S. Army Special Forces and other military personnel trained hundreds of Rwandan troops. But Kagame and his colleagues had designs of their own. While the Green Berets trained the Rwandan Patriotic Army, that army was itself secretly training Zairian rebels.(…) [In] Rwanda, U.S. officials publicly portrayed their engagement with the army as almost entirely devoted to human rights training. But the Special Forces exercises also covered other areas, including combat skills… Hundreds of soldiers and officers were enrolled in U.S. training programs, both in Rwanda and in the United States… [C]onducted by U.S. Special Forces, Rwandans studied camouflage techniques, small-unit movement, troop-leading procedures, soldier-team development, [etc.]… And while the training went on, U.S. officials were meeting regularly with Kagame and other senior Rwandan leaders to discuss the continuing military threat faced by the [former Rwandan] government [in exile] from inside Zaïre… Clearly, the focus of Rwandan-U.S. military discussion had shifted from how to build human rights to how to combat an insurgency. (…) With [Ugandan President] Museveni's support, Kagame conceived a plan to back a rebel movement in eastern Zaire [headed by Laurent Desire Kabila]. (. . .) The operation was launched in October 1996, just a few weeks after Kagame's trip to Washington and the completion of the Special Forces training mission. (…) Once the war [in the Congo] started, the United States provided "political assistance" to Rwanda, (…) An official of the U.S. Embassy in Kigali traveled to eastern Zaire numerous times to liaise with Kabila. Soon, the rebels had moved on. Brushing off the Zairian army with the help of the Rwandan forces, they marched through Africa's third-largest nation in seven months, with

only a few significant military engagements. Mobutu fled the capital, Kinshasa, in May 1997, and Kabila took power, changing the name of the country to Congo…U.S. officials deny that there were any U.S. military personnel with Rwandan troops in Zaire during the war, although unconfirmed reports of a U.S. advisory presence have circulated in the region since the war's earliest days.[39]

American Mining Interests

At stake in these military operations in the Congo were the extensive mining resources of Eastern and Southern Zaire including strategic reserves of cobalt – of crucial importance for the US defense industry. During the civil war, several months before the downfall of Mobutu, Laurent Desire Kabila based in Goma, Eastern Zaire had renegotiated the mining contracts with several US and British mining companies, including American Mineral Fields (AMF) – a company headquartered in President Bill Clinton's hometown of Hope, Arkansas.[40]

Meanwhile, back in Washington, IMF officials were busy reviewing Zaire's macro-economic situation. No time was lost. The post-Mobutu economic agenda had already been decided upon. In a study released in April, 1997 – barely a month before President Mobutu Sese Seko fled the country – the IMF had recommended *"halting currency issue completely and abruptly"* as part of an economic recovery programme.[41] And a few months later, upon assuming power in Kinshasa, the new government of Laurent Kabila Desire was ordered by the IMF to freeze civil service wages with a view to "restoring macro-economic stability." Eroded by hyperinflation, the average public sector wage had fallen to 30,000 new Zaires (NZ) a month, the equivalent of one US dollar.[42]

The IMF's demands were tantamount to maintaining the entire population in abysmal poverty. They precluded, from the outset, a meaningful post-war economic reconstruction, thereby contributing to fuelling the continuation of the Congolese civil war in which close to two million people have died.

Concluding Remarks

The civil war in Rwanda was a brutal struggle for political power between the Hutu-led Habyarimana government supported by France, and the Tutsi Rwandan Patriotic Front (RPF) backed financially and militarily by

Washington. Ethnic rivalries were used deliberately in the pursuit of geopolitical objectives. Both the CIA and French intelligence were involved.

In the words of former Cooperation Minister Bernard Debre in the government of Prime Minister Henri Balladur:

> What one forgets to say is that, if France was on one side, the Americans were on the other, arming the Tutsis who armed the Ugandans. I don't want to portray a showdown between the French and the Anglo-Saxons, but the truth must be told.[43]

In addition to military aid to the warring factions, the influx of development loans played an important role in "financing the conflict." In other words, both the Ugandan and Rwanda external debts were diverted into supporting the military and paramilitary. Uganda's external debt increased by more than two billion dollars, – i.e. at a significantly faster pace than that of Rwanda (an increase of approximately 250 million dollars from 1990 to 1994). In retrospect, the RPA – financed by US military aid and Uganda's external debt – was much better equipped and trained than the Forces Armees du Rwanda (FAR) loyal to President Habyarimana. From the outset, the RPA had a definite military advantage over the FAR.

According to the testimony of Paul Mugabe, a former member of the RPF High Command Unit, Major General Paul Kagame had personally ordered the shooting down of President Habyarimana's plane with a view to taking control of the country. He was fully aware that the assassination of Habyarimana would unleash "a genocide" against Tutsi civilians. RPA forces had been fully deployed in Kigali at the time the ethnic massacres took place and did not act to prevent it from happening:

> The decision of Paul Kagame to shoot Pres. Habyarimana's aircraft was the catalyst of an unprecedented drama in Rwandan history, and Major-General Paul Kagame took that decision with all awareness. Kagame's ambition caused the extermination of all of our families: Tutsis, Hutus and Twas. We all lost. Kagame's take-over took away the lives of a large number of Tutsis and caused the unnecessary exodus of millions of Hutus, many of whom were innocent under the hands of the genocide ringleaders. Some naive Rwandans proclaimed Kagame as their savior, but time has demonstrated that it was he who caused our suffering and misfortunes… Can Kagame explain to the Rwandan people why he sent Claude Dusaidi and Charles Muligande to New York and Washington to stop the UN military intervention

which was supposed to be sent and protect the Rwandan people from the genocide ? The reason behind avoiding that military intervention was to allow the RPF leadership the takeover of the Kigali Government and to show the world that they - the RPF - were the ones who stopped the genocide. We will all remember that the genocide occurred during three months, even though Kagame has said that he was capable of stopping it the first week after the aircraft crash. Can Major-General Paul Kagame explain why he asked MINUAR to leave Rwandan soil within hours while the UN was examining the possibility of increasing its troops in Rwanda in order to stop the genocide ?[44]

Paul Mugabe's testimony regarding the shooting down of Habyarimana's plane ordered by Kagame is corroborated by intelligence documents and information presented to the French parliamentary inquiry. Major General Paul Kagame was an instrument of Washington. The loss of African lives did not matter. The civil war in Rwanda and the ethnic massacres were an integral part of US foreign policy, carefully staged in accordance with precise strategic and economic objectives.

Despite the good diplomatic relations between Paris and Washington and the apparent unity of the Western military alliance, *it was an undeclared war between France and America.* By supporting the build up of Ugandan and Rwandan forces, and by directly intervening in the Congolese civil war, Washington also bears a direct responsibility for the ethnic massacres committed in the Eastern Congo including several hundred thousand people who died in refugee camps.

US policy-makers were fully aware that a catastrophe was imminent. In fact, four months before the genocide, the CIA had warned the US State Department in a confidential brief that the Arusha Accords would fail and "that if hostilities resumed, then upward of half a million people would die".[45] This information was withheld from the United Nations: "it was not until the genocide was over that information was passed to Maj.-Gen. Dallaire [who was in charge of UN forces in Rwanda]."[46]

Washington's objective was to displace France, discredit the French government (which had supported the Habyarimana regime) and install an Anglo-American protectorate in Rwanda under Major General Paul Kagame. Washington deliberately did nothing to prevent the ethnic massacres.

When a UN force was put forth, Major General Paul Kagame sought to delay its implementation stating that he would only accept a peacekeeping force once the RPA was in control of Kigali. Kagame "feared [that] the proposed United Nations force of more than 5,000 troops (...) [might] intervene to deprive them [the RPA] of victory".[47] Meanwhile, the Security Council, after deliberation and a report from Secretary General Boutros Boutros Ghali, decided to postpone its intervention.

The 1994 Rwandan "genocide" served strictly strategic and geopolitical objectives. The ethnic massacres were a stumbling blow to France's credibility which enabled the US to establish a neocolonial foothold in Central Africa. From a distinctly Franco-Belgian colonial setting, the Rwandan capital Kigali has become – under the expatriate Tutsi-led RPF government – distinctly Anglo-American. English has become the dominant language in government and the private sector. Many private businesses owned by Hutus were taken over in 1994 by returning Tutsi expatriates. The latter had been exiled in Anglophone Africa, the US and Britain.

The Rwandan Patriotic Army (RPA) functions in English and Kinyarwanda; the University, previously linked to France and Belgium, functions in English. While English had become an official language alongside French and Kinyarwanda, French political and cultural influence will eventually be erased. Washington has become the new colonial master of a francophone country.

Several other francophone countries in sub-Saharan Africa have entered into military cooperation agreements with the US. These countries are slated by Washington to follow suit on the pattern set in Rwanda. Meanwhile in francophone West Africa, the US dollar is rapidly displacing the CFA Franc – which is linked in a currency board arrangement to the French Treasury.

Endnotes

1. The system of export quotas of the International Coffee Organization (ICO) was lifted in the aftermath of the Florida meetings in July 1989. The fob price in Mombasa declined from US$ 1.31 a pound in May 1989 to $ 0.60 in December, *Marchés tropicaux,* 18 May 1990, p. 1369; 29 June 1990, p. 1860.

2. See Jean Rumiya, *Le Rwanda sous le régime du mandat belge (1916-1931)*, L'Harmattan, Paris, 1992, pp. 220-26; Andre Guichaoua, *Destins paysans et politiques agraires en Afrique centrale,* L'Harmattan, Paris, 1989.

3. See Ferdinand Nahimana, *Le Rwanda, Émergence d'un État,*

L'Harmattan, Paris, 1993.

4. *New African*, June 1994, p. 16.

5. See United Nations Conference on the Least Developed Countries, *Country Presentation by the Government of Rwanda*, Geneva, 1990, p. 5. See also République Rwandaise, Ministère des Finances et de *l'Economie, L'Economie rwandaise, 25 ans d'efforts* (1962-87), Kigali, 1987.

6. See the study of A. Guichaoua, *Les paysans et l'investissement-travail au Burundi et au Rwanda*, Bureau international du Travail, Geneva, 1987.

7. United Nations Conference on the Least Developed Countries, *op. cit.*, p. 2.

8. A 5 percent growth in exports was to take place under Scenario II as opposed to 2.5 percent under Scenario I.

9. Debt forgiveness amounting to US$ 46 million was granted in 1989.

10. World Bank, *World Debt Tables, 1993-94*, Washington DC, p. 383. The outstanding debt had increased by more than 400 percent since 1980 (from US$ 150.3 million in 1980 to $ 804.3 million in 1992).

11. See Myriam Gervais, "Etude de la pratique des ajustements au Niger et au Rwanda", *Labor, Capital and Society*, Vol. 26. No. 1, 1993, p. 36.

12. This figure is a conservative estimate. Economist Intelligence Unit, *Country Profile, Rwanda/Burundi 1993/1994*, London, 1994, p. 10.

13. In 1993, a third devaluation of the order of 30 percent had been recommended by the World Bank as a means of eliminating the debts of the *Fonds d'égalisation*.

14. The International Committee of the Red Cross (ICRC) had estimated in 1993 that more than a million people were affected by famine, *Marchés tropicaux*, 2 April 1993, p. 898. A FAO communiqué released in March 1994 pointed to a 33 percent decline in food production in 1993. See *Marchés tropicaux*, 25 March 1994, p. 594.

15. There has been no official communiqué or press report confirming or denying the channeling of balance-of-payments aid towards military expenditure. According to the Washington-based Human Rights Watch, Egypt agreed with Kigali to supply US$ 6 million worth of military equipment. The deal with South Africa was for US$ 5.9 million. See *Marchés tropicaux*, 28 January 1994, p. 173.

16. See *New African*, June 1994, p. 15. See also the interview with Colette Braeckman on France's military aid in Archipel, No. 9, July 1994, p. 1.

17. See *Marchés tropicaux*, 26 February 1992, p. 569.

18. See *Marchés tropicaux*, 8 October 1993, p. 2492.

19. Part I of this chapter was written in 1994 for the first edition of

Globalization of Poverty". Part II is in part based on a study conducted by the author and Belgian economist Pierre Galand on the use of Rwanda's 1990-94 external debt to finance the military and paramilitary.

20. Africa Direct, Submission to the UN Tribunal on Rwanda, http://www.junius.co.uk/africa- direct/tribunal.html.

21. *Ibid.*

22. Africa's New Look, *Jane's Foreign Report*, August 14, 1997.

23. Jim Mugunga, Uganda foreign debt hits Shs 4 trillion, The Monitor, Kampala, 19 February 1997.

24. Michel Chossudovsky and Pierre Galand, *L'usage de la dette extérieure du Rwanda: La responsabilité des créanciers*, mission report, United Nations Development Program and Government of Rwanda, Ottawa and Brussels, 1997.

25. *Ibid.*

26. *Ibid.*

27. *Ibid.* The imports recorded were of the order of kg. 500.000 of machetes or approximately one million machetes.

28. *Ibid.* See also schedule 1.2 of the Development Credit Agreement with IDA, Washington, 27 June 1991, CREDIT IDA 2271 RW.

29. Chossudovsky and Galand, *op cit.*

30. *Ibid.*

31. *Ibid.*

32. *World Bank Completion Report*, quoted in Chossudovsky and Galand, *op cit.*

33. *Ibid.*

34. *Ibid.*

35. See World Bank, *Rwanda at* http://www.worldbank.org/afr/rw2.htm.

36. *Ibid.*, italics added.

37. A ceiling on the number of public employees had been set at 38,000 for 1998 down from 40,600 in 1997. See Letter of Intent of the Government of Rwanda including cover letter addressed to IMF Managing Director Michel Camdessus, IMF, Washington, http://www.imf.org/external/np/loi/060498.htm,1998.

38. *Ibid.*

39. Lynne Duke Africans Use US Military Training in Unexpected Ways, *Washington Post.* July 14, 1998. p. A01.

40. *Musengwa Kayaya*, U.S. Company To Invest in Zaire, Pan African News, 9 May 1997.

41. International Monetary Fund, *Zaire Hyperinflation 1990-1996*, Washington, April 1997.

42. Alain Shungu Ngongo, Zaire-Economy: How to Survive On a Dollar a Month, *International Press Service*, 6 June 1996.

43. Quoted in Therese LeClerc. "Who is responsible for the genocide in Rwanda ?", World Socialist website at http://www.wsws.org/index.shtml, 29 April 1998.

44. Paul Mugabe, "The Shooting Down Of The Aircraft Carrying Rwandan President Habyarimana", testimony to the International Strategic Studies Association (ISSA), Alexandria, Virginia, 24 April 2000.

45. Linda Melvern, "Betrayal of the Century", *Ottawa Citizen*, Ottawa, 8 April 2000.

46. *Ibid.*

47. Scott Peterson, "Peacekeepers will not halt carnage, say Rwanda, rebels", *Daily Telegraph*, London, May 12, 1994.

Chapter 8
"Exporting Apartheid" to sub-Saharan Africa

Under President Nelson Mandela, the right wing Afrikaner Freedom Front (FF) headed by General Constand Viljoen was promoting the development of a "Food Corridor" extending across the southern part of the continent from Angola to Mozambique. In the post-Apartheid era, Afrikaner agri-business was to extend its grip into neighbouring countries with large scale investments in commercial farming, food processing and eco-tourism. The Afrikaner unions of the Orange Free State and Eastern Transvaal are part-ners; the objective is to set up white-owned farms beyond South Africa's borders.[1]

The "Food Corridor", however, does not mean "food for the local peo-ple". On the contrary, under the scheme the peasants will loose their land; small-holders will become farm laborers or tenants on large scale planta-tions owned by the Boers. Moreover, the South African Chamber for Agricultural Development (SACADA), which acts as an umbrella organi-zation, is integrated by several right wing organizations including the Freedom Front (FF) led by Viljoen and the secret Afrikaner Broederbond. As South African Defence Force (SADF) Commander in Chief during the Apartheid regime, General Viljoen had been implicated in the attacks on so-called "African National Congress Targets" including the blow up of suspected anti-apartheid activists and critics.[2] The Freedom Front, although "moderate" in comparison to Eugene Terre'Blanche's far-right Afrikaner Weerstandsbeweging (AWB), is a racist political movement committed to the Afrikaner Volksstaat.[3] The SACADA-Freedom Front ini-tiative had, nonetheless, received the political backing of the African National Congress as well as the personal blessing of President Nelson Mandela.

In discussions with President Mandela, General Viljoen had argued that:

> settling Afrikaner farmers would stimulate the economies of neigh-
> bouring states, would provide food and employment for locals, and

that this would stem the flow of illegal immigrants into South Africa.[4]

Viljoen had also held high-level meetings on Afrikaner agricultural investments with representatives of the European Union, the United Nations and other donor agencies.[5]

In turn, Pretoria was negotiating with several African governments on behalf of SACADA and the Freedom Front. The ANC government was anxious to facilitate the expansion of corporate agri-business into neighbouring countries. "Mandela has asked the Tanzanian government to accept Afrikaner farmers to help develop the agricultural sector. SACADA has approached some 12 African countries interested in White South African farmers".[6] In a venture set up in 1994 under the South African Development Corporation (SADEVCO), the government of the Congo had granted to the Boers 99 year leases on agricultural land. President Mandela endorsed the scheme calling on African nations "to accept the migrants as a kind of foreign aid".[7]

An earlier trek of White farmers to Zambia and the Congo dating to the early 1990s met with mixed results. Rather than tied to the interests of corporate agri-business (as in the case of SACADA), the impetus was based on the resettlement of individual (often bankrupt) Afrikaner farmers without political backing, financial support and the legitimacy of the New South Africa.

Pressured by the World Bank and the World Trade Organization (WTO), the host national governments had, on the whole, welcomed the inflow of Afrikaner investments. The liberalization of trade and investment under WTO auspices was supporting the extension of Afrikaner business interests throughout the region.

The Expropriation of Peasant Lands

The "Food Corridor" will eventually displace a pre-existing agricultural system; it not only appropriates the land, it takes over the host country's economic and social infrastructure, and it spells increased levels of poverty in the countryside. It weakens subsistence agriculture, as well as the peasant cash crop economy; it displaces local level agricultural markets and aggravates the conditions of endemic famine prevailing in the region. Jen Kelenga, a spokesperson for a pro-democracy group in the Congo (former Zaire) sees the Boers "in search of new territories to apply their racist way of living".[8]

The "Food Corridor" potentially alters the rural landscape of the

Southern African region, requiring the uprooting and displacement of small farmers over an extensive territory. Under the proposed scheme, millions of hectares of the best farmland are to be handed over to South African agri-business. The Boers will manage large-scale commercial farms using the rural people both as "labor tenants" as well as seasonal agricultural workers.

While the project is meant to "bring development" and "transfer much needed agricultural expertise", the initiative is largely intent upon *"exporting Apartheid"* to neighbouring countries. The latter objective is in turn supported by the gamut of IMF-World Bank-WTO-sponsored economic reforms.

Afrikaner investments in agriculture go hand-in-hand with the World Bank sponsored Land Law. The expropriation of peasant lands is often demanded by creditors as a condition for the rescheduling of Paris Club debts. Peasant lands (which formally belonged to the state) are sold (at very low prices) or leased out to international agribusiness (eg. on a 50-99 years concession). The meagre proceeds of the land sales will be used to service the external debt.

The World Bank had also put forward changes in land legislation, which could eventually abrogate the right to land of millions of smallholders. Identical land legislation was being enforced throughout the region, the national level land laws (drafted under technical advice from the World Bank Legal Department) are with some variations "exact carbon copies of each other":

> The constitution [in Mozambique] says that the land is the property of the State and cannot be sold or mortgaged. There has been strong pressure particularly from the United States and the World Bank for land to be privatized and to allow mortgages.[9]

South African companies and banks are also participating in the country-level privatization programmes (under the structural adjustment programme) acquiring – at rock bottom prices – the ownership of state assets in mining, public utilities and agriculture. With regard to the latter, experimental farms, government research stations, state-owned plantations, seed producing facilities, etc. have been put on the auction block. With the deregulation of agricultural markets under World Bank advice, the state marketing system is either closed down or taken over by private investors.

Derogating Customary Land Rights

Under the proposed land legislation, both SACADA and the World Bank, nonetheless, tout the protection of traditional land rights. The small peasantry is to be "protected" through the establishment of "customary land reserves" established in the immediate vicinity of the white commercial farms. In practice, under the new land legislation, the majority of the rural people will be caged into small territorial enclaves ("communal lands") while the bulk of the best agricultural land will be sold or leased to private investors.

This also means that peasant communities which practice shifting cultivation over a large land area as well as pastoralists, will henceforth be prosecuted for encroaching on lands earmarked for commercial farming, often without their prior knowledge. Impoverished by the macro-economic reforms, with no access to credit and modern farm inputs, these customary enclaves will constitute "labor reserves" for large scale agri-business.

Afrikaner Farms in Mozambique

Sacada had plans to invest in Mozambique, Zaire, Zambia and Angola, "with Mozambique being the test case".[10] President Joaquim Chissano of Mozambique and President Nelson Mandela had signed an intergovernmental agreement granting rights to Afrikaner agri-business to develop investments in at least six provinces encompassing territorial concessions of some eight million hectares:[11]

> Mozambique needs the technical expertise and the money, and we
> have the people. . . We favor an area which is not heavily populated
> because it is an Achilles heal if there are too many people on the land.
> For the Boers, Land is next to God and the Bible.[12]

In SACADA's concessionary areas in Mozambique, the "socialist" Frelimo government was to ensure that there would be no encroachment; rural small-holders and subsistence farmers (who invariably do not possess legal land titles) will either be expelled or transferred into marginal lands.[13] In turn, members of the military and government ministers who sought to become "business partners" of international agri-business were granted concessions over millions of hectares of land which is already occupied by the peasantry.[14] The World Bank, together with bilateral donors, had proposed – on behalf of potential foreign investors – a system of land registration including the extensive mapping of land areas through aerial photography in view of generating digitized maps.[15]

In Mozambique's Niassa province, the best agricultural land was leased in concession to the Afrikaners for fifty years. "There are just so many beautiful, fertile places to choose from. . .", said Egbert Hiemstra who owns two farms in Lydenburg and wants a third in Mozambique.[16] At the token price of some $ 0.15 per hectare per annum, the land lease is a give-away.[17]

Through the establishment of Mosagrius (a joint venture company), SACADA is now firmly established in the fertile valley of the Lugenda river. But the Boers also have their eyes on agricultural areas along the Zambezi and Limpopo rivers as well as on the road and railway facilities linking Lichinga, Niassa's capital to the deep see port of Nagala. The railway line is being rehabilitated and modernized (by a French contractor) with development aid provided by France.

> Our intention [the Afrikaner farmers] is to develop the highveld areas in maize, wheat and beef cattle linked up with agro-processing and the export market. In the lowvelds we will plant a variety of tropical fruit trees as well as establish modern juice factories. Our agricultural institutes will establish research stations in the area with a view to supporting SACADA's initiative. . .Eventually we would also like to get into the cotton areas of Nampulo and Cabo Delgado provinces.[18]

The available infrastructure, including several state buildings and enterprises, will be handed over; several state-owned farms in Niassa will be transferred to the Afrikaners alongside the Technical College in Lichinga.[19] The Agricultural Research Station is also to be taken over: "They want out", they are seeking Afrikaner investment to keep the Research Station afloat.[20] Eventually, Afrikaner agri-business is intent on taking over the government's seed producing facilities (SEMOC) in Niassa.[21]

In the Mosagrius project, "The main thrust will come from the successful farmers in South Africa who are now seeking for new lands, and who are able to mobilize considerable financial resources".[22] They will operate their new farms as part of their business undertakings in South Africa, dispatching white Afrikaner managers and supervisors to Mozambique. "Family farms with a good track record but without funding capabilities are also eligible. They will rely on SACADA for funding".[23] No provision is made, however, to help Afrikaner farmers driven into bankruptcy as a result of Pretoria's economic liberalization programme. These farmers may, nonetheless, be hired to work as managers in Mozambique.

In turn, the Boers will bring their black right-hand men, their tractor operators, their technicians. In the words of the Mosagrius liaison officer at the South African High Commission in Maputo: "Each and every Afrikaner farmer will bring his tame Kaffirs" who will be used to supervise the local workers.[24]

SACADA had carefully mapped out the designated areas by helicopter. South Africa's agricultural research institutes had surveyed the area, providing an assessment of prevailing environmental, climatic and social conditions. South African demographers have been called in as consultants to evaluate the implications of displacing the rural people.

Creating "Rural Townships"

Under the SACADA scheme, the rural communities in Niassa which occupy the Afrikaner concessionary areas are to be regrouped into "rural townships" similar to those of the Apartheid regime:

> What you do is to develop villages along the roadside close to the [White] farms. These villages have been planned very carefully [by SACADA] in proximity to the fields so that farm-workers can go back and forth; you give the villages some infrastructure and a plot of land for each household so that the farm-laborers can set up their food gardens.[25]

Unless token customary land rights are entrenched within or in areas contiguous to the concessions, the peasants will become landless farm laborers or "labor tenants". Under the latter system applied by the Boers in South Africa since the 19th century, black peasant households perform labor services (corvée) in exchange for the right to farm a small parcel of land. Formally outlawed in South Africa in 1960 by the Nationalist government, "labor tenancy" remains in existence in many parts of South Africa including East Transvaal and Kwa-Zulu Natal.[26] It has evolved towards the payment of a (very low) nominal wage largely to disguise the (outlawed) feudal relationship. Since 1995, it has been the target of the Land Reform (Labor Tenants) Bill of Land Affairs Minister Derek Hanekom.[27]

The rural townships established in the concessions constitute "reserves" of cheap labor for the white commercial farms. Wages in Mozambique are substantially lower than in South Africa. For seasonal workers, the wage was set at the statutory minimum wage – a meagre $ 18 a month – which the IMF Representative Sergio Leite, considered in his statement to a donors' meeting in 1995, to be "excessive" by international standards. He also pointed to the inflationary pressures resulting from wage demands.[28]

The derogation of workers rights, as well as the deregulation of the labor market under IMF advice, enable the Boers not only to pay their Mozambican workers excessively low wages, but also to escape the demands of black agricultural workers in South Africa. It also allows corporate agri-business investing in neighboring countries to more effectively lobby the ANC government against Land Reform and "affirmative action" programmes within South Africa.

Moreover, under the Mosagrius Agreement (clause 42) the Mozambican government will be fully responsible in dealing with land disputes and ensuring the expropriation of peasant lands "without prejudice or loss that may occur from such claims to SDM [Mosagrius] and other Mosagrius participants".[29]

Foreign Aid Supports the Establishments of White Farms

South Africa's major commercial banks, the World Bank and the European Union have firmly backed the project. "The Food Corridor" has become an integral part of the IMF-World Bank-sponsored structural adjustment programme. In the words of SACADA Secretary Willie Jordaan: "SACADA had endeavoured to bring its policies in line with the World Bank and the International Monetary Fund, and claimed that it was set to become an international development agency" with a mandate to contract with donor institutions and carry out "foreign aid programmes" on their behalf.[30]

While the West had endorsed the ANCs struggle against the Apartheid regime, it was providing – in the post Apartheid era – financial support to a racist Afrikaner development organization. Under the disguise of "foreign aid", Western donors had contributed to the extension of the Apartheid system into neighbouring countries. The European Union provided money to SACADA out of a development package explicitly earmarked by Brussels for South Africa's Reconstruction and Development Programme. According to an EU spokesman, the project "was the best noise out of Africa in 30 years".[31] The EU Ambassador to South Africa Mr. Erwan Fouéré met General Viljoen to discuss the project. Fouéré confirmed that if all goes well, further EU money could be made available to cover the costs of "settling Afrikaner farmers in South Africa's neighbouring countries". The fact that the scheme derogated the land rights of small-holders, while replicating the system, of "labor tenancy" prevalent in South Africa under Apartheid was not a matter for discussion.

Fostering Ecotourism

Most of Mozambique's coastline on lake Niassa – including a 160 km. stretch in the Riff Valley from Meponda to Mapangula extending further North to Ilha sobre o Lago close to the Tanzanian border – had been designated "for tourism and other complementary and subsidiary activities [which are] ecologically sustainable".[32] The latter also included designated areas for South African investments in fishing and aquaculture on lake Niassa displacing the local fishing industry.[33]

In turn, the Agreement handed over to Mosagrius, the development and operation rights over the Niassa Game Reserve on the Tanzanian border. The Reserve includes an extensive area of some 20,000 hectares earmarked for a so-called "ecologically sustainable ecotourism". SACADA is to fence the entire area and establish up-market tourist lodges on the periphery of the Game Park; hunting of wild game is also envisaged for wealthy individuals "in strictly controlled areas".[34] According to the Mosagrius liaison officer, "fauna restocking of the Reserve may, however, be required to ensure that tourists see the real thing".[35] A specialist from South Africa's Department of Nature Conservation is assisting SACADA in planning the venture, as well as securing financial resources. International funding of the lodges and the Game Reserve is in the process of being secured from a number of wealthy private investors. . .[36]

In a much larger undertaking, James Ulysses Blanchard III – the right-wing Texan tycoon – has been granted a concession over a vast territory, which includes the Maputo Elephant Reserve and the adjoining Machangula Peninsula. During the Mozambican civil war, Blanchard provided financial backing to Renamo, the rebel organization directly supported by the Apartheid regime and trained by the South African Defence Force (SADF).

> But it now seems that the man who once bankrolled a rebel army to wage a war of incredible destruction and brutality (the US State Department once described Renamo atrocities as worse than those of the Pol Pot regime in Cambodia) is likely to be rewarded with control over a huge chunk of Mozambique's richest province.[37]

Blanchard intends to create an Indian Ocean Dream Park with a floating hotel, deluxe tourist lodges at $ 600-800 a night and a casino. Large parcels of land in Manchangula have also been allocated to agricultural investors from Eastern Transvaal.[38] Local communities in Blanchard's concessionary area will be expropriated; in the words of his general manager, John Perrot:

> We gonna come here and say [to the local villagers] `Okay, now you're in a national park. Your village can either get fenced or you can have them wild animals walking right through your main street'.[39]

In this scramble for territory, the Mozambican government agreed to hand over several million hectares of so-called "unused land" to a religious organization, the Dutch based Maharashi Heaven on Earth Company.[40] President Chissano is a devotee of Maharishi Mahesh Yogi, founder of the Natural Law Party. Since the signing of the agreement in July 1993, however, the government seems to have backtracked on the deal stating that the Maharashi Church would "be treated like any other foreign investor – no more, no less".[41]

Carving up the National Territory

An autonomous territory, "a State within a State" is being developed initially in Niassa province; Mosagrius (overriding the national and provincial governments) is the sole authority concerning the utilization rights of land in its concessionary areas (clause 34); similarly, the territory is defined as a free trade zone allowing for the unimpeded movement of goods, capital and people (meaning white South Africans). All investments in the concessionary areas "will be free from customs duties, or other fiscal impositions".[42]

In turn, with concessions granted to foreign investors in various parts of the country, the national territory is once again being carved up into a number of separate "corridors" reminiscent of the colonial period. This system of territorial concessions – with each of the corridors integrated separately into the world market – tends to favor the demise of the national economy.

The decline of the Mozambican State apparatus, as well the fragmentation of the national economy, favors the transformation of entire regions of the country (eg. Niassa province) into concessionary areas or "corridors" under the political custody of donors, non-governmental organizations and foreign investors. The latter constitute a de facto "parallel government" which increasingly bypasses the state system. Moreover, in several areas in Northern Mozambique, the former pro-Apartheid rebel group Renamo (which has also established its links to the donors) is formally in command of local government. In the war's aftermath, several Renamo leaders have become "business partners" of South African companies investing in Mozambique, including SACADA sponsored investments: "It would appear that there is a secret understanding as part of the [1992] Peace Agreement that Renamo and its backers will get land".[43]

Endnotes

1. Ten Years Ago, *Weekly Mail and Guardian*, Johannesburg, 23 June 1995.

2. See Stefaans Brummer, The Web of Stratcoms, Johannesburg, *Weekly Mail and Guardian*, 24 February 1995. See also, *Antifa Info Bulletin*, Vol 1, No. 1, 23 January 1996.

3. In founding the Freedom Front, Viljoen parted from the Afrikaner Volksfront (AVF) of which he was the co-leader. He also abandoned his threats of armed resistance shortly before the 1994 elections.

4. "EU Backs Boers Trek to Mozambique", Johannesburg, *Weekly Mail and Guardian*, 1 December 1995.

5. "Trade Block planned for Eastern Regions", Johannesburg, *Weekly Mail and Guardian*, 12 May 1995.

6. *Ibid.*

7. "The Boers are Back", *South Africa: Programme Support Online,* No. 4. 1996. See also "Boers Seek Greener Pastures", *Los Angeles Times*, 2 September 1995.

8. "The Boers are Back", *South Africa: Programme Support Online*, No. 4, 1996.

9. Joseph Hanlon, *Supporting Peasants in their Fight for Land*, Christian Aid, London, November 1995.

10. "The Second Great Trek", *op. cit.*

11. See "Boers are Back" *op cit* and "Boers seek Greener Pastures" *op. cit.*

12. Author's interview with officials of the South African High Commission responsible for the SACADA project, Maputo, July 1996.

13. See the documents of the Land Conference, *Conferencia Nacional de terras, documento de trabalho*, Maputo, July 1996.

14. Hanlon, *op. cit.*, p. 1.

15. *Ibid.*

16. See "EU Backs Boer Trek", *op cit.*

17. *Ibid* The amount quoted for the land lease is Rand 0.60 per annum per hectare.

18. Interview with officials of the South African High Commission in Maputo, July 1996.
19. According to press reports and officials of the South African High Commission in Maputo, July 1996. The agreement itself explicitly refers to some 170,000 hectares plus the prospect of development rights on lake Niassa. See "The Agreement on Basic Principles and Understanding concerning the Mosagrius Development Programme", Maputo, May 1996.
20. Interview with officials of the South African High Commission, responsible for the Mosagrius project.
21. *Ibid.*
22. *Ibid.*
23. *Ibid.*
24. *Ibid.*
25. Interview with South African agricultural experts, South African High Commission, Maputo, July 1996.
26. See Eddie Koch and Gaye Davis, "Hanekom's Bill to bury Slavery", Johannesburg, *Weekly Mail and Guardian*, 2 June 1995.
27. *Ibid.*
28. "FMI nao concorda", *Mediafax*, Maputo, 26 September 1995, p. 1.
29. Clause 42 of the Mosagrius Agreement.
30. "FMI nao concorda," Mediafax, Maputo, 26 September 1995, p. 1. See also "The Second Great Trek", *Weekly Mail and Guardian*.
31. "EU Backs Boers Trek to Mozambique", Johannesburg, *Weekly Mail and Guardian*, 1 December 1995.
32. See clauses 38 and 39 of the Mosagrius agreement.
33. Addendum 1, art. 1d of the Mosagrius Agreement.
34. Interview with officials of the South African High Commission, Maputo, July 1996.
35. Interview of officials of the South African High Commission in Maputo, July 1996.
36. *Ibid.*
37. Eddie Koch, "The Texan who Plans a Dream Park Just Here", Johannesburg, *Mail and Guardian*, 18 January 1996.
38. "O A, B, C do projecto de Blanchard", *Mediafax*, Maputo, 19 February 1996, p. 1.
39. Eddie Koch, *op. cit.*
40. Philip van Niekerk, "Land for Peace, TM Group pursues Mozambique Haven", *The Boston Globe*, 4 December 1994.
41. *Ibid.*

42. Clause 35.2 of the Mosagrius Agreement, *op. cit.*

43. Hanlon, *op cit*, p. 9.

Chapter 9
Wreaking Ethiopia's Peasant Economy, Destroying Biodiversity

Having sowed the seeds of famine in Ethiopia through structural adjustment, the IMF and the World Bank are enabling US multinationals to exploit the disaster by providing genetically modified seed as aid.

The "economic therapy" imposed under IMF-World Bank jurisdiction is, in large part, responsible for triggering famine and social devastation in Ethiopia and the rest of sub-Saharan Africa, wreaking the peasant economy and impoverishing millions of people. With the complicity of branches of the US government, it has also opened the door for the appropriation of traditional seeds and landraces by US biotech corporations, which behind they have been peddling the adoption of their own genetically modified seeds under the disguise of emergency aid and famine relief.

Crisis in the Horn

More than 8 million people in Ethiopia – representing 15% of the country's population – had been locked into "famine zones". Urban wages had collapsed and unemployed seasonal farm workers and landless peasants were driven into abysmal poverty. The international relief agencies concurred, without further examination, that climatic factors are the sole and inevitable cause of crop failure and the ensuing humanitarian disaster. What the media tabloids failed to disclose was that – despite the drought and the border war with Eritrea – several million people in the most prosperous agricultural regions had also been driven into starvation. Their predicament was not the consequence of grain shortages but of "free markets" and "bitter economic medicine" imposed under the IMF-World Bank-sponsored Structural Adjustment Programme (SAP).

Ethiopia produces more than 90% of its consumption needs. Yet at the height of the crisis, the nation-wide food deficit for 2000 was estimated by the Food and Agriculture Organization (FAO) at 764,000 metric tons of grain – representing a shortfall of 13 kilos per person per annum.[1] In Amhara, grain production (1999-2000) was twenty percent in excess of consumption needs. Yet 2.8 million people in Amhara (representing 17% of the region's population) became locked into famine zones and were "at risk" according to the FAO.[2] Whereas Amhara's grain surpluses were in excess of 500,000 tons (1999-2000), its "relief food needs" had been tagged by the international community at close to 300,000 tons.[3] A similar pattern prevailed in Oromiya – the country's most populated state where 1.6 million people were classified "at risk", despite the availability of more than 600,000 metric tons of surplus grain.[4] In both these regions, which include more than 25% of the country's population, scarcity of food was clearly not the cause of hunger, poverty and social destitution. Yet no explanations were given by the panoply of international relief agencies and agricultural research institutes.

The Promise of the "Free Market"

In Ethiopia, a transitional government came into power in 1991 in the wake of a protracted and destructive civil war. After the pro-Soviet Dergue regime of Colonel Mengistu Haile Mariam was unseated, a multi-donor financed Emergency Recovery and Reconstruction Project (ERRP) was hastily put in place to deal with an external debt of close to 9 billion dollars that had accumulated during the Mengistu government. Ethiopia's outstanding debts with the Paris Club of official creditors were rescheduled in exchange for far-reaching macro-economic reforms. Upheld by US foreign policy, the usual doses of bitter IMF economic medicine were prescribed. Caught in the straightjacket of debt and structural adjustment, the new Transitional Government of Ethiopia (TGE), led by the Ethiopian People's Revolutionary Democratic Front (EPRDF) – largely formed from the Tigrean People's Liberation Front (PLF) – had committed itself to far-reaching "free market reforms", despite its leaders' Marxist leanings. Washington soon tagged Ethiopia, alongside Uganda, as Africa's post Cold War free market showpiece.

While social budgets were slashed under the structural adjustment programme (SAP), military expenditure – in part financed by the gush of fresh development loans – quadrupled since 1989.[5] With Washington supporting both sides in the Eritrea-Ethiopia border war, US arms sales spiralled. The bounty was being shared between the arms manufacturers and the agri-business conglomerates. In the post-Cold War era, the latter positioned themselves in the lucrative procurement of emergency aid to war-torn countries. With mounting military spending financed on borrowed money, almost half of Ethiopia's export revenues had been earmarked to meet debt-servicing obligations.

A Policy Framework Paper (PFP) stipulating the precise changes to be carried out in Ethiopia had been carefully drafted in Washington by IMF and World Bank officials on behalf of the transitional government, and was forwarded to Addis Ababa for the signature of the Minister of Finance. The enforcement of severe austerity measures virtually foreclosed the possibility of a meaningful post-war reconstruction and the rebuilding of the country's shattered infrastructure. The creditors demanded trade liberalization and the full-scale privatization of public utilities, financial institutions, state farms and factories. Civil servants, including teachers and health workers, were fired, wages were frozen and the labor laws were rescinded to enable state enterprises "to shed their surplus workers". Meanwhile, corruption became rampant. State assets were auctioned off to foreign capital at bargain prices and Price Waterhouse Cooper was entrusted with the task of coordinating the sale of state property.

In turn, the reforms had led to the fracture of the federal fiscal system. Budget transfers to the state governments were slashed leaving the regions to their own devices. Supported by several donors, "regionalization" was heralded as "a devolution of powers from the federal to the regional governments". The Bretton Woods institutions knew exactly what they were doing. In the words of the IMF, "[the regions] capacity to deliver effective and efficient development interventions varies widely, as does their capacity for revenue collection".[6]

Wrecking the Peasant Economy

Patterned on the reforms adopted in Kenya in 1991 (See Box 9.1), agricultural markets were wilfully manipulated on behalf of the agri-business conglomerates. The World Bank demanded the rapid removal of price controls and all subsidies to farmers. Transportation and freight prices were deregulated serving to boost food prices in remote areas affected by drought. In turn, the markets for farm inputs, including fertilizer and seeds, were handed over to private traders including Pioneer Hi-Bred International which entered into a lucrative partnership with Ethiopia Seed Enterprise (ESE) – the government's seed monopoly.[7]

Box 9.1

Famine in the Breadbasket

A "free market" in grain – imposed by the IMF and the World Bank – destroys the peasant economy and undermines "food security". Malawi and Zimbabwe were once prosperous grain surplus countries; Rwanda was virtually self-sufficient in food until 1990 when the IMF ordered the dumping of EU and US grain surpluses on the domestic market precipitating small farmers into bankruptcy. In 1991-92, famine had hit Kenya – East Africa's most successful bread-basket economy. The Nairobi government had been previously placed on a black list for not having obeyed IMF prescriptions. The deregulation of the grain market had been demanded as one of the conditions for the rescheduling of Nairobi's external debt with the Paris Club of official creditors.

For the lifting of economic sanctions, the government of President Daniel arap Moi required the IMF green light. The international donor community had demanded that the Kenyan State not interfere or otherwise regulate the distribution of food to remote areas. The foreseeable outcome: the price of food staples in Kenya's semi-arid East and Northeast regions bordering Ethiopia and Somalia had skyrocketed. According to the United Nations, close to 2 million people were locked into "famine zones". The crisis, however, was not limited to Kenya's remote semi-arid regions.

Famine had also struck in the Rift Valley – Kenya's thriving agricultural heartland. Throughout the country food was available but purchasing power had collapsed under the brunt of the IMF sponsored reforms. And surplus grain was being exported.

At the outset of the reforms in 1992, USAID under its Title III program "donated" large quantities of US fertilizer "in exchange for free market reforms":

> [V]arious agricultural commodities [will be provided] in exchange for reforms of grain marketing...and [the] elimination of food subsidies...The reform agenda focuses on liberalization and privatization in the fertilizer and transport sectors in return for financing fertilizer and truck imports. (...) These program initiatives have given us [an] "entrée" (...) in defining major [policy] issues.[8]

While the stocks of donated US fertilizer were rapidly exhausted; the imported chemicals contributed to displacing local fertilizer producers. The same companies involved in the fertilizer import business were also in control of the domestic wholesale distribution of fertilizer using local level merchants as intermediaries.

Increased output was recorded in commercial farms and in irrigated areas (where fertilizer and high yielding seeds had been applied). The overall tendency, however, was towards greater economic and social polarization in the countryside, marked by significantly lower yields in less productive marginal lands occupied by the poor peasantry. Even in areas where output had increased, farmers were caught in the clutch of the seed and fertilizer merchants.

In 1997, the Atlanta based Carter Center – which was actively promoting the use of biotechnology tools in maize breeding – proudly announced that "Ethiopia [had] become a food exporter for the first time".[9] Yet in a cruel irony, the donors ordered the dismantling of the emergency grain reserves (set up in the wake of the 1984-85 famine) and the authorities acquiesced.

Instead of replenishing the country's emergency food stocks, grain was exported to meet Ethiopia's debt servicing obligations. Close to one million tons of the 1996 harvest was exported – an amount which would have been amply sufficient (according to FAO figures) to meet the 1999-2000 emergency. In fact, the same food staple which had been exported (namely maize) was re-imported barely a few months later. The world market had confiscated Ethiopia's grain reserves.

In return, US surpluses of genetically engineered maize (banned by the European Union) were being dumped on the horn of Africa in the form of emergency aid. The US had found a convenient mechanism for "laundering its stocks of dirty grain". The agri-business conglomerates not only cornered Ethiopia's commodity exports, they were also involved in the procurement of emergency shipments of grain back into Ethiopia. During the 1998-2000 famine, lucrative maize contracts were awarded to giant grain merchants such as Archer Daniels Midland (ADM) and Cargill Inc.[10]

Laundering America's GM Grain Surpluses

US grain surpluses peddled in war-torn countries also served to weaken the agricultural system. Some 500,000 tons of maize and maize products were "donated" in 1999-2000 by USAID to relief agencies including the World

Food Programme (WFP) which, in turn, collaborates closely with the US Department of Agriculture. At least 30% of these shipments (procured under contract with US agri-business firms) were surplus genetically modified grain stocks.[11]

Boosted by the border war with Eritrea and the plight of thousands of refugees, the influx of contaminated food aid had contributed to the pollution of Ethiopia's genetic pool of indigenous seeds and landraces. In a cruel irony, the food giants were, at the same time, gaining control – through the procurement of contaminated food aid – over Ethiopia's seed banks. According to South Africa's Biowatch: "Africa is treated as the dustbin of the world…To donate untested food and seed to Africa is not an act of kindness but an attempt to lure Africa into further dependence on foreign aid."[12]

Moreover, part of the "food aid" had been channelled under the "food for work" program which served to further discourage domestic production in favor of grain imports. Under this scheme, impoverished and landless farmers were contracted to work on rural infrastructural programmes in exchange for "donated" US corn.

Meanwhile, the cash earnings of coffee smallholders plummeted. Whereas Pioneer Hi-Bred positioned itself in seed distribution and marketing, Cargill Inc. established itself in the markets for grain and coffee through its subsidiary Ethiopian Commodities.[12] For the more than 700,000 smallholders with less than two hectares that produce between 90 and 95% of the country's coffee output, the deregulation of agricultural credit, combined with low farmgate prices of coffee, had triggered increased indebtedness and landlessness, particularly in East Gojam (Ethiopia's breadbasket).

Biodiversity up for Sale

The country's extensive reserves of traditional seed varieties (barley, teff, chick peas, sorghum, etc.) were being appropriated, genetically manipulated and patented by the agri-business conglomerates: "Instead of compensation and respect, Ethiopians today are (…) getting bills from foreign companies that have "patented" native species and now demand payment for their use."[13] The foundations of a "competitive seed industry" were laid under IMF and World Bank auspices.[14] The Ethiopian Seed Enterprise (ESE), the government's seed monopoly, joined hands with Pioneer Hi-Bred in the distribution of hi-bred and genetically modified (GM) seeds (together with hybrid resistant herbicide) to smallholders. In turn, the marketing of seeds had been transferred to a network of private contractors and "seed enterprises" with financial support and technical assistance from the World Bank. The "informal" farmer-to-farmer seed exchange was slated to be converted under the World Bank programme into a "formal" market-oriented system of "private seed producer-sellers."[15]

In turn, the Ethiopian Agricultural Research Institute (EARI) was collaborating with the International Maize and Wheat Improvement Center (CIMMYT) in the development of new hybrids between Mexican and Ethiopian maize varieties.[16] Initially established in the 1940s by Pioneer Hi-Bred International with support from the Ford and Rockefeller foundations, CIMMYT developed a cozy relationship with US agri-business. Together with the UK based Norman Borlaug Institute, CIMMYT constitutes a research arm as well as a mouthpiece of the seed conglomerates. According to the Rural Advancement Foundation (RAFI) "US farmers already earn $ 150 million annually by growing varieties of barley developed from Ethiopian strains. Yet nobody in Ethiopia is sending them a bill."[17]

Impacts of Famine

The 1984-85 famine had seriously threatened Ethiopia's reserves of landraces of traditional seeds. In response to the famine, the Dergue government, through its Plant Genetic Resource Centre – in collaboration with Seeds of Survival (SoS) – had implemented a programme to preserve Ethiopia's biodiversity.[18] This programme – which was continued under the transitional government – skilfully "linked on-farm conservation and crop improvement by rural communities with government support services".[19] An extensive network of in-farm sites and conservation plots was established involving some 30,000 farmers. In 1998, coinciding chronologically with the onslaught of the 1998-2000 famine, the government clamped down on Seeds of Survival (SoS) and ordered the programme to be closed down.[20]

The hidden agenda was eventually to displace the traditional varieties and landraces reproduced in village-level nurseries. The latter were supplying more than 90 percent of the peasantry through a system of farmer-to-farmer exchange. Without fail, the 1998-2000 famine led to a further depletion of local level seed banks: "The reserves of grains [the farmer] normally stores to see him through difficult times are empty. Like 30,000 other households in the [Galga] area, his family has also eaten their stocks of seeds for the next harvest."[21] And a similar process was unfolding in the production of coffee where the genetic base of the arabica beans was threatened as a result of the collapse of farmgate prices and the impoverishment of small-holders.

The famine – itself in large part a product of the economic reforms imposed to the advantage of large corporations by the IMF, World Bank and the US Government – served to undermine Ethiopia's genetic diversity to the benefit of the biotech companies. With the weakening of the system of traditional exchange, village level seed banks were being replenished with commercial hi-bred and genetically modified seeds. In turn, the distribution of seeds to impoverished farmers had been integrated with the "food aid" programmes. WPF and USAID relief packages often include "donations" of seeds and fertilizer, thereby favoring the inroad of the agribusiness-biotech companies into Ethiopia's agricultural heartland. The emergency programs are not the "solution" but the "cause" of famine. By deliberately creating a dependency on GM seeds, they had set the stage for the outbreak of future famines.

This destructive pattern – invariably resulting in famine – is replicated throughout sub-Saharan Africa. From the onslaught of the debt crisis of the early 1980s, the IMF-World Bank had set the stage for the demise of the peasant economy across the region with devastating results. Now in Ethiopia, fifteen years after the last famine left nearly one million dead, hunger is once again stalking the land. This time, as eight million people face the risk of starvation, we know that it isn't just the weather that is to blame.

Endnotes

1   Food and Agriculture Organization (FAO), *Special Report: FAO/WFP Crop Assessment Mission to Ethiopia*, Rome, January 2000.

2.   *Ibid.*

3.   *Ibid.*

4.   *Ibid.*

5.   Philip Sherwell and Paul Harris, "Guns before Grain as Ethiopia Starves, *Sunday Telegraph*, London, April 16, 2000.

6.   IMF, Ethiopia, Recent Economic Developments, Washington, 1999.

7.   Pioneer Hi-Bred International, General GMO *Facts*, http://www.pioneer.com/usa/biotech/value_of_products/product_value.htm#.

8.   United   States   Agency   for   International   Development   (USAID),

"*Mission to Ethiopia, Concept Paper: Back to The Future*", Washington, June 1993.

9. Carter Center, *Press Release*, Atlanta, Georgia, January 31, 1997.

10. Declan Walsh, "America Finds Ready Market for GM Food", *The Independent*, London, March 30, 2000, p. 18.

11. *Ibid.*

12. Maja Wallegreen, "The World's Oldest Coffee Industry In Transition", *Tea & Coffee Trade Journal*, November 1, 1999.

13. Laeke Mariam Demissie, "A vast historical contribution counts for little; West reaps Ethiopia's genetic harvest", *World Times*, October, 1998.

14. World Bank, *Ethiopia-Seed Systems Development Project*, Project ID ETPA752, 6 June 1995.

15. *Ibid.*

16. See CIMMYT Research Plan and Budget 2000-2002 http://www.cimmyt.mx/about/People-mtp2002.htm#.

17. Laeke Mariam Demissie, *op. cit.*

18. "When local farmers know best", *The Economist*, 16 May 1998.

19. *Ibid.*

20. Laeke Mariam Demissie, *op. cit.*

21. Rageh Omaar, "Hunger stalks Ethiopia's dry land", BBC, London, 6 January, 2000.

PART III

SOUTH AND SOUTHEAST ASIA

Chapter 10

India: The IMF's "Indirect Rule"

Indirect rule in India has a long history: the Rajputs and princely states had a fair degree of autonomy in relation to the British colonial government. In contrast, under the IMF-World Bank tutelage, the Union Minister of Finance reports directly to 1818 H Street N.W., Washington D.C. bypassing parliament and the democratic process. The Union budget text, formally written by Indian bureaucrats in Delhi, has become a repetitious and redundant document. Its main clauses are included in the loan agreements signed with the World Bank and the IMF.

Introduction

The IMF bail-out to the minority Congress government of Prime Minister P. V. Narasimha Rao in 1991 did not, at first glance, point towards a major economic breakdown and disintegration of civil society comparable to that which had occurred in many debt-stricken countries in Latin America and Eastern Europe undergoing IMF "shock treatment". While India did not experience hyperinflation nor the collapse of its foreign exchange market, the social impact in a country of 900 million people was devastating: in India, the IMF program initiated in July 1991 directly affected the livelihood of several hundred million people. There was evidence of widespread chronic starvation and social destitution which resulted directly from the macro-economic measures.

In India, the IMF-World Bank program was set in motion with the fall of the Janata Dal government of V.P. Singh in 1990, and the assassination of Rajiv Gandhi during the election campaign in Tamil Nadu in 1991. The government was obliged to airlift some 47 tons of gold to the vaults of the Bank of England for "safe custody" to satisfy the requirements of international creditors.[1] The IMF agreement, implemented shortly thereafter, was to provide, at best, a short breathing-space: with a debt of more than US$

80 billion, the IMF and World Bank loans (already earmarked to pay back international creditors) barely provided the cash required to fund six months of debt servicing.

The IMF's "economic surgery", under the 1991 New Economic Policy, required the Indian government to cut spending in social programs and infrastructure, eliminate state subsidies and price support programs (including food subsidies) and sell off the more profitable public enterprises at "a good price" to the large business houses and foreign capital. Other reform measures included the closing down of a large number of so-called "sick public enterprises", the liberalization of trade, the free entry of foreign capital, as well as major reforms in banking, financial institutions and the tax structure.

The IMF loan agreement, together with the World Bank structural adjustment loan (SAL) signed in December 1991 (of which the contents and conditions were a closely guarded state secret), were intended to "help India" alleviate its balance-of-payments difficulties, reduce the fiscal deficit and relieve inflationary pressures. The IMF-World Bank package, however, accomplished exactly the opposite results: it pushed the economy into a stagflation (the price of rice increased by more than 50 percent in the months following the 1991 economic measures) and heightened the balance-of-payments crisis (as a result of the increased cost of imported raw materials and the influx of imports in support of luxury consumption). Moreover, trade liberalization, combined with the compression of internal purchasing power and the free entry of foreign capital, pushed a large number of domestic producers into bankruptcy.

A National Renewal Fund (NRF) was created in July 1991. This "social safety net", devised by World Bank advisors and targeted towards so-called "vulnerable groups", did not provide adequate compensation to an estimated 4 to 8 million public- and private-sector workers (out of a total organized labor force of 26 million) who were to be laid off as a result of the program. The NRF was intended to buy out trade-union opposition. In the textile industry, approximately one third of the workers were to be laid off. A large share of the automobile and engineering industry was to be phased out with the entry of foreign capital and the establishment of joint ventures. The G-7 countries were anxious to "export their recession"; Western and Japanese transnationals were eager to capture a part of India's domestic market as well as obtain – with the help of the GATT rules on intellectual property rights – the abrogation of India's 1970 Patent Law. This would enable them to register product patents in manufacturing as well as in agriculture (through plant breeders' rights), thereby virtually gaining control over a large portion of the Indian economy.

It should be noted that the "exit policies" as such did not address in a meaningful way the serious problems of bureaucracy and mismanagement of public-sector enterprises, as well as the necessity to modernize Indian industry. While the IMF program denied India the possibility of an autonomous national capitalist development (its hidden agenda), the reforms, nonetheless, received the firm backing of India's largest business houses (in a fragile alliance with the upper-caste landlord lobby). The Tatas and the Birlas identify increasingly with foreign capital and the global market economy rather than with the "national interest". The tendency is towards increased concentration of ownership. Preferential credit to small and medium-sized enterprises is eliminated and the big business families, in partnership with foreign capital, are rapidly entering into a variety of areas previously preserved for small-scale industry (i.e. small-scale industrial units).

The so-called "exit policy" proposed by the government and the IMF was viewed by the large industrial corporations as "an opportunity to change the labor laws and to get rid of our workers. For us it is more profitable to sub-contract with small factories which employ casual and unorganized labor".[2] Bata, the multinational shoe manufacturer, pays its unionized factory workers 80 rupees a day (US$ 3). With the reforms of the labor laws, it would be able to lay off its workers and subcontract with independent cobblers at no more than 25 rupees a day (approximately $ 1). In the jute industry, in small engineering and in the garment industry the large corporate monopolies tend to subcontract thereby reducing their modern-sector labor force.

Crushing the Rural and Urban Poor

Instead of extending the labor laws to protect casual and seasonal workers, the IMF program proposed "to help the poor" by scrapping the labor laws altogether because "these laws favor the labor aristocracy" and "discriminate against" the non-unionized sectors of the labor force. Neither the government nor the IMF had addressed the broader social impact of the New Economic Policy on farm-workers, artisans and small enterprises.

In India, more than 70 percent of rural households are small marginal farmers or landless farm workers, representing a population of over 400 million people. In irrigated areas, agricultural workers are employed for

200 days a year, and in rain-fed farming for approximately 100 days. The phasing-out of fertilizer subsidies (an explicit condition of the IMF agreement) and the increase in the prices of farm inputs and fuel were pushing a large number of small and medium-sized farmers into bankruptcy. The price of chemical fertilizer shot up by 40 percent in the immediate aftermath of the 1991 New Economic Policy.

In turn, millions of landless farm workers belonging to the scheduled and backward castes – already well below the official poverty line – were being crushed by Finance Minister Manmohan Singh's New Economic Policy. These are "the untouchables of economic policy". For the upper-caste élites, the Harijans are people who really do not matter. The impact of the IMF's "economic medicine" on these sectors of the labor force was carefully overlooked. For the IMF and the government, there were no "exit policies" for the unorganized sectors. In the words of the Finance Minister Manmohan Singh: "the cottage industries have no problems because the wages will go down".[3]

In Tamil Nadu, for instance, the minimum wage for farmworkers set by the state government was 15 rupees a day (US$ 0.57) in 1992. Labor legislation, however, was not enforced and actual wages paid to farm workers were (with the exception of the harvest period), substantially lower than the minimum daily wage: for paddy transplanting, for instance, workers were paid between 3 and 5 rupees a day; in heavy construction work, men received 10 to 15 rupees a day and women 8 to 10 rupees.[4] With perhaps the exception of the states of Kerala and West Bengal, minimum wage legislation has largely been ineffective in protecting the rights of farm workers.

On the Hyderabad-Bangalore national highway, one can observe the child laborers of the Dhone limestone mines transport heavy loads in bamboo baskets up a flight of some 60 steps where the limestone is emptied into tall brick kilns. Both adult workers and children are paid 9.50 rupees a day; there have been no wage increases since the July 1991 Union Budget: "we have to work here regardless of poisonous fumes, heat and dust. The wages are higher than on the farms. . ."[5]

"Eliminating the Poor" through Starvation Deaths

In the post-independence period, starvation deaths were limited largely to peripheral tribal areas (e.g. in Tripura or Nagaland). This is no longer the case, there is evidence that famine has become widespread since the adoption of the New Economic Policy in 1991. A study on starvation deaths among handloom weavers in a relatively prosperous rural community in Andhra Pradesh, which occurred in the months following the implementation of the 1991 New Economic Policy, enables us to pinpoint the transmission mechanism underlying the IMF-sponsored program: with the devaluation and the lifting of controls on cotton-yarn exports, the jump in the domestic price of cotton yarn led to a collapse in the pacham (24 meters) rate paid to the weaver by the middle-man (through the putting-out system).

> Radhakrishnamurthy and his wife were able to weave between three and four pachams a month bringing home the meager income of 300-400 rupees for a family of six, then came the Union Budget of 24 July 1991, the price of cotton yarn jumped and the burden was passed on to the weaver. Radhakrishnamurthy's family income declined to 240-320 rupees a month.[6]

Radhakrishnamurthy of Gollapalli village in Guntur district died of starvation on 4 September, 1991. Between 30 August and 10 November 1991, at least 73 starvation deaths were reported in only two districts of Andhra Pradesh. The IMF-World Bank program, rather than "eliminating poverty" as claimed by the then World Bank president Lewis Preston, actually contributed to "eliminating the poor". Combined with a 50 percent rise in the price of rice (which resulted from the devaluation and the removal of food and fertilizer subsidies), the real earnings of handloom workers declined by more than 60 percent in the six-month period after the adoption of the IMF program in 1991.[7] There are 3.5 million handlooms throughout India supporting a population of some 17 million people.

A similar situation prevails in most small-scale rural and urban cottage industries which operate through the putting-out system. For instance, there are in India more than a million diamond cutters supporting a population of nearly five million people. The large diamond export houses based in Bombay import rough diamonds from South Africa, and subcontract the work through middle-men to rural workshops in Maharashtra. Seven out of 10 diamonds sold in Western Europe and the US are cut in India. Whereas in the rich countries, diamonds are said to be "a girl's best friend", in India poverty is the necessary input into this profitable export activity: in the words of a major diamond exporter:

> Making jewelry is cheap labor (. . .)[Food prices have gone up] but we have not increased the rupee payments to village workers. With the devaluation, our dollar labor costs go down, we are more competitive. We pass on some of the benefits to our overseas customers.[8]

The IMF Supports Caste Exploitation

The IMF-World Bank program recommended the repeal of minimum wage legislation as well as the deindexation of earnings. The proposed "liberalization" of the labor market contributed to reinforcing despotic social relations thereby providing, in practice, a greater legitimacy to caste exploitation, semi-slavery and child labor. Under World Bank guidelines, the tendency was towards dispossession (through the formal removal of land ceilings), as well as the expropriation of communal village lands by feudal landlords and kulaks. The liberalization of banking (e.g. by doing away with the rural credit cooperatives) contributed to strengthening the village money-lender.[9]

The IMF program converted itself into an instrument of "economic genocide": several hundred million people (farm-workers, artisans, small traders, etc.) were surviving on per capita incomes substantially lower than 50 cents a day (with domestic prices, in the logic of the IMF measures, moving up to world levels).[10] An increase in the price of rice and wheat of more than 50 percent (in the year following the July 1991 New Economic Policy), combined with a decline in the average number of days worked in both rain-fed and irrigated agriculture, was pushing large sectors of the rural population into "chronic starvation" – a process without precedent on this scale since the great famines in Bengal in the early 1940s.[11] In contrast, the drop in internal consumption of food had been matched by an increase in rice exports. In the words of Tata Exports:

> The devaluation was very good for us. Together with the lifting of quantitative restrictions on rice exports, we expect to increase our sales of rice to the world market by 60 percent.[12]

Poverty Supports Exports to the Rich Countries

The IMF-World Bank reforms feed on the poverty of the people and on the contraction of the internal market. While India's population is substantially larger than that of all OECD countries combined (approximately 750 million), the economic reforms entail a major redirection of the Indian economy towards exports. In the logic of the structural adjustment program, the only viable market is that of the rich countries. The IMF program compresses internal consumption and reorients India's productive system towards the international market. Poverty is an input on the supply side: labor costs in dollars are low, internal purchasing power is low. For instance, following the 1991 IMF-sponsored measures, the sale of cloth in India fell to 8 meters per capita per annum (16 meters in 1965, 10 meters in 1985) – barely sufficient for a saree and a blouse.

Towards Political Collapse

With active secessionist movements in Kashmir, Punjab and Assam, disturbances in Amritsar and an uncertain truce along the "Line of Control" with Pakistan, the Imo's economic medicine has contributed to polarizing further Indian society, as well as potentially creating the pre-conditions for the political break-up of the Indian union. The austerity measures imposed by the IMF have exacerbated tensions between the union and the state governments. More generally, the economic program has contributed to embittering religious and ethnic strife.

In the aftermath of the reforms, the Congress Party remained deeply divided on economic policy with several cabinet ministers coming out openly against the IMF package. Moreover, the rise in food prices has weakened Congress' grass-root support, while its *rapprochement* with Israel since the Gulf War (in part as a result of US pressures) has tarnished its image as a secular party, leading to a strengthening of the Muslim League.

Both Hindu, as well as Islamic fundamentalism, feed on the poverty of the masses. The major opposition party, the Hindu Bharatiya Janata Party (BJP) had rhetorically condemned the government's "open-door" policy. Invoking Mahatma Gandhi's swadeshi (self-reliance), the Rashtriya Swayam Sevak Sangh (RSS) – the BJP's parent fundamentalist movement – called for a massive boycott of foreign goods. In turn, the National Front (NF) and the Leftist Front (LF), led by the Communist Party of India (Marxist), feared that if the minority Congress government were to fall, the BJP would take over. In 1996, with the defeat of Congress in parliamentary elections, the BJP formed a government which has largely continued the IMF reforms initiated under the Congress government in the early 1990s.

The IMF's Indirect Rule

The Washington-based international bureaucracy has installed in India "a parallel government" which builds upon these internal social, religious and ethnic divisions ("divide and rule"). Since the Emergency Period in the mid-1970s, and more forcefully since Indira Gandhi's return to power in 1980, former IMF and World Bank employees have moved into key advisory positions in central government ministries. Not surprisingly, the IMF feels that:

> It has on the whole been easy to negotiate with Indian officials. . .compared to other Third World countries, where you see a lot of grim faces at the bargaining table. Economic thinking has largely been in the same direction, their attitude has been most conciliatory.[13]

A quarterly monitoring system was set up under the close guard of the IMF. Under this computerized system, located in the Ministry of Finance, IMF and World Bank officials have access to key macro-economic data no later than six weeks after the end of the quarter. In the words of the IMF liaison officer in Delhi: "We take the monitoring very seriously, we scrutinize all the information we get (. . .) we are very careful that they [the government] do not cheat". Some 40 key economic variables are subject to quarterly verification by the IMF:

> We have also included in the agreement ten "structural benchmarks", these are not explicit conditions of the loan agreement, they pertain to broad areas of structural reform which we would like the government to address [in future loan negotiations].[14]

Despite precise targets for the fiscal deficit (contained in the loan agreements), the IMF's main objective was, however, to enforce the process of fiscal collapse and establish a system whereby the government is in a strait-jacket and no longer controls the main instruments of fiscal and monetary policy. These conditions forestalled, virtually from the outset, the possibility of economic growth. The IMF did not, however, quibble over numbers. In fact, the "structural benchmarks" rather than the quantitative targets are what really matters. Conformity to things which are understood by both sides but which are not necessarily stated as explicit conditions in the loan agreement is what counts: "the government must give us 'signals' that they are moving in the right direction. . ."[15]

Within the framework of the government's "relationship" to the Washington-based institutions, key government policy documents were drafted directly by the IMF and the World Bank on behalf of the Union Ministry of Finance. In this regard, the Indian press was careful to point out (with a touch of humor) that the Memorandum on Economic Policies of 27 August, 1991 (a key document in the government's initial agreement with the IMF), together with the covering letter addressed to the IMF

Managing Director Mr. Michel Camdessus, was drafted in "American script" (most probably by Washington-based officials) against the habitual British construction, style and spelling used by Indian bureaucrats:[16] "Yes sir, there are awful mistakes of grammar, spelling and syntax. But I did not type it, sir. It came from the World Bank for your signature".[17] A few days prior to the 29 February, 1992 Union Budget speech in the Lok Sabha, it became apparent that the main budget proposals had not only been "leaked" by the minister of finance in a letter to World Bank president Lewis Preston, but more importantly that the budget was already an integral part of the conditionalities contained in the structural adjustment loan agreement signed with the World Bank in December 1991.[18]

Endnotes

1. See M. K. Pandhe, *Surrender of India's Sovereignty and Self-Reliance*, Progressive Printers, New Delhi, 1991, p. 2.
2. Interview in Bombay with a major industrialist, January 1992.
3. Interview with Finance Minister Manmohan Singh, New Delhi, January 1992.
4. Interviews with leaders of farm-workers' organizations in Tamil Nadu, February 1992.
5. See "Around a Kiln, the Child Laborers of Dhone", *Frontline*, 13 March 1992, p. 52.
6. See the excellent study of K. Nagaraj *et al.*, "Starvation Deaths in Andhra Pradesh", Frontline, 6 December, 1991, p. 48.
7. *Ibid.*
8. Interview with a major diamond export house in Bombay, January 1992.
9. The Narasimhan Commission Report, *India: Financial Sector Report*, is a near "photocopy" of World Bank proposals; see S. Sanhar's scrutiny of the Narasimhan Report in Indian Express, 8 December, 1991.
10. For a majority of the rural and urban population, household income (with five to six family members) is less than R1,000 a month, – i.e. a per capita income of less than R7 a day (less than US30 cents).
11. According to the National Nutrition Monitoring Bureau (NNMB), the diet and nutrition surveys conducted between 1977 and 1989 would indicate some improvement in "severe" malnutrition among children. While abject poverty according to these figures had declined in India, the levels of average poverty have remained very high. See "Starvation Deaths and Chronic Deprivation", Frontline, 6 December, 1991, p. 81.

Chronic starvation is defined as "a situation in which the subjects subsist on diets which are very deficient in energy for a long period of time", *Frontline*, 6 December 1991, p. 79.

12. Interview with Tata Exports in Bombay, January 1992.

13. Interview with the IMF liaison officer in Delhi, January 1992.

14. *Ibid.*

15. *Ibid.*

16. See Praful Bidwani, *Times of India*, 18 December, 1991.

17. See Laxman (the famous cartoonist) in Times of India, reproduced in *Structural Adjustment, Who Really Pays*, Public Interest Research Group, New Delhi, March 1992, p. 44.

18. *Economic Times*, 28 February 1992, p. 1.

Chapter 11

Bangladesh: Under the Tutelage of the "Aid" Consortium

The 1975 Military Coup

The military coup of August 1975 led to the assassination of President Mujibur Rahman and the installation of a military junta. The authors of the coup had been assisted by key individuals within the Bangladesh National Security Intelligence and the CIA office at the American Embassy in Dhaka.[1] In the months which preceded the assassination plot, the US State Department had already established a framework for "stable political transition" to be carried out in the aftermath of the military take-over.

Washington's initiative had been firmly endorsed by the Bretton Woods institutions: less than a year before the assassination of Sheik Mujib, Dhaka's international creditors had demanded the formation of an "aid consortium" under the custody of the World Bank. Whereas the "structural adjustment" program had not yet been launched officially, the Bangladesh economic package of the mid-1970s contained most of its essential ingredients. In many respects, Bangladesh was "a laboratory test-case" – a country in which the IMF "economic medicine" could be experimented with on a trial basis (prior to the debt crisis of the early 1980s). An economic stabilization program had been established: devaluation and price liberalization contributed to exacerbating a situation of famine which had broken out in several regions of the country.

In the aftermath of Sheik Mujib's overthrow and assassination, continued US military aid to Bangladesh was conditional upon the country's abiding by the Imo's policy prescriptions. The US State Department justified its aid program to the new military regime on the grounds that the government's foreign policy was "pragmatic and nonaligned". The United States was to support this non-alignment and help Bangladesh in its economic development.[2]

The Establishment of a Parallel Government

Bangladesh has been under continuous supervision by the international donor community since the accession of General Ziaur Rahman to the presidency in 1975 (in turn assassinated in 1981), as well as during the reign of General Hussein Mahommed Ershad (1982-90).[3] The state apparatus was firmly under the control of the IFIs and "aid agencies" in collusion with the dominant clique of the military. Since its inauguration, the "aid consortium" has met annually in Paris. The Dhaka government is usually invited to send observers to this meeting.

The IMF had established a liaison office on the fourth floor of the Central Bank; World Bank advisors were present in most of the ministries. The Asian Development Bank, controlled by Japan, also played an important role in the shaping of macro-economic policy. A monthly working meeting, held under the auspices of the World Bank Dhaka office, enabled the various donors and agencies to "coordinate" efficiently (outside the ministries) the key elements of government economic policy.

In 1990, mounting opposition to the military dictatorship, as well as the resignation of General Hussein Mahommed Ershad, accused of graft and corruption, was conducive to the formation of a provisional government and the holding of parliamentary elections. The transition towards "parliamentary democracy" under the government of Mrs. Khaleda Zia, the widow of President General Ziaur Rahman, was not conducive, however, to a major shift in the structure of state institutions. Continuity has in many respects been maintained: many of General Ershad's former cronies were appointed to key positions in the new "civilian" government.

Establishing a Bogus Democracy

The IMF-sponsored economic reforms contributed to reinforcing a "rentier economy" controlled by the national élites and largely dependent on foreign trade and the recycling of aid money. With the restoration of "parliamentary democracy", powerful individuals within the military had strengthened their business interests.[4] The government party, the Bangladesh National Party (BNP), was under the protection of the dominant clique of the military.

With the restoration of formal democracy in 1991, the daughter of assassinated president Mujib Rahman Sheik Hasina Wajed of the Awami League Party became the leader of the opposition. With public opinion focussing on the rivalry in parliament between the "widow" and the "orphan", the dealings of local power groups, including members of the military, with the "aid agencies" and donors passed virtually unnoticed. The donor community had become, in the name of "good governance", the defender of a bogus democratic facade controlled by the armed forces and allied closely to the fundamentalist movement Jamaat-i-islami. In some respects, Begum Zia had become a more compliant "political puppet" than the deposed military dictator General Ershad.

Supervising the Allocation of State Funds

The "aid consortium" had taken control of Bangladesh's public finances. This process, however, did not consist solely in imposing fiscal and monetary austerity: the donors supervised directly the allocation of funds and the setting of development priorities. According to a World Bank advisor:

> We do not want to establish an agreement for each investment project, what we want is to impose discipline. Do we like the list of projects ? Which projects should be retained ? Are there "dogs" in the list ? [5]

Moreover, under the clauses of the Public Resources Management Credit (1992), the World Bank gained control over the entire budgetary process including the distribution of public expenditure between line ministries and the structure of operational expenditures in each of the ministries:

> Of course we cannot write the budget for them ! The negotiations in this regard are complex. We nonetheless make sure they're moving in the right direction (. . .). Our people work with the guys in the ministries and show them how to prepare budgets. [6]

The aid consortium also controlled the reforms of the banking system implemented under the government of Mrs Khaleda Zia. Lay-offs were ordered, parastatal enterprises were closed down. Fiscal austerity prevented the government from mobilizing internal resources. Moreover, for most public investment projects the "aid consortium" required a system of international tender. Large international construction and engineering companies took over the process of domestic capital formation to the detriment of local-level enterprises.

Undermining the Rural Economy

The IMF also imposed the elimination of subsidies to agriculture – a process, which contributed, as of the early 1980s, to the bankruptcy of small and medium-sized farmers. The result was a marked increase in the number of landless farmers who were driven into marginal lands affected by recurrent flooding. Moreover, the liberalization of agricultural credit not only contributed to the fragmentation of land-holdings (already under considerable stress as a result of demographic pressures), but also to the reinforcement of traditional usury and the role of the village money lender.

As a result of the absence of credit to small farmers, the owners of irrigation equipment reinforced their position as a new "water-lord" rentier class. These developments did not lead, however, to the "modernization" of agriculture (e.g. as in the Punjab) based on the formation of a class of rich farmer-entrepreneurs. The structural adjustment program thwarted the development of capitalist farming from the outset. In addition to the neglect of agricultural infrastructure, the Bretton Woods institutions required the liberalization of trade and the deregulation of grain markets. These policies contributed to the stagnation of food agriculture for the domestic market.

A blatant example of restructuring imposed by the IMF pertains to the jute industry. In spite of the collapse of world prices, jute was one of Bangladesh's main earners of foreign exchange in competition with synthetic substitutes produced by the large textile multinationals. Unfair competition ?(. . .) The IMF required, as a condition attached to its soft loan under the enhanced structural adjustment facility (ESAF), the closing down of one third of the jute industry (including public and private enterprises) and the firing of some 35,000 workers.[7] Whereas the latter were to receive severance payments, the IMF had neglected to take into account the impact of the restructuring program on some three million rural households (18 million people) which depended on jute cultivation for their survival.

Dumping US Grain Surpluses

The deregulation of the grain market was also used to support (under the disguise of "US Food Aid") the dumping of American grain surpluses. The "Food for Work" programs under the auspices of USAID were used to "finance" village-level public works projects through payments of grain (instead of money wages) to impoverished peasants thereby destabilizing local-level grain markets.

It is worth noting that US grain sales on the local market served two related purposes. First, heavily subsidized US grain was allowed to compete directly with locally produced food staples thereby undermining the development of local producers. Second, US grain sales on the local market were used to generate "counterpart funds". The latter were, in turn, channeled into development projects controlled by USAID – i.e. which by their very nature maintained Bangladesh's dependency on imported grain. For instance, counterpart funds generated from grain sales (under PL 480) were used in the early 1990s to finance the Bangladesh Agricultural Research Institute. Under this project, USAID determined the areas of priority research to be funded.

Undermining Food Self-Sufficiency

There is evidence that food self-sufficiency in Bangladesh could indeed have been achieved through the extension of arable lands under irrigation, as well as through a comprehensive agrarian reform.[8] Moreover, a recent study suggested that the risks of flooding could be reduced significantly through the development of appropriate infrastructure.

The structural adjustment program constituted, however, the main obstacle to achieving these objectives. First, it obstructed the development of an independent agricultural policy; second, it deliberately placed a lid (through the Public Investment Program [PIP] under World Bank supervision) on state investment in agriculture. This "programmed" stagnation of food agriculture also served the interests of US grain producers. Fiscal austerity imposed by the "aid consortium" prevented the mobilization of domestic resources in support of the rural economy.

The Fate of Local Industry

The war of independence had resulted in the demise of the industrial sector developed since 1947 and the massive exodus of entrepreneurs and professionals.[9] Moreover, the economic impact of the war was all the more devastating because no "breathing space" was provided to Bangladesh by the "aid consortium" to reconstruct its war-torn economy and develop its human resources.

The structural adjustment program, adopted in several stages since 1974, provided a final lethal blow to the country's industrial sector. The macro-economic framework imposed by the Bretton Woods institutions contributed to undermining the existing industrial structure while, at the same time, preventing the development of new areas of industrial activity geared towards the internal market.

Moreover, with a fragmented agricultural system and the virtual absence of rural manufacturing, non-agricultural employment opportunities in Bangladesh's countryside were more or less non-existent. Urban-based industry was limited largely to the export garment sector which relied heavily on cheap labor from rural areas. According to the IMF resident representative in Dhaka, the only viable industries are those using abundant supplies of cheap labor for the export sector:

> What do you want to protect in this country ? There is nothing to protect. They want permanent protection but they mainly have a comparative advantage in the labor-intensive industries.[10]

From the IMF's perspective, the garment industry was to constitute the main source of urban employment. There are some 300,000 garment workers most of whom are young girls. Sixteen percent of this labor force is children between the ages of 10 and 14. Most of the workers come from impoverished rural areas.[11] Production in the factories is marked by compulsory overtime and despotic management: wages including overtime (1992) are of the order of US$ 20 a month. In 1992, a public gathering of garment workers was brutally repressed by the security forces. According to the government, the demands of the workers constituted a threat to the balance of payments.

The Recycling of Aid Money

Whereas many aid and non-governmental organizations are involved in meaningful projects at the grass-roots level, several of the "poverty alleviation schemes", rather than helping the poor, constitute an important source of income for urban professionals and bureaucrats. Through the various local executing agencies based in Dhaka, the local élites had become development brokers and intermediaries acting on behalf of the international donor community. The funds earmarked for the rural poor often contributed to the enrichment of military officers and bureaucrats. This "aid money" was then recycled into commercial and real-estate investments including office buildings, luxury condominiums, etc.

"The Social Dimensions of Adjustment"

With a population of over 130 million inhabitants, Bangladesh is among the world's poorest countries. Per capita income is of the order of US$ 170 per annum (1992). Annualexpenditures on health in 1992 were of the order of $ 1.50 per capita (of which less than 25 cents per capita was spent on essential pharmaceuticals).[12] With the exception of family planning, social expenditures were considered to be excessive: in 1992-93, the Bangladesh "aid consortium" required the government to implement a further round of "cost-effective" cuts in social-sector budgets.

Undernourishment was also characterized by a high prevalence of Vitamin-A deficiency (resulting from a diet made up almost exclusively of cereals). Many children and adults particularly in rural areas had become blind as a result of Vitamin-A deficiency.

A situation of chronic starvation prevailed in several regions of the country. The Bangladesh "aid consortium" meeting in Paris in 1992 urged the government of Mrs. Khaleda Zia to speed up the implementation of the reforms as a means of "combating poverty". The government of Bangladesh was advised (in conformity with World Bank president Lewis Preston's new guidelines) that donor support would only be granted to countries "which make a serious effort in the area of poverty reduction".

In 1991, 140,000 people died as a result of the flood which swept the country (most of whom were landless peasants driven into areas affected by recurrent flooding). Ten million people (almost ten percent of the population) were left homeless.[13] Not accounted, however, in these "official" statistics were those who died of famine in the aftermath of the disaster. While the various relief agencies and donors underscored the detrimental role of climatic factors, the 1991 famine was aggravated as a result of the IMF-supported macro-economic policy. First, the ceilings on public investment in agriculture and flood prevention imposed by the donor since the 1970s had been conducive to the stagnation of agriculture. Second, the devaluation implemented shortly after the 1991 flood, spurred on a 50 percent increase in the retail price of rice in the year which followed the disaster. And this famine was all the more serious because a large share of the emergency relief provided by the donors had been appropriated by the privileged urban élites.

Endnotes

1. According to the study of Lawrence Lifschutz, *Bangladesh, the Unfinished Revolution*, Zed Books, London, 1979, part 2.

2. According to a report of the US State Department published in 1978, quoted in Lawrence Lifschultz, *op. cit.*, p. 109.

3. General Ziaur Rahman becomes head of state as Commander in Chief of the Armed Forces in 1975 during the period of martial law. He was subsequently elected president in 1978.

4. Interview with the leader of an opposition party in Dhaka, February 1992.

5. Interview with a World Bank advisor in Dhaka, 1992.

6. *Ibid.*

7. Many of the smaller jute enterprises were pushed into bankruptcy as a result of the liberalization of credit.

8. See Mosharaf Hussein, A. T. M. Aminul Islam and Sanat Kumar Saha, *Floods in Bangladesh, Recurrent Disaster and People's Survival*, Universities' Research Centre, Dhaka, 1987.

9. See Rehman Sobhan, *The Development of the Private Sector in Bangladesh: a Review of the Evolution and Outcome of State Policy*, Research Report No: 124, Bangladesh Institute of Development Studies, pp. 4-5.

10. Interview with the resident representative of the IMF, Dhaka, 1992.

11. Seventy percent of the garment workers are female, 74 percent are from rural areas, child labor represents respectively 16 and 8 percent of the female and male workers. See Salma Choudhuri and Pratima Paul-Majumder, *The Conditions of Garment Workers in Bangladesh, An Appraisal,* Bangladesh Institute of Development Studies, Dhaka, 1991.

12. See World Bank, Staff Appraisal Report, Bangladesh, Fourth Population and Health Project, Washington DC, 1991.

13. See Gerard Viratelle, "Drames naturels, drames sociaux au Bangladesh", Le Monde diplomatique, Paris, June 1991, pp. 6-7.

Chapter 12

The Post-War Economic Destruction of Vietnam

The social consequences of structural adjustment applied in Vietnam since the mid-1980s are devastating. Health clinics and hospitals have closed down, local-level famines have erupted, affecting up to a quarter of the country's population, and three quarters of a million children have dropped out from the school system. There has been a resurgence of infectious diseases with a tripling of recorded malaria deaths during the first four years of the reforms. Five thousand (out of a total of 12,000) state enterprises have been driven into bankruptcy, more than a million workers and some 200,000 public employees, including tens of thousands of teachers and health workers, have been laid off.

A secret agreement reached in Paris in 1993, which in many regards was tantamount to forcing Vietnam "to compensate Washington" for the costs of the war, required Hanoi to recognise the debts of the defunct Saigon regime of General Thieu as a condition for the granting of fresh credit and the lifting of the US embargo.

The achievements of past struggles and the aspirations of an entire nation are undone and erased almost "with the stroke of a pen". No orange or steel-pellet bombs, no napalm, no toxic chemicals: a new phase of economic and social (rather than physical) destruction has unfolded. The seemingly "neutral" and "scientific" tools of macro-economic policy (under the guidance of the Bretton Woods institutions) constitute, in the aftermath of the Vietnam War, an equally "effective" and formally "non-violent" "instrument of re-colonization" and impoverishment affecting the livelihood of millions of people.

Rewriting the History of the War

In 1940, the Vichy government had appointed Admiral Jean Decoux as governor-general to negotiate the terms of Indochina's integration into Japan's "Greater East Asia Co-Prosperity Sphere" while formally retaining France's colonial territories under the mandate of the Vichy administration. The Viet Minh Front, which had led the resistance movement against the Vichy regime and Japanese occupation forces, received Washington's assent as of 1944, with weapons and financial support provided through the Office of Strategic Services (OSS), the predecessor of today's Central Intelligence Agency (CIA). September 2, 1945: at the Declaration of Independence on Ba Dinh Square in Hanoi proclaiming the founding of the Democratic Republic of Vietnam, American OSS agents were present at the side of Ho Chi Minh. Almost 30 years of history separate this event from the equally momentous surrender of General Duong Vanh Minh in Saigon's Independence Hall on 30 April 1975, marking the end of the Vietnam War and the opening of the period of national reconstruction.

The devastation left by the war created, from the outset of the post-war era, an atmosphere of helplessness and policy inertia. The subsequent outbreak of the Cambodian civil war – fuelled by Washington's covert support to Pol Pot's forces after 1979 – and China's invasion on the northern border further thwarted the reconstruction of the civilian economy. With reunification, two divergent socio-economic systems were united: the reforms in the South were enforced narrowly following central committee guidelines, with little discernment of the social forces at work: small-scale trade in Ho Chi Minh City was suppressed while a hasty process of collectivization was carried out in the Mekong River Delta with strong opposition from the middle peasantry. Political repression affected not only those sectors of society that had ties to the Saigon regime, but also many of those who had opposed General Thieu.

In turn, the international environment had changed: the transformations of the global market system and the breakdown of the Soviet Bloc (which was Vietnam's main trading partner) backlashed, creating a situation of disarray in the national economy. The Communist Party was unable to formulate a coherent program of economic reconstruction. Profound divisions and shifts within the Communist Party leadership unfolded from the early 1980s.

Today, after more than 50 years of struggle against foreign occupation, the history of the Vietnam War is being cautiously rewritten: neoliberalism constitutes (with the technical support of the Bretton Woods institutions) the

Communist's Party's official doctrine. Bureaucrats and intellectuals are called upon unreservedly to support the new dogma in the name of socialism. With the adoption in 1986 of *Renovation (Doi moi)*, references to America's brutal role in the war are increasingly considered improper. The Communist Party leadership has recently underscored the "historic role" of the United States in "liberating" Vietnam from Japanese occupation forces in 1945. In turn, the symbols of the US period have gradually returned to the streets of Saigon. At the "Museum of American War Crimes", now renamed "Exhibition House of Aggression War Crimes", a model light fighter-jet used by the US Air Force in bombing-raids can be purchased at the souvenir kiosk with an encoated Coca-cola logo on its fuselage, alongside a vast selection of manuals on foreign investment and macro-economic reform. Not a single text on the history of the war is in sight. Outside the museum, the frenzy of an incipient consumer economy is in sharp contrast with the squalor of beggars, street children and cyclo-drivers, many of whom were war veterans in the liberation of Saigon in 1975.

The New Vietnam War

The stylized image portrayed by much of the Western media is that the free-market mechanism has propelled Vietnam into the status of a prospective "Asian tiger". Nothing could be further from the truth: the economic reforms launched in 1986 under the guidance of the Bretton Woods institutions have, in the war's brutal aftermath, initiated a new historical phase of economic and social devastation. Macro-economic reform has led to the impoverishment of the Vietnamese people striking simultaneously at all sectors of economic activity.

The first step in 1984-85 (prior to the formal launching of *Doi moi* by the Sixth Party Congress) consisted in crushing the Vietnamese currency: inflation and the "dollarization" of domestic prices were engineered by repeated devaluations reminiscent of the spectacular tumble of the piastre in 1973 under the Saigon regime, in the year following the Paris agreement and the formal "withdrawal" of American combat troops.[1] Today, Vietnam is once again inundated with US dollar notes, which have largely replaced the Vietnamese dong as a "store of value". Whereas the IMF closely monitors monetary emissions by Vietnam's Central Bank, the US Federal Reserve Bank has, in a de facto sense, taken over the responsibility of issuing currency (i.e. a massive credit operation in its own right) for America's former wartime enemy. The delusion of "economic progress" and prosperity – narrowly portrayed in the Western press – is based on the rapid growth of small, yet highly visible, "pockets" of Western-style consumerism, concentrated largely in Saigon and Hanoi. The harsh economic and social realities are otherwise: soaring food prices, local-level famines, massive lay-offs of urban workers and civil servants and the destruction of Vietnam's social programmes.[2]

Reimbursing the "Bad Debts" of the Saigon Regime

Vietnam never received war reparations payments, yet Hanoi was compelled as a condition for the "normalization" of economic relations and the lifting of the US embargo in February 1994 to "foot the bill" of the multilateral debts incurred by the US-backed Saigon regime. At the donor conference held in Paris in November 1993, a total of US$ 1.86 billion of loans and "aid" money was generously pledged in support of Vietnam's market reforms. Yet immediately after the conference, another (separate) meeting was held – this time behind closed doors with the Paris Club of official creditors.[3] On the agenda: the rescheduling of the "bad debts" incurred by the Saigon regime prior to 1975. Who gives the green light to whom ? The IMF gave its stamp of approval to Vietnam's economic reforms prior to the Paris donor conference. However, it was ultimately the results of the meetings with the Paris Club which were decisive in providing the green light to Washington. And it was only after the formal lifting of the embargo that multilateral and bilateral disbursements were allowed to proceed.

The reimbursement of arrears of US$ 140 million (owed by Saigon) to the IMF was also demanded as a condition for the resumption of credit. To this effect, Japan and France (Vietnam's former colonial masters of the Vichy period) formed a so-called "friends of Vietnam" committee to "lend to Hanoi" the money needed to reimburse the IMF. By fully recognizing the legitimacy of these debts, Hanoi had, in effect, accepted to repay loans which had been utilized to support the US war effort. Ironically, these negotiations were undertaken with the participation of a former minister of finance (and acting prime minister) in the military government of General Duong Vanh Minh which had been installed by the US military mission in 1963 in the aftermath of the assassination of President Ngo Dinh Diem and his younger brother. Dr Nguyen Xian Oanh (a prominent economist who also happened to be a former staff member of the IMF) occupied the position of economic advisor to Prime Minister Vo Van Kiet. (Oanh had worked closely with Kiet since the early 1980s when the latter was Communist Party Secretary in Ho Chi Minh City).[4]

Destroying the National Economy

Through the seemingly innocuous mechanism of the "free" market (and without the need for warfare and physical destruction), the reforms had contributed to a massive demobilization of productive capacity: more than 5,000 out of 12,300 state-owned enterprises (SOEs) had, by 1994, been closed down or steered into bankruptcy. This process was further exacerbated as a result of the collapse of trade with the countries of the former Soviet bloc. Rules on the liquidation of state enterprises were adopted in 1990, leading to a further "down-sizing" of the industrial base through the restructuring of the remaining enterprises.[5] More than a million workers and some 136,000 public employees (of which the majority were health workers and teachers) had been laid off by the end of 1992.[6] The government's target, under "decision no: 111", was to lay off another 100,000 employees by the end of 1994, reducing the size of the civil service by 20 percent. Moreover, with the withdrawal of Vietnamese troops from Cambodia, an estimated 500,000 soldiers had been demobilized and 250,000 "guest workers" had returned from Eastern Europe and the Middle East with few prospects for employment.[7]

According to World Bank data, the growth in private-sector employment was insufficient to accommodate the new entrants into the labor force. With soaring prices, the real earnings of those who remain employed had dropped to abysmally low levels: unable to subsist on government salaries of US$ 15 a month, a variety of survival activities, including frequent moonlighting by state employees, had unfolded, leading to high rates of absenteeism and the de facto paralysis of the entire administrative apparatus. With the exception of joint-venture enterprises, where the recommended minimum wage had been set at $ 30-35 a month (1994) (it is not enforced), there is no minimum wage legislation nor are there any guidelines pertaining to the indexation of wages. "The Party's free market policy is that the labor market should also be free."[8]

Whereas many of the SOEs were grossly "inefficient" and "uncompetitive" by Western standards, their demise had been engineered through the deliberate manipulation of market forces: the restructuring of state banking and financial institutions (including the elimination of the commune-level credit cooperatives) was conducive to the "freeze" of all medium- and long-term credit to domestic producers. Short-term credit was available at an interest rate of 35 percent per annum (1994). Moreover, the state was not permitted, under the terms of its agreement with the IMF, to provide budget support either to the state-owned economy or to an incipient private sector.

The demise of the state economy had also been engineered as a result of a highly discriminatory tax system: whereas SOEs continued to pay (in a situation where all subsidies and state credits had been removed) the 40-50 percent profit-withholding tax inherited from the system of central planning, foreign investors (including all joint ventures) enjoyed generous exemptions and tax holidays. Moreover, the profit-withholding tax was no longer collected on a regular basis from private-sector enterprises.[9]

The reforms' hidden agenda was to destabilize Vietnam's industrial base: heavy industry, oil and gas, natural resources and mining, cement and steel production were to be reorganized and taken over by foreign capital with the Japanese conglomerates playing a decisive and dominant role. The most valuable state assets were to be transferred to joint-venture companies. No concern was expressed by the leadership to reinforce and preserve its industrial base, or to develop, for that matter, a capitalist economy owned and controlled by "nationals". The prevailing view within the "donor community" was that a "downsizing" of the state economy was required to make room for the spontaneous development of a Vietnamese private sector. State investment was said to "crowd out" private capital formation. The reforms not only demobilized the state economy, they also prevented a transition towards national capitalism.

Moreover, the relative weakness of Vietnam's business groups, combined with the freeze on credit and the virtual absence of state support, contributed to thwart the development of a domestic private- sector economy. While various token incentives had been offered to returning Viet Kieu ("overseas Vietnamese"), much of the Vietnamese Diaspora, including the refugees of the Vietnam War and the "Boat People", had little in terms of financial resources or savings. With some exceptions, their activities were largely concentrated in family-owned and medium-sized enterprises in the commercial and services economy.[10]

A blatant example of "economic engineering", set in motion by the market reforms, concerns the fate of Vietnam's steel industry. Nearly eight million tons of bombs together with a bounty of abandoned military hardware had provided Vietnam's heavy industry with an ample supply of scrap metal. Irony of history, America's only tangible "contribution" to post-war reconstruction had been revoked: with the "open-door policy", large quantities of scrap metal were being freely re-exported (at prices substantially below world-market values). Whereas production at Vietnam's five major steel mills was stalled due to the shortage of raw materials (not to mention a legal ban on the import of scrap metal by state enterprises), a Japanese conglomerate made up of the Kyoei, Mitsui and Itochu corporations had established in 1994 a modern joint-venture steel plant in Ba-Ria Vung Tau province which imports the scrap metal (at world-market prices) "back" into Vietnam.

Excluding Domestic Producers from their Own Market

Through the deliberate manipulation of market forces, domestic producers were being literally *excluded from their own market* – even in areas where they were considered to have "a comparative advantage". Tariff barriers were removed and much of Vietnam's light manufacturing industry was displaced by a massive influx of imported consumer goods. Since 1986, a large share of Vietnam's meager foreign exchange earnings had been allocated to the import of consumer goods, creating a vacuum in the availability of capital equipment for domestic industry. The reforms allowed SOEs involved in the export trade freely to use their hard-currency earnings to import consumer goods. A network had been established between the managers of SOEs involved in the import-export business, local-level bureaucrats and private merchants. Hard-currency earnings were squandered and large amounts of money were appropriated. With the market reforms, many of the SOEs escaped state control and became involved in a variety of illicit activities. With the lifting of state budget support and the freeze on credit, productive activities were abandoned.

In the new areas of light manufacturing and industrial processing promoted as a result of the "open door", the internal market is "off limits" to Vietnamese companies. Cheap-labor garment producers, involved in joint ventures or subcontracting agreements with foreign capital, will usually export their entire output. In contrast, the domestic Vietnamese market is supplied with imported second-hand garments and factory rejects from Hong Kong, leading also to the demise of tailors and small producers in the informal economy. (The price of used garments purchased in the developed countries is US$ 80 a ton.)

Thwarting the Channels of Internal Trade

The reforms promoted the "economic Balkanization" of the regions, each of which is separately integrated into the world market: the deregulation of the transport industry led to skyrocketing freight prices. State transport companies were also driven into bankruptcy with a large share of the transport industry taken over by joint-venture capital.

Moreover, with the freeze on budget transfers from the central to the provincial and municipal governments recommended by the World Bank, provincial and local authorities became increasingly "free" to establish their own investment and trading relations with foreign companies to the detriment of internal trade. The provinces were negotiating numerous investment and trade agreements, including the granting of land to foreign investors, as well as concessions which allowed foreign capital (in a completely unregulated environment) to plunder Vietnam's forest resources. In the context of the budget crisis, these various agreements often constituted the only means of covering central and provincial government expenditures, including the salaries of state officials.

Moreover, in a situation where the salaries of public employees are exceedingly low (US\$ 15 to 30 a month), foreign cooperation and joint-venture linkages inevitably constitute a means for obtaining "salary supplements" in the form of consulting fees, expense accounts, travel allowances, etc. The latter – invariably disbursed in hard currency – enable the foreign donors and contractors to secure the allegiance of professional cadres and local-level officials. The state is bankrupt and unable (under the clauses of its agreements with the creditors) to remunerate its civil servants. Foreign contractors and "aid agencies" not only appropriate human capital in research institutes and government departments, they become the main source of income for senior and middle-level bureaucrats involved in the management of foreign trade and investment.

The Disintegration of the State's Public Finances

The reforms have pushed the state's public finances into a straitjacket. The Central Bank is not allowed to expand the money supply or issue currency without IMF approval. Neither is it allowed to grant credit or finance the SOEs. The latter are, in turn, precipitated into bankruptcy as a result of the freeze on credit and state funding. In turn, the bankruptcy of the state enterprises was conducive to the collapse of state tax revenues which backlashed on the state's public finances.

A similar situation existed with regard to the state banks. The latter had been affected by the decline of dong deposits by the population (who preferred to hold their savings in the form of hoards in dollar notes), not to mention the lifting of state subsidies, strict reserve requirements and high withholding taxes. In turn, the contraction of credit, as well as increased loan default by SOEs, was pushing the state banks into receivership to the advantage of the numerous foreign and joint-venture banks operating in Vietnam. In 1994, more than 10,000 out of the 12,300 enterprises were heavily indebted to the state banks.

The state enterprises were not, however, allowed to approach foreign banks directly for credit. On the other hand, the foreign banks had access to this lucrative short-term credit market by providing collateral loans to Vietnamese state banks.

Collapse of State Capital Formation

The reforms contributed to triggering an impressive collapse of public investment. From 1985 to 1993, the share of government capital expenditure in GDP declined by 63 percent, from 8.2 to 3.1 percent. In agriculture and forestry the decline (90 percent) was even more dramatic, – i.e. from 1.0 to 0.1 percent of GDP. In industry and construction, capital expenditure fell from 2.7 to 0.1 percent of GDP (a decline of 96 percent).[11]

New rules pertaining to the levels of recurrent and investment expenditure had been established under the policy-based loan agreements negotiated with the Bretton Woods institutions. Precise ceilings were placed on all categories of expenditure, public employees were laid off, allocations to health and educations were frozen, etc. The underlying objective was to reduce the budget deficit. The state was no longer permitted to mobilize its own resources for the building of public infrastructure, roads or hospitals, etc. – i.e. the creditors not only became the "brokers" of all major public investment projects, they also decided in the context of the "Public Investment Program" (PIP) (established under the technical auspices of the World Bank) on what type of public infrastructure was best suited to Vietnam, and what should or should not be funded by the "donor community". The process of funding public investment created debt, which, in turn, reinforced the grip of the creditors on economic policy.

This supervision applied not only to the *amount of public investment*, it affected the precise composition of public expenditure and the setting of investment priorities by the creditors. It also required divestiture and privatization of most SOEs involved in infrastructure and strategic sectors of the economy. In turn, the loans pledged at the Paris Donor Conference in November 1993 required a system of international tender (and "competitive bidding") which allocated the entire execution of all public-works projects to international construction and engineering firms. The latter in turn skimmed off large amounts of money (which Vietnam will ultimately have to repay) into a variety of consulting and management fees. In turn, Vietnamese companies (whether public or private) were excluded from the tendering process, although much of the actual construction work was undertaken by local companies (using Vietnamese labor at very low wages) in separate sub-contracting deals reached with the transnationals.

Reintegrating the Japanese Empire

The tendency is towards the reintegration of Vietnam into the Japanese sphere of influence, a situation reminiscent of World War II when Vietnam was part of Japan's "Great East Asia Co-Prosperity Sphere". This dominant position of Japanese capital was brought about through the control of over more than 80 percent of the loans for investment projects and infrastructure. These loans channeled through Japan's Overseas Economic Cooperation Fund (OECF), as well as through the Asian Development Bank (ADB), supported the expansion of the large Japanese trading companies and transnationals.

With the lifting of the US embargo in February 1994, American capital scrambled to restore its position in a highly profitable investment and trading arena dominated by Japan (and to a lesser extent by the European Union). The Japanese have a "head lead" not only in key investments, they also control much of the long-term credit to Vietnam. Confrontations between Washington and Tokyo are likely to unfold as American transnationals attempt to restore the position they held in South Vietnam (e.g. in offshore oil) prior to 1975. Other important players are the Koreans, and the Chinese from Taiwan and Hong Kong. A clear demarcation prevails; however, the latter tend to concentrate in manufacturing and export processing, whereas the large infrastructural, oil and gas and natural resources projects are in the hands of Japanese and European conglomerates.

It is worth noting that Japan also controls a large share of the loans used to finance consumer imports. This consumer frenzy of Japanese brand products is now largely sustained on borrowed money fuelled by the infusion of hundreds of millions of dollars of so-called "quick disbursing loans" pledged by Japan and the multilateral banks (including the ADB, the World Bank and the IMF).[12] These loans (which in the official jargon are said to constitute "balance-of-payments aid") are earmarked explicitly for commodity imports. Administered by Vietnam's Central Bank, the disbursements under these loans are allocated in the form of foreign-exchange quotas to thousands of state enterprises involved in the import trade. This process accelerates the deluge of consumer goods while contributing to swelling the external debt. With the exception of a small number of larger state corporations (and those involved in the import trade), the reforms have contributed to demobilizing entire sectors of the national economy: the only means for a national enterprise to "survive" is to enter the lucrative import business or to establish a "joint-venture" in which the "foreign partner" has access to credit (in hard currency) and control over technology, pricing and the remittance of profits. Moreover, the entire international trading system is prone (from the lower echelons to top state officials) to corruption and bribery by foreign contractors.

Vietnam's economic crisis did not signify, however, a concurrent decline in the "recorded" rate of GDP growth. The latter has increased largely as a result of the rapid redirection of the economy towards foreign trade (development of oil and gas, natural resources, export of staple commodities and cheap-labor manufacturing). Despite the wave of bankruptcies and the compression of the internal market, there has been a significant growth in the new export-oriented joint ventures. In turn, the "artificial" inflow of imported goods was conducive to the enlargement of the commercial sector and its share of the GDP.

Economic growth was being fuelled by debt. The burden of debt servicing increased more than tenfold from 1986 to 1993. It was also boosted as a result of the government's agreement with the Paris Club in late 1993 to recognize the bad debts of the defunct Saigon regime.

The Outbreak of Famine

The adoption of a more flexible "farm contract system" among the reforms of 1981 in support of household production was broadly welcomed by the rural people. In contrast, however, the second wave of agricultural reforms adopted since 1986 has contributed to the impoverishment of large sectors of that same population. Under the guidance of the World Bank and the FAO, the authorities abrogated the policy of "local-level self-sufficiency in food" which was devised to prevent the development of regional food shortages. In the highland areas of central Vietnam, farmers were encouraged to specialize "according to their regional comparative advantage" – namely, to give up food farming and switch to "high-value" cash crops for export. Over-cropping of coffee, cassava, cashew-nuts and cotton, combined with the plummeting of world commodity prices and the high cost of imported farm inputs, was conducive to the outbreak of local-level famines.

Ironically, the process of "switching" into export crops also resulted in a net decline in foreign-exchange earnings because large shipments of agricultural commodities were sold by the state trading companies to international contractors at substantial financial losses:

> We mobilize farmers to produce cassava and cotton, but they cannot export at a profit because the international price has gone down (. . .) What happens is that the state trading companies are obliged to export the coffee or the cassava at a loss. They manage, however, to compensate for these losses because they use the foreign-exchange proceeds to import consumer goods. They also make large profits through price mark-ups on imported fertilizer.[13]

The state export corporations, while showing a book-value profit, were, in fact, contributing to generating debt (in foreign exchange) by routinely selling staple commodities below their world-market price. In many of the food-deficit areas, export crops by farmers (who had abandoned food farming) remained unsold due to the situation of oversupply which characterized the world market. The result was famine because the farmers could neither sell the industrial cash crops nor produce their own food.

A similar situation prevailed with regard to the SOEs involved in the rice trade. The latter preferred to export at a financial loss rather than sell in the domestic market. With the complete deregulation of the grain market and sales in the hands of private merchants, domestic prices soared particularly in the food-deficit areas. Whereas rice was being exported below world-market prices, severe food shortages had unfolded in regions where paddy production had been abandoned as a result of the policy of "regional specialization". In 1994, for instance, the authorities acknowledged the existence of a famine in Lai Cai province on the border with China affecting more than 50,000 people. Whereas food shortages had built up in Lai Cai over a five-month period (without any emergency relief being provided), two million tons of rice remained unsold in the Mekong Delta as a result of the collapse of the state-owned rice-trading companies.

Famine was not limited to the food-deficit areas. It was affecting all major regions, including the urban areas and the "food-surplus economy" of the Mekong Delta. In the latter region, 25.3 percent of the adult population had a daily energy intake below 1,800 calories.[14] In the cities, the devaluation of the dong, together with the elimination of subsidies and price controls, had led to soaring prices of rice and other food staples. Deindexation of salaried earnings and massive urban unemployment (resulting from the retrenchment of civil servants and workers in SOEs) had also resulted in lower levels of food intake and a deterioration in the nutritional status of children in urban areas.

Child Malnutrition

The deregulation of the grain market had triggered famine and a high incidence of child malnutrition. Despite the increased "availability" of staple foods, as suggested by FAO data, a nutrition survey confirmed an abrupt overall deterioration in the nutritional status of both children and adults. The adult mean energy intake (per capita/per day) for the country was 1,861 calories with 25 percent of the adult population below 1,800 calories (1987-90) indicating a situation of extreme undernourishment.15 In 9 per cent of the sample households, energy intake by adults was less than 1,500 calories. Recorded energy intakes for young children under six were on average 827 calories per capita.

The situation with regard to child malnutrition was acknowledged by the World Bank:

> Vietnam has a higher proportion of underweight and stunted children [of the order of 50 percent] than in any other country in South and Southeast Asia with the exception of Bangladesh. . . The magnitude of stunting and wasting among children certainly appears to have increased significantly. . . it is also possible that the worsening macro-economic crisis in the 1984-86 period may have contributed to the deterioration in nutritional status.[16]

It is also worth noting (according to the survey) that Vitamin-A deficiency, which causes blindness (resulting from a diet composed almost exclusively of cereals), is widespread among children in all regions of the country except Hanoi and the southeast. This situation compares to that of Bangladesh. (See Chapter 11.)

The deregulation of the grain market (under World Bank guidance) allowed easy access to the world market (although at very low commodity prices) while disrupting the channels of internal trade and triggering local-level famines.[17] This pattern was candidly acknowledged by the World Bank:

> Of course since private sector flows typically respond to price incen-

tives, the problem of food availability in the food deficit areas will not disappear overnight, since consumers in these areas do not have the purchasing power to bid up the price paid for foodgrains from the surplus regions. In fact at present it is financially more rewarding to export rice outside Vietnam than to transfer it to the deficit regions within the country. Indeed as private sector grain trade expands, the availability of food in the deficit regions may initially decline before it improves.[18]

Into the Net of International Agri-business

The general direction of the government's grain policy largely coincided with the interests of international agri-business: a switch out of paddy into a variety of crops (citrus trees, hybrid maize, cashew-nuts, etc.) was being encouraged even in regions (e.g. Mekong Delta) which were favorable to paddy cultivation. In Dong Nai province in the south, for instance, farmers were encouraged to move out of paddy; hybrid maize seedlings were purchased from an international grain conglomerate with short-term loans (at 2.5 percent per month) financed by the State Agricultural Bank. The harvested maize was then "purchased back" by Proconco, a French agro-industrial joint venture exporting as well as selling animal feed in the domestic market to produce meat products for Taiwan and Hong Kong.[19] Short-term credit was available only for designated commercial crops with loan periods (less than 180 days) shorter than those required to complete the entire cycle of agricultural production and marketing of the commodity.

Vietnam as a Major Exporter of Rice

An impressive increase in paddy production took place between 1987-89 and 1992, which enabled Vietnam to move from a position of net importer to that of an exporter of rice. This tendency was sustained without an increase in the land areas allocated to paddy. It was largely the result of a shift into new varieties, as well as increased use of chemical fertilizer and pesticides entailing substantially higher costs to the small farmer. The government had moved out of supplying farm inputs; the SOEs producing pesticides had collapsed. Increasingly, a large share of farm inputs were being imported:

> Our productivity has gone up but our income has not gone up, we must pay for the new seed varieties, insecticide and fertilizer.

Transport costs have increased. If the costs continue to rise, we will not be able to continue farm activities; off-farm employment including handicrafts and labor in the city are essential; farming does not provide enough money to survive.[20]

Largely centered in the Mekong Delta, this expanded paddy output (and the corresponding surge in exports) had also been conducive to increased land concentration. In the Red River delta, small farmers were paying royalties to the International Rice Research Institute (IRRI) (supported by the World Bank and the Rockefeller Foundation) for a new variety of paddy which was being reproduced in local nurseries. Agricultural research institutes, whose funds had been cut off by the state, had entered the lucrative business of seed development and production.[21]

The expansion in paddy production seems, however, to have reached a peak: the withdrawal of state support in the provision of irrigation infrastructure, water conservancy and maintenance, since 1987, will affect future output patterns. Large-scale irrigation and drainage have been neglected: the World Bank recommends cost recovery and the commercialization of water resources while, nonetheless, acknowledging that "farmers outside the Mekong Delta are too poor to bear increased rates [irrigation charges] at this time".[22] The risk of recurrent flooding and drought has also increased as a result of the collapse of state enterprises responsible for routine operation and maintenance. A similar situation exists in agricultural support and extension services:

> Provision of agricultural support services – the supply of fertilizer, seed, credit, pest control, veterinary services, machinery services, research and extension advice, was until the late 1980s a predominantly governmental function. (…) This system, while still functioning on paper, has now largely collapsed in reality due to the restoration of a family-based farming system, increasing real budgetary shortfalls, and civil service salary rates devalued to almost nothing by inflation. Those support services involving a marketable product or service have been semi-privatized with some success, and the remainders are hardly functioning. In the support service bureaucracy, a large number of employees survive on moonlighting activities, while some 8,000 graduates of the agro-technical schools reportedly are "unemployed".[23]

The Concentration of Land

The tendency is towards a major crisis in production, increased social polarization in the countryside and a greater concentration of land ownership: large sectors of the rural population in the Red River and Mekong delta areas are being driven off the land; famines have also occurred in the rice-surplus regions. The Law, passed in the National Assembly in October 1993, had been drafted with the support of the World Bank's Legal Department. Legal experts and World Bank seminars were organized to focus on the implications of the Law:

> The foreign experts brought in by the World Bank think that the Law is suitable to our particular conditions: if farmers lack capital or resources they can "transfer" the or they can move to the cities or work for "an advanced household". (…) The lack of is not the cause of poverty, the poor lack knowledge, experience and have limited education, and the poor also have too many children.[24]

Under the law, farm (under a formal system of long-term leases) can be freely "transferred" (i.e. sold) and mortgaged as "enforceable collateral" (officially only with a state banking institution but, in practice, also with private money-lenders). The can then be "transferred" or sold if there is loan default.

The consequence has been the re-emergence (particularly in the south) of usury and tenancy, forcing the peasant economy back to the struggles for and credit waged at the end of the French colonial period. In the south, concentration is already fairly advanced, marked by the development of medium-sized plantations (including numerous joint ventures with foreign capital). Many state farms had been transformed into joint-venture plantations using both permanent and seasonal workers. Landless farmers, who constitute an increasingly large share of the rural population, are confined to seeking employment in the cities or as seasonal wage laborers in commercial plantations operated by rich farmers or joint ventures. Rural wages in the Red River delta were of the order of 50 cents a day (1994). While land forfeiture of small farmers in North Vietnam is still at an incipient level, the Land Law opens the way for the appropriation of large tracts of agricultural land by urban merchants and money-lenders.

It is worth mentioning that the agricultural policies of the defunct Saigon regime of General Thieu are resurfacing. In the south, land titles granted by US, "aid" programs in 1973 as a means of "pacifying" rural areas are fully recognized by the authorities. In contrast, thousands of peasants who left their villages to fight alongside the liberation forces are without formal claims to agricultural land. We will recall that the US land-distribution program was implemented in the aftermath of the 1973 Paris agreement during the last years of the Thieu regime. This period of so-called "Vietnamization" of the war coincided with the formal withdrawal of American combat troops and the propping up of the Saigon government with massive amounts of US "aid". According to the Ministry of Agriculture, the United States wartime program is a useful "model": "Our present policy is to emulate the US land-distribution program of that period, although we lack sufficient financial resources."

The Destruction of Education

Perhaps the most dramatic impact of the reforms has been in the areas of health and education. Universal education and literacy was a key objective of the struggle against French colonial rule.

From 1954 (following the defeat of the French at Dien Bien Phu) to 1972, primary and secondary school enrolment in North Vietnam had increased sevenfold (from 700,000 to nearly five million). After reunification in 1975, a literacy campaign was implemented in the south. According to UNESCO figures, the rates of literacy (90 percent) and school enrolment were among the highest in South-East Asia.

The reforms have deliberately and consciously destroyed the educational system by massively compressing the educational budget, depressing teachers' salaries and "commercializing" secondary, vocational and higher education through the exaction of tuition fees. The movement is towards the transformation of education into a commodity. In the official jargon of the UN agencies, this requires:

> ...consumers of [educational] services to pay increased amounts, encouraging institutions to become self-financing, and by using incentives to privatize delivery of education and training where appropriate.[25]

Virtually repealing all previous achievements – including the struggle against illiteracy carried out since 1945 – the reforms have engineered an unprecedented collapse in school enrolment with a high drop-out rate observed in the final years of primary school. The obligation to pay tuition fees is now entrenched in the constitution, which was carefully redrafted in 1992. According to official data, the proportion of graduates from primary education who entered the four-year lower-secondary education program declined from 92 percent in 1986/87 (prior to the inauguration of the tuition fees) to 72 percent in 1989/90 – a drop of more than half a million students. Similarly, some 231,000 students out of *a total of 922,000 dropped out of the upper secondary education program. In other words, a total of nearly three quarters of a million children were pushed out of the secondary-school system during the first three years of the reforms* (despite an increase of more than 7 percent in the population of school age). While recent enrolment data is unavailable, there is no evidence that this trend has been reversed.[26] The available data of the 1980s suggests a drop-out rate of 0.8 percent per annum in primary education with total enrolment increasing but substantially behind the growth in the population of school age. The structure of underfunding will trigger a speedy erosion of primary education in the years ahead.

The state allocated (1994) an average of US$ 3 to 4 per annum per child at the primary school level. In the Red River delta region, the cost to parents of school materials and books (previously financed by the government) was in 1994 equivalent to 100 kg. of paddy per child per annum (a significant fraction of total household consumption).

"Concern" was, nonetheless, expressed by the government and "the donors" that with a rapidly declining enrolment rate, "unit costs have increased" and there is now "an oversupply of teachers".[27] With a "downsized" school system, consideration should be given "to quality rather than quantity" requiring (according to "the donors") the lay-off of surplus teachers. All echelons of the educational system are affected by this process: state-supported pre-primary crèches are being phased out, and will henceforth be run as commercial undertakings.

Cost recovery was also enforced for universities and all centers of higher learning. Institutes of applied research were called upon to recover their costs by commercializing the products of their research: "Universities and research institutes are so poorly funded that their survival depends on generating independent sources of income". The state covered only 25 percent of total salaries of research and other operating expenditures of major research institutes.[28] Research establishments were, nonetheless, granted a preferential rate of interest on short-term credit (1.8 percent per month instead of 2.3 percent).

In vocational and technical education, including the teachers' training colleges, a freeze on enrolment (with precise "ceilings") was established under guidelines agreed with external donor agencies. The result: a major curtailment in the supply of human capital and qualified professionals.

In the above context, financial control and supervision of most research and training institutes is in the hands of external donor agencies which selectively fund salary supplements in foreign exchange, research contracts, etc., while also dictating the orientations for research and the development of academic curricula.

Collapse of the Health System

In health, the most immediate impact of the reforms was the collapse of the district hospitals and commune-level health centers. Until 1989, health units provided medical consultations as well as essential drugs free of charge to the population. The disintegration of health clinics in the south is on the whole, more advanced where the health infrastructure had been developed after reunification in 1975. With the reforms, a system of user fees was introduced. Cost recovery and the free-market sale of drugs were applied. The consumption of essential drugs (through the system of public distribution) declined by 89 percent pushing Vietnam's pharmaceutical and medical supply industry into bankruptcy.[29]

By 1989, the domestic production of pharmaceuticals had declined by 98.5 percent in relation to its 1980 level with a large number of drug companies closing down. With the complete deregulation of the pharmaceutical industry, including the liberalization of drug prices, imported drugs (now sold exclusively in the "free" market at exceedingly high prices) have now largely displaced domestic brands. A considerably "down-sized", yet highly profitable commercial market has unfolded for the large pharmaceutical transnationals. The per capita annual consumption of pharmaceuticals purchased in the "free" market is of the order of US$ 1 per annum (1993) which even the World Bank considers to be too low.[30] The impact on the levels of health of the population are dramatic.

The government (under the guidance of the "donor community") also discontinued budget support to the provision of medical equipment and maintenance, leading to the virtual paralysis of the entire public-health system. Real salaries of medical personnel and working conditions declined dramatically: the monthly wage of medical doctors in a district hospital was as low as US$ 15 a month (1994). With the tumble in state salaries and the emergence of a small sector of private practice, tens of thousands of doctors and health workers abandoned the public-health sector. A survey conducted in 1991 confirmed that most of the commune-level health centers had become inoperative: with an average staff of five health workers percenter, the number of patients had dropped to less than six a day (slightly more than one patient per health worker per day).[31] Since the reforms, there has also been a marked downturn in student admissions to the country's main medical schools which are currently suffering from a massive curtailment of their operating budgets.

The Resurgence of Infectious Diseases

The resurgence of a number of infectious diseases including malaria, tuberculosis and diarrhea was acknowledged by the Ministry of Health and the donors. A WHO study confirmed that the number of malaria deaths increased threefold in the first four years of the reforms, alongside the collapse of curative health and soaring prices of anti-malarial drugs. What is striking in this data is that the number of malaria deaths increased at a faster rate than the growth in reported cases of malaria suggesting that the collapse in curative health services played a decisive role in triggering an increase in (malaria) mortality.[32] These tendencies are amply confirmed by commune-level data:

> The state of health used to be much better, previously there was an annual check-up for tuberculosis, now there are no drugs to treat malaria, the farmers have no money to go to the district hospital, they cannot afford the user fees.[33]

The World Bank has acknowledged the collapse of the health system (the underlying macro-economic "causes", however, were not mentioned):

> [D]espite its impressive performance in the past, the Vietnamese health sector is currently languishing (. . .) there is a severe shortage of drugs, medical supplies and medical equipment and the government health clinics are vastly underutilized. The shortage of funds to the health sector is so acute that it is unclear where the grass-roots facilities are going to find the inputs to continue functioning in the future.[34]

Whereas the World Bank conceded that the communicable disease control programs for diarrhea, malaria and acute respiratory infections "have [in the past] been among the most successful of health interventions in Vietnam", the proposed "solutions" consisted of the "commercialization" (i.e. commodification) of public health as well as the massive lay-off of surplus doctors and health workers. The World Bank proposed that the wages of health workers should be increased within the same budgetary envelope: "an increase in the wages of government health workers will almost necessarily have to be offset by a major reduction in the number of health workers."[35]

The reforms brutally dismantle the social sectors, undoing the efforts and struggles of the Vietnamese people during nearly 40 years, reversing the fulfillment of past progress. There is a consistent and coherent pattern: the deterioration in health and nutrition (in the years immediately following the reforms) is similar (and so is the chronology) with that observed in school enrolment. In the aftermath of a brutal and criminal war, the world community must take cognizance of the "deadly" impact of macro-economic policy applied to a former wartime enemy.

Endnotes

1. The devaluations of 1984-85 under the advice of the IMF were conducive to a tenfold collapse of the Vietnam dong, largely of the same magnitude as that which occurred in South Vietnam in 1973. The dong was worth US$ 0.10 at the official exchange rate in 1984; one year later it was worth US$ 0.01.

2. The reforms have triggered a collapse in the standard of living in many ways comparable to that which occurred in South Vietnam under the defunct regime of General Thieu. An eightfold increase in the price of rice was recorded between 1973 and 1974 after the US "withdrawal" of combat troops.

3. For a breakdown and composition of the international aid and loans pledged at the donor conference, see *Vietnam Today*, Singapore, Vol. 2, Issue 6, 1994, p. 58.

4. Interview with Dr Nguyen Xian Oanh in Ho Chi Minh City, April 1994.

5. From mid-1991 to mid-1992, some 4,000 enterprises ceased operations with some 1,259 being liquidated. Some of the enterprises which ceased operating were merged with other state enterprises. See World Bank, *Viet Nam, Transition to Market Economy*, Washington DC, 1993, p. 61.

6. In the sector of SOEs, decision no: 176 passed in 1989 was conducive to 975,000 workers (36 percent of labor force) being laid off between 1987 and 1992. The growth in private-sector employment has not been sufficient to accommodate new entrants into the labor market. See World Bank, *Viet Nam, Transition to Market Economy*, pp. 65-66, see also Table 1.3, p. 233.

7. *Ibid*, p. 65. See also Socialist Republic of Vietnam, *Vietnam: A Development Perspective* (main document prepared for the Paris Donor Conference), Hanoi, September 1993, p. 28.

8. Interview conducted with state officials in Hanoi, April 1994.

9. See World Bank, *Viet Nam, Transition to Market Economy*, p. 47.

10. In contrast to the "Overseas Chinese", the Vietnamese Diaspora cannot be considered as constituting an "economic élite".

11. See World Bank, *Viet Nam, Transition to Market Economy*, p. 246. It is worth noting that the statistics in current and constant dong are considered to be unreliable.

12. At the November 1993 Paris Donor Conference, over US$ 1.8 billion of multilateral and bilateral credit was pledged.

13. Interview with the Ministry of Agriculture and Food Industry (MAFI), Hanoi, April 1994.

14. See World Bank, *Vietnam, Population, Health and Nutrition Review*, Washington DC, 1993, Table 3.6, p. 47.

15. The percentage of children under five suffering from malnutrition is estimated at 45 percent according to the weight for age criterion and 56.5 percent according to height for age. *Ibid*, pp. 38-46 and p. 62.

16. See World Bank, *Viet Nam, Transition to Market Economy*, p. 182.

17. The policy of local food self-sufficiency had been dictated by the deficiencies of the internal rail and road transport network, destroyed during the war.

18. World Bank, *Vietnam, Population, Health and Nutrition Sector Review*, p. 42.

19. Interviews conducted in Dong Nai Province as well as with members of the Agricultural Research Institute, Ho Chi Minh, April 1994.

20. Interviews with farmers in Da Ton Commune, Gia Lam district near Hanoi, April 1994.

21. World Bank, *Viet Nam, Transition to Market Economy*, p. 144.

22. *Ibid*, p. 141.

23. *Ibid*, p. 143.

24. Interview with the Ministry of Agriculture and Food Industry (MAFI), Hanoi, April 1994.

25. See Ministry of Education, UNDP, UNESCO (National Project Education Sector Review and Human Resources Sector Analysis), *Vietnam Education and Human Resources Analysis*, Vol. 1, Hanoi, 1992, p. 39.

26. Ministry of Education, UNDP, UNESCO, *op. cit.* p. 65.

27. *Ibid,* p. 60.

28. World Bank, *Viet Nam, Transition to Market Economy*, p. 145.

29. Figures of the Ministry of Health quoted in World Bank, *Vietnam: Population, Health and Nutrition Sector Review*, Table 4.6, p. 159.

30. *Ibid,* p. 89.

31. *Ibid,* p. 86.

32. *Ibid*, Table 4.2, p. 154.

33. Interview conducted in Phung Thuong Commune, Phue Tho district, Hay Tay Province, North Vietnam.

34. World Bank, *Viet Nam, Transition to Market Economy*, p. 169.

35. *Ibid*, p. 171.

PART IV

LATIN AMERICA

Chapter 13

Debt and "Democracy" in Brazil

Political scandal during the presidency of Fernando Collor de Mello played a significant role in the restructuring of the Brazilian State. This first "democratically elected" presidency marked the demise of military dictatorship, as well as the transition towards a new "authoritarian democracy" under the direct control of the creditors and the Washington-based international financial institutions.

A few weeks after the Rio Earth Summit in June 1992, a congressional inquiry confirmed that President Collor was personally involved, through his front-man and former campaign manager P. C. Farias, in a multi-million extortion racket involving the use of public funds. The money from the kick-back operation (involving government contracts to construction companies) had been channeled into "phantom bank accounts" or was diverted to pay for the personal expenses of the president's household – including his wife Rosane's wardrobe. Public opinion had its eye riveted on the political scandal and the disgrace of the president: the viewing figures for the televized congressional hearings were higher than those of the Olympic Games.

Meanwhile backstage (removed from the public eye), another much larger multi-billion dollar deal was being negotiated between Collor's minister of finance and Brazil's international creditors: these negotiations unfolded from June to September of 1992, behind closed doors, coinciding chronologically with the impeachment process. Government ministers resigned and declared publicly their lack of support for the president. The "internationally respected" minister of finance Mr. Marcilio Marques Moreira stood firm ensuring the necessary liaison with the IMF and the commercial creditors. The weakening of the state combined with instability on the Sao Paulo stock exchange and capital flight also served to put further pressure on the government. The negotiations with the commercial banks were announced by President Collor in June 1992 at the outset of the scandal.[1] A preliminary agreement on the "restructuring" formula (under the Brady Plan) of US$ 44 billion owed to international banks was disclosed shortly before Collor's impeachment by the senate on 29 September 1992. It was a sell-out: Brazil's burden of debt servicing would increase substantially as a result of the deal.[2]

The campaign to impeach the president had usefully distracted public attention from the real social issues: the large majority of the population had been impoverished as a result of the *Plan Collor* launched in March 1990 by the controversial minister of economy and finance Ms Zelia Cardoso de Mello, followed by the more orthodox, yet equally damaging, economic therapy of her successor Marcilio Marques Moreira: unemployment was widespread, real wages had collapsed, social programs had been crushed.

The devaluation of the cruzeiro had been imposed by the creditors and inflation was running at more than 20 percent a month – largely as a result of the IMF's "anti-inflation program". A hike in real interest rates imposed on Brazil in 1991 by the IMF had contributed to fuelling the internal debt, as well as attracting large amounts of "hot" and "dirty" money into Brazil's banking system.[3] Tremendous profits were made by some 300 large financial and industrial enterprises. These groups were largely responsible for "a profit-led inflation"; the share of capital in GDP increased from 45 percent in 1980 to 66 percent in the early 1990s. "Democracy" had secured for the economic élites (in alliance with the international creditors) what the nationalist military regimes were not capable of achieving fully.

The IMF's hidden agenda consisted of supporting the creditors while, at the same time, weakening the central state. Ninety billion dollars in interest payments had already been paid during the 1980s, almost as much as the total debt itself (US$ 120 billion). Collecting the debt, however, was not the main objective. Brazil's international creditors wanted to ensure that the country would remain indebted well into the future and that the national economy and the state would be restructured to their advantage through the continued pillage of natural resources and the environment, the consolidation of the cheap-labor export economy and the taking over of the most profitable state enterprises by foreign capital.

State assets would be privatized in exchange for debt; labor costs would be depressed as a result of the deindexation of wages and the firing of workers. Inflation was directly engineered by the macro-economic reforms. Poverty was not only "the result" of the reforms, it was also "an explicit condition" of the agreement with the IMF.

Brazil's Debt Saga: Act I: Plan Collor

Who are the "characters" in Brazil's "debt saga"?

The Plan Collor, initiated in 1990, was an unusual "cocktail" combining an interventionist monetary policy with IMF-style privatization, trade liberalization and a floating exchange rate. A US$ 31 billion budget deficit was to be eliminated, 360,000 federal employees were to be fired and six ministries were abolished. Introduced in March 1990, shortly after the presidential inauguration, the Plan Collor was, in many respects, a continuation of the Plan Verao adopted in 1989 under the Sarney government. The target of 360,000 employees was not met because the government lay-offs did not receive congressional approval. Only 14,000 were laid off with severance pay. Many of them were rehired under Itamar Franco's presidency.

Savings accounts were frozen by Finance Minister Ms Zelia Cardoso de Mello in a naive monetarist attempt to control inflation: "Inflation is a tiger, we must kill the tiger". Instead, the measures largely "killed economic activity", unemployment grew to record levels and small businesses were crippled due to the freeze on bank deposits, leading to at least 200,000 lay-offs in 1990 alone. Organized labor responded to the *Plan Collor* in September 1990 with a strike, regrouping more than one million workers. In the words of economist Paulo Singer: "the shock was cruel, monstrous and unnecessary".

The hidden agenda of Plan Collor consisted in curtailing public expenditure and cutting wages so as to release the money required to service the external and internal debts. The formula for repayment of Brazil's external debt, however, was still tainted by former-President Sarney's 1989 nationalist stance regarding the debt, – i.e. "a partial moratorium" (much to the dislike of the international banks) limiting debt servicing to 30 percent of total interest payments.

The IMF had provided its "stamp of approval" to the *Plan Collor*, yet a US$ 2 billion stand-by loan, approved in September 1990, was still on hold. In the words of IMF Managing Director Mr. Michel Camdessus: "before asking approval of the [IMF] executive council, I must be sure that the negotiations with the banks are moving in the right direction and that their results will be satisfactory".[4]

A few weeks later, the government reopened debt talks with the international creditors. Mr. Jorio Dauster, Collor's chief debt negotiator, argued unconvincingly that "debt payments must be limited to Brazil's ability to pay".[5] The advisory group of 22 commercial banks, led by Citicorp, retaliated by vetoing the IMF loan agreement and by instructing the multilateral banks not to grant "new money" to Brazil.[6] This veto was officially sanctioned by the G7 at a meeting in Washington. In turn, the United States Treasury directed the World Bank and the Inter-American Development Bank (IDB) to postpone all new loans to Brazil. The IMF, also responding to precise directives from the commercial banks and the US administration, postponed its mission to Brasilia. The IMF was a mere financial bureaucracy responsible for carrying out economic policy reform in indebted countries on behalf of the creditors.

The Brazilian government was caught in a vicious circle: the granting of "fresh money" from the IMF needed to repay the commercial banks was being blocked by the advisory group representing those same commercial banks – an impossible situation. The government had satisfied all the conditions laid down by the IMF, yet Brazil was still on the blacklist. And failure to meet the demands of the commercial creditors could easily become a pretext for further reprisals and blacklisting. Tension was mounting. Ms Zelia Cardoso de Mello, Brazil's finance minister, angrily accused the G7 at the Inter-American Development Bank meetings in Nagoya, Japan in April 1991 of using unfair political pressure in blocking multilateral credit to Brazil.[7]

Act II: Conforming to "The Washington Consensus"

The Nagoya meetings marked an important turning point. Nationalist rhetoric and recrimination against the international financial community were regarded as untimely and improper. Zelia Cardoso was fired in early May. A new economic team, more in line with the "Washington Consensus", was set up. The appointment of Marcilio Marques Moreira as minister of economy and finance, was welcomed by the US administration and the international financial institutions (IFIs)[8]. While ambassador in Washington, Marques Moreira had developed a close personal relationship with the IMF's Michel Camdessus and David Mulford, under-secretary of the US Treasury. Zelia Cardoso's debt negotiator Jorio Dauster was also dismissed and replaced by Pedro Malan, an advisor to the Inter-American Development Bank and a former World-Bank executive director. Malan's association, for more than ten years, with the Washington scene, as well as Marques Moreira's personal ties were significant factors in the evolution of Brazil's debt negotiations in the second part of Collor's presidency.

In June 1991, the IMF sent a new mission to Brasilia headed by José

Fajgenbaum. The IMF had withdrawn its "stamp of approval" on the instructions of the advisory group headed by Citicorp. New negotiations on macro-economic reform had to be initiated. José Fajgenbaum – speaking on behalf of the IMF mission – stated that if Brazil wanted to reach a new loan agreement with the IMF "structural economic reforms implying amendments to the Constitution were required".[9] There was uproar in the parliament, with the IMF accused of "gross interference in the internal affairs of the state". President Collor requested the IMF to replace Fajgenbaum as head of mission "with a more qualified individual". "A populist victory for President Collor" in his battle with the IMF, said the *New York Times.*[10]

While the incident was identified as "an unfortunate misunderstanding", Fajgenbaum's statement was very much in line with established IMF practice.[11] The IMF was demanding the adoption of "a much stronger economic medicine" to allow a larger share of state revenues to be redirected towards servicing the debt with the commercial banks. Yet, several clauses of the 1988 Constitution stood in the way of achieving these objectives. The IMF was fully aware that the budget targets could not be met without a massive firing of public-sector employees. And, yet, the latter required an amendment to a clause of the 1988 Constitution guaranteeing security of employment to federal civil servants. Also at issue was the financing formula (entrenched in the Constitution) of state and municipal-level programs from federal government sources. This formula limited the ability of the federal government to slash social expenditures and shift revenue towards debt servicing.[12] From the standpoint of the IMF and the commercial banks, the amendment of the constitution was imperative. The clauses of the state pension plan *(A Previdencia Social)* included in the 1988 Constitution were also considered a barrier to the servicing of the federal government's debt. The privatization of state enterprises in strategic sectors of the economy (e.g. petroleum and telecommunications) also required a constitutional revision.

The second round of negotiations with the IMF was completed in late 1991: Michel Camdessus gave his approval to a new agreement after consultations with President Bush's Secretary of the Treasury Nicholas Brady and Under-Secretary David Mulford.[13] The second Letter of Intent, prepared by Marcilio Marques Moreira, was handed personally by President Collor de Mello to Michel Camdessus at a breakfast meeting held during the Latin-American Summit in Cartagena, Colombia in December. (Remember, the first one signed by Zelia Cardoso in September 1990 had been torn up.)

This new loan agreement (US$ 2 billion), however, was to commit the Brazilian government over a period of 20 months to a far more destructive set of economic reforms.[14] The fiscal adjustment was particularly brutal: 65 percent of current expenditures were already earmarked for debt servicing and the IMF was demanding further cuts in social spending.

The agreement was signed on the explicit (unwritten) understanding that the Brazilian authorities would resume negotiations with the Paris Club and reach a satisfactory agreement with the commercial banks on debt-servicing arrears. In the words of Marcilio Marques Moreira the deal on the commercial debt represented "a new chapter full of opportunities. This is the 'new Brazil' reinserting itself into the international community in a dynamic, competitive and sovereign way".[15]

Act III: In the Aftermath of Collor's Impeachment

Act III of the debt saga commenced with the inauguration of Itamar Franco as acting president.[16] A clumsy beginning: the new president promised to increase real wages, bring down the prices of public utilities and modify the privatization program without realizing that his hands were tied as a result of the agreement signed a year earlier with the IMF. Despite an impressive Congressional majority based on a coalition of parties extending from left to right (led by the former head of the Communist Party), Itamar Franco's cabinet failed to receive the immediate assent of the Washington institutions.

Franco's populist statements displeased both the creditors and the national élites. The IMF had decided to be much tougher on the new government: three ministers of finance were appointed during the first seven months of Itamar Franco's presidency, none of them receiving a friendly endorsement from the IMF. In the meantime, the IMF had sent in its auditors to monitor economic progress under the loan agreement: the quarterly targets for the budget deficit had not been met (and could not be met without amendments to the constitution). Even though the tax-reform legislation had been passed through Congress as required by the IMF, the program was considered to be "no longer on track". The disbursements under the stand-by loan were discontinued, Brazil was back on the blacklist and negotiations with the IMF on economic reform were once again back to square one.

At another breakfast meeting, this time in Washington in February 1993, with Itamar's second minister of finance, Paulo Haddad, Michel Camdessus insisted upon the development of a new economic program to be submitted for IMF approval within a 60-day period. Moreover, it was also made clear by the IMF that a stand-by loan would not be granted prior to the formal signing of the final agreement with the commercial banks, and that it was therefore necessary to synchronize the deadline dates set respectively for policy reform and debt restructuring.[17]

No time was lost. A few weeks later, an IMF mission had arrived in Brasilia headed by the same notorious José Fajgenbaum, who two years earlier had hinted of the need for constitutional reform. Continuity in personnel on the IMF side. . .not on the Brazilian side! Paulo Haddad was no longer in charge. Upon arrival of the mission, the ministry's economic team was in a state of disarray; the economy and finance portfolio had been switched a few days earlier. Itamar Franco's third minister of finance, Mr. Eliseu Resende, would go to Washington to meet Camdessus in late April. He was dismissed in May.[18]

Act IV: A Marxist Sociologist as Finance Minister

A new phase of the "debt saga" was initiated with the appointment of Fernando Henrique Cardoso, a prominent intellectual and Marxist sociologist, as minister of finance. The business community, somewhat apprehensive at first, was soon reassured: despite his leftist writings (*inter alia* on "social classes under peripheral capitalism"), the new minister pledged relentless support to the tenets of neo-liberalism: "forget everything I have written. . .", he said at a meeting with leading bankers and industrialists. A few years earlier Cardoso had been nominated "intellectual of the year" for his critical analysis of social classes in Brazil.

By July 1993, President Itamar Franco had virtually abdicated from exercising any real political power, having fully entrusted the conduct of the economic reforms to his new minister. As a former opposition senator, the finance minister understood that passage of the IMF reforms would require the manipulation of civil society, as well as the mustering of support in the legislature. Public opinion was led to believe that the proposed deindexation of wages was the only means "of combating inflation". In June 1993, Cardoso announced budget cuts of 50 percent in education, health and regional development while pointing to the need for revisions to the constitution at the upcoming sessions of Congress. Under Cardoso's wages' proposal – which received Congressional approval – wages could decline (in real terms) by as much as 31 percent, representing an estimated "savings" of US$ 11 billion for the public purse (and for the creditors !).[19]

Act V: Rescheduling the Commercial Debt[20]

The debt saga reached its final stage in April 1994. An agreement was sealed in New York on the "restructuring" of US$ 49 billion of commercial debt under the Brady Plan. The deal had been carefully negotiated by Cardoso and Citibank Corp Vice-Chairman Mr. William Rhodes who was acting on behalf of some 750 international creditor banks.

In contrast to previous rounds of negotiations, precise deadline dates had been set for the safe passage of major pieces of "prescribed" legislation including amendments to the 1988 Constitution. The IMF had been entrusted with the bureaucratic task of enforcing and carefully monitoring the legislative process on behalf of the commercial banks. However, despite Finance Minister Cardoso's efforts to manipulate civil society, muster political support and jostle the various reforms through a "sovereign" parliament, time had been running out. The 16 March deadline for the signing of a "Letter of Intent" with the IMF could not be met. A tight schedule, the so-called "notification deadline" for a deal with the commercial banks' steering committee, had been set for 17 March.

While the 15 April agreement was formally reached against established practice (which requires prior approval of an IMF standby loan as collateral for the debt restructuring program), the economic reforms were, nonetheless, considered "to be on track". IMF Managing Director Michel Camdessus stated that he was impressed with steps already taken and promised to cooperate closely with the government. In turn, Cardoso (who in the meantime had become presidential candidate) stated that the "IMF's promise of further cooperation" (once key elements of the economic program were in place) should be enough for the debt restructuring deal to go ahead. Despite "unfortunate delays" in the parliamentary process, the main condition – requiring a massive release of state financial resources in favor of the creditors – had been met: the legislature had approved the IMF's fiscal reforms, including the creation of a "Social Emergency Fund" (SEF) (on the World-Bank model). The vote in Congress (requiring a constitutional amendment) obliged the government to slash the federal budget (including public investment) by 43 percent while redirecting state revenue towards debt servicing.

The measures imposed by the creditors constituted a final lethal blow to Brazil's social programs, already in an advanced stage of decay as a result of successive "shock therapies". The SEF was "financed from the budget cuts" (implying transfers of funds to the SEF) through the concurrent phasing out of regular government programs and the massive dismissal of government employees. Its inauguration represented an important political landmark: sovereignty in social policy was foregone; henceforth, budgets and organizational structures would be monitored directly by the Washington-based Bretton Woods institutions acting on behalf of the international creditor banks. The collapse and destruction of the state's social programs and the phasing out of part of the government pension plan (Previdencia Social) were "pre-conditions" for the signing of the agreement. Moreover, the reforms also engineered a squeeze of real wages by establishing "a salary ceiling" in the public sector,[21] as well as the "switching" of all wage contracts into a new currency unit, the URV (or "Real").[22] The latter reform, requiring a separate piece of legislation, had been worked out well in advance (in high-level meetings behind closed doors) in close consultation with the Washington-based bureaucracy: Winston Fritsch, Brazil's secretary of state in charge of economic policy, had inadvertently leaked to the press in October 1993 that he would "deliver to the IMF, the skeleton of a plan of deindexation".[23]

The IMF's "economic therapy" had also redefined, in a fundamental way, the relationship between the central and regional governments entrenched in the 1988 Constitution. The proposed "model" of fiscal reform was, in this regard, analogous to that imposed by the international creditors on the Yugoslav Federation in 1990. (See Chapter 17.) Federal transfers to state and municipal governments earmarked for health, education and housing were frozen, the regions were to become "fiscally autonomous" and the savings accruing to the federal Treasury were to be redirected towards interest payments.

But the IMF had also pointed to the need for constitutional amendments which would allow for the speedy privatization of Petrobras and Telebras – the petroleum and telecommunications parastatals.

Cardoso had "performed much better" than his predecessors in the finance portfolio under the Collor presidency. "Success" in carrying out the IMF program was rewarded. The minister of finance was elected president in the 1994 elections supported by a massive multi-million-dollar media campaign, as well as an (unwritten) agreement by the country's major business interests not to increase prices during the election campaign. The introduction of the new currency by Cardoso while he was minister of finance had engineered the deindexation of wages. Yet the remarkably low rates of inflation in the months preceding his election as president were instrumental in providing support to Cardoso's candidacy, particularly among the poorest sections of the population which survived on the fringe of the labor market.[24]

Continuity with the authoritarian democratic regime established under Fernando Collor de Mello had been ensured. In the words of a senior executive of one of Brazil's largest creditor banks:

> Collor had a double personality, he was very committed to economic reform, he acted as a catalyst in implementing what the Brazilian people wanted. (. . .). His second cabinet under Finance Minister Marcilio Marques Moreira was the best. Today [1993] Fernando Henrique Cardoso is doing the right thing at a lesser speed. (. . .) To reach the deficit targets set by the IMF, the Congress must accept the US$ 6 billion budget cut, another US$ 6 billion will have to come from the Constitutional revision, essentially through the lay-off of public employees. (…) What we would need in Brazil is a "soft Pinochet government", preferably civilian, something like Fujimori, the military is not an option.

Act VI, Epilogue: The Management of Poverty at Minimal Cost to the Creditors

Macro-economic policy had accelerated the "expulsion" of landless peasants from the countryside leading to the formation of a nomadic migrant labor force moving from one metropolitan area to another. In the cities, an entirely new "layer of urban poverty" (socially distinct from that which characterized the *favelas*) had unfolded: thousands of salaried workers and white-collar employees hitherto occupying middle and lower-class residential areas had been evicted, socially marginalized and often "excluded" from the slum areas.

The SEF set up by Fernando Henrique Cardoso in 1994 required a "social engineering" approach, a policy framework for "managing poverty" and attenuating social unrest at minimal cost to the creditors. So-called "targeted programs" earmarked "to help the poor", combined with "cost recovery" and the "privatization" of health and educational services were said to constitute "a more efficient" way of delivering social programs. Concurrently, the Institute for National Security Studies (INSS) was to become increasingly "self-financing" by substantially raising its premium contributions from both urban and rural workers.[25] The state, which withdraws many programs under the jurisdiction of line ministries, will henceforth be managed by the organizations of civil society under the umbrella of the SEF. The latter will also finance "a social safety net" (in the form of severance payments) earmarked for public-sector workers laid off as a result of the constitutional reform process.

The establishment of the SEF was carried out "in the name of poverty alleviation". The "Citizens' campaign against famine", initiated after Collor's impeachment in the Senate in 1992, provided the government of Itamar Franco with the necessary ideological backbone, as well as a populist mouthpiece. The campaign had lost its original momentum as a broad democratic grass-roots movement directed against the policies of the state. Although the campaign was officially non-partisan, both the opposition Workers Party (PT) and the government were involved. A deal had also been struck between the leader of the campaign Dr. Herbert de Souza ("Betinho") and Mr. Alcyr Calliari, president of the Bank of Brazil. The Bank of Brazil (a powerful financial arm of the central state) was entrusted with setting up local campaign committees throughout the country. More than two thirds of these grass-roots committees were controlled by employees of the Bank of Brazil.[26] In turn, the powerful business tycoon Roberto Marinho, who controls the "Globo" television network, offered to grant free Hollywood-style commercials to the campaign during prime TV time.

Poverty and famine were portrayed in a stylized tabloid form in the Brazilian press; with funding in the hands of the financial élites, no pervasive linkage was made between the IMF's "economic medicine" and the occurrence of famine. As the economic crisis deepened, the "Citizens' campaign" served the "useful" purpose of diverting attention from the real policy issues; it sought a broad national consensus, avoided controversy and refrained from directly indicting either the government or Brazil's privileged social élites.

The campaign against famine also served another related function: the main "poverty indicators" put forth by the campaign were based on the "estimates" of the government's official "economic think tank", the Institute of Applied Economic Research (IPEA), now entrusted with supportive "research" on famine and poverty. Grossly manipulated and falsified, IPEA's "estimates" suggested that a mere 21 percent of the Brazilian population was situated below the "critical poverty" line.[27] Double standards: 32 million people in Brazil against 35.7 million in the United States (according to the definition of the US government).

The campaign portrayed poverty as pertaining essentially to a "social minority" thereby vindicating the World Bank's framework of "selective targeting in favor of the poor". It not only distorted, but tacitly denied the obvious (amply confirmed by official statistics) – namely, that most sectors of society, including the middle classes, were being impoverished as a result of the economic reforms adopted since the outset of the Collor government.[28]

The SEF officially sanctioned the withdrawal of the state from the social sectors (a process which was already ongoing), and "the management of poverty" (at the micro-social level) by separate and parallel organizational structures. Since the outset of the Collor government, various non-governmental organizations (NGOs), funded by international "aid programs", had gradually taken over many of the functions of the municipal governments whose funds had been frozen as a result of the structural adjustment program.

Small-scale production and handicraft projects, sub-contracting for export processing firms, community-based training and employment programs, etc. were set up under the umbrella of the "social safety net". A meager survival to local-level communities was ensured while, at the same time, containing the risk of social upheaval. An example of "micro-level management of poverty" is in Pirambu – a sprawling slum area of 250,000 inhabitants in the Northeastern city of Fortaleza. Pirambu had been "carved up", each slice of the urban space was under the supervision of a separate international aid organization or NGO. In the Couto Fernandes neighborhood of Pirambu, the German Aid Agency GTZ supported the establishment of a model of "community management".[29]

This "micro-democracy", installed under the watchful eye of the "donor community", also served the purpose of subduing the development of independent grass-roots social movements. German funding financed the salaries of the expatriate experts, whereas the investment funds earmarked for small-scale manufacturing were to be "self-financed" through a "revolving fund" managed by the local community.

The "management of poverty" in rural areas served the same broad objectives: to subdue the peasant movement on behalf of Brazil's powerful land-owning class while ensuring a meager survival to millions of landless peasants uprooted and displaced by large-scale agri-business. In the northeastern Sertâo, for instance, a region affected by recurrent drought, a minimum works program *(frentes de trabalho)* provided employment (at US\$ 14 a month) to some 1.2 million landless farm workers (1993).[30] The latter, however, were often hired by the large landowners at the expense of the federal government. The distribution of US grain surpluses, financed under Public Law 480 (Washington's food aid program-PL 480) to impoverished farmers (through government and relief agencies), also served the related purpose of weakening local-level food agriculture and uprooting the small peasantry. The food distribution programs were adopted in the name of the "Citizens' Campaign against Famine".

The expropriation of peasant lands was an integral part of the IMF-World Bank structural adjustment program. In this context, the National Institute for Colonization and Agrarian Reform (INCRA), among several government agencies, was in charge of "the rural safety net" through token land distribution programs and the development of cooperatives for the "posseiros" (landless farmers). These schemes were invariably established in marginal or semi-arid lands which do not encroach upon the interests of the land-owning class. In the states of Para, Amazonas and Maranhao, several international donors, including the World Bank and the Japanese Aid Agency (JICA), had contributed to financing (through INCRA) so-called "areas of colonization".[31] The latter served largely as "labor reserves" for large-scale plantations. It is also worth mentioning that the proposed constitutional amendments implied the *de facto* derogation of customary land rights of the indigenous people – a process which was already underway with the transformation (under the jurisdiction of INCRA) of the "Indian reserves" in the Amazon into areas of settlement for plantation workers.[32]

Consolidating a Parallel Government

The IMF-sponsored reforms had contributed to social polarization and the impoverishment of all sectors of the population including the middle classes. Moreover, as the federal fiscal structure breaks down, there is the added risk of regional Balkanization: instability within the military, routine violation of fundamental human rights, urban and rural violence, and an increasingly vocal secessionist movement in the south.

Since the presidency of Fernando Collor de Mello, a *de facto* "parallel government" reporting regularly to Washington has developed. Under the presidency of Fernando Henrique Cardoso (1994-2001), the creditors are in control of the state bureaucracy and of its politicians. The state is bankrupt and its assets are being impounded under the privatization program.

Endnotes

1. The Senate provided its approval to the debt restructuring formula in December 1992.

2. Interest payments to international creditors had been limited to 30 percent in a partial moratorium negotiated with the commercial banks in 1989 under the government of Joseph Sarney. Under the restructuring plan, interest payments would increase to 50 percent.

3. Contained in the Letter of Intent to the IMF of December 1991.

4. Quoted in *Jornal do Brasil*, 21 September 1990.

5. See Simon Fisher and Stephen Fidler, "Friction likely as Brazil reopens Debt Talks", *Financial Times*, London, 10 October 1990.

6. Prior to the payment of debt-servicing arrears amounting to some US$ 8 billion.

7. See Christina Lamb, "Brazil Issues Angry Protest at Suspension of Development Loans", *Financial Times*, London, 4 April 1991.

8. See Luiz Carlos Bresser Pereira, "O FMI e as carrocas", *Folha de São Paulo*, 27 July 1991, pp. 1-3.

9. In an interview with the *Jornal do Brasil, quoted in Estado de São Paulo*, 23 June 1991. See also "Missão do FMI adota discurso moderado", *Folha de São Paulo*, 19 June 1991.

10. See *O Globo*, 27 June 1991.

11. See *Folha de São Paulo*, 19 July 1991.

12. The right to strike is also entrenched in the 1988 Constitution.

13. See José Meirelles Passos, "FMI e EUA apoiam programa brasilieira", *O Globo,* 7 December 1991.

14. The Letter of Intent was approved by the IMF in January 1992. See also, "Carta ao FMI preve 'aperto brutal' em 92", *Folha de São Paulo,* 6 December 1991.

15. Quoted in Stephen Fidler and Christina Lamb, "Brazil sets out Accord on 44 billion Debt", *Financial Times*, London, 7 July 1992.

16. Itamar Franco was appointed acting president pending a court decision on the Senate impeachment vote.

17. Pedro Malan (the debt negotiator appointed under Collor) confirmed in March from his Washington office that 802 banks, including Chase Manhattan and Lloyds Bank, had already approved the debt-restructuring formula. Yet, in practice, the veto of the advisory committee on the granting of multilateral loans to Brazil was still in effect. See Fernando Rodrigues, "Bancos aderem ao acordo da divida externa", *Folha de São Paulo*, 16 March 1993.

18. See Claudia Sofatle, "Missão do FMI volta sem acordo", *Gazeta Mercantil*, 17 March 1993.

19. *Financial Times*, 20 August 1993. The US$ 11 billion are the "savings" for the state in relation to a congressional wage-adjustment proposal which provided for a 100 percent cost-of-living adjustment to salaried workers. This proposal, adopted by the Congress in July, was vetoed by the government. Cardoso's wages proposal was meant to constitute a compromise solution. See also *Folha de São Paulo*, 30 July 1993.

20. The latter part of this chapter was written in collaboration with Micheline Ladouceur.

21. The "salary ceiling" is established in the context of Provisional Measure no: 382. *O Globo*, 8 December 1993, pp. 2-11.

22. Initially operating as an accounting unit.

23. Quoted in *Folha de São Paolo*, 3 March 1994, pp. 1-10.

24. Interview with Fernando Henrique Cardoso, who at the time was Finance Minister, Brasilia, August 1993.

25. In accordance with the clauses of provisional measure no: 381; see *O Globo*, 8 December 1993, pp. 2-11.

26. See *Veja*, Rio de Janeiro, December 1993.

27. See Instituto de Pesquisa Econômica Aplicada (IPEA), *O Mapa da Fome II: Informações sobre a Indîgencia por Municipios da Federação*, Brasilia, 1993.

28. Eighty percent of the labor force had earnings below US$ 300 a month in 1991 according to the Brazilian Institute of Geography and Statistics (IBGE).

29. Interviews conducted in Pirambu, Fortaleza, July 1993.

30. Interviews with rural farm workers in the region of Monsenhor Tabosa, Ceara, July 1993.

31. Celia Maria Correa Linhares and Maristela de Paula Andrade, "A Açao Oficial e os Conflitos Agrarios no Maranãho", *Desenvolvimento e Cidadania*, No. 4. São Luis de Maranhão, 1992.

32. See *Panewa*, Porto Velho, Vol. VI, No. 18, November-December 1993 and Vol. VII, No. 19, January 1994.

Chapter 14

IMF Shock Treatment in Peru

The August 8, 1990 "Fujishock", named after President Alberto Fujimori, was announced in a message to the nation by Prime Minister Juan Hurtado Miller: "Our major objectives are to curtail the fiscal deficit and eliminate price distortions": from one day to the next, *the price of fuel increased by 31 times* (2,968 percent) and the *price of bread increased by more than twelve times* (1,150 percent). In the true "spirit of Anglo-Saxon liberalism", these prices were "fixed" through presidential decree rather than by the "free" market (a form of "planned liberalism"). The Fujishock was intended to crush hyperinflation: this was achieved, however, through a 446 percent increase in food prices in a single month ! Inflation during the first year of the Cambio 90 government had "fallen" to a modest 2,172 percent.

Many countries in Latin America had experienced "shock treatment", yet the extent of "economic engineering" in Peru was unprecedented. The social consequences were devastating: whereas an agricultural worker in Peru's northern provinces was (in August 1990) receiving US$ 7.50 a month (the equivalent of the price of a hamburger and a soft drink), consumer prices in Lima were higher than in New York.[1] Real earnings declined by 60 percent in the course of August 1990; by mid-1991 the level of real earnings was less than 15 percent of their 1974 value (a decline of more than 85 percent). The average earnings of government employees had declined by 63 percent during the first year of the Fujimori government and by 92 percent in relation to 1980 (see Table 14.3).[2] On the IMF blacklist since the mid-1980s, Peru had been "rewarded" for President Alan Garcia's (1985-90) rhetorical stance to limit debt-servicing payments to 10 percent of export earnings.

Table 14.1
The Impact of the August 1990 Shock Treatment
on Consumer Prices

Lima Metropolitan Area, August 1990

Percentage Increase	INEI	Cuanto
Food and beverages	446.2	288.2
Transport and communication	571.4	1428.0
Health and medical services	702.7	648.3
Rent, fuel and electricity	421.8	1035.0
Consumer price index	397.0	411.9

Source: Instituto Nacional de Estadistica (INEI), Anuario estadistico, 1991, *Cuanto*, Peru en Numeros, chapter 21, Lima, 1991.

Historical Background

Peru's first macro-economic stabilization program was initiated in the mid-1970s after the 1975 *coup d'état* directed against the populist military government of General Velasco Alvarado. The economic reforms had been carried out by the military junta under General Morales Bermudez, Velasco's successor, as a condition for the rescheduling of Peru's external debt with the commercial banks and the official creditors. These reforms had been directly negotiated with the creditor banks without the involvement of the IMF. In 1978, a second "economic package" was put in motion – this time in the context of a formal agreement with the IMF.

These earlier economic reforms, adopted prior to the formal launching of the structural adjustment program in the early 1980s, had been modeled on those applied in Chile (under General Pinochet and the Chicago Boys in 1973). The conditionality clauses were, on balance, less stringent and coherent in comparison to the policy-based loan agreements under the structural adjustment programs initiated in the early 1980s.

The macro-economic reforms of the mid- to late 1970s, nonetheless, were instrumental in initiating in Peru a historical process of impoverishment: successive currency devaluations unleashed an inflationary spiral and real purchasing power in the modern urban sector declined by approximately 35 percent from 1974 to 1978 (Table 14.3). This compression of real wages (and labor costs) was not conducive, however, to enhancing

Peru's export potential as claimed by the Bretton Woods institutions.

With the accession of President Fernando Belaunde Terry in 1980, macro-economic policy became more cohesive. Those policies firmly supported by the IMF contributed to weakening the state and the system of state enterprises established under the government of General Velasco Alvarado. Generous exploration and exploitation contracts were granted to foreign capital (e.g. in petroleum to Occidental). Reduced tariff barriers also contributed to undermining key sectors of the national economy. The state's participation in the banking sector was curtailed and the influx of foreign capital into commercial banking was encouraged, as was the establishment of subsidiaries of a number of international banks including Chase, Commerzbank, Manufacturer's Hannover and Bank of Tokyo.[3]

This IMF-supported program was implemented by the Belaunde government at the very outset of the debt crisis: a bonanza of imported consumer goods, resulting from the liberalization of trade, coincided (chronologically) with the collapse of export revenues and the decline in the terms of trade (1981-82). The combination of these two factors contributed to exacerbating the balance of payments crisis, resulting in a decline of GDP of the order of 12 percent in 1982 and a rate of inflation of more than 100 percent in 1983.

From 1980 to 1983, the levels of infant malnutrition increased dramatically. In 1985, estimated food consumption had fallen by 25 percent in relation to its 1975 level. In the course of Belaunde's five-year presidential term (1980-85), real earnings at the minimum wage (remuneración minima vital) declined by more than 45 percent. All categories of the labor force were affected: the average decline of real earnings for blue- and white-collar workers was respectively of 39.5 and 20.0 percent. (See Table 14.3.)

In the 10-year period, from the end of the Velasco government (1975) to the end of Belaunde's term of office (1985), the minimum wage had declined (according to official data) by 58.2 percent, the average wage by 55.0 percent (blue collar workers) and the average earnings of middle-income white-collar workers by 51.7 percent.

Table 14.2

The Impact of the August 1990 Shock Treatment
on Consumer Prices

Lima Metropolitan Area, August 1990
(Intis)

Commodity	Before 3 August 1990	After 9 August 1990	Percentage Increase
Kerosene (gal.)	19	608	3100
Gasoline (84oct)(gal.)	22	675	2968
Propane gas (924 lbs.)	41	1120	2632
Bread (36 gr/unit)	2	25	1150
Beans (kg.)	240	2800	1067
White Potatoes (kg.)	40	300	650
Flour (kg.)	220	1500	531
Milk (litre)	60	290	383
Spaghetti (kg.)	180	775	331
Vegetable oil (litre)	220	850	286
Rice (grade A)(kg.)	94	310	230
Powdered Milk (410 gr.)	100	330	230
Egg (kg.)	170	540	218
Chicken (kg.)	213	600	182

Source: *Cuanto*, vol. 2, No. 19, August 1990, p.5.

The APRA's Non-Orthodox Economic Policy (1985-87)

The Acción Popular government of President Fernando Belaunde Terry had been discredited. In the 1985 election campaign, the opposition American Popular Revolutionary Alliance (APRA) (a populist party founded in the 1920s) had presented an "alternative economic program". In overt confrontation with the Bretton Woods institutions, the newly-elected APRA government of President Alan Garcia put forth its so-called "Economic Emergency Plan" *(Plan Economico de Emergencia)* in July 1985. This program went directly against the IMF's usual economic prescriptions.

At the outset of Alan Garcia's presidency, the annual rate of inflation was in excess of 225 percent. The government's program consisted of reactivating consumer demand. A price freeze on essential consumer goods and public services was implemented. Interest rates were brought down and the

Table 14.3
Index of Real Wages (1974-1991)
(1974=100)*

Year	Minimum Legal Income	White- Collar Private Sector	Blue- Collar Private Sector	Wages in Govt Sector
1974	100.0	100.0	100.0	
1975	93.1	100.6	88.3	
1976	85.6	83.3	95.1	
1977	75.3	72.4	79.2	
1978	58.4	62.2	71.3	
1979	63.6	56.9	70.9	
1980	79.9	61.1	75.0	
1981	67.9	62.1	73.5	100.0
1982	62.2	67.0	74.4	91.7
1983	64.4	57.4	61.6	66.3
1984	49.7	59.6	52.5	58.2
1985	43.5	48.8	45.4	46.4
1986	45.1	61.0	60.8	48.4
1987	49.0	63.9	65.6	59.2
1988	41.5	44.2	41.3	53.5
1989	25.1	36.3	37.6	35.3
1990	21.4	18.7	20.1	18.8
July	20.9	13.8	16.2	21.1
August		7.5	8.3	8.9
September	19.4	11.1	12.9	8.6
December[1]	13.8	14.6	16.3	6.1
1991				
April	15.3	15.7	19.4	8.6
May	14.1			7.8

Source: Estimated from official data of INEI, *Anuario estadistico*, 1991.
Cuanto, *Peru en Numéros*, 1991, ch.21 and *Cuanto suplemento*, No.13, July 1991.
*: The base year of the index for Government Sector Wages is 1981.
[1]/Includes *gratificación*.
The private sector categories include white-collar and blue-collar earnings in private sector employment in the Lima Metropolitan Area.
Since 1963, the Minimum Legal Income was equal to the reference unit *(unidad de referencia)*. From June 1984 to August 1990 it was equivalent to the reference unit plus additional bonus payments. From August 1990, the government abolished the Minimum Legal Income *(Ingreso Minimo Legal)* and replaced it by the so-called *Remuneración Minima Vital*. (The category General Government includes earnings in the central and regional governments and decentralised public institutions.)

exchange rate was "stabilized". The economy had been stagnating under the Belaunde government and operating with a considerable amount of excess capacity. It was, therefore, possible for the APRA government to reactivate economic activity "on the demand-side" without creating undue inflationary pressures on production costs.[4]

President Alan Garcia had committed himself during the election campaign to paying higher producer prices to farmers with a view to reactivating production and bringing about a redistribution of income in favor of the rural areas. During the first year of operation of the economic package, there was (according to World Bank estimates) an improvement of 75 percent of the rural-urban terms of trade and a significant short-term growth of agricultural production.[5]

In the urban economy, the authorities decreed increases in wages and salaries somewhat in excess of inflation. A temporary employment program was established, an expansionary fiscal policy was adopted and credit was characterized by negative real interest rates. Various tax incentives and subsidies were devised in support of this reactivation of aggregate demand. These exemptions, however, largely benefited the national economic and financial élites. The state's tax base, as well as its international foreign exchange reserve position were consequently weakened.

The APRA's Debt-Negotiating Strategy

Upon assuming office, President Garcia declared a moratorium on the payment of debt-servicing obligations. The latter were not to exceed ten percent of export earnings. Peru was immediately put on the blacklist by the international financial community. The inflow of fresh money was frozen; the international commercial banks cut off their support to Peru in 1985. By 1986 no new commercial loans were granted. Official agencies and OECD governments also substantially curtailed their levels of disbursements to Peru.[6]

Despite the moratorium, the Peruvian external debt increased dramatically – on average by 9 percent per annum during the APRA government.[7] In terms of net flows of capital, President Garcia's rhetorical stance on debt-servicing did not serve its purpose: actual debt-servicing payments were on average of the order of 20 percent of export earnings during the 1985-89 period. With the freeze on new loans, not to mention capital flight to offshore bank accounts, the 1985-89 period was marked by a massive outflow of real resources.[8]

The Economic Program Enters a Deadlock

During the first 18 months of the APRA government, there was significant growth of GDP. Inflation was brought down largely as a result of the system of "price freezes", the dollarization process of the national economy was reduced and levels of consumption increased markedly.

But the program could not be sustained beyond the short run. Whereas economic growth had been supported by an expansionary fiscal policy, the tax base remained extremely fragile. Indirect taxes had been reduced, there was massive tax evasion and the various subsidies and exemptions to large corporations were "funded" through deficit financing and an expansion of the money supply. The system was prone to corruption and speculation. The structure of multiple exchange rates *(mercado unico de cambios)*, theoretically intended as an instrument of income redistribution, ultimately benefited the wealthiest segment of Peruvian society.[9]

In 1988, the level of foreign-exchange reserves plummeted to minus US$ 252 million.[10] While levels of purchasing power had expanded, a large portion of the country's foreign-exchange earnings had been appropriated by the economic élites in the form of subsidies and tax exemptions. The state had implemented a standard Keynesian "counter-cyclical" policy in support of aggregate demand without tackling more fundamental structural issues. While these measures exhibited some minimal level of technical coherence under conditions of extreme stagnation and underutilization of industrial capacity, they were unable to sustain the economic recovery beyond the short term.

In practice, the APRA government had supported vested economic interests through the manipulation of its various regulatory policy instruments. The economic model had been defined in narrow technical terms supported by populist rhetoric: the APRA did not have the required social basis, nor the political will, let alone the grass-roots support to implement substantive and sustainable economic and social reforms in such areas as tax reform, regionalization, reactivation of agriculture and support to small-scale productive units of the informal economy.

Beyond its populist rhetoric, the APRA government was unwilling to take actions which encroached directly upon the vested interests of the economic elites. In 1987, the proposed nationalization of the banking sector (which did not even concur with a politically defined mandate), announced rhetorically with a view to "democratizing credit", was easily circumvented by the commercial banks and financial institutions in a drawn-out legal battle which led ultimately to the abandonment of the nationalization project. The intent marked the end of the APRA's "populist honeymoon" with the financial élites. It created divisions within the APRA, discredited the government and generated an aura of economic uncertainty and mistrust on the part of the business sector which, according to some observers, unleashed the hyperinflationary process of 1988-90. The economic élites had "declared war on the government".

Similarly, in tackling the issue of ownership rights, in 1990 the APRA government presented the issue demagogically at the level of formal "registration" *(registro predial)* of ownership rights which would enable, for instance, units of the rural economy *(parceleros)* and informal economy to accede to formal ownership. The question of concentration of ownership of real assets and wealth-formation by the privileged classes was carefully avoided.

De Facto "Shock Treatment" (1988-90)

The growth in real purchasing power achieved in 1985 and 1986 was short-lived. Economic activity started to slow down by the beginning of 1987. Expansion was replaced by contraction: the movement of real earnings was reversed in a matter of months. Between December 1987 and October 1988, real earnings plummeted by 50 to 60 percent, the wages of public employees declined by two-thirds.[11] By mid-1988, real wages were 20 percent below their 1985 level.

In July 1988, the government initiated a new emergency plan and in September a more "orthodox" anti-inflationary program was introduced. The September 1988 package contained most of the essential ingredients of the standard IMF program without the neoliberal ideology and the support of international creditors.

In many respects, the September 1988 package set the pace for the economic shock measures to be adopted by the Fujimori government in August 1990. The economic package included all the essential elements: devaluation and unification of the exchange rate, the enactment of price increases of public services and gasoline, substantial cuts in government expenditure and the introduction of cost recovery for most public enterprises. The package also implied the deindexation of wages and salaries.

Failure of the APRA's Non-orthodox Economic Package

The failure of the non-orthodox economic package under President Alan Garcia does not vindicate the neoliberal framework. The economic program was politically ambivalent from the outset. The APRA failed to take a stance with regard to the regulation of profit margins and the setting of prices by powerful commercial and agro industrial interests. Keynesian instruments were adopted mechanically without addressing fundamental structural issues. To succeed, the program required a positive influx of foreign exchange. Exactly the opposite occurred: the net outflow of resources continued unabated. The international creditors maintained their grip on Peru's balance of payments.

The Restoration of IMF Rule

During the 1990 election campaign, Alberto Fujimori had confronted his opponent author Mario Vargas Llosa of the Democratic Front Coalition (Fredemo). Vargas Llosa had proposed "economic shock treatment" as a solution to Peru's economic crisis. Fujimori's party, Cambio 90, had rejected the neoliberal recipe promising an economic program which would lead to "stabilization without recession" combining a solution to hyperinflation while protecting workers' purchasing power.[12]

An expansionary economic policy had been envisaged by Fujimori in the months preceding his inauguration as president on the 28 July 1990. This program, however, had been defined in narrow technical terms (debated within a closed circle of professional and academic economists) without focusing on the political process required to carry it out. The program had been defined as a technical "solution" to the economic crisis in isolation from the broader political debate and without the participation of representative organizations of civil society in its formulation.

On the plane to Washington to meet IMF Managing Director Michel Camdessus, the president-elect is reported to have stated thoughtfully to his principal economic advisor: "If the economic shock were to work, the Peruvian people would no doubt forgive me." Strong internal and external political pressures were being exercized on the president-elect to abandon the "alternative program" in favor of an orthodox IMF-sponsored package. Upon his return from Washington and Tokyo, from his meetings with Peru's international creditors, the president-elect had become an unbending supporter of "strong economic medicine". Yet this shift in policy direction was known only within his immediate political entourage: nothing was revealed to the Peruvian people who had voted against Fredemo's "economic shock treatment".

Divisions developed within the economic advisory team and the president-elect developed close links with another group of economists firmly committed to the "Washington Consensus" and the IMF package. His main economic advisors resigned shortly before his accession to the presidency, and a new economic stabilization package – not markedly different from that proposed by Mario Vargas Llosa during the election campaign – was put together in a hurry with the technical support of the IMF and the World Bank.

The August 1990 IMF-Fujishock

The August 1990 shock treatment not only conformed to IMF prescriptions, it went far beyond what was normally expected of an indebted country as a condition for the renegotiation of its external debt. Despite the high levels of critical poverty prevailing in the last months of the APRA government, a further "adjustment" in real earnings was considered necessary to "alleviate inflationary pressures". Peru's hyperinflation was said to be caused by "demand factors", requiring a further compression in wages and social expenditures, together with massive lay-offs of public-sector workers.

The spread of the cholera epidemic in 1991 – while largely attributable to poverty and the breakdown of the country's public health infrastructure since the Belaunde government – was also a result of the IMF-sponsored program. With a thirty-fold increase in the price of cooking oil, people in Lima's *"pueblos jovenes"*, including the "middle classes", were no longer able to afford to boil their water or cook their food.

The international publicity surrounding the outbreak of the cholera epidemic (approximately 200,000 declared cases and 2,000 registered deaths in a six-month period) overshadowed in the international press a more general process of social destruction: since the August 1990 Fujishock, tuberculosis had also reached epidemic proportions heightened by malnutrition and the breakdown of the government's vaccination program. The collapse of the public-health infrastructure in the Selva region had led to a resurgence of malaria, dengue and leishmaniasis.[13] Public schools, universities and hospitals had been closed down as a result of an indefinite strike by teachers and health workers (their wages were an average US$ 45-70 a month [July 1991] – 40 times lower than in the US).

More than 83 percent of the population (mid-1991 estimate) (includ-

Table 14.4
Undernourishment, Malnutrition and Infant Mortality

1.Undernourishment (deficient calorie and protein intake according to WHO/FAO standards)

at national level (1991)   in excess of 83 % of population*

2. Infant malnutrition (1985-86)

at national level	38.5 %
rural areas	57.6 %
urban areas	24.2 %

3. Infant mortality less than one year (per thousand) (1985-86)

Lima	61.4 o/oo
Sierra***	130-134 o/oo

4. Child Mortality less than five (1985-86)**

Lima	16.5 %
Sierra***	26.5 %

5. Life expectancy at birth (years) (1985-86)

Lima	67.7
Sierra	47.6-49.0

Source: Ministry of Health and ENNIV.
   *author's estimate based on household expenditure data.
  **percentage of children who die before age five estimated
   from mortality rates by specific age groups (Ministry of Health).
***based on rates recorded in Huancavelica and Cusco.

ing the middle class) did not meet minimum calorie and protein requirements. The recorded rate of child malnutrition at the national level was of the order of 38.5 percent (the second highest in Latin America). One child in four in the Sierra died before the age of five. One child in six in Lima died before age five. The recorded total fertility rate was of the order of 4.8 (four live births per mother) which suggests that for the Sierra there was, on average, an incidence of at least one child death per family unit. (See Table 14.4.) Yet the international financial community for his successful economic policies had commended Fujimori.

The IMF-World Bank Tutelage

"Get a serious economic program in place and we will help you". The implementation of what the IMF calls a "serious economic program" (in the words of Mr. Martin Hardy, head of the IMF mission which visited Peru in 1991) is usually a precondition for the granting of bridge-financing by an "international support group". There were no "promises" by the international financial institutions attached to the implementation of the August 1990 economic package. The latter was an "IMF Shadow Program" with no loan money attached to it. (See chapter 3.) While there were no undue pressures from the IMF, it was made clear that Peru would remain on the "black list" as long as it did not conform to IMF economic prescriptions.

The economic package, however, was implemented by the Fujimori government prior to the signing of a loan agreement and "before" reaching an agreement on the rescheduling of Peru's external debt. Once the first set of measures had been adopted, there was little left to negotiate. Moreover, immediately after the August 1990 "economic stabilization" phase, the Peruvian authorities initiated a number of major structural reforms ("phase two") in conformity with IMF-World Bank prescriptions.

The Fujimori government had expected that the "economic shock" of August 1990 would immediately lead the way to the formation of an International Support Group and the granting of a "rescue package". There was, however, reluctance on the part of the creditors to form a support group. Peru was faithfully paying all its current debt-servicing obligations and macro-economic policy was in conformity with the IMF menu.[14] From the point of view of the international creditors, there was, therefore, no need to grant "favors" to Peru (as in the cases of Egypt or Poland).

It was, of course, difficult for the government to adopt an independent stance, – i.e. "negotiate with the IMF" when IMF and World Bank officials were sitting in the Ministry of Economics and Finance. These advisors to the government were directly on IMF and World Bank payrolls "on loan" to Peru.[15] One of the senior advisors to Minister of Economics and Finance Carlos Boloña was an IMF staff member directly on the IMF payroll.

The Granting of Fictitious Money

At the outset, the government's main objective was to be removed from the IMF blacklist by unconditionally accepting to reimburse Peru's debt arrears to the International Financial Institutions (IFIs). This objective was to be achieved through the negotiation of "new loans" from the IFIs earmarked "to pay back old debts".[16] (For further details see Chapter 3.) Not one dollar of this money would actually enter Peru. These new loans were money which the IFIs were "giving to themselves"; they uncondi tionally legitimized the external debt (without a write-down), and obliged Peru to start servicing its debt arrears immediately. The loans from the IFIs granted in 1991 would have to be repaid over a period of three to five years. As a direct result of these new loans, Peru's debt-servicing obliga- tions more than doubled in 1991 (from US$ 60 million a month to over $ 150 million).

The Role of the Military

Peru conformed faithfully to Washington's model of "democratization". Prior to his inauguration in July 1990, Fujimori retreated in the armed forces compound in Lima for daily discussions with the military high command. A deal was struck between the president-elect, the military and a major reorganization of the armed forces was carried out. This uncondi- tional support of the armed forces was required to repress civil dissent and enforce the IMF program. A few days before the Fujishock, a state of emer- gency was declared in the whole country. On 8 August 1990, the military and security forces had carefully cornered the entire Lima downtown area with troops, anti-riot forces and armored vehicles.

Under the veil of "parliamentary democracy", the military, under Fujimori, increasingly took on a more active role in "civilian" administra- tion. The situation at the outset of the Fujimori government was, in some regards, comparable to that which had developed in the early 1970s in Uruguay under President Bordaberry where the military ruled under the formal disguise of a civilian government.

The Collapse of the State

The IMF austerity measures were conducive to the phasing out of government programs: the reduction of health and educational expenditures, and the collapse of civil administration in the regions, etc. This state of affairs also contributed to discrediting the central government to the benefit of the Shining Path insurgents *(Sendero luminoso)* directed against the state.

From its involvement in civilian politics during the 1960s and 1970s, Sendero had developed as a clandestine organization during the Belaunde government. Sendero was able to control and establish a parallel administration in some regions of the Selva and Sierra. In certain parts of the country, the Peruvian state had lost control over normal functions of civilian government. The application of the IMF's economic surgery in 1990-91 contributed to exacerbating this situation.

The state was losing control over the national territory, and this applied not only to areas of the Sierra and the Selva. Increasingly the insurgency by Sendero had permeated the Lima Metropolitan Area. The "pacification program", initiated during the Belaunde government (and continued during the APRA and Cambio 90 governments), implied the handing over of the functions of civilian administration in the southern-central Sierra to the armed forces. Instead of curtailing Sendero, however, this strategy – combined with the failures of economic and social policy – contributed to the advancement of the insurgency. Moreover, the state, through its military and police apparatus, had officially sanctioned indiscriminate arrests, arbitrary and extra-judicial executions and torture of political prisoners, and the arrest of family members and presumed "sympathizers" (amply documented by Amnesty International). State counter-insurgency was marked by the curtailment of civil liberties, particularly among the poorer segments of society.[17] In 1988, right-wing death squadrons appeared under the name "Comando Rodrigo Franco"; their targets were left-wing personalities and trade-union leaders.

Under Fujimori, repression of the Shining Path insurgency became a pretext for systematic harassment by the security forces of civilian opposition to the IMF program. From the outset of the Cambio 90 government, the indiscriminate torture and execution of "suspects" were applied far more systematically. The strategy of assassination and intimidation of civilian opposition directed against trade union, peasant and student leaders emanated directly from the military high command. In the so-called "dirty war" *(la guerra sucia)* with the Shining Path, the official guideline (with regard to the treatment of suspects) was "Neither prisoners nor wounded" *(ni prisoneros, ni heridos)* (as contained in a secret military document leaked to the press in 1991).[18]

The Plight of the Rural Economy

The IMF program had an immediate impact on the rural economy: with the exception of the illegal coca cultivation, there was a major contraction in agricultural production in the year which followed the August 1990 shock treatment.

The impoverishment of the rural population was worsened by the continued control of marketing and distribution channels by powerful agro-industrial monopolies. Domestic producers were displaced as a result of the import of cheap agricultural staples. The 1990 economic measures were conducive to immediate and abrupt hikes in the prices of fuel, farm inputs, fertilizers and agricultural credit: in many rural areas in the Sierra, costs of production increased well in excess of the farmgate price. The result was the bankruptcy of the small independent farmer. In the Sierra, for instance, some 800,000 producers of wool and alpaca fibers, who are among the poorest segment of the rural population, were further impoverished as a result of the decline of the real price of wool and alpaca fibers in 1990-91.

The Concentration of Land

The privatization of agricultural land was conducive to undermining the existing structure of the rural economy characterized by small-scale individual production *(parcelero)* and agricultural communities *(comunidades agricolas)*. The 1991 Land Law required a minimum unit of ownership of ten hectares. Land concentration was thus encouraged, leading to the strengthening of medium-sized holdings and the consolidation of a middle peasantry. *Parceleros pushed* into bankruptcy as a result of the economic reforms were obliged to sell or give up their land.[19] This initial process of land concentration was, however, but a first step towards the restructuring of agricultural ownership. Agricultural credit was also reformed. Production units below ten hectares were no longer eligible for agricultural credit.

In turn, the middle peasantry became firmly subordinated to banking and commercial interests through the mortgaging of their newly acquired land titles. The legislation introduced in 1991 was conducive to land forfeiture by the *parcelero* and the purchase of large amounts of land by urban commercial interests.

Whereas the peasant communities of the Sierra were formally "protected" from the privatization of land, the increased prices of fuel and transportation contributed to cutting them out of the market economy. Farmgate prices had been pushed below costs. Many peasant communities which had previously sold their agricultural surplus in local markets were forced to withdraw totally from commercial agriculture.

There was a de facto return to subsistence agriculture. Commercial farm inputs such as seeds, fertilizer, etc. were no longer applied; the tendency was towards the consolidation of "traditional agriculture" marked by a dramatic decline in the levels of productivity of both the *parceleros* and the peasant communities. The countryside became increasingly polarized. The peasant communities impoverished as a result of structural adjustment could no longer survive without outside sources of income. Increasingly the peasant communities became "reserves of labor" for commercial agriculture.

The Illegal Narco-economy

The August 1990 economic shock created the conditions for the further growth of the drug trade. The contraction of internal demand for food, coupled with the lifting of tariffs on imported food staples, contributed to a serious recession in agricultural production. Combined with the subsequent repeal of the Agrarian Reform, impoverished peasants from the Sierra migrated to the coca producing areas in the Alto Huallaga Valley. In the Sierra, coca-cultivation as a cash crop for export started to develop on a significant scale.

Peru is by far the largest world producer of coca leaf used to produce cocaine (more than 60 percent of total world production, the second most important producer being Bolivia). (See Chapter 14) Both Peru and Bolivia are the direct producers, selling coca paste to the Colombian drug cartels which process it into cocaine powder. With the clamping down of the Medellin cartel, however, there was in the early 1990s a shift in the marketing and processing channels and the development within Peru of commercial intermediaries and an increased use of the Peruvian banking system as a safe financial haven for transferring funds in and out of the country. The weakening of the Medellin cartel and the development of the Cali cartel initially favored a greater "autonomy" of both Peru and Bolivia in the drug trade.

Moreover, a large amount of dollar bills from the drug economy had been channeled into the informal foreign-exchange market on Lima street corners *(el mercado Ocoña)*. Since the Belaunde government (1980-85), the Central Bank had used the Ocoña street market periodically to replenish its failing international reserves. Peru's ability to meet its debt-servicing obligations depends on the recycling of narco-dollars into the local foreign-exchange market. In 1991, it was estimated that the Central Bank purchased some 8 million dollars a day in the informal foreign-exchange market of which a large part was earmarked to service Peru's external debt.

With the freeze of wages and government expenditure (imposed by the IMF), monetary issues by the Central Bank had been dramatically curtailed. Ironically, this tight monetary policy – combined with the inundation of the Ocoña market with dollar bills brought into the country with the illegal cocaine trade – had been conducive, as of early 1991, to the tumble of the American dollar against the Peruvian currency much to the dismay of the IMF which had insisted on a "real devaluation" in support of the export sector.

Internal demand had been compressed but so had exports. As a result of the economic measures, all sectors of the national economy – with the exception of the illegal coca production – were marked by deep recession.

The Anti-Drug Agreement with Washington

"Coca eradication programs" by Washington had invariably been combined with counterinsurgency and "pacification" programs, with strong military and intelligence backing to the Peruvian military and the police from the United States military and the US Drug Enforcement Administration (DEA). The latter had established a military base in Santa Lucia in the Huallaga region.[20]

Rather than weakening Sendero in the Alto Huallaga, however, these military operations enabled Shining Path to gain some element of support among coca producers. It is worth noting that under Fujimori, the military had become increasingly involved in the marketing of coca paste and the laundering of drug money.

The Anti-Drug Agreement signed in May 1991 with the US had a direct bearing on macro-economic policy. In the words of a witness to the US Senate committee:

The President's [George Bush] national drug control strategy . . . says that [US] economic aid is conditioned on drug control performance and the existence of sound economic policies.[21]

Yet, ironically, these same "sound economic policies" had largely contributed to the rapid development of the narco-economy. The economic reforms had encouraged the migration of impoverished peasants to the coca-producing areas.

Moreover, the macro-economic policies adopted under Fujimori, including the privatization of agricultural land and the reform of the system of agricultural credit, had virtually destroyed from the outset the possibility of "an alternative development" in the Alto Huallaga valley as envisaged in the Anti-Drug Agreement. The latter was based on the substitution of coca by alternative cash crops (tobacco, maize, etc.). Yet as a result of the IMF-sponsored reforms (which were also included as "cross-conditionalities" in the Anti-Drug Agreement), commercial agriculture in the Huallaga region – with the exception of the illegal coca production – was no longer viable.

The illicit narcotics trade had been reinforced as a result of the structural adjustment program. The legal economy had been undermined: the process of crop substitution was from the "alternative crops" (e.g. tobacco, maize, etc.) into coca marked by a steady increase in the acreage allocated to the cultivation of coca leaf.[22] (See Table 14.5.)

US Military and Security Objectives

A large part of US support under the agreement had been granted in the

Table 14.5 Coca Production in the Alto Huallaga Region (1974-91)			
Year	Area (hectares)	Production in metric tons	Population
1974	16,700	12,200	7,000
1978	21,540	18,120	9,900
1982	50,600	47,000	23,500
1986	60,200	61,000	27,350
1991	90,000	84,750	50,000

Source: Cooperativa "Alto Huallaga", Uchiza, *Agronoticias*, No. 138, June 1991, p.14.

form of military aid. Debt conditionalities were also being used by the US to pursue military and security objectives in the Andean region under the formal umbrella of the Anti-Drug Program. The latter had also strengthened the Peruvian military in the Alto Huallaga and consequently its ability to "protect" the narco-economy.

It is worth mentioning in this regard that there is ample evidence that the United States Central Intelligence Agency (CIA) has used laundered drug money to fund its covert operations and support pro-US military and paramilitary groups throughout the world.[23]

If Washington had really been interested in a solution to the drug trade, it would not have obliged Peru to adopt an economic policy under IMF guidance which strengthened the position of the narco-traders in alliance with the military.

Whereas one arm of the American state was involved in bona fide drug eradication programs, another arm was doing exactly the opposite. The laundering of "dirty money" was also being reinforced by the IMF-sponsored reforms of the banking system and the foreign-exchange regime, allowing for the "free" movement of money in and out of the country. This strengthening of the narco-economy, however, also served the interests of Peru's international creditors because it contributed to generating the dollar revenues required for Peru to meet its debt-servicing obligations.

Macro-economic reform undermined the legal economy, reinforced illicit trade and contributed to the recycling of "dirty money" towards Peru's official and commercial creditors.

Endnotes

1. *Cuanto*, Lima, September 1990.

2. These estimates are based on official statistics; *see Peru en Numeros, 1991, Annuario estadistico,* chapter 21, Cuanto, Lima, 1991, *and Cuanto Suplemento,* No. 13, July 1991.

3. Carlos Malpica, *El poder economico en el Peru,* Vol. I, Mosca Azul Editores, Lima, 1989.

4. The expansion of farm output was achieved through the expansion of aggregate demand and necessary consumption *(consumo popular)* rather than through the readjustment of the preferential exchange rate applying to the imports of basic food staples and the elimination of the subsidies (which essentially supported the agro-industrial monopolies). This indicated that the development of agriculture required the maintenance of urban consumer

demand.

5. See World Bank, *Peru, Policies to Stop Hyperinflation and Initiate Economic Recovery*, Washington, 1989, p. 10.

6. See Drago Kisic and Veronica Ruiz de Castilla, *La Economia peruana en el contexto internacional*, CEPEI, Vol. 2, No. 1, January 1989, pp. 58-59.

7. *Peru Economico*, August 1990, p. 26.

8. Another important factor was the decision of the Aprista government to revoke the convertibility of the foreign-exchange deposit certificates. This measure was adopted without assessing the nature of the foreign-exchange market and its relationship to the narco-economy.

9. The abuses pertaining to the (subsidized) "dollar MUC" have been amply documented: requests for MUC dollar allotments for the purpose of importing commodities were submitted to the Central Bank, the imports were not undertaken (or receipts were falsified indicating a transaction for a larger amount and the money was then converted into bona fide foreign exchange or back into local currency at a considerable profit). See for instance "Quien volo con los MUC", Oiga, No. 468, Lima, 5 February 1990, pp. 18-19.

10. See Kisic and Ruiz, *op. cit*, p. 60.

11. See Fernando Rospigliosi, "Izquierdas y clases populares: democracia y subversion en el Peru", in Julio Cotler (editor), *Clases populares, crisis y democracia en America Latina,* Instituto de Estudios Peruanos, Lima, 1989, p. 127.

12. See "Plan de Gobierno de Cambio 90: una propuesta para el Peru", *Pagina Libre,* 21 May 1990, pp. 17-24.

13. Based on author's interviews of health workers conducted in Peru in July 1991.

14. For further details see "Peru, Situación economica", *Situación latinoamericana,* Vol. 1, No. 2, April 1991, pp. 122-128.

15. Their daily consulting incomes of US$ 500-700 a day (including a "daily subsistence allowance" of some US$ 130 a day) was only slightly less than Peru's annual per capita income.

16. The IMF loans were to be granted in the form of "an accumulation of rights" clause. Debt arrears were estimated (1991) at approximately US$ 14 billion of which US$ 2.3 billion were with the IFIs.

17. A report by Amnesty International confirmed that approximately 3,000 people had "disappeared" *(desaparecidos)* between 1982 and 1989 and another 3,000 had been executed "extrajudicially". Amnesty also pointed to the practice of illegal detention and torture by the security forces and the absence of sanctions directed against members of the security forces involved in assassinations and torture. Pagina Libre, 17 March 1990, p. A2. Cf. also *La Republica,* 11 February, 1990, p. 14.

18. See the secret documents revealed by the journalist Cesar Hildebrandt in the

TV series *En Persona,* July 1991, which led to the closing down of the program and the curtailment of most public-affairs TV programs.

19. See *Alerta Agraria,* June 1991, p. 2.

20. Several other US institutions operated out of the Santa Lucia military Base: the NAS (an affiliate of the DEA) and CORAH (a US project geared towards coca-crop eradication).

21. United States Senate, Committee on Governmental Affairs, *Cocaine Production, Eradication and the Environment: Policy, Impact and Options,* Washington, August 1990, p. 51 (italics added).

22. In the San Martin region (in the coca-producing region), areas under cultivation in "alternative crops" such as maize, rice and cocoa supported by credits from the Banco Agrario declined by 97% between 1988/89 to 1990/91, from 101,100 to 6,730 hectares. For further details see *Revista Agronoticias,* No. 138, Lima, June 1991, p. 7.

23. For a review of alleged CIA support to drug laundering in Indochina and the Golden Triangle since the early 1950s see Alfred McCoy, *The Politics of Heroin in Southeast Asia.* 1991.

Chapter 15

Debt and the Illegal Drug Economy:
The Case of Bolivia

The Bolivian experience is regarded by the Bretton Woods institutions as a "successful" model of structural adjustment to be emulated by countries "who want to stabilize their economy and establish a sustained process of economic growth". It is also worth noting the similarity between the Bolivian and Peruvian adjustment processes. Both economies depend heavily on illegal coca exports as their major source of foreign exchange. In both countries the "recycling" of narco-dollars constitutes a means for servicing the external debt.

Bolivia's New Economic Policy

In September 1985, the MNR government of Victor Paz Estenssoro initiated an orthodox economic stabilization package *("Decreto Supremo 21,060")* geared towards "combating inflation" and "eliminating internal and external imbalances". The economic package contained all the essential ingredients of the IMF structural adjustment program. The currency was devalued, the exchange rate was unified and a foreign-exchange auction *(bolsin)* was set up.

Government expenditure was curtailed and some 50,000 public employees were laid off. A tight monetary policy was adopted together with the elimination of price controls. The deindexation of wages and the "liberalization" of the labor market were adopted. The package also included the liberalization of trade involving substantial reductions in import tariffs.[1]

The stabilization program was followed by a reorganization of the state mining industry, the closing down of unprofitable mines and the firing of some 23,000 workers.

The architect of the Bolivian economic adjustment package, Gonzalo Sanchez de Losada (who became President of Bolivia in 1993), described the events which followed the adoption of the New Economic Policy or Nueva Politica Economica (NPE) in August 1985 as follows:

> Once we implemented the measures, we had a general strike, the country was paralyzed for ten days in September 1985 (. . .) On the tenth day, the union leaders declared a Hunger Strike, that was their big mistake. It was then that we decided to declare a state of emergency. [President] Paz had hoped that the people would be of the opinion that the situation could not continue that way. So we captured the union leaders and deported them to the interior of the country. This disarticulated the labor movement. We closed down COMIBOL, the state mining consortium and fired 24,000 workers in addition to some 50,000 public employees fired at a national level. We eliminated job security.[2]

The policy was, nonetheless, "successful" in bringing inflation under control within a matter of months. Prior to the adoption of the September 1985 measures, the rate of inflation was running at approximately 24,000 percent per annum. The objective of price stabilization, however, was achieved through the "dollarization" of prices (rather than as a result of the economic stabilization measures): "since most prices were de facto indexed to the exchange rate, stabilization of the latter implied an almost immediate stabilization of the former".[3]

A debt-reduction scheme was negotiated. Under this scheme, official donors would finance the "buy back" of Bolivia's commercial debt at a substantial discount from the commercial banks. The debt buy-back was conditional upon the adoption of the IMF program.

Economic and Social Impact

The stabilization package was conducive to a significant decline in the levels of employment and real earnings. In turn, the contraction of salaried earnings backfired on the informal urban sector and the rural economy. Reduced levels of purchasing power, combined with the impact of trade liberalization (and the influx of cheap food imports), contributed to undermining the peasant economy which relied heavily on the internal market. Similarly, the lifting of tariffs contributed to the displacement of the national manufacturing industry. Commercial imports flourished largely at the expense of domestic production.

The levels of earnings and government expenditure had already declined dramatically in the first part of the 1980s during the Siles-Zuazo government. Yet in the immediate aftermath of the 1985 economic reforms, real government expenditure (particularly in the areas of health and education) was trimmed by a further 15 percent.[4] While wages in the modern sector had declined (according to official data) by only 20 percent, the number of people employed had fallen to abysmally low levels. With the reduction in modern-sector employment, largely through dismissals, the collapse in earnings was substantially higher than 20 percent.

Programmed Economic Stagnation

The IMF program initiated in 1985 contributed to the stagnation of all major sectors of the national economy (mining, industry and agriculture) with the exception of the illegal coca economy and the urban services sector. This pattern is comparable to that observed in Peru under Fujimori. (See Chapter 14)

Stagnation in the mining industry (made up largely of the state mining consortium COMIBOL and a small sector of privately operated mines) resulted from the closing down of "unprofitable mines" (and the firing of workers) and the collapse of the international tin market. The decline in the terms of trade further exacerbated the impact of the economic reforms.

Severance payments to redundant miners were invested in the acquisition of land in the coca-producing areas by workers who had been laid off to the extent that both capital and labor were redirected towards the coca economy. The NPE provided no other alternative source of employment for workers laid off by COMIBOL.

The manufacturing sector (mainly geared towards the internal market) was in part displaced (e.g. textiles and agro-industry) as a result of the liberalization of imports. The decline in internal purchasing power and the surge of smuggling activities also played an important role in pushing small-scale manufacturing enterprises into bankruptcy.

The Impact on the Rural Economy

Bolivia's agriculture consists of three distinct sub-sectors:

a) the peasant economy *(economia campesina)* characterized by small-scale agriculture *(parceleros)* and peasant communities *(comunidades campesinas)* concentrated in the Andean valleys and the Altiplano *(high-plateaux)*. The peasant economy is the product of the Agrarian Reform of the 1950s and the dismantling of the landed estates *(haciendas)*. As in Peru, the highlands' peasant communities are characterized by a high incidence of critical poverty (97 percent of the rural population is classified as "poor" and between 48 and 77 percent as "critically poor" *(pobreza critica)*.[5]

b)   a sub-sector of commercial farming geared largely towards the export market and characterized by medium to large-sized plantations, particularly in the new (lowland) areas of agricultural colonization *(llanos orientales)* (e.g. in the area of Santa Cruz).

c)   the production of coca both for processing into coca paste and export as well as for "traditional" sale in the domestic market.

The NPE contributed to undermining the peasant economy. Local grain markets were affected by the influx of cheap food imports (e.g. wheat), including food aid and smuggling from Argentina and Brazil. This influx depressed the real prices of domestically produced food staples. Real agricultural wholesale prices declined by 25.9 percent in the three years following the adoption of the NPE in 1985.

The decline in the (real) farmgate price was also accompanied by a significant rise in the margins between retail and wholesale prices. Merchants and intermediaries to the detriment of the direct agricultural producers were appropriating a larger share of the surplus. The dramatic increase in transport costs was also a major factor in compressing the revenues of the peasantry and increasing the gap between the farmgate price and the wholesale price.[6]

The 1985 IMF-sponsored program did not – with the exception of soya beans (located largely in the lowland areas of commercial farming) – contribute to increasing the production of cash crops for exports. As in Peru, there was a shift out of traditional export crops into the illegal coca economy.

The Laundering of Dirty Money

The national economic élites, including the commercial banks, were tied into the illegal drug trade. Government monetary and foreign-exchange policy upheld the role of commercial banking in the laundering of coca dollars.

The liberalization of the foreign-exchange market through the Dutch auction system *(bolsin)* was accompanied by measures, which provided legitimacy to the laundering of narco-dollars in the domestic banking system. The secrecy of foreign-exchange transactions *(el secreto bancario)* was introduced, the development of dollar deposits and the repatriation of capital to the domestic banking system were encouraged. Abnormally high interest rates (5 percent above LIBOR) contributed to attracting "hot money deposits" into Bolivia's commercial banks.

These deposits also included the earnings from the drug trade accruing to Bolivian intermediaries. The bank secrecy *("no questions asked")*, the reforms of the foreign-exchange regime which allowed for the free movement of money in and out of the country, combined with the high interest rates encouraged the deposit of narco-dollars in the Bolivian commercial banking sector.

The reforms of the banking system contributed to a significant decline in real productive investment. From 1986 to 1988, the lending interest rate (in US dollars) was between 20 and 25 percent per annum and credit to agriculture and manufacturing had been frozen.[7]

"Eradication" of Coca Production

While the macro-economic framework directly supported the narco-economy and the laundering of dirty money, the government had also adopted legislation, with the support of the US Drug Enforcement Administration (DEA), with a view to curbing coca production. In accordance with their mandate under the relevant legislation *(Ley del regimen de la coca)*, the government had set up mobile rural surveillance units (UMOPAR, *Unidad Movil de Patrullaje Rural*) in the coca-producing areas. These units, however, were largely involved in repressive actions directed against the small coca producer (often in areas of traditional production). Their activities had little impact on the narco-trade and the various powerful interests involved in the commercialization and export of coca paste. According to one report, it has been suggested that UMOPAR was controlled by the drug mafia.[8]

The Narco-State

The coca economy had been "protected" at the highest level by officials of the Bolivian government during the dictatorship of Garcia Meza (1980-82), which was commonly labeled in international circles as the "government of cocaine".9 The structure of the state was not modified, however, as a result of the restoration of parliamentary democracy.

Important financial and industrial interests continue to have direct links to the coca trade, including the use of coca-revenues to finance investments in the modern economy.

Since the mid-1970s, the development of the urban-services economy geared towards the upper-income market was largely financed by the narco-economy. The recycling of narco-dollars into domestic capital formation had been conducive to the development of residential real estate, shopping centers, tourist and entertainment infrastructure, etc. This process had been reinforced as a result of the IMF-sponsored program.

With the adoption of the NPE in 1985, the ruling MNR party abandoned its populist stance and shifted its political allegiance by combining forces with the rightist Nationalist Democratic Action Party (ADN) of former dictator General Hugo Banzer. (This represented a political turnaround since historically the MNR had depended on the support of organized labor.)

Banzer had allegedly been a key figure in the illegal coca trade since the mid-1970s and there was firm evidence that members of the ADN parliamentary caucus, together with senior officers of the military, were connected to the drug mafia.[10]

The MNR/ADN "Pact for Democracy" enabled the MNR government to carry out the various components of the NPE legislation in parliament including, the deregulation of the labor market and the repression of the labor movement.

ADN retained its involvement in the government coalition with the accession of President Paz Zamora of the MIR (Revolutionary Left) in 1989. Paz Zamora was the second runner-up in the 1989 presidential race after Hugo Banzer and the MNR candidate Gonzalo Sanchez de Losada. Paz acceded in 1989 to the presidency in the context of a political arrangement with General Hugo Banzer. Whereas Paz Zamora occupied the presidential seat, General Banzer and the ADN controlled key cabinet appointments.

The ADN/MIR government coalition pursued the macro-economic policies initiated with the NPE in 1985 under the MNR. ADN and its leader, Hugo Banzer, have thus provided, in the two "democratically elected" civilian governments, both political continuity as well as the maintenance of a cohesive link between government policy and the interests of the illegal coca trade.

Endnotes

1. For further details see Juan Antonio Morales, *The Costs of the Bolivian Stabilization Program,* documento de trabajo, no: 01/89, Universidad Catolica Boliviana, 1989, La Paz, p. 4.

2. Interview with Gonzalo Sanchez de Lozada, minister of finance under the MNR government of Paz Estenssoro and architect of the Bolivian economic package, *Caretas,* No: 1094, Lima, 5 February, 1990, p. 87 (our translation). Sanchez de Losada was subseuently elected president of Bolivia.

3. Morales, *op. cit.*, p. 6.

4. Morales, *op. cit.*, p. 9a.

5. See Morales, *op. cit.*, p. 6. See also Juan Antonio Morales, *Impacto de los ajustes estructurales en la agricultura campesina boliviana,* mimeo, Universidad Catolica Boliviana, 1989, La Paz.

6. See Morales, The Costs of the *Bolivian Stabilization Program,* pp. 24a-25a.

7. The borrowing rate was between 12 and 16 percent with a spread between lending and borrowing rates of between 6.8 and 14.0 percent. For further details see Morales, *The Costs of the Bolivian Stabilization Program,* p. 14, Table 7.

8. For details on the involvement of major political and social personalities in the narco-trade, see Amalia Barron, "Todos implicados en el narcotrafico", *Cambio 16,* Madrid, 8 August 1988.

9. See Henry Oporto Castro, "Bolivia: El complejo coca-cocaina" in Garcia Sayan (editor), *Coca, cocaina y narcotrafico,* Comision Andina de Juristas, Lima, 1989, p. 177.

10. See G. Lora, *Politica y burguesia narcotraficante,* Mi Kiosco, La Paz, 1988.

PART V

THE FORMER SOVIET UNION AND THE BALKANS

Chapter 16

The "Thirdworldization"
of the Russian Federation

Macro-Economic Reform in the Russian Federation

Phase I: The January 1992 Shock Treatment

"In Russia we are living in a post-war situation. . .", but there is no post-war reconstruction. "Communism" and the "Evil Empire" have been defeated, yet the Cold War, although officially over, has not quite reached its climax: the heart of the Russian economy is the military-industrial complex and "the G-7 wants to break our high tech industries. (. . .) The objective of the IMF economic program is to weaken us" and prevent the development of a rival capitalist power.[1]

The IMF-style "shock treatment", initiated in January 1992, precluded from the outset a transition towards "national capitalism" – i.e. a national capitalist economy owned and controlled by a Russian entrepreneurial class and supported, as in other major capitalist nations, by the economic and social policies of the state. For the West, the enemy was not "socialism" but capitalism. How to tame and subdue the polar bear, how to take over the talent, the science, the technology, how to buy out the human capital, how to acquire the intellectual property rights ? "If the West thinks that they can transform us into a cheap labor high technology export haven and pay our scientists US$ 40 a month, they are grossly mistaken, the people will rebel."[2]

While narrowly promoting the interests of both Russia's merchants and the business mafias, the "economic medicine" was killing the patient, destroying the national economy and pushing the system of state enterprises into bankruptcy. Through the deliberate manipulation of market forces, the reforms had defined which sectors of economic activity would be allowed to survive. Official figures pointed to a decline of 27 percent in industrial production during the first year of the reforms; the actual collapse of the Russian economy in 1992 was estimated by some economists to be of the order of 50 percent.[3]

The IMF-Yeltsin reforms constitute an instrument of "Thirdworldization"; they are a carbon copy of the structural adjustment program imposed on debtor countries in Latin America and sub-Saharan Africa. Harvard economist Jeffrey Sachs, advisor to the Russian government, had applied in Russia the same "macro-economic surgery" as in Bolivia where he was economic advisor to the MNR government in 1985. (See Chapter 15.) The IMF-World Bank program, adopted in the name of democracy, constitutes a coherent program of impoverishment of large sectors of the population. It was designed (in theory) to "stabilize" the economy, yet consumer prices in 1992 increased by more than one hundred times (9,900 percent) as a direct result of the "anti-inflationary programme".[4] As in Third World "stabilization programs", the inflationary process was largely engineered through the "dollarization" of domestic prices and the collapse of the national currency. The price liberalization program did not, however, resolve (as proposed by the IMF) the distorted structure of relative prices which existed under the Soviet system.

The price of bread increased (by more than a hundred times) from 13-18 kopeks in December 1991 (before the reforms) to over 20 rubles in October 1992; the price of a (domestically produced) television set rose from 800 rubles to 85,000 rubles. Wages, in contrast, increased approximately ten times – i.e. real earnings had declined by more than 80 percent and billions of rubles of life-long savings had been wiped out. Ordinary Russians were very bitter: "the government has stolen our money".[5] According to an IMF official, it was necessary to "sop up excess liquidity, purchasing power was too high".[6] "The government opted for 'a maximum bang'" so as to eliminate household money holdings "at the beginning of the reform programme".[7] According to one World Bank advisor, these savings "were not real, they were only a perception because [under the Soviet system] they [the people] were not allowed to buy anything".[8] An economist of the Russian Academy of Science saw things differently:

> Under the Communist system, our standard of living was never very high. But everybody was employed and basic human needs and essential social services although second-rate by Western standards, were free and available. But now social conditions in Russia are similar to those in the Third World.[9]

Average earnings were below US$ 10 a month (1992-3), the minimum wage (1992) was of the order of US$ 3 a month, a university professor earned US$ 8, an office worker US$ 7, a qualified nurse in an urban clinic earned US$ 6.[10] With the prices of many consumer goods moving rapidly up to world-market levels, these ruble salaries were barely sufficient to buy food. A winter coat could be purchased for US$ 60 – the equivalent of nine months pay.[11]

The collapse in the standard of living, engineered as a result of macro-economic policy, is without precedent in Russian history: "We had more to eat during the Second World War".

Under IMF-World Bank guidelines, social programs are to become self-financing: schools, hospitals and kindergartens (not to mention state-supported programs in sports, culture and the arts) were instructed to generate their own sources of revenue through the exaction of user fees.[12] Charges for surgery in hospitals were equivalent to two to six months earnings which only the *"nouveaux riches"* could afford. Not only hospitals, but theatres and museums were driven into bankruptcy. The famous Taganka Theatre was dismantled in 1992; many small theatres no longer had the funds to pay their actors. The reforms were conducive to the collapse of the welfare state. Many of the achievements of the Soviet system in health, education, culture and the arts (broadly acknowledged by Western scholars) have been undone.[13]

Continuity with the *ancien régime* was nonetheless maintained. Under the masque of liberal democracy, the totalitarian state remained unscathed: a careful blend of Stalinism and the "free" market. From one day to the next, Yeltsin and his cronies had become fervent partisans of neoliberalism. One totalitarian dogma was replaced by another, social reality was distorted, official statistics on real earnings were falsified: the IMF claimed in late 1992, that the standard of living "had gone up" since the beginning of the economic reform programme.[14] The Russian Ministry of Economy maintained that "wages were growing faster than prices".[15] In 1992, the consumer price index computed with the technical support of the IMF, pointed to a 15.6 times increase in prices (1,660 percent).[16] "But the people are not stupid, we simply do not believe them [the government]; we know that prices have gone up one hundred times".[17]

The Legacy of Perestroika

During the period of perestroika, buying at state-regulated prices and reselling in the free market, combined with graft and corruption were the principal sources of wealth formation. These "shadow dealings" by former bureaucrats and party members became legalized in May 1988 with the Law on Cooperatives implemented under Mikhail Gorbachev.[18] This law allowed for the formation of private commercial enterprises and joint-stock companies which operated alongside the system of state enterprises. In many instances, these "cooperatives" were set up as private ventures by the managers of state enterprises. The latter would sell (at official prices) the output produced by their state enterprise to their privately owned "cooperatives" (i.e. to themselves) and then re-sell on the free market at a very large profit. In 1989, the "cooperatives" were allowed to create their own commercial banks, and undertake foreign-trade transactions. By retaining a dual price system, the 1987-89 enterprise reforms, rather than encouraging bona fide capitalist entrepreneurship, supported personal enrichment, corruption and the development of a bogus "bazaar bourgeoisie".

Developing a Bazaar Bourgeoisie

In the former Soviet Union, "the secret of primitive accumulation" is based on the principle of "quick money": stealing from the state and buying at one price and re-selling at another. The birth of Russia's new *"biznesmany"*, an offshoot of the Communist nomenclature of the Brezhnev period, lies in the development of "apparatchik capitalism". "Adam bit the apple and original sin fell upon 'socialism'".[19]

Not surprisingly, the IMF program had acquired unconditional political backing by the "Democrats"– i.e. the IMF reforms supported the narrow interests of this new merchant class. The Yeltsin government unequivocally upheld the interests of these "dollarized élites". Price liberalization and the collapse of the ruble under IMF guidance advanced the enrichment of a small segment of the population. The dollar was handled on the Interbank currency auction; it was also freely transacted in street kiosks across the former Soviet Union. The reforms have meant that the ruble is no longer considered a safe "store of value" – i.e. the plunge of the national currency was further exacerbated because ordinary citizens preferred to hold their household savings in dollars: "people are willing to buy dollars at any price". [20]

Distorting Social Relations

The Cold War was a war without physical destruction. In its cruel aftermath, the instruments of macro-economic policy perform a decisive role in dismantling the economy of a defeated nation. The reforms are not intent (as claimed by the West) in building market capitalism and Western style socio-democracy, but in neutralizing a former enemy and forestalling the development of Russia as a major capitalist power. Also of significance is the extent to which the economic measures have contributed to destroying civil society and distorting fundamental social relations: the criminalization of economic activity, the looting of state property, money laundering and capital flight are bolstered by the reforms. In turn, the privatization program (through the public auction of state enterprises) also favored the transfer of a significant portion of state property to organized crime. The latter permeates the state apparatus and constitutes a powerful lobby broadly supportive of Yeltsin's macro-economic reforms. According to a recent estimate, half of Russia's commercial banks were, by 1993, under the control of the local mafias, and half of the commercial real estate in central Moscow was in the hands of organized crime.[21]

Pillage of the Russian Economy

The collapse of the ruble was instrumental in the pillage of Russia's natural resources: oil, non-ferrous metals and strategic raw materials could be bought by Russian merchants in rubles from a state factory and re-sold in hard currency to traders from the European Community at ten times the price. Crude oil, for instance, was purchased at 5,200 rubles (US$ 17) a ton (1992), an export license was acquired by bribing a corrupt official and the oil was re-sold on the world market at $ 150 a ton.[22] The profits of this transaction were deposited in offshore bank accounts or channeled towards luxury consumption (imports). Although officially illegal, capital flight and money laundering were facilitated by the deregulation of the foreign-exchange market and the reforms of the banking system. Capital flight was estimated to be running at over $ 1 billion a month during the first phase of the IMF reforms (1992).[23] There is evidence that prominent members of the political establishment had been transferring large amounts of money overseas.

Undermining Russian Capitalism

What role will "capitalist Russia" perform in the international division of labor during a period of global economic crisis ? What will be the fate of

Russian industry in a depressed global market? With plant closures in Europe and North America, "is there room for Russian capitalism" on the world market? Macro-economic policy under IMF guidance shapes Russia's relationship to the global economy. The reforms tend to support the free and unregulated export of primary goods including oil, strategic metals and food staples, while consumer goods including luxury cars, durables and processed food are freely imported for a small privileged market but there is no protection of domestic industry, nor are there any measures to rehabilitate the industrial sector or to transform domestic raw materials. Credit for the purchase of equipment is frozen, the deregulation of input prices (including oil, energy and freight prices) is pushing Russian industry into bankruptcy.

Moreover, the collapse in the standard of living has backlashed on industry and agriculture – i.e. the dramatic increase in poverty does not favor the growth of the internal market. Ironically, from "an economy of shortage" under the Soviet system (marked by long queues), consumer demand has been compressed to such an extent that the population can barely afford to buy food.

In contrast, the enrichment of a small segment of the population has encouraged a dynamic market for luxury goods including long queues in front of the dollar stores in Moscow's fashionable Kuznetsky area. The *"nouveaux riches"* look down on domestically produced goods: Mercedes Benz, BMW, Paris *haute couture*, not to mention high-quality imported "Russian vodka" from the United States at US$ 345 in a crystal bottle (four years of earnings of an average worker) are preferred. This "dynamic demand" by the upper-income groups is, therefore, largely diverted into consumer imports financed through the pillage of Russia's primary resources.

Acquiring State Property "at a Good Price"

The enormous profits accruing to the new commercial élites are also recycled into buying state property "at a good price" (or buying it from the managers and workers once it has gone through the government's privatization scheme). Because the recorded book-value of state property (denominated in current rubles) was kept artificially low (and because the ruble was so cheap), state assets could be acquired for practically nothing.[24] A high-tech rocket production facility could be purchased for US$ 1 million. A downtown Moscow hotel could be acquired for less than the price of a Paris apartment. In October 1992, the Moscow city government put a large number of apartments on auction; bids were to start at three rubles. While the former nomenclature, the new commercial élites and the local mafias are the only people who have money (and who are in a position to acquire property), they have neither the skills nor the foresight to manage Russian industry. It is unlikely that they will play a strong and decisive role in rebuilding Russia's economy. As in many Third World countries, these "compradore" élites prosper largely through their relationship to foreign capital.

Moreover, the economic reforms favor the displacement of national producers (whether state or private) and the taking over of large sectors of the national economy by foreign capital through the formation of joint ventures. Marlboro and Philip Morris, the American tobacco giants, for instance, have already acquired control over state production facilities for sale in the domestic market; British Airways has gained access to domestic air-routes through Air Russia, a joint venture with Aeroflot.

Important sectors of light industry are being closed down and replaced by imports whereas the more profitable sectors of the Russian economy (including the high-tech enterprises of the military-industrial complex) are being taken over by joint ventures. Foreign capital, however, has adopted a wait-and-see attitude. The political situation is uncertain, the risks are great: "we need guarantees regarding the ownership of land, and the repatriation of profits in hard currency".[25] Many foreign enterprises prefer to enter "through the back door" with small investments. These often involve joint ventures or the purchase of domestic enterprises at a very low cost, largely to secure control over (highly qualified) cheap labor and factory space.

Weakening Russia's High-Tech Economy

Export processing is being developed in the high-tech areas. It constitutes a very lucrative business: Lockheed Missile and Space Corporation, Boeing and Rockwell International among others have their eye on the aerospace and aircraft industries. American and European high-tech firms (including defense contractors) can purchase the services of top Russian scientists in fiber optics, computer design, satellite technology, nuclear physics (to name but a few) for an average wage below US$ 100 a month, at least 50 times less that in Silicon Valley. There are 1.5 million scientists and engineers in the former Soviet Union representing a sizeable reserve of "cheap human capital".[26]

Macro-economic policy supports the interests of Western high-tech firms and military contractors because it weakens the former Soviet aerospace and high-tech industries and blocks Russia (as a capitalist power in its own right) from competing on the world market. The talent and scientific know-how can be bought up and the production facilities can either be taken over or closed down.

A large share of the military-industrial complex is under the jurisdiction of the Ministry of Defense. Carried out under its auspices, the various "conversion programs" negotiated with NATO and Western defense ministries aim at dismantling that complex, including its civilian arm, and preventing Russia from becoming a potential rival in the world market. The conversion schemes purport physically to demobilize Russia's productive capabilities in the military, avionics and high-tech areas while facilitating the take-over and control by Western capital of Russia's knowledge base (intellectual property rights) and human capital, including her scientists, engineers and research institutes. AT&T Bell Laboratories, for instance, has acquired through a "joint venture" the services of an entire research laboratory at the General Physics Institute in Moscow. McDonnell Douglas has signed a similar agreement with the Mechanical Research Institute.[27]

Under one particular conversion formula, military hardware and industrial assets were "transformed" into scrap metal which was sold on the world commodity market. The proceeds of these sales were then deposited into a fund (under the Ministry of Defense) which could be used for the imports of capital goods, the payment of debt-servicing obligations or investment in the privatization programs.

Taking Over Russia's Banking System

Since the 1992 reforms and the collapse of many state banks, some 2,000 commercial banks have sprung up in the former Soviet Union of which 500 are located in Moscow. With the breakdown of industry, only the strongest banks and those with ties to international banks will survive. This situation favors the penetration of the Russian banking system by foreign commercial banks and joint-venture banks.

Undermining the Ruble Zone

The IMF program was also intent on abolishing the ruble zone and under-mining trade between the former republics. The latter were encouraged from the outset to establish their own currencies and central banks with technical assistance provided by the IMF. This process supported "economic Balkanization": with the collapse of the ruble zone, regional economic power serving the narrow interests of local tycoons and bureaucrats unfolded.

Bitter financial and trade disputes between Russia and the Ukraine have developed. Whereas trade is liberalized with the outside world, new "internal boundaries" were installed, impeding the movement of goods and people within the Commonwealth of Independent States.[28]

Phase II: The IMF Reforms Enter an Impasse

The IMF-sponsored reforms (under Prime Minister Yegor Gaidar) entered an impasse in late 1992. Opposition had built up in parliament as well as in the Central Bank. The IMF conceded that if the government were to meet the target for the fiscal deficit, up to 40 percent of industrial plants might have been forced to close down. The president of the Central Bank, Mr. Gerashchenko with support from Arcady Volsky of the Civic Union Party, took the decision (against the advice of the IMF) to expand credit to the state enterprises, while at the same time cutting drastically expenditures in health, education and old-age pensions. The Civic Union had put forth an "alternative program" in September 1992. Despite the subsequent replacement of Yegor Gaidar as prime minister in the parliamentary crisis of December 1992, the Civic Union's program was never carried out.

The IMF had, nonetheless, agreed in late 1992 to the possibility of "the less orthodox" approach of the centrist Civic Union prior to Gaidar's dismissal. In the words of the IMF resident representative in Moscow: "the IMF is not married to Gaidar, he has a similar economic approach but we will work with his successor".

At the beginning of 1993, the relationship between the government and the parliament evolved towards open confrontation. Legislative control over the government's budgetary and monetary policy served to undermine the "smooth execution" of the IMF program. The parliament had passed legislation which slowed down the privatization of state industry, placed restrictions on foreign banks and limited the government's ability to slash subsidies and social expenditures as required by the IMF.[29]

Opposition to the reforms had largely emanated from within the ruling political élites, from the moderate centrist faction (which included former Yeltsin collaborators). While representing a minority within the parliament, the Civic Union (also involving the union of industrialists led by Arcady Volsky) favored the development of national capitalism while maintaining a strong role for the central state. The main political actors in Yeltsin's confrontation with the parliament (e.g. Alexander Rutskoi and Ruslan Khasbulatov), therefore, cannot be categorized as "Communist hard-liners".

The government was incapable of completely bypassing the legislature. Both houses of parliament were suspended by presidential decree on 21 September 1993.

Abolishing the Parliament in the Name of "Governance"

On 23 September, two days later, Mr. Michel Camdessus, the IMF managing director, hinted that the second tranche of a US$ 3 billion loan under the IMF's systemic transformation facility (STF) would not be forthcoming because "Russia had failed to meet its commitments" largely as a result of parliamentary encroachment. (The STF loan is similar in form to the structural adjustment loans negotiated with indebted Third World countries). (See Chapter 3.)

President Clinton had stated at the Vancouver Summit in April 1993 that Western "aid" was tied to the implementation of "democratic reform". The conditions set by the IMF and the Western creditors, however, could only be met by suspending parliament altogether (a not unusual practice in many indebted Third World countries). The storming of the White House by élite troops and mortar artillery was thus largely intent on neutralizing political dissent from within the ranks of the nomenclature both in Moscow and the regions, and getting rid of individuals opposing IMF-style reform.

The G7 had endorsed President Yeltsin's decree abolishing both houses of parliament prior to its formal enactment and their embassies in Moscow had been briefed ahead of time. The presidential decree of 21 September was immediately followed by a wave of decrees designed to speed up the pace of economic reform and meet the conditionalities contained in the IMF loan agreement signed by the Russian government in May: credit was immediately tightened and interest rates raised, measures were adopted to increase the pace of privatization and trade liberalization.

In the words of Minister of Finance Mr. Boris Fyodorov, now freed from parliamentary control: "we can bring in any budget that we like"[30]

The timing of President Yeltsin's decree was well chosen: Yeltsin's finance minister Boris Fyodorov was scheduled to report to the G7 meeting of finance ministers on 25 September, the foreign minister Mr. Andrei Kosyrev was in Washington meeting President Clinton, the IMF-World Bank annual meeting was scheduled to commence in Washington on the 28 September, and 1 October had been set as a deadline for a decision on the IMF's standby loan prior to the holding in Frankfurt of the meeting of the London Club of commercial bank creditors (chaired by the Deutsche Bank) on 8 October. And on 12 October, President Yeltsin was to travel to Japan to initiate negotiations on the fate of four Kuril islands in exchange for debt relief and Japanese "aid".

Following the suspension of parliament, the G7 expressed "their very strong hope that the latest developments will help Russia achieve a decisive breakthrough on the path of market reforms"[31] The German minister of finance Mr. Theo Wagel said that "Russian leaders must make it clear that economic reforms would continue or they would lose international financial aid". Mr. Michel Camdessus expressed hope that political developments in Russia would contribute to "stepping up the process of economic reform".

Yet despite Western encouragement, the IMF was not yet prepared to grant Russia the "green light": Mr. Viktor Gerashchenko, the pro-Civic Union president of the Central Bank, was still formally in control of monetary policy; an IMF mission which traveled to Moscow in late September 1993 (during the heat of the parliamentary revolt), had advised Michel Camdessus that "plans already announced by the government for subsidy cuts and controls over credit were insufficient".[32]

The impact of the September 1993 economic decrees was almost immediate: the decision to further liberalize energy prices and to increase interest rates served the objective of rapidly pushing large sectors of Russian industry into bankruptcy. With the deregulation of Roskhlebprodukt, the state bread distribution company, in mid-October 1993, bread prices increased overnight by three to four times.[33] It is worth emphasizing that this "second wave" of impoverishment of the Russian people was occurring in the aftermath of an estimated 86 percent decline in real purchasing power in 1992 ![34] Since all subsidies were financed out of the state budget, the money saved could be redirected (as instructed by the IMF) towards the servicing of Russia's external debt.

The reform of the fiscal system, proposed by Finance Minister Boris Fyodorov in the aftermath of the September 1993 coup, followed the World Bank formula imposed on indebted Third World countries. It required "fiscal autonomy" for the republics and local governments by cutting the flow of revenue from Moscow to the regions and diverting the central state's financial resources towards the reimbursement of the creditors. The consequences of these reforms were fiscal collapse, economic and political Balkanization, and enhanced control of Western and Japanese capital over the economies of Russia's regions.

"Western Aid" to Boris Yeltsin

By 1993, the reforms had led to the massive plunder of Russia's wealth resulting in a significant outflow of real resources: the balance of payments deficit for 1993 was of the order of US$ 40 billion –approximately the amount of "aid" ($ 43 billion) pledged by the G7 at its Tokyo Summit in 1993. Yet most of this Western "aid" was fictitious: it was largely in the form of loans (rather than grant aid) which served the "useful" purpose of enlarging Russia's external debt (of the order of $ 80 billion in 1993) and strengthening the grip of Western creditors over the Russian economy.

Russia was being handled by the creditors in much the same way as a Third World country: out of a total of US$ 43.4 billion which had been pledged in 1993, less than $ 3 billion was actually disbursed. Moreover, the agreement reached with the Paris Club regarding the rescheduling of Russia's official debt – while "generous" at first sight – in reality offered Moscow a very short breathing space.[35] Only the debt incurred during the Soviet era was to be rescheduled;[36] the massive debts incurred by the Yeltsin government (ironically largely as a result of the economic reforms) were excluded from these negotiations.

With regard to bilateral pledges, President Clinton offered a meager US$ 1.6 billion at the Vancouver Summit in 1993; $ 970 million was in the form of credits – mainly for food purchases from US farmers; $ 630 million was arrears on Russian payments for US grain to be financed by tapping "The Food for Progress Program" of the US Department of Agriculture, thus putting Russia on the same footing as countries in sub-Saharan Africa in receipt of US food aid under PL 480. Similarly, the bulk of Japanese bilateral "aid" to Russia were funds earmarked for "insurance for Japanese companies" investing in Russia.[37]

Into the Strait-Jacket of Debt-Servicing

The elimination of parliamentary opposition in September 1993 resulted in an immediate shift in Moscow's debt-negotiation strategy with the commercial banks. Again, the timing was of critical importance. No "write-off" or "write-down" of Russia's commercial debt was requested by the Russian negotiating team at the Frankfurt meetings of the London Club held in early October 1993, only four days after the storming of the White House. Under the proposed deal, the date of reckoning would be temporarily postponed; US$ 24 out of US$ 38 billion of commercial debt would be rescheduled. All the conditions of the London Club were accepted by Moscow's negotiating team, with the exception of Russia's refusal to waive its "sovereign immunity to legal action". This waiver would have enabled the creditor banks to impound Russia's state enterprises and confiscate physical assets if debt-servicing obligations were not met. For the commercial banks, this clause was by no means a formality: with the collapse of Russia's economy, a balance of payments crisis, accumulated debt-servicing obligations due to the Paris Club, Russia was being pushed into a "technical moratorium" – i.e. a situation of de facto default.

The foreign creditors had also contemplated mechanisms for converting Russia's foreign exchange reserves (at the Central Bank as well as dollar deposits in Russian commercial banks) into debt-servicing. They also had their eye on foreign exchange holdings held by Russians in offshore bank accounts.

The IMF's economic medicine was not only devised to enforce debt-servicing obligations, it was also intent on "enlarging the debt". The reforms contributed to crippling the national economy thereby creating a greater dependency on external credit. In turn, debt default was paving the way towards a new critical phase in Moscow's relationship to the creditors. In the image of a subservient and compliant Third World regime, the Russian state was caught in the strait-jacket of debt and structural adjustment: state expenditures were brutally slashed to release state funds to reimburse the creditors.

The Collapse of Civil Society

As the crisis deepened, the population became increasingly isolated and vulnerable. "Democracy" had been formally installed but the new political parties, divorced from the masses, were largely heeding the interests of merchants and bureaucrats. The impact of the privatization program on employment was devastating: more than 50 percent of industrial plants had been driven into bankruptcy by 1993.[38] Moreover, entire cities in the Urals and Siberia belonging to the military-industrial complex and dependent on state credits and procurements were in the process of being closed down. In 1994 (according to official figures), workers at some 33,000 indebted enterprises, including state industrial corporations and collective farms, were not receiving wages on a regular basis.[39]

The tendency was not solely towards continued impoverishment and massive unemployment. A much deeper fracturing of the fabric of Russian society was unfolding, including the destruction of its institutions and the possible break-up of the Russian Federation. G7 policy-makers should carefully assess the consequences of their actions in the interests of world peace. The global geopolitical and security risks are far-reaching; the continued adoption of the IMF economic package spells disaster for Russia and the West.

Table 16.1

Storming the Russian Parliament, a Macro-Economic Chronology

September–October 1993

13 September	President Yeltsin calls back Yegor Gaidar into the government.
20 September	G7 embassies are advised of the suspension of parliament.
21 September	Boris Yeltsin dissolves parliament and abrogates the constitution.
22 September	G7 messages of support to Boris Yeltsin.
23 September	Michel Camdessus, managing director of IMF, states that Russia's economic reforms are not on track.
	A wave of economic decrees is initiated by Yegor Gaidar.
24 September	Troops and riot police encircle the White House.
25 September	The finance minister Mr. Boris Fyodorov meets G7 finance ministers.
28 September	The annual meeting of the IMF and World Bank opens in Washington; Boris Fyodorov meets Michel Camdessus.
	IMF mission of economists is in Moscow to monitor progress of economic reforms.
1 October	Deadline date for decision by IMF regarding stand-by loan.
4 October	Storming of the White House.
4 October	Decision by the IMF (based on economists' mission report) to delay loan disbursements.
5 October	The US, the European Community and Japan support Yeltsin's decision to crush the parliamentary revolt.
	Massive purges of Yeltsin opponents begin in Moscow and the regions.
8 October	Meeting in Frankfurt of the London Club pertaining to the rescheduling of Russia's debt with the commercial banks.
12 October	Boris Yeltsin arrives in Tokyo.
14 October	Price of bread increases from 100 to 300 rubles.

Source: *Financial Times*, September and October 1993, several issues.

Endnotes

1. Interview with an economist of the Russian Academy of Science, Moscow, October 1992.
2. *Ibid.*
3. A 50 percent decline in relation to the average of the previous three years. Interviews with several economists of the Russian Academy of Science, Moscow, September 1992.
4. Based on author's compilation of price increases over the period December 1991-October 1992 of some 27 essential consumer goods including food, transportation, clothing and consumer durables.
5. According to the government's official statement to the Russian Parliament, wages increased 11 times from January to September 1992.
6. Interview with the head of the IMF Resident Mission, Moscow, September 1992.
7. See World Bank, *Russian Economic Reform, Crossing the Threshold of Structural Reform,* Washington DC, 1992, p. 18.
8. Interview with a World Bank advisor, Moscow, October 1992.
9. Interview with an economist of the Russian Academy of Science, Moscow, September 1992.
10. Interview in a Moscow polyclinic, interviews with workers in different sectors of economic activity, Moscow and Rostow on the Don, September-October 1992. See also Jean-Jacques Marie, "Ecole et santé en ruines", *Le Monde diplomatique,* June 1992, p. 13.
11. The price and wage levels are those prevailing in September-October 1992. The exchange rate in September 1992 was of the order of 300 rubles to the dollar.
12. For further details see Jean Jacques Marie, *op. cit.*
13. There is a failure on the part of the Russian economic advisors to uncover the theoretical falsehoods of the IMF economic framework. There is no analysis on how the IMF policy package actually works, and little knowledge in the former Soviet Union of policy experiences in other countries, including sub-Saharan Africa, Latin America and Eastern Europe.
14. Interview with IMF official, Moscow, September 1992.
15. See *Delovoi Mir (Business World),* No. 34, 6 September 1992, p. 14.
16. During the first nine months of 1992.
17. Interview with ordinary Russian citizens, Rostov on the Don, October 1992.
18. See International Monetary Fund, World Bank, Organization for Economic Cooperation and Development and European Bank for Reconstruction and Development, *A Study of the Soviet Economy,* Vol. 1, Paris, 1991, part II, chapter 2.

19. Paraphrase of "Adam bit the apple and thereupon sin fell on the human race" in Karl Marx "On Primitive Accumulation", *Capital* (book 1).

20. See "Ruble Plunges to New Low", *Moscow Times*, 2 October 1992, p. 1.

21. See Paul Klebnikov, "Stalin's Heirs", *Forbes*, 27 September 1993, pp. 124-34.

22. The government is said to have issued export licenses in 1992 covering two times the recorded exports of crude petroleum.

23. According to estimates of the Washington-based International Institute of Banking.

24. It is estimated that with a purchase of US$ 1,000 of state property (according to the book value of the enterprise), one acquires real assets of a value of $ 300,000.

25. Interview with a Western commercial bank executive, Moscow, October 1992.

26. See Tim Beardsley, "Selling to Survive", *Scientific American*, February 1993, pp. 94-100.

27. *Ibid.*

28. With technical assistance from the World Bank, a uniform tariff on imports was designed for the Russian Federation.

29. The Central Bank was under the jurisdiction of parliament. In early September 1993, an agreement was reached whereby the Central Bank would be responsible to both the government and the parliament.

30. Quoted in *Financial Times*, 23 September 1993, p. 1.

31. *Ibid*, p. 1.

32. According to *Financial Times*, 5 October 1993.

33. See Leyla Boulton, "Russia's Breadwinners and Losers", *Financial Times*, 13 October 1993, p. 3.

34. Chris Doyle, *The Distributional Consequences of Russia's Transition*, Discussion Paper no. 839, Center for Economic Policy Research, London, 1993. This estimate is consistent with the author's evaluation of price movements of basic consumer goods over the period December 1991–October 1992. Official statistics (which are grossly manipulated) acknowledge a 56 percent collapse in purchasing power since mid-1991.

35. The amount eligible for restructuring pertained to the official debt contracted prior to January 1991 (US$ 17 billion). Two billion were due in 1993, 15 billion were rescheduled over 10 years with a five-year grace period.

36. Only debt incurred prior to the cut-off date (January 1991) was to be rescheduled; 15 out of $ 17 billion were rescheduled, $ 2 billion were due to the Paris Club in 1993.

37. See *The Wall Street Journal*, New York, 12 October 1993, p. A17. See also Allan Saunderson, "Legal Wrangle Holds Up Russian Debt Deal", *The European*, 14-17 October 1993, p. 38.

38. The World Bank has recommended to the government to "fracturize", large enterprises, that is to break them up into smaller entities.
39. See *Financial Times*, 1 August 1994, p. 1.

Chapter 17

Dismantling Former Yugoslavia, Recolonizing Bosnia-Herzegovina

As heavily-armed US and NATO troops enforced the peace in Bosnia, the press and politicians alike portrayed Western intervention in the former Yugoslavia as a noble, if agonizingly belated, response to an outbreak of ethnic massacres and human rights violations. In the wake of the November 1995 Dayton peace accords, the West was eager to touch up its self-portrait as savior of the Southern Slavs and get on with "the work of rebuilding" the newly "sovereign states."

But following a pattern set early on, Western public opinion had been skillfully misled. The conventional wisdom exemplified by the writings of former US Ambassador to Yugoslavia Warren Zimmermann, held that the plight of the Balkans was the outcome of an "aggressive nationalism", the inevitable result of deep-seated ethnic and religious tensions rooted in history.[1] Likewise, much was made of the "Balkans power-play" and the clash of political personalities: "Tudjman and Milosevic are tearing Bosnia-Herzegovina to pieces".[2]

Lost in the barrage of images and self-serving analyses are the economic and social causes of the conflict. The deep-seated economic crisis, which preceded the civil war, had long been forgotten. The strategic interests of Germany and the US in laying the groundwork for the disintegration of Yugoslavia go unmentioned, as does the role of external creditors and international financial institutions. In the eyes of the global media, Western powers bear no responsibility for the impoverishment and destruction of a nation of 24 million people.

But through their domination of the global financial system, the Western powers, in pursuit of national and collective strategic interests, helped bring the Yugoslav economy to its knees and stirred its simmering ethnic and social conflicts. Now it is the turn of Yugoslavia's war-ravaged successor states to feel the tender mercies of the international financial community.

As the world focused on troop movements and cease-fires, the international financial institutions were busily collecting former Yugoslavia's external debt from its remnant states, while transforming the Balkans into a safe-haven for free enterprise. With a Bosnian peace settlement holding under NATO guns, the West had in late 1995 unveiled a "reconstruction" program that stripped that brutalized country of sovereignty to a degree not seen in Europe since the end of World War II. It consisted largely of making Bosnia a divided territory under NATO military occupation and Western administration.

Neocolonial Bosnia

Resting on the Dayton accords, which created a Bosnian "Constitution," the US and its European allies had installed a full-fledged colonial administration in Bosnia. At its head was their appointed High Representative, Carl Bildt, a former Swedish prime minister and European Union representative in the Bosnian peace negotiations.[3] Bildt was given full executive powers in all civilian matters, with the right to overrule the governments of both the Bosnian Federation and the Republika Srpska (Serbian Bosnia). To make the point crystal clear, the Accords spelled out that "the High Representative is the final authority in theater regarding interpretation of the agreements."[4] He is to work with the multinational military implementation force (IFOR) military High Command as well as with creditors and donors.

The UN Security Council had also appointed a "Commissioner" under the High Representative to run an international civilian police force.[5] Irish police official Peter Fitzgerald, with UN policing experience in Namibia, El Salvador and Cambodia, was to preside over some 1,700 police from 15 countries. Following the signing of the Dayton Accords in November 1995, the international police force was dispatched to Bosnia after a five-day training program in Zagreb.[6]

The new "Constitution", included as an Appendix to the Dayton Accords, handed the reins of economic policy over to the Bretton Woods institutions and the London based European Bank for Reconstruction and Development (EBRD). The IMF was empowered to appoint the first governor of the Bosnian Central Bank who, like the High Representative, "shall not be a citizen of Bosnia and Herzegovina or a neighboring state."[7]

Under the IMF regency, the Central Bank is not allowed to function as a Central Bank: "For the first six years . . . it may not extend credit by creating money, operating in this respect as a currency board."[8] Neither was Bosnia to be allowed to have its own currency (issuing paper money only when there is full foreign exchange backing), nor permitted to mobilize its internal resources. Its ability to self-finance its reconstruction through an independent monetary policy was blunted from the outset.

While the Central Bank was in IMF custody, the EBRD heads the Commission on Public Corporations, which supervises, since 1996, operations of all public sector enterprises in Bosnia, including energy, water, postal services, telecommunications and transportation. The EBRD president appoints the commission chair and is in charge of public sector restructuring – i.e. the sell-off of state and socially-owned assets, and the procurement of long-term investment funds[9] Western creditors explicitly created the EBRD "to give a distinctively political dimension to lending".[10]

As the West proclaimed its support for democracy, actual political power rests in the hands of a parallel Bosnian "state" whose executive positions are held by non-citizens. Western creditors have embedded their interests in a constitution hastily written on their behalf. They have done so without a constitutional assembly and without consultations with Bosnian citizens' organizations. Their plans to rebuild Bosnia appear more suited to sating creditors than satisfying even the elementary needs of Bosnians. The neocolonization of Bosnia was a logical step of Western efforts to undo Yugoslavia's experiment in "market socialism" and workers' self-management, and to impose the dictate of the "free market".

Historical background

Multi-ethnic, socialist Yugoslavia was once a regional industrial power and economic success. In the two decades before 1980, annual gross domestic product (GDP) growth averaged 6.1 percent, medical care was free, the rate of literacy was 91 percent and life expectancy was 72 years.[11] But after a decade of Western economic ministrations and a decade of disintegration, war, boycott and embargo, the economies of the former Yugoslavia were prostrate, their industrial sectors dismantled.

Yugoslavia's implosion was partially due to US machinations. Despite Belgrade's non-alignment and its extensive trading relations with the European Community and the US, the Reagan administration had targeted the Yugoslav economy in a "Secret Sensitive" 1984 National Security Decision Directive (NSDD 133) entitled "US Policy towards Yugoslavia." A censored version, declassified in 1990, elaborated on NSDD 64 on

Eastern Europe issued in 1982. The latter advocated "expanded efforts to promote a 'quiet revolution' to overthrow Communist governments and parties," while reintegrating the countries of Eastern Europe into a market-oriented economy.[12]

The US had earlier joined Belgrade's other international creditors in imposing a first round of macroeconomics reform in 1980, shortly before the death of Marshall Tito. That initial round of restructuring set the pattern.

Secessionist tendencies, feeding on social and ethnic divisions, gained impetus precisely during a period of brutal impoverishment of the Yugoslav population. The economic reforms "wreaked economic and political havoc. . . Slower growth, the accumulation of foreign debt and especially the cost of servicing it as well as devaluation led to a fall in the standard of living of the average Yugoslav. . . The economic crisis threatened political stability . . . it also threatened to aggravate simmering ethnic tensions".[13]

These reforms, accompanied by the signing of debt restructuring agreements with the official and commercial creditors, also served to weaken the institutions of the federal state creating political divisions between Belgrade and the governments of the Republics and Autonomous Provinces. "The [Federal] Prime Minister Milka Planinc, who was supposed to carry out the program, had to promise the IMF an immediate increase of the discount rates and much more for the Reaganomics arsenal of measures. . ."[14] And throughout the 1980s, the IMF and World Bank periodically prescribed further doses of their bitter economic medicine as the Yugoslav economy slowly lapsed into a coma.

From the outset, successive IMF sponsored programs hastened the disintegration of the Yugoslav industrial sector. Following the initial phase of macro-economic reform in 1980, industrial growth plummeted to 2.8 percent in the 1980-87 period, plunging to zero in 1987-88 and to a negative 10 percent growth rate by 1990.[15] This process was accompanied by the piecemeal dismantling of the Yugoslav welfare state, with all the predictable social consequences. Debt restructuring agreements, meanwhile, increased foreign debt, and a mandated currency devaluation also hit hard at Yugoslavs' standard of living.

Mr. Markovic goes to Washington

In Autumn 1989, just before the fall of the Berlin Wall, Yugoslav federal Premier Ante Markovic met in Washington with President George Bush to cap negotiations for a new financial aid package. In return for assistance, Yugoslavia agreed to even more sweeping economic reforms, including a new devalued currency, another wage freeze, sharp cuts in government spending and the elimination of socially owned, worker-managed companies.[16]

The Belgrade nomenclature, with the assistance of Western advisers, had laid the groundwork for Markovic's mission by implementing beforehand many of the required reforms, including a major liberalization of foreign investment legislation.

"Shock therapy" began in January 1990. Although inflation had eaten away at earnings, the IMF ordered that wages be frozen at their mid November 1989 levels. Prices continued to rise unabated, and real wages collapsed by 41 percent in the first six months of 1990.[17]

The IMF also effectively controlled the Yugoslav central bank. Its tight money policy further crippled the country's ability to finance its economic and social programs. State revenues that should have gone as transfer payments to the republics went instead to service Belgrade's debt with the Paris and London clubs. The republics were largely left to their own devices. The economic package was launched in January 1990 under an IMF Stand-by Arrangement (SBA) and a World Bank Structural Adjustment Loan (SAL II). The budget cuts requiring the redirection of federal revenues towards debt servicing, were conducive to the suspension of transfer payments by Belgrade to the governments of the Republics and Autonomous Provinces.

In one fell swoop, the reformers had engineered the final collapse of Yugoslavia's federal fiscal structure and mortally wounded its federal political institutions. By cutting the financial arteries between Belgrade and the republics, the reforms fueled secessionist tendencies that fed on economic factors, as well as ethnic divisions, virtually ensuring the de facto secession of the republics. The IMF-induced budgetary crisis created an economic fait accompli that paved the way for Croatia's and Slovenia's formal secession in June 1991.

Crushed by the Invisible Hand

The reforms demanded by Belgrade's creditors also struck at the heart of Yugoslavia's system of socially-owned and worker-managed enterprises. As one observer noted, 'the objective was to subject the Yugoslav economy to massive privatization and the dismantling of the public sector.' "The Communist Party bureaucracy, most notably its military and intelligence sector, was canvassed specifically and offered political and economic backing on the condition that wholesale scuttling of social protections for Yugoslavia's workforce was imposed."[18] It was an offer that a desperate Yugoslavia could not refuse. By 1990, the annual rate of growth of GDP had collapsed to -7.5 percent. In 1991, GDP declined by a further 15 percent, industrial output collapsed by 21 percent.[19]

The restructuring program, demanded by Belgrade's creditors, was intended to abrogate the system of socially owned enterprises. The *Enterprise Law* of 1989 required abolishing the Basic Organizations of Associated Labor (BOAL). The latter were socially-owned productive units under self-management with the Workers' Council constituting the main decision making body. The 1989 Enterprise Law required the transformation of the BOALs into private capitalist enterprises with the Worker's Council replaced by a so-called "Social Board" under the control of the enterprise's owners including its creditors.[20]

Overhauling the Legal Framework

Advised by Western lawyers and consultants, a number of supporting pieces of legislation were put in place in a hurry. The Financial Operations Act of 1989 was to play a crucial role in engineering the collapse of Yugoslavia's industrial sector, it was to provide for an "equitable" and so-called "transparent trigger mechanism" which would steer so-called "insolvent" enterprises in bankruptcy or liquidation. A related act entitled the Law on Compulsory Settlement, Bankruptcy and Liquidation was to safeguard "the rights of the creditors". The latter could call for the initiation of bankruptcy procedures enabling them to take over and/or liquidate the assets of debtor enterprises.[21]

The earlier 1988 Foreign Investment Law had allowed for unrestricted entry of foreign capital not only into industry, but also into the banking, insurance and services' sectors. Prior to the enactment of the law, foreign investment was limited to joint ventures with the socially-owned enterprises.[22] In turn, the 1989 Law on the Circulation and Management of

Social Capital and the 1990 Social Capital Law allowed for the divestiture of the socially-owned enterprises, including their sale to foreign capital. The Social Capital Law also provided for the creation of "Restructuring and Recapitalization Agencies" with a mandate to organize the "valuation" of enterprise assets prior to privatization. As in Eastern Europe and the former Soviet Union, however, the valuation of assets was based on the recorded "book-value" expressed in local currency. This book-value tended to be unduly low thereby securing the sale of socially-owned assets at rock-bottom prices. Slovenia and Croatia had by 1990 already established their own draft privatization laws.[23]

The assault on the socialist economy also included a new banking law designed to trigger the liquidation of the socially-owned Associated Banks. Within two years, more than half the country's banks had vanished, to be replaced by newly-formed "independent profit-oriented institutions."[24] By 1990, the entire "three-tier banking system" consisting of the National Bank of Yugoslavia, the national banks of the eight Republics and autonomous provinces and the commercial banks had been dismantled under the guidance of the World Bank. A Federal Agency for Insurance and Bank Rehabilitation was established in June 1990 with a mandate to restructure and *reprivatize* restructured banks under World Bank supervision.[25] This process was to be undertaken over a five-year period. The development of non-banking financial intermediaries including, brokerage firms, investment management firms and insurance companies was also to be promoted.

The Bankruptcy Program

Industrial enterprises had been carefully categorized. Under the IMF-World Bank sponsored reforms, credit to the industrial sector had been frozen with a view to speeding up the bankruptcy process. So-called *exit mechanisms* had been established under the provisions of the 1989 Financial Operations Act.[26] Under the new law, if a business was unable to pay its bills for 30 days running, or for 30 days within a 45-day period, the government would launch bankruptcy proceedings within the next 15 days. This mechanism allowed creditors (including national and foreign banks) to routinely convert their loans into a controlling equity in the insolvent enterprise. Under the Act, the government was not authorized to intervene. In case a settlement was not reached, bankruptcy procedures would be initiated – in which case, workers would not normally receive severance payments.[27]

In 1989, according to official sources, 248 firms were steered into bankruptcy or were liquidated and 89,400 workers had been laid off.[28] During the first nine months of 1990, directly following the adoption of the IMF program, another 889 enterprises with a combined work-force of 525,000 workers were subjected to bankruptcy procedures.[29] In less than two years the World Bank's so-called *trigger mechanism* (under the Financial Operations Act) had led to the lay-off of 614,000 (out of a total industrial workforce of the order of 2.7 million). The largest concentrations of bankrupt firms and lay-offs were in Serbia, Bosnia-Herzegovina, Macedonia and Kosovo.[30]

Many socially-owned enterprises attempted to avoid bankruptcy through the non payment of wages. Half a million workers, representing some 20 percent of the industrial labor force, were not paid during the early months of 1990, in order to meet the demands of creditors under the "settlement" procedures stipulated in the Law on Financial Organizations. Real earnings were in a free fall, social programs had collapsed. With the bankruptcies of industrial enterprises, unemployment had become rampant, creating within the population an atmosphere of social despair and hopelessness.

The January 1990 IMF-sponsored package contributed to increasing enterprise losses, while precipitating many of the large electric, petroleum refinery, machinery, engineering and chemical enterprises into bankruptcy. Moreover, with the deregulation of the trade regime, a flood of imported commodities contributed to further destabilizing domestic production. These imports were financed with borrowed money granted under the IMF package (i.e. the various "quick disbursing loans" granted by the IMF, the World Bank and bilateral donors in support of the economic reforms). While the import bonanza was fueling the build-up of Yugoslavia's external debt, the abrupt hikes in interest rates and input prices imposed on national enterprises had expedited the displacement and *exclusion of domestic producers from their own national market.*

"Shedding Surplus Workers"

The situation prevailing in the months preceding the Secession of Croatia and Slovenia (mid-1991) (confirmed by the 1989-90 bankruptcy figures) points to the sheer magnitude and brutality of the process of industrial dismantling. The figures, however, provide but a partial picture, depicting the situation at the outset of the *bankruptcy program*, which continued unabated in Yugoslavia's successor states in the years following the Dayton Accords.

The World Bank had estimated that there were *still*, in September 1990, 2,435 "loss-making" enterprises out of a remaining total of 7,531.[31] In other words, these 2,435 firms, with a combined work-force of more than 1.3 million workers, had been categorized as "insolvent" under the provisions of the Financial Operations Act, requiring the immediate implementation of bankruptcy procedures. Bearing in mind that 600,000 workers had already been laid off by bankrupt firms prior to September 1990, these figures suggest that some 1.9 million workers (out of a total of 2.7 million) had been classified as "redundant". The "insolvent" firms concentrated in the energy, heavy industry, metal processing, forestry and textile sectors were among the largest industrial enterprises in the country representing (in September 1990) 49.7 percent of the total *(remaining and employed)* industrial work-force.[32]

As 1991 dawned, real wages were in free fall, social programs had collapsed, and unemployment ran rampant. The dismantling of the industrial economy was breathtaking in its magnitude and brutality. Its social and political impact, while not as easily quantified, was tremendous. Yugoslav President Borisav Jovic warned that the reforms were "having a markedly unfavorable impact on the overall situation in society. . . Citizens have lost faith in the state and its institutions. . . The further deepening of the economic crisis and the growth of social tensions has had a vital impact on the deterioration of the political-security situation."[33]

The Political Economy of Disintegration

Some Yugoslavs joined together in a doomed battle to prevent the destruction of their economy and polity. As one observer found, "worker resistance crossed ethnic lines, as Serbs, Croats, Bosnians and Slovenians mobilized . . . shoulder to shoulder with their fellow workers."[34] But the economic struggle also heightened already tense relations among the republics and between the republics and Belgrade.

Serbia rejected the austerity plan outright, and some 650,000 Serbian workers struck against the federal government to force wage hikes.[35] The other republics followed different and sometimes self-contradictory paths.

In relatively wealthy Slovenia, for instance, secessionist leaders such as Social Democratic party chair Joze Pucnik supported the reforms: "From an economic standpoint, I can only agree with socially harmful measures in our society, such as rising unemployment or cutting workers' rights, because they are necessary to advance the economic reform process."[36]

But at the same time, Slovenia joined other republics in challenging the federal government's efforts to restrict their economic autonomy. Both Croatian leader Franjo Tudjman and Serbia's Slobodan Milosevic joined Slovene leaders in railing against Belgrade's attempts to impose harsh reforms on behalf of the IMF.[37]

In the multiparty elections in 1990, economic policy was at the center of the political debate as separatist coalitions ousted the Communists in Croatia, Bosnia and Slovenia. Just as economic collapse spurred the drift toward separation, separation in turn exacerbated the economic crisis. Cooperation among the republics virtually ceased. And with the republics at each others' throats, both the economy and the nation itself embarked on a vicious downward spiral.

The process sped along as the republican leadership deliberately fostered social and economic divisions to strengthen their own hands: "The republican oligarchies, who all had visions of a 'national renaissance' of their own, instead of choosing between a genuine Yugoslav market and hyperinflation, opted for war which would disguise the real causes of the economic catastrophe."[38]

The simultaneous appearance of militias loyal to secessionist leaders only hastened the descent into chaos. These militias (covertly financed by the US and Germany), with their escalating atrocities, not only split the population along ethnic lines, they also fragmented the workers' movement.[39]

"Western Help"

The austerity measures had laid the basis for the recolonization of the Balkans. Whether that required the breakup of Yugoslavia was subject to debate among the Western powers, with Germany leading the push for secession and the US, fearful of opening a nationalist Pandora's box, originally arguing for Yugoslavia's preservation.

Following Franjo Tudjman's and the rightist Democratic Union's decisive victory in Croatia in May 1990, German Foreign Minister Hans-Dietrich Genscher, in almost daily contact with his counterpart in Zagreb, gave his go-ahead for Croatian secession.[40] Germany did not passively support secession; it "forced the pace of international diplomacy" and pressured its Western allies to recognize Slovenia and Croatia. Germany sought a free hand among its allies "to pursue economic dominance in the whole of Mittel Europa".[41]

Washington, on the other hand, "favored a loose unity while encouraging democratic development . . . [Secretary of State] Baker told Tudjman and [Slovenia's President] Milan Kucan that the United States would not encourage or support unilateral secession . . . but if they had to leave, he urged them to leave by a negotiated agreement."[42] In the meantime, the US Congress had passed the 1991 Foreign Operations Appropriations Act which curtailed all financial assistance to Yugoslavia. The provisions of the Act had been casually referred to by the CIA as "a signed death warrant" for Yugoslavia.[43] The CIA had correctly predicted that "a bloody civil war would ensue".[44] The law also demanded the IMF and the World Bank to freeze credit to Belgrade. And the US State Department had insisted that the Yugoslav republics (considered as de facto political entities) "uphold separate election procedures and returns before any further aid could be resumed to the individual republics".[45]

Post War Reconstruction and the "Free Market"

In the wake of the November 1995 Dayton Accords, Western creditors turned their attention to Yugoslavia's "successor states". Yugoslavia's foreign debt had been carefully divided and allocated to the successor republics, which were strangled in separate debt rescheduling and structural adjustment agreements.[46]

The consensus among donors and international agencies was that past IMF macro-economics reforms inflicted on federal Yugoslavia had not quite met their goal and further shock therapy was required to restore "economic health" to Yugoslavia's successor states. Croatia, Slovenia and Macedonia had agreed to loan packages to pay off their shares of the Yugoslav debt that required a consolidation of the process begun under Ante Markovic's bankruptcy program. The all too familiar pattern of plant closings, induced bank failures, and impoverishment has continued unabated since 1996. And who was to carry out IMF diktats ? The leaders of the newly sovereign states have fully collaborated with the creditors.

In Croatia, the government of President Franjo Tudjman was obliged to sign already in 1993, at the height of the civil war, an agreement with the IMF. In return for fresh loans, largely intended to service Zagreb's external debt, the government of President Franjo Tudjman agreed to implementing further plant closures and bankruptcies, driving wages to abysmally low levels. The official unemployment rate increased from 15.5 percent in 1991 to 19.1 percent in 1994.[47]

Zagreb had also instituted a far more stringent bankruptcy law, together with procedures for "the dismemberment" of large state-owned public utility companies. According to its "Letter of Intent" to the Bretton Woods institutions, the Croatian government had promised to restructure and fully privatize the banking sector with the assistance of the European Bank for Reconstruction and Development (EBRD) and the World Bank. The latter had also demanded a Croatian capital market structured to heighten the penetration of Western institutional investors and brokerage firms.

Under the agreement signed in 1993 with the IMF, the Zagreb government was not permitted to mobilize its own productive resources through fiscal and monetary policy. The latter were firmly under the control of its external creditors. The massive budget cuts demanded under the agreement had also forestalled the possibility of post-war reconstruction. The latter could only be carried out through the granting of fresh foreign loans, a process which has contributed to fueling Croatia's external debt well into the 21st century.

Macedonia had also followed a similar economic path to that of Croatia. In December 1993, the Skopje government agreed to compress real wages and freeze credit in order to obtain a loan under the IMF's Systemic Transformation Facility (STF). In an unusual twist, multi-billionaire business tycoon George Soros participated in the International Support Group composed of the government of the Netherlands and the Basel-based Bank of International Settlements. The money provided by the Support Group, however, was not intended for "reconstruction" but rather to enable Skopje to pay back debt arrears owed the World Bank.[48]

Moreover, in return for debt rescheduling, the government of Macedonian Prime Minister Branko Crvenkovski had to agree to the liquidation of remaining "insolvent" enterprises and the lay off of "redundant" workers – which included the employees of half the industrial enterprises in the country. As Deputy Finance Minister Hari Kostov soberly noted, with interest rates at astronomical levels because of donor-sponsored banking reforms, "it was literally impossible to find a company in the country which would be able to (. . .) to cover [its] costs." [49]

Overall, the IMF economic therapy for Macedonia was a continuation of the "bankruptcy program" launched in 1989-90 under federal Yugoslavia. The most profitable assets were put on sale on the Macedonian stock market, but this auction of socially owned enterprises had led to industrial collapse and rampant unemployment.

And global capital applauds. Despite an emerging crisis in social welfare and the decimation of his economy, Macedonian Finance Minister Ljube Trpevski proudly informed the press in 1996 that "the World Bank and the IMF place Macedonia among the most successful countries in regard to current transition reforms".[50]

The head of the IMF mission to Macedonia, Paul Thomsen, agreed. He avowed that "the results of the stabilization program were impressive" and gave particular credit to "the efficient wages policy" adopted by the Skopje government. Still, his negotiators had insisted that despite these achievements, even more budget cutting was necessary.[51]

Reconstruction Colonial Style

But Western intervention was making its most serious inroads on national sovereignty in Bosnia. The neocolonial administration imposed under the Dayton Accords and supported by NATO's firepower had ensured that Bosnia's future would be determined in Washington, Bonn, and Brussels rather than in Sarajevo.

The Bosnian government had estimated in the wake of the Dayton Accords that reconstruction costs would reach $ 47 billion. Western donors had initially pledged $ 3 billion in reconstruction loans, of which only a part was actually granted. Moreover, a large chunk of the fresh money lent to Bosnia had been tagged to finance some of the local civilian costs of IFOR's military deployment, as well as repay international creditors.[52]

Fresh loans will pay back old debt. The Central Bank of the Netherlands had generously provided "bridge financing" of $ 37 million to allow Bosnia to pay its arrears with the IMF, without which the IMF will not lend it fresh money. But in a cruel and absurd paradox, the sought-after loans from the IMF's newly created "Emergency Window" for "post-conflict countries" will not be used for post-war reconstruction. Instead, they will repay the Dutch Central Bank, which had coughed up the money to settle IMF arrears in the first place.[53]

Debt piles up, and little new money goes for rebuilding Bosnia's war torn economy.

While rebuilding is sacrificed on the altar of debt repayment, Western governments and corporations show greater interest in gaining access to strategic natural resources. With the discovery of energy reserves in the region, the partition of Bosnia between the Federation of Bosnia-Herzegovina and the Bosnian-Serb Republika Srpska under the Dayton Accords has taken on new strategic importance. Documents in the hands of Croatia and the Bosnian Serbs indicate that coal and oil deposits have been identified on the eastern slope of the Dinarides Thrust, retaken from Krajina Serbs by the US-backed Croatian army in the final offensives before the Dayton Accords. Bosnian officials had reported that Chicago-based Amoco was among several foreign firms that subsequently initiated exploratory surveys in Bosnia.54

"Substantial" petroleum fields also lie "in the Serb-held part of Croatia" just across the Sava River from Tuzla, the headquarters for the US military zone.55 Exploration operations went on during the war, but the World Bank and the multinationals that conducted the operations kept local governments in the dark, presumably to prevent them from acting to grab potentially valuable areas.[56]

With their attention devoted to debt repayment and potential energy bonanzas, both the US and Germany have devoted their efforts – with 70,000 NATO troops on hand to "enforce the peace" – to administering the partition of Bosnia in accordance with Western economic and strategic interests.

While local leaders and Western interests share the spoils of the former Yugoslav economy, they have entrenched socio-ethnic divisions in the very structure of partition. This permanent fragmentation of Yugoslavia along ethnic lines thwarts a united resistance of Yugoslavs of all ethnic origins against the recolonization of their homeland.

But what's new ? As one observer caustically noted, all of the leaders of Yugoslavia's successor states have worked closely with the West: "All the current leaders of the former Yugoslav republics were Communist Party functionaries and each in turn vied to meet the demands of the World Bank and the IMF, the better to qualify for investment loans and substantial perks for the leadership."[57]

From Bosnia to Kosovo

Economic and political dislocation has been the pattern in the various stages of the Balkans war: from the initial military intervention of NATO in Bosnia in 1992 to the bombing of Yugoslavia on "humanitarian grounds" in 1999. Bosnia and Kosovo are stages in the recolonization of the Balkans. The pattern of intervention under NATO guns in Bosnia under the Dayton Accords has been replicated in Kosovo under the formal mandate of United Nations "peace-keeping".

In post-war Kosovo, state terror and the "free market" go hand in hand. In close consultation with NATO, the World Bank had carefully analyzed the consequences of an eventual military intervention leading to the occupation of Kosovo. Almost a year prior to the onslaught of the war, the World Bank had conducted relevant "simulations" which "anticipated the possibility of an emergency scenario arising out of the tensions in Kosovo".[58] This suggests that NATO had already briefed the World Bank at an early stage of military planning.

While the bombing was still ongoing, the World Bank and the European Commission had been granted a special mandate for "coordinating donors' economic assistance in the Balkans"[59] The underlying terms of reference did not exclude Yugoslavia from receiving donor support. It was, however, clearly stipulated that Belgrade would be eligible for reconstruction loans *"once political conditions there change"*.[60]

In the wake of the bombings, "free market reforms" were imposed on Kosovo largely replicating the clauses of the Rambouillet agreement, which had in part been modeled on the Dayton Accords imposed on Bosnia. Article I (Chapter 4a) of the Rambouillet Agreement stipulated that: "The economy of Kosovo shall function in accordance with free market principles".

Along with NATO troops, an army of lawyers and consultants was sent into Kosovo under World Bank auspices. Their mandate: create an "enabling environment" for foreign capital and ensure Kosovo's speedy transition to a "thriving, open and transparent market economy".[61] In turn, the Kosovo Liberation Army (KLA) provisional government had been called upon by the donor community to "establish transparent, effective and sustainable institutions".[62] The extensive links of the KLA to organized crime and the Balkans narcotics trade were not seen by the "international community" as an obstacle to the installation of "democracy" and "good governance".

In occupied Kosovo, under UN mandate, the management of state-owned enterprises and public utilities was taken over by appointees of the Kosovo Liberation Army (KLA). The leaders of the Provisional Government of Kosovo (PGK) had become "the brokers" of multinational capital committed to handing over the Kosovar economy at bargain prices to foreign investors.

Meanwhile, Yugoslav state banks operating in Pristina had been closed down. The Deutschmark was adopted as legal tender and almost the entire banking system in Kosovo was handed over to Germany's Commerzbank A.G., which gained full control over commercial banking functions for the province including money transfers and foreign exchange transactions.63

Taking over Kosovo's Mineral Wealth

Under Western military occupation, Kosovo's extensive wealth in mineral resources and coal was slated to be auctioned off at bargain prices to foreign capital. Prior to the bombings, Western investors already had their eyes riveted on the massive Trepca mining complex which constitutes "the most valuable piece of real estate in the Balkans, worth at least $ 5 billion".[64] The Trepca complex not only includes copper and large reserves of zinc, but also cadmium, gold and silver. It has several smelting plants, 17 metal treatment sites, a power plant and Yugoslavia's largest battery plant. Northern Kosovo also has estimated reserves of 17 billion tons of coal and lignite.

Barely a month after Kosovo's military occupation under NATO guns, the head of the United Nations Mission in Kosovo (UNMIK) Bernard Kouchner issued a decree to the effect that: "UNMIK shall administer movable or immovable property, including monetary accounts, and other property of, or registered in the name of the Federal Republic of Yugoslavia or the Republic of Serbia or any of its organs, which is in the territory of Kosovo".[65]

No time was lost – a few months after the military occupation of Kosovo, the International Crisis Group (ICG) – a think tank supported by Financier George Soros – issued a paper on "Trepca: Making Sense of the Labyrinth", which advised the United Nations Mission in Kosovo (UNMIK) "to take over the Trepca mining complex from the Serbs as quickly as possible and explained how this should be done".[66] And in August 2000, UNMIK Head Bernard Kouchner sent in heavily armed "peacekeepers" ("wearing surgical masks against toxic smoke") to occupy the mine on the pretense that it was creating an environmental hazard through excessive air pollution.

Meanwhile, the United Nations had handed over the management of the entire Trepca complex to a Western consortium. With a stake in the Trepca deal was Morrison Knudsen International, now regrouped with Rayethon Engineering and Construction. The new conglomerate is the Washington Group, one of the world's most powerful engineering and construction firms, as well as a major Defense contractor in the US. Junior partners in the deal are TEC-Ingenierie of France and Sweden's consulting outfit Boliden Contech.

The Installation of a Mafia State

While Financier George Soros was investing money in Kosovo's reconstruction, the George Soros Foundation for an Open Society had opened a branch office in Pristina establishing the Kosovo Foundation for an Open Society (KFOS) as part of the Soros' network of "non-profit foundations" in the Balkans, Eastern Europe and the former Soviet Union. Together with the World Bank's Post Conflict Trust Fund, the Kosovo Open Society Foundation (KOSF) was providing "targeted support" for "the development of local governments to allow them to serve their communities in a transparent, fair and accountable manner".[67] Since most of these local governments are in the hands of the KLA, which has extensive links to organized crime, this program is unlikely to meet its declared objective.[68]

In turn, "strong economic medicine" imposed by external creditors has contributed to further boosting a criminal economy (already firmly implanted in Albania) which feeds on poverty and economic dislocation.

With Albania and Kosovo at the hub of the Balkans drug trade, Kosovo was also slated to reimburse foreign creditors through the laundering of dirty money. Narco-dollars will be recycled towards servicing Kosovo's debt, as well as "financing" the costs of "reconstruction". The lucrative flow of narco-dollars thus ensures that foreign investors involved in the "reconstruction" programme will be able reap substantial returns.

Neoliberalism, the Only Possible World ?

Administered in several doses since the 1980s, NATO-backed neo-liberal economic medicine has helped destroy Yugoslavia. Yet, the global media has carefully overlooked or denied its central role. Instead, they have joined the chorus singing praises of the "free market" as the basis for rebuilding a war shattered economy. The social and political impact of economic restructuring in Yugoslavia has been carefully erased from our collective understanding. Opinion-makers instead dogmatically present cultural, ethnic, and religious divisions as the sole cause of war and devastation. In reality, they are the consequence of a much deeper process of economic and political fracturing.

Such false consciousness not only masks the truth, it also prevents us from acknowledging precise historical occurrences. Ultimately, it distorts the true sources of social conflict. When applied to the former Yugoslavia, it obscures the historical foundations of South Slavic unity, solidarity and identity in what constituted a multi-ethnic society.

At stake in the Balkans are the lives of millions of people. Macro-economic reform, combined with military conquest and UN "peace keeping", has destroyed livelihoods and made a joke of the right to work. It has put basic needs such as food and shelter beyond the reach of many. It has degraded culture and national identity. In the name of global capital, borders have been redrawn, legal codes rewritten, industries destroyed, financial and banking systems dismantled and social programs eliminated. No alternative to global capital, be it Yugoslav "market socialism" or "national capitalism", will be allowed to exist.

Endnotes

1. See, e.g., former US Ambassador to Yugoslavia Warren Zimmerman, 'The Last Ambassador, A Memoir of the Collapse of Yugoslavia', *Foreign Affairs*, Vol 74, no. 2, 1995.

2. For a critique, see Milos Vasic, *et al.*, War Against Bosnia, *Vreme News Digest Agency*, Apr. 13, 1992.

3. Testimony of Richard C. Holbrooke, Assistant Secretary of State, Bureau of European and Canadian Affairs, before the Senate Appropriations Committee, Subcommittee on Foreign Operations, Washington, 19 December 1995.

4. Dayton Peace Accords, Agreement on High Representative, Articles I and II, 16 December 1995.

5. Dayton Peace Accords, Agreement on Police Task Force. Article II.

6. According to a United Nations statement, United Nations, New York, 5 January 1996. See also *Seattle Post Intelligencer*, 16 January 1996, p. A5.

7. Dayton Peace Accords, Agreement on General Framework, Article VII.

8. *Ibid.*

9. *Ibid*, Agreement on Public Corporations, Article I.10.

10. Stabilizing Europe, *The Times* (London), Nov 22, 1990.

11. World Bank, World Development Report 1991, Statistical Annex, Tables 1 and 2, Washington, 1991.

12. Sean Gervasi, 'Germany, the US, and the Yugoslav Crisis', Covert Action Quarterly, No. 43, Winter 1992-93, p. 42.

13. *Ibid.*

14. Dimitrije Boarov, "A Brief Review of Anti-inflation Programs, the Curse of Dead Programs", *Vreme New Digest Agency*, No. 29, 13 April 1992.

15. World Bank, Industrial Restructuring Study: Overview, Issues, and Strategy for Restructuring, Washington, D C, June 1991, pp. 10,14.

16. Gervasi, *op. cit.*, p. 44.

17. World Bank, Industrial Restructuring *Study, op. cit.*, p. viii.

18. Ralph Schoenman, Divide and Rule Schemes in the Balkans, *The Organizer*, San Francisco, Sept. 11, 1995.

19. Judit Kiss, Debt Management in Eastern Europe, *Eastern European Economics*, May June 1894, p 59.

20. See Barbara Lee and John Nellis, *Enterprise Reform and Privatization in Socialist Economies*, The World Bank, Washington DC, 1990, pp. 20-21.

21. For further details see World Bank, *Yugoslavia, Industrial Restructuring*, p. 33.

22. World Bank, *Yugoslavia, Industrial Restructuring*, p. 29.

23. *Ibid*, p. 23.

24. *Ibid*, p. 38.

25. *Ibid*, p. 39.

26. *Ibid*, p. 33.

27. *Ibid*, p. 33.

28. *Ibid*, p. 34. Data of the Federal Secretariat for Industry and Energy. Of the total number of firms, 222 went bankrupt and 26 were liquidated.

29. *Ibid*, p. 33. These figures include bankruptcy and liquidation.

30. *Ibid*, p. 34.

31. *Ibid*, p. 13. Annex 1, p. 1.

32. "Surplus labor" in industry had been assessed by the World Bank mission to be of the order of 20 percent of the total labor force of 8.9 million, – i.e. approximately 1.8 million. This figure is significantly below the actual number of redundant workers based on the categorization of "insolvent" enterprises. Solely in the industrial sector, there were 1.9 million workers (September 1990) out of 2.7 million employed in enterprises classified as insolvent by the World Bank. See World Bank, *Yugoslavia, Industrial Restructuring*, Annex 1.

33. British Broadcasting Service, Borisav Jovic Tells SFRY Assembly Situation Has Dramatically Deteriorated, 27 April 1991.

34. Schoenman, *op. cit.*

35. Gervasi, op *cit.*, p. 44.

36. Federico Nier Fischer, Eastern Europe: Social Crisis, *Inter Press Service*, 5 September 1990.

37. Klas Bergman, 'Markovic Seeks to Keep Yugoslavia One Nation', Christian

Science Monitor, July 11,1990, p. 6.

38. Dimitrue Boarov, "Brief Review of Anti-Inflation Programs: the Curse of the Dead Programs", Vreme News Digest Agency, Apr. 13, 1992.

39. Ibid.

40. Gervasi, op cit., p. 65.

41. Ibid, p. 45.

42. Zimmerman, op. cit.

43. Jim Burkholder, Humanitarian Intervention ? Veterans For Peace, undated, www.veteransforpeace.org.

44. Ibid.

45. Ibid.

46. In June 1995, the IMF, acting on behalf of creditor banks and Western governments, proposed to redistribute that debt as follows: Serbia and Montenegro, 36%, Croatia 28%, Slovenia 16%, Bosnia-Herzegovina, 16% and Macedonia 5%.

47. "Zagreb's About Turn", The Banker, January 1995, p. 38.

48. See World Bank, Macedonia Financial and Enterprise Sector, Public Information Department, 28 November 1995.

49. Statement of Macedonia's Deputy Minister of Finance Mr. Hari Kostov, reported in MAK News, 18 April 1995. Macedonian Information and Liaison Service, MILS News, 11 April 1995.

50. Ibid.

51. According to the terms of the Dayton Accords (Annex1-A), "the government of the Republic of Bosnia and Herzegovina shall provide free of cost such facilities NATO needs for the preparation and execution of the Operation".

52. IMF to Admit Bosnia on Wednesday, United Press International, 18 December 1995.

53. Frank Viviano and Kenneth Howe, "Bosnia Leaders Say Nation Sit Atop Oil Fields", The San Francisco Chronicle, 28 August 1995. See also Scott Cooper, "Western Aims in Ex-Yugoslavia Unmasked", The Organizer, 24 September.

54. Ibid.

55. Ibid.

56. Schoenman, op. cit.

57. World Bank Development News, Washington, 27 April 1999.

58. World Bank Group Response to Post Conflict Reconstruction in Kosovo: General Framework For an Emergency Assistance Strategy, http://www.worldbank.org/html/extdr/kosovo/kosovo_st.htm undated).

59. Ibid.

60. World Bank, The World Bank's Role in Reconstruction and Recovery in

Kosovo, http://www.worldbank.org/html/extdr/pb/pbkosovo.htm, undated.

61. *Ibid.*

62. International Finance Corporation (IFC), International Consortium Backs Kosovo's First Licensed Bank, http://www.ifc.org, Press Release, Washington, 24 January 2000.

63. *New York Times*, July 8, 1998, report by Chris Hedges.

64. Quoted in Diana Johnstone, "How it is Done, Taking over the Trepca Mines: Plans and Propaganda", http://www.emperors- clothes.com/articles/Johnstone/howitis.htm, Emperors Clothes, 28 February 2000.

65. See Johnstone, *op cit.*

66. For the ICG report see http://www.emperorsclothes.com/artiches/Johnstone/icg.htm

67. World Bank, KOSF and World Bank, World Bank Launches First Kosovo Project, Washington, http://www.worldbank.org/html/extdr/extme/097.htm, November 16, 1999, News Release No. 2000/097/ECA.

68. Out of the 20 million dollars budget for this program, only one million dollars was being provided by the World Bank.

Chapter 18

Albania's IMF Sponsored Financial Disaster

Historical Background of the Crisis

Following the demise of the Communist State in 1991, Western capitalism had come to symbolize, for many Albanians, the end of an era, as well as the uncertain promise of a better life. In a cruel irony, production and earnings had plummeted under the brunt of the free market reforms inflicted by donors and creditors. Since 1991, the national economy had been thoroughly revamped under the supervision of the Bretton Woods institutions. With most of the state-owned enterprises spearheaded into liquidation, unemployment and poverty had become rampant.

President Ramiz Alia, Enver Hoxha's chosen successor had already initiated an overture to Western capitalism. Diplomatic relations had been restored with Bonn in 1987 leading to expanded trade with the European Community. In 1990 at its Ninth Plenum, the Albanian Workers' Party (AWP) adopted an economic reform programme, which encouraged foreign investment and provided greater autonomy to managers of state-owned enterprises. These reforms also allowed for the accumulation of private wealth by members of the Communist nomenclature. In April 1990, Prime Minister Adil Carcani announced confidently that Albania was eager to participate in the Conference on European Cooperation and Security, opening the door to the establishment of close ties with Western Defence institutions including NATO.

President Ramiz Alia was re-elected by a multi-party Parliament in May 1991. The defunct Albanian Workers Party was re-baptized and a coalition government between the new "Socialists" and the opposition Democratic Party was formed. Also in 1991, full diplomatic relations with Washington were restored; Secretary of State James Baker visited Tirana, and Albania requested full membership in the Bretton Woods institutions.

Meanwhile, amidst the chaos of hyperinflation and street riots, which preceded the 1992 elections, German, Italian and American business interests had carefully positioned themselves forging political alliances as well as "joint ventures" with the former Communist establishment. The opposition Democratic Party (in principle committed to Western style democracy) was led by Sali Berisha, a former Secretary of the Communist Party and a member of Enver Hoxha's inner circle. Berisha's election campaign had been generously funded by the West.

The IMF-World Bank Sponsored Reforms

Western capital was anxious to secure a firm grip over the reigns of macroeconomic policy. The IMF-World Bank sponsored reforms were set in motion immediately after the electoral victory of the Democrats and the inauguration of President Sali Berisha in May 1992. Economic borders were torn down, Albanian industry and agriculture were "opened up". Adopted in several stages, the ill-fated IMF sponsored reforms reached their inevitable climax in late 1996 with the ruin of the industrial sector and the near disintegration of the banking system. The fraudulent "pyramid" investment funds, which had mushroomed under the Berisha regime, had closed their doors. The faded promises of the "free market" had evaporated, millions of dollars of life long savings had been squandered; the money had been siphoned out of the country. One third of the population was defrauded with many people selling their houses and land.

Some 1.5 billion dollars had been deposited in the "ponzi" schemes with remittances from Albanian workers in Greece and Italy representing a sizeable portion of total deposits. Yet the amounts of money which had transited in and out of the investment funds were significantly larger. The Puglian Sacra Corona Unita and the Neapolitan Camorra Mafias had used the pyramids to launder vast amounts of dirty money, part of which was reinvested in the acquisition of state property and land under Tirana's privatization programme. The ponzi schemes were allegedly also used by Italy's crime syndicates as a point of transit – i.e. to re-route dirty money towards safe offshore banking havens in Western Europe.

These shady investment funds were an integral part of the economic reforms inflicted by Western creditors. The application of "strong economic medicine", under the guidance of the Washington-based Bretton Woods institutions, had contributed to wrecking the banking system and precipitating the collapse of the Albanian economy. Since their inception in 1991-92, the free market reforms had also generated an environment which fostered the progress of illicit trade (noticeably in narcotics and arms sales) as well as the criminalization of state institutions.

Controlled by the ruling Democratic Party, Albania's largest financial "pyramid" –VEFA Holdings – had been set up by the Guegue "families" of Northern Albania with the support of Western banking interests. According to one report, VEFA is now under investigation in Italy for its ties to the Mafia, which allegedly used VEFA to launder large amounts of dirty money.[1]

The pyramids not only financed the campaign of the Democratic Party ahead of the June 1996 elections, they were also used by Party officials to swiftly transfer money out of the country.[2]

> Several of the multi-million-dollar schemes lent their support to the ruling Democratic Party in last year's [1996] parliamentary and local elections. (. . .) To date, no country has investigated the link between governments and the schemes, and critics point to a dearth of fraud-related legislation.[3]

"Foundation fever" was also used to bolster Berisha's euphoric 1996 re-election bid. Widely accused of poll-rigging, the Democratic Party had branded the logos of the pyramids in its 1996 campaign posters. Echoing the get-rich-quick frenzy of the ponzi schemes, the Berisha regime had promised: "with us everybody wins". . .

An "Economic Success Story"

The alleged links of the Albanian state apparatus to organized crime were known to Western governments and intelligence agencies, yet President Sali Berisha had been commended by Washington for his efforts toward establishing a multi-party democracy "with legal guarantees of human rights". Echoing the US State Department, the Bretton Woods institutions (which had overseen the deregulation of the banking system), had touted Albania as an "economic success story": "Albania's performance on macro-economic policy and structural reforms has been remarkably good since 1992".[4] World Bank Director for Central Europe and Asia Mr. Jean Michel Severino on a visit to Tirana in the Fall of 1996, had praised Berisha for the country's "fast growth and generally positive results"; the economy "has bounced back quicker than in other [transition] countries". . . A few months later, the scam surrounding the fraudulent "pyramids" and their alleged links to organized crime were unveiled.

In all the euphoria about double-digit growth rates, few bothered to notice that the revenue was almost all coming from criminal activity or artificial sources, such as foreign aid and remittances sent home by Albanians working abroad.[5]

In February 1997, Prime Minister Alekxander Meksi grimly admitted in a statement to Parliament that the country was on "the brink of macro-economic chaos, (. . .) a real economic catastrophe (. . .) even worse than in 1992," following the initial injection of IMF shock treatment.[6] President Berisha had himself re-appointed by Parliament; a state of emergency was in force which "gave police power to shoot stone-throwers on sight. The main opposition newspaper was set afire, apparently by the secret police, less than 12 hours after the introduction of draconian press censorship laws".[7] Prime Minister Meksi was sacked in early March 1997, the Commander in chief of the Armed Forces General Sheme Kosova was put under house arrest and replaced by General Adam Copani. The latter – who over the years had established close personal ties to NATO headquarters – was responsible for coordinating with Western governments the activities of the military-humanitarian operation ordered by the UN Security Council.

The economy had come to a standstill, poverty was rampant, the Albanian State was in total disarray leading to mass protest and civil unrest. Yet the West's endorsement of the Berisha regime remained impervious.

The Bankruptcy Programme

The pyramid scam was the consequence of economic and financial deregulation. Under the IMF-World Bank sponsored reforms initiated since the outset of the Berisha regime in 1992, most of the large public enterprises had been earmarked for liquidation or forced bankruptcy leading to mass unemployment. Under the World Bank programme, budgetary support for the State Owned Enterprises (SOEs) would be slashed while "clearly identifying which enterprises are to be allowed access to public resources and under which conditions".[8] This mechanism contributed to rendering inoperative a large part of the nation's productive assets. Moreover, credit to state enterprises had been frozen with a view to speeding up the bankruptcy process.

A bankruptcy law was enacted (modelled on that imposed on Yugoslavia in 1989); the World Bank had demanded that:

restructuring efforts include splitting of SOEs [state owned enterprises] to make them more manageable (. . .) and prepare them for privatization. The state-owned medium-sized and large enterprises including public utilities, would be privatized through the mass privatization program (MPP), (. . .), for which vouchers are being distributed to the citizens.[9]

The most profitable state enterprises were initially transferred to holding companies controlled by members of the former nomenclature state assets within the portfolio of these holding companies were to be auctioned off to foreign capital according to a calendar agreed upon with the Bretton Woods institutions.

The privatization programme had led virtually overnight to the development of a property owning class firmly committed to the tenets of neoliberalism. In Northern Albania, this class was associated with the Guegue "families" linked to the Democratic Party. According to one report, the Northern tribal clans or "fares" had also developed links with Italy's crime syndicates.[10]

In turn, this rapid accumulation of private wealth had led to the spurt of luxury housing and imports (including large numbers of shiny Mercedes cars) (...) The import of cars has been boosted by the influx of dirty money (...) Moreover, the gush of hard currency loans granted by multilateral creditors had also contributed to fuelling the import of luxury goods. (Imports had almost doubled from 1989 to 1995. Exports, on the other hand, had dwindled exacerbating the country's balance of payments crisis).[11]

Financial Deregulation

The Albanian Parliament had passed a banking law in 1992 allowing for the creation (with little or no restrictions) of "foundations" and "holding companies" involved in commercial banking activities. The World Bank had insisted on "an appropriate framework for creating new [small and medium-sized] private banks and encouraging informal money lenders and non-bank financial intermediaries to enter the formal financial intermediation circuit".[12] The "pyramids" had thereby become an integral part of the untamed banking environment proposed by the Bretton Woods institutions. The various funds and "foundations" were to operate freely alongside the state banks composed of the National Commercial Bank, the Rural Commercial Bank and the Savings Bank. The law, while spurting the expansion of private financial intermediaries, nonetheless, retained certain "supervisory functions" for the Central Bank authorities. Article 28 of the law provided for the establishment of a Reserve Fund at the Central Bank with a view to "safeguarding the interests of depositors".[13]

The provisions of Article 28 were later incorporated into a special article on banks and financial institutions contained in the World Bank sponsored Draft Law on Bankruptcy presented to Parliament in late 1994. This article provided for the establishment of a "deposit insurance fund" under the supervision of the Central Bank.

While the law was being debated in the Legislature, the IMF advisory team at the Central Bank intervened and demanded:

> that this clause be scrapped because it was "at this time inconsistent with Fund staff advice". (No other reason was given.) Also, the IMF experts advised, normal bankruptcy procedure should not be applied to banks because that would have meant that the creditors of an insolvent bank could ask that bank to stop operations. This was inadvisable, an IMF expert claimed, because "in Albania, which has so few banks, this is perhaps a matter solely for the bank regulatory authorities" – and that meant the Central Bank.[14]

In turn, the foreign consultant who had drafted the Bankruptcy Law (on behalf of the government with support from the World Bank) had advised the authorities that the removal of the deposit insurance clause from the draft law might result in:

> 'Small creditors' rallies in front of closed banks, waving red flags and posters accusing National Bank officials of conspiracy with Western capital, or the Mafia, to exploit and destroy the people". The IMF experts did not listen. On their advice, the deposit insurance scheme and the full application of insolvency law to banks were scrapped.[15]

Despite this forewarning, the IMF's decision (over-ruling both the government and the World Bank) was to be formally embodied in the draft of a new banking law presented to Parliament in February 1996 "at a time when the danger represented by fraudulent banking enterprises should have been evident to everybody".[16] The new banking law also scrapped the three-tier banking system contained in the 1992 Law:

> It [the 1996 draft law] was written in an Albanian so awful that the poor deputies can hardly have understood it; that may have been the reason why they passed it, certainly very much impressed by its arcane technicality. It evidently was a verbatim translation from an English original, so one may safely assume that this, again, was the work of

those IMF experts at the Central Bank everybody believed in – just as, at that same time, nearly everybody believed in those pyramids.[17]

The IMF team at the Albanian Central Bank had:

thwarted pending legislation for the safety of depositors. (. . .) The IMF team at the Albanian Central Bank did not use its influence to make the Central Bank carry out its supervisory duties and stop the pyramids in time – perhaps because the IMF experts believed that Albania needed all the banks it could get, honest or fraudulent.[18]

And it was only when the financial scam had reached its climax in late 1996, that the IMF retreated from its initial position and "asked President Berisha to act. At that time it was far too late, any sort of soft landing was impossible".[19]

In parallel with these developments, the World Bank (which was busy overseeing the enterprise restructuring and privatization programme) had demanded in 1995 the adoption of legislation, which would transform the state-owned banks into holding companies. This transformation had been included in the "conditionalities" of the World Bank Enterprise and Financial Sector Adjustment Credit (EFSAC).

The World Bank had carefully mapped out the process of industrial destruction by demanding a freeze of budget support to hundreds of SOEs targeted for liquidation. It had also required the authorities to set aside large amounts of money to prop up SOEs which had been earmarked for privatization. Thus, prior to putting the National Commercial Bank, the Rural Commercial Bank and the Savings Bank on the auction block, the government (following World Bank advice) was required to "help restore the banks' balance sheets by assuming their non-performing loan portfolio. This will be done so that they can be really sound banks and be turned into shareholding companies, which will then be sold".[20] Making the SOEs (including state-owned public utilities) "more attractive" to potential foreign investors had predictably contributed to fuelling the country's external debt. This "strengthening of SOEs in preparation for privatiza-tion" was being financed from the gush of fresh money granted by multi-lateral and bilateral creditors. Ironically, the Albanian State was "funding its own indebtedness" – i.e. by providing financial support to SOEs ear-marked for sale to Western investors.

Moreover, part of the foreign exchange proceeds, generated by the influx of overseas remittances and dirty money into the "foundations", were also being used to prop up the state's debt-stricken enterprises ultimately to the benefit of foreign buyers who were acquiring state property at rock bottom prices.

In 1996, the Tirana stock exchange was set up with a view to "speeding up the privatization programme". In the true spirit of anglo-saxon liberalism, only ten players (carefully selected by the regime) would be licensed to operate and "compete" in the exchange. [21]

The Scramble for State Property

As the banking system crumbled and the country edged towards disaster, foreign investors (including Italy's crime syndicates) scrambled to take over the most profitable state assets. In February 1997, Anglo-Adriatic, Albania's first voucher privatization fund, was busy negotiating deals with foreign investors in areas ranging from breweries to cement and pharmaceuticals. The Privatization Ministry – hastily set up in response to Western demands after the rigged June 1996 elections – reaffirmed the government's determination "to conclude this undertaking to privatize the economy and to do it soundly, steadily and legally. We are determined to go on."[22]

At midday on March 10, on the third floor of the Albanian Finance Ministry, an auction is due to take place for the sale of a 70 percent stake in the Elbasan cement plant for cash. A day later, a 70 percent stake is due to be sold in the associated limestone quarry.[23]

The World Bank had also recommended that all public utilities including, water distribution, electricity and infrastructure, be placed in private hands. In turn, civil unrest had served to further depress the book-value of state assets to the benefit of foreign buyers: "This is the Wild East", says one Western investor in Tirana. "There is going to be trouble for some time, but that also offers opportunities. We are pressing on regardless." [24]

Selling Off Strategic Industries

Despite mounting protest from the trade-unions, the government had established (in agreement with Western financial institutions) a precise calendar for the sale of its strategic holdings in key industries including oil, copper and chrome. These sales had been scheduled for early 1997... With a modest investment of 3.5 million dollars, Preussag AG, the German mining group was to acquire an 80 percent stake in the chrome industry, giving it control over the largest reserves of chrome ore in Europe.

The stakes in the 1996 elections were high for both America and

Germany. The Adenauer Foundation had been lobbying in the background on behalf of German economic interests. Berisha's former Minister of Defence Safet Zoulali (alleged to have been involved in the illegal oil and narcotics trade) was the architect of the agreement with Preussag against the competing bid of the US-led consortium of Macalloy Inc. in association with Rio Tinto Zimbabwe (RTZ).

Several Western oil companies including Occidental, Shell and British Petroleum had their eyes rivetted on Albania's abundant and unexplored oil-deposits in the regions of Durres, Patos and Tirana. Occidental was also drilling off-shore on Albania's coastline on the Adriatic.

A "favorable mining law", set up under Western advice in 1994, had enticed several Western mining companies into Mirdita, Albania's main copper producing area. But Western investors were also gawking Albania's gold, zinc, nickel and platinum reserves in the Kukes, Kacinari and Radomira areas. A spokesman for a major Western mining company had been inspired by the fact that "Albania [was] stable politically, unlike some of its Balkan neighbours". [25] In 1996, the government established regulations for the privatization of the entire mining industry.

Foreign Control over Infrastructure

Under the agreements signed with the Bretton Woods institutions, the Albanian government was in a strait-jacket. It was not permitted to mobilize its own productive resources through fiscal and monetary policy. Precise ceilings were imposed on all categories of expenditure. The state was no longer permitted to build public infrastructure, roads or hospitals without the assent of its creditors, – i.e. the latter had not only become the "brokers" of all major public investment projects, they also decided in the context of the "Public Investment Programme" (PIP) (established under the guidance of the World Bank) on what type of public infrastructure is best suited to Albania.

The Grey Economy

Alongside the demise of the state-owned corporations, more than 60,000 small scale "informal" enterprises had mushroomed overnight. According to the World Bank, this was clear evidence of a buoyant free enterprise economy: "the decline of the state sector was compensated by the rapid growth of private, small-scale, often informal, activities in retail trade, handicrafts, small-scale construction, and services" (World Bank, Public Information Department, 5 December 1995). Yet upon closer scrutiny of official data, it appears that some 73 percent of total employment (237,000 workers) in this incipient private sector was composed of "newly created enterprises [which] have only one employee". [26]

An expansive "grey economy" had unfolded: most of these so-called "enterprises" were "survival activities" (rather than bona fide productive units) for those who had lost their jobs in the public sector. [27] In turn, this "embryonic" market capitalism was supported by the Albanian Development Fund (ADF) – a "social safety net" set up in 1992 by the World Bank, the European Union and a number of bilateral donors with a view to "helping the development of rural and urban areas by creating new jobs". ADF was also to provide support "with small credits and advice to the unemployed and economically disadvantaged people helping them start their own business".[28] As in the case of VEFA Holdings, the ADF was managed by appointees of the Democratic Party.

Albania had also become a new cheap labor frontier, competing with numerous low wage locations in the Third World: some 500 enterprises and joint ventures (some of them with suspected Mafia connections) were involved in cheap labor assembly in the garment and footwear industries, largely for export back to Italy and Greece. Legislation had also been approved in 1996 to create "free economic areas" offering foreign investors – among other advantages – a seven-year tax holiday. [29]

Rural Collapse

The crisis had brutally impoverished Albania's rural population; food self-sufficiency had been destroyed; wheat production for sale in the domestic market had tumbled from 650,000 tons in 1988 (a level sufficient to feed Albania's entire population) to an estimated 305,000 tons in 1996. Local wheat production had declined by 26 percent in 1996.[30]

The dumping of surplus agricultural commodities, alongside the disintegration of rural credit, had contributed to steering Albania's agriculture into bankruptcy. The United States was supplying the local market with grain surpluses imported under the 1991 Food for Progress Act. Government trading companies had also entered into shady deals through Swiss and Greek commodity brokers involving large shipments of imported wheat.

Moreover, a large chunk of Western financial support was granted in the form of food aid. Dumped on the domestic market, "US Food for

Progress" not only contributed to demobilizing domestic agriculture, it also contributed to the enrichment of a new merchant class in control of the sale of commodity surpluses on the domestic market.

Locally produced food staples had been replaced by imports. In turn, retail food prices had skyrocketed. In the 1980s, Albania was importing less than 50,000 tons of grain.[31]; in 1996 grain imports were (according to FAO estimates) in excess of 600,000 tons of which 400,000 tons were wheat.

By 1996, more than 60 percent of the food industry was in the hands of foreign capital.[32] Agro-processing for export to the European Union had developed largely to the detriment of the local market. The World Bank was providing low interest loans, seeds and fertilizers solely in support of non-traditional export crops. According to one observer, neither credit nor seeds were available to produce grain staples obliging farmers to "shift away from wheat and corn into higher value added products like fruits, vegetables, and pork".[33] What goes unmentioned, however, is that one of the "high value crops" for the export market was the illicit production of marijuana. Moreover, Italian intelligence sources have confirmed the establishment of coca plantations in mountainous areas on the border with Greece. "The Sicilian Mafia, with the support of Colombians, is believed to have set up the plantations."[34] The FAO describes the situation with regard to grain production as follows:

> [Wheat] plantings are estimated to have dropped [in 1996] to only some 127,000 hectares, well below the average 150,000 hectares sown from 1991 to 1995. This reduction was mainly as a result of farmers opting for other crops offering better returns relative to wheat. Yields are also estimated to have dropped further below the previous year's already reduced level. As in the past few years, yield potential was already limited by farmers' limited access to inputs such as fertilizer, crop protection chemicals, and new seeds (farmers have simply been keeping part of the previous season's crop to plant in the next year which has led to a degeneration of the quality of the seed). [35]

Moreover, the production of traditional seeds (reproduced in local nurseries) had been destroyed; farmers now depend largely on seed varieties distributed by international agri-business, yet the prices of commercial seeds has skyrocketed. In a cruel irony, the market for imported seeds and farm inputs had been totally paralysed. According to a spokesman of the Ministry of Agriculture:

Some 35,000 tonnes of wheat are needed this year [1996] as seed, which is a great amount and may be ensured through import only. 'But not a kilogram of seed has been imported until now from private businessmen and the state enterprises.' [36]

This manipulation of the market for seeds and farm inputs had heightened Albania's dependence on imported grain to the benefit of Western agri-business.

The dumping of EU and US grain surpluses on domestic markets had led to the impoverishment of local producers. Fifty percent of the labor force in farming now earns a mere $ 165 per annum. According to the United Nations Development Programme [37] the average income per peasant household in 1995 was a meagre $ 20.40 a month with farms in mountainous areas earning $ 13.30 dollars per month. Several hundred thousand people have flocked out of the rural areas; Tirana's population has almost doubled since 1990. A sprawling slum area has developed at Kanza, on the north-western edge of Tirana.

Macro-economic Chaos

From 1989 to 1992, Albania's industrial output had declined by 64.8 percent and its GDP by 41.2 percent. [38] Recorded GDP later shot up by 7.4 percent in 1994, 13.4 percent in 1995 and 10 percent in 1996. [39] Yet, these "positive results", hailed by the Bretton Woods institutions, had occurred against a background of industrial decline spurted by the World Bank sponsored bankruptcy programme. In 1995, industrial output stood at 27.2 percent of its 1989 level, – i.e. a decline of more than 70 percent. [40]

Despite the impressive turn-around in recorded GDP, living standards, output and employment continued to tumble. While domestic prices had skyrocketed, monthly earnings had fallen to abysmally low levels. Real wages stood at an average of $ 1.50 a day (less than 50 dollars a month) in 1990 declining by 57.1 percent from 1990 to 1992. [41] This collapse in real earnings continued unabated after 1992. According to recent data, conscripts in the Armed forces are paid 2 dollars a month, old age pensions receive between 10 and 34 dollars a month. The highest salaries for professional labor were of the order of $ 100 a month (1996). With the devaluation of the lek in late 1996, real earnings collapsed further (almost overnight) by 33 percent.

The Outbreak of Endemic Diseases

Widespread poverty had led to the resurgence of infectious diseases. There was an outbreak of cholera in 1995. A polio epidemic spread in 1996 from the Northwestern region to Tirana and the rest of the country. [42] According to the United Nations, average life expectancy was 72.2 years in the period prior to the adoption of the market reforms; adult literacy was of the order of 85 percent. [43] The economic reforms had also precipitated the disintegration of health and educational services. The World Bank was assisting the government in slashing social sector budgets through a system of cost recovery. Teachers and health workers were laid off and health spending was squeezed through the adoption of "new pricing policies and payment mechanisms for outpatient services, hospital services and drugs" devised by the World Bank. [44] In collaboration with the World Bank, the Phare program of the European Union had granted support to the privatization of health care.

Criminalization of the State

An expansive underground economy had unfolded. A triangular trade in oil, arms and narcotics had developed largely as a result of the embargo imposed by the international community on Serbia and Montenegro and the blockade enforced by Greece against Macedonia. In turn, the collapse of industry and agriculture had created a vacuum in the economic system which boosted the further expansion of illicit trade. The latter had become a "leading sector", an important source of foreign exchange and a fertile ground for the criminal mafias.

The influx of overseas remittances from some 300,000 Albanian workers in Greece and Italy had increased (according to official figures) threefold from 1992 to 1996. The actual influx, including unrecorded inflows of dirty money was much larger. Several reports confirm that the pyramid schemes had been used extensively to launder the proceeds of organized crime as well as channel dirty money towards the acquisition of state assets.

A Tirana banker, who declined to be named, told Reuters that the last major shipment of dirty money arrived at the start of 1997, with the Mafia paying $ 1.5 million to a fund which laundered $ 20 million. He is quoted as saying that: "The dirty money is plunged into the pyramids and clean money sent out under the guise of bogus import deals," adding that "it is easy to watch the money clear the system." [45]

The Italian mafias were involved in drug-trafficking, cigarette-smuggling and prostitution:

> Pier Luigi Vigna, Italy's chief anti-Mafia prosecutor, confirmed a report by a small business association that Italian-organized crime groups had sunk money into the schemes to raise start-up capital for new ventures. He noted that Albania had become a significant producer of marijuana and was dabbling in the cultivation of coca, the raw material for cocaine. [46]

Local politicians were said to "benefit from the ambient disorder, they even seem to bank on it which hardly encourages efforts towards the modernization and restructuring of Albania". [47] According to one press report (based on intelligence sources), senior members of the government, including cabinet members and members of the secret police SHIK, are alleged to be involved in drugs trafficking and illegal arms trading:

> The allegations are very serious. Drugs, arms, contraband cigarettes all are believed to have been handled by a company run openly by Albania's ruling Democratic Party, Shqiponja (. . .). In the course of 1996 Defence Minister, Safet Zhulali [was alleged] to had used his office to facilitate the transport of arms, oil and contraband cigarettes. (. . .) Drugs barons from Kosovo, the Albanian-dominated region controlled by Serbia, operate in Albania with impunity, and much of the transportation of heroin and other drugs across Albania, from Macedonia and Greece en route to Italy, is believed to be organized by Shik, the state security police (. . .). Intelligence agents are convinced the chain of command in the rackets goes all the way to the top and have had no hesitation in naming ministers in their reports. [48]

Amidst massive protests against the government handling of the pyramid schemes, Safet Zhulali had fled the country to Italy by boat.

"Guns and Ammo for Greater Albania"

The trade in narcotics and weapons was allowed to prosper despite the presence, since 1993, of more than 800 American troops at the Albanian-Macedonian border with a mandate to enforce the embargo. The West had turned a blind eye. The revenues from oil and narcotics were used to finance the purchase of arms (often in terms of direct barter): "Deliveries of oil to Macedonia (skirting the Greek embargo [in 1993-4]) can be used to cover heroin, as do deliveries of kalachnikov rifles to Albanian 'brothers' in Kosovo." [49]

These extensive deliveries of weapons were tacitly accepted by the Western powers on geopolitical grounds; both Washington and Bonn had favored the idea of "a Greater Albania" encompassing Albania, Kosovo and parts of Macedonia. [50] Not surprisingly, there was a "deafening silence" of the international media regarding the Kosovo arms-drugs trade: "the trafficking [of drugs and arms] is basically being judged on its geostrategic implications (. . .) In Kosovo, drugs and weapons trafficking is fuelling geopolitical hopes and fears." [51]

In turn, the financial proceeds of the trade in drugs and arms were recycled towards other illicit activities (and vice versa), including a vast prostitution racket between Albania and Italy. Albanian criminal groups operating in Milan "have become so powerful running prostitution rackets that they have even taken over the Calabrians in strength and influence." [52] Dirty money, originating from payments from the mafias for the dispatch of Albanian women to Italy, has also been deposited in the pyramid funds. . . According to the Albanian Helsinki Committee, up to one third of Italy's prostitutes are Albanians. [53] Other estimates place the number of Albanian prostitutes in Italy at 4000-7000.

Organized Crime Invests in Legal Business

Legal and illegal activities had become inextricably intertwined. The evidence suggests that the involvement of Italy's crime syndicates in Albania was not limited to the mafias' traditional money spinners (drugs, prostitution, arms smuggling, etc.). Organized crime was also suspected to have invested in a number of legal economic activities including the garment industry, tourism and the services economy. According to The Geopolitical Drug Watch "the pyramid cooperatives of southern Albania mostly invested in medium sized Italian firms, establishing joint ventures, some of which are being investigated by the Italian authorities". [54] Conversely, there is evidence that Albanian criminal groups have invested in land and real estate in Italy.

The four main pyramids were Sudja, Populli, Xhaferri and VEFA Holdings. The latter, upheld by the West "as a model of post-communist free enterprise", is the country's largest pyramid investment fund, closely controlled by the Democratic Party. VEFA, which continues to play a key role in the World Bank sponsored privatization programme, owns a large number of former state-owned enterprises including supermarkets, import-export, transportation and manufacturing companies. The supermarket run by VEFA is partly owned by the Italian Aldes supermarket chain.

VEFA is currently under investigation in Italy for its alleged ties to the Mafia. VEFA has been advised by the Naples-based accounting firm Cecere and Caputo, which is alleged to have connections to the Mafia. The brother of the (deceased) founder of the accounting firm Gennaro Cecere, was arrested in early 1997 on Mafia-associated charges. [55] A consultant for the firm, Gianni Capizzi, led a seven-member team in February 1997 with the mandate to restructure VEFA Holdings and give a hand to its chairman, Vehbi Alimucaj, a former army supplies manager "who has no training in economics". Alimucaj is alleged to be involved in the illegal trading of arms:

> Capizzi said by telephone that he had no reason to believe that VEFA operated in an illegal way (. . .) [T]he brother had no connection with the firm, (. . .) Nicola Caputo, the other principal in the Italian firm, has met Alimucaj several times while on business in Albania, Capizzi said.[56]

Recycling Dirty Money Towards Western Creditors

International creditors, anxious to collect interest payments on Tirana's mounting external debt, had their eyes rivetted on the expansive foreign exchange proceeds of this illegal trade. As Albania fell deeper in debt and legal industries and agriculture collapsed, income from illicit trade and overseas remittances became the only available source of essential foreign exchange, and creditors and the Tirana government alike shared a vested financial interest in the uninterrupted flow of lucrative contraband.

The gush of remittances and dirty money into the country was being transformed into domestic currency (lek) and funnelled into the pyramid funds (as well as into the acquisition of state assets and land under the privatization programme).

In turn, the hard currency proceeds were being funnelled from the inter-bank market towards the Treasury. In conformity with its agreements with the Bretton Woods institutions, the government would eventually be obligated to use these hard currency reserves to pay the interest and arrears on Albania's external debt. In fact, a large part of the foreign exchange influx (including money of criminal origin) will eventually be used to meet the demands of Tirana's external creditors leading to a corresponding outflow of resources. According to one report, the creditors had a vested interest in keeping the pyramids afloat as long as possible:

The IMF waited until October 1996 to raise the alarm. For four years, international institutions, American and European lenders and the foreign ministries of Western countries had been content to back the activities of the Albanian political class, which is an offshoot of the "fares", a name given the extended family clans without which nothing can be done in Albania. [57]

Western finance capital had relied on Berisha's Democratic Party which, in turn, was alleged to be associated with Italy's crime syndicates. In turn, the Bretton Woods institutions (which were responsible in advising the government), had insisted on the total deregulation of the banking system. No impediment were to be placed on the development of the pyramids, no restrictions on the movement of money. . . The conventional wisdom would no doubt argue that this influx of hot and dirty money was helping the country "improve its balance of payments".

The West had not only tolerated, during the government of President Berisha, a financial environment in which criminals and smugglers were allowed to prosper, the "free market" system had also laid the foundations for the criminalization of the state apparatus. The evidence suggests that "strong economic medicine" imposed by external creditors contributed to the progress of an extensive criminal economy, which feeds on poverty and economic dislocation.

What Prospects under the Socialists ?

The political protest movement did not identify the role played by international financial institutions and Western business interests in triggering the collapse of the Albanian economy. The people's movement was largely directed against a corrupt political regime. The Democrats were discredited because society had been impoverished. In the eyes of the people, the Berisha government was to blame.

The West's stake in Albania remains unscathed; – i.e. Western interference was not the prime object of political protest. Moreover, the West has been able to enforce its free market reforms on the Berisha government while, at the same time, laying the groundwork for Berisha's downfall. By simultaneously co-opting the Socialist opposition, Western business interests were able to sidetrack political dissent while ensuring the installation of a successor regime.

The West has ensured the replacement of an unpopular government whose legitimacy is challenged, by a freshly-elected "Socialist" regime formed from the ranks of the opposition. Successive governments bear the sole brunt of social discontent while shielding the interests of creditors and MNCs. Needless to say, this change of regime does not require a shift in the direction of macro-economic policy. On the contrary, it enables the Bretton Woods institutions to negotiate with the new authorities a fresh wave of economic reforms.

Under the arrangement reached with Socialist Party leaders at the Rome Conference on 31 July 1997, a residual contingent of Italian troops will remain in Albania. In the words of Franz Vranitzky, mediator for Albania from the Organization for Security and Cooperation in Europe (OSCE), at the close of the Conference: "We will continue to fill the framework with substance with regard to the reconstruction of the Albanian police force, of the army, of commerce, of financial systems and of the constitution."

On the economic front, the Bretton Woods institutions will ensure that the Socialists continue to apply "sound macro-economic policies". In the words of Vranitzky: "The International Monetary Fund (IMF) and the World Bank would send teams to Tirana in August [1997] to help with economic programmes, including setting up banking systems and advising on how to deal effectively with pyramid schemes." [58]

Prime Minister Fatos Nano stated triumphantly at the close of the Rome Conference: "Our [government] programme has not only received a [parliamentary] vote of confidence but today it has received a vote of confidence from the international community."

The July 1997 Rome Agreement safeguards the West's strategic and economic interests in Albania; it transforms a country into a territory; it serves as a bulwark blocking a united resistance of the Albanian people against the plunder of their homeland by foreign capital.

Endnotes

1. Andrew Gumbel, "The Gangster Regime We Fund", *The Independent*, February 14, 1997, p. 15.
2. "Albania, More than a Bankruptcy, the Theft of a Century", *The Geopolitical Drug Dispatch,* No. 66, April 1977, p. 1.
3. *Christian Science Monitor*, 13 February 1997.
4. World Bank Public Information Department, 5 December 1995.
5. Andrew Gumbel, *op. cit.*, p. 15.
6. *Albanian Daily News*, February 28, 1997.

7. Jane Perlez, "Albania Tightens Grip, Cracks Down on Protests", *New York Times*, March 4, 1997.

8. World Bank, Public Information Department, 5 December 1995.

9. *Ibid.*

10. *Geopolitical Drug Watch*, No 66, p. 4.

11. United Nations Economic Commission for Europe (UNECE), Economic Survey of Europe 1996, Geneva, 1996, p 188-189.

12. World Bank, Public Information Department, 5 December 1995.

13. See F. Münzcl, "IMF Experts Partially Responsible for Albanian Unrest", Kosova Information Office, Stockholm, 13 March 1997.

14. *Ibid.*

15. *Ibid.*

16. *Ibid.*

17. *Ibid.*

18. *Ibid.*

19. *Ibid.*

20. *Albanian Times*, Vol. 2, No. 18, May 1996.

21. *Ibid.*

22. *Ibid.*

23. Kevin Done, *Financial Times*, February 19, 1997.

24. Ibid.

25. *Albanian Times*, Vol. 2, No. 19, 1996.

26. *Albanian Times*, Vol. I, No. 8 December 1995.

27. World Bank Public Information Department, 5 December 1995.

28. *Albanian Times,* Vol 2, No. 19, 1995.

29. *Albanian Times*, Vol 2, No 7, February 1996.

30. FAO Release, 8 October 1996.

31. World Bank, World Development Report, 1992.

32. *Albanian Times*, Vol 2. No. 15.

33. *Albanian Times*, Vol 1, No. 2, 1995.

34. Helena Smith, "Italy fears Influx will set back War on Mafia", *The Guardian*, March 25, 1997.

35. FAO Release, October 8, 1996.

36. *Albanian Observer*, Vol 2, No 1.

37. Albania Human Development Report.

38. United Nations Economic Commission for Europe (UNECE), Economic Survey of Europe 1996, Geneva, 1996, p. 184.

39. *Ibid.* The 1996 figure is an estimate.

40. *Ibid,* p. 185.

41. Statistical Yearbook of Albania, 1991, p. 131.
42. WHO, Press Release WHO/59, 18 September 1996; *Albanian Times*, Vol 2, No. 40.
43. See UNDP, Report on Human Development 1992.
44. World Bank Public Information Department, Albania-Health Financing and Restructuring Project, Washington, January 1994.
45. Fabian Schmidt, "Is There A Link Between The Albanian Government And Organized Crime ?", *Bulletin of the Open Media Research Institute*, 17 February 1997, Vol 1, No. 553.
46. Andrew Gumbel, The Gangster Regime We Fund, *The Independent*, February 14, 1997, p. 15.
47. *Geopolitical Drug Watch*, No. 35, September 1994, p. 3.
48. Andrew Gumbel, The Gangster Regime We Fund, *The Independent*, February 14, 1997, p. 15.
49. *Geopolitical Drug Watch*, No. 35, 1994, p. 3.
50. *Geopolitical Drug Watch*, No 32, June 1994, p. 4.
51. *Ibid.*
52. *The Guardian*, 25 March 1997.
53. Ismije Beshiri and Fabian Schmidt, Organized Criminal Gangs Force Albanian Women Into Prostitution Abroad, *Open Media Research Institute Brief*, 14 August 1996.
54. *Ibid*, No. 66, April 1997, p. 3.
55. Daniel J. Wakin, Associated Press Dispatch, 19 February 1997.
56. *bid.*
57. *Geopolitical Drug Watch*, No 66, p. 2.
58. *Ibid.*

PART VI

THE NEW WORLD ORDER

Chapter 19

Structural Adjustment in the Developed Countries

In virtually all sectors of the Western economy, factories are closing down and workers are being laid-off. Agricultural producers in North America and Western Europe are facing impending bankruptcy. Corporate restructuring of the aerospace and engineering industries, relocation of automobile production to Eastern Europe and the Third World, closure of Britain's coal mines. . . In turn, the recession in industry backlashes on the service economy: deregulation and collapse of major airlines, failure of major retail companies, collapse of real estate empires in Tokyo, Paris and London. . . And the plunge in property values has led to loan default, which, in turn, has sent a cold shiver through the entire financial system. During the Reagan-Thatcher era, the recession was marked by several waves of bankruptcies of small enterprises, the collapse of local-level banks (e.g. the US savings and loans crisis) and a bonanza of corporate mergers which spurted the stock market crash of "Black Monday" October 19, 1987. In the 1990s, with the wave of mega-corporate mergers and financial deregulation, the global economic crisis had entered a new phase culminating in a global financial meltdown.

Dismantling the Welfare State

At the very heart of the crisis in the West are the markets for public debt where hundreds of billions of dollars of government bonds and Treasury bills are transacted on a daily basis. The accumulation of large public debts has provided financial and banking interests with "political leverage" as well as the power to dictate government economic and social policy. "Surveillance" by creditor institutions (without the formal involvement of the IMF and the World Bank) is routinely enforced in the European Union and North America. Since the 1990s, the macro-economic reforms adopted in the developed countries contain many of the essential ingredients of the "structural adjustment programs" applied in the Third World and Eastern Europe. Ministers of finance are increasingly expected to report to the large investment houses and commercial banks. Targets for the budget deficit are imposed. The Welfare State is slated to be phased out.

The debts of parastatal enterprises, public utilities, state, provincial and municipal governments are carefully categorized and "rated" by financial markets (e.g. Moody's and Standard and Poor ratings). Moody's downgrading of Sweden's sovereign debt rating in 1995 was instrumental in the decision of the minority Social Democratic government to curtail core welfare programmes, including child allowances and unemployment insurance benefits.[1] Similarly, Moody's credit rating of Canada's public debt was a major factor in the lay-offs of public employees and the closing down of provincial-level hospitals. Canadian provinces (devoid of adequate funding) have been obliged to "downsize" health, education and social security. In turn, under the Canadian privatization programme imposed by Wall Street, large amounts of state property were put on the auction block with the entire railway network of Canadian National (CN) (developed since the 19th century) sold off on international capital markets for the modest sum of 2 billion dollars (somewhat less than the price demanded for the purchase of the Canadian Labatt brewery consortium).[2]

This dismantling of the state, however, is not limited to the privatization of public utilities, airlines, telecoms and railways; corporate capital also aspires to privatize health and education, and eventually acquire control over all state-supported activities. Under WTO definition of "investment", cultural activities, the performing arts, sports, municipal level community services, etc. are slated to be transformed into money-making operations. In turn, corporations vie to establish their control over water, electricity, national highways, the inner-city road network, national parks, etc.

The Conversion of Private Debts

Since the early 1980s, large amounts of debt of large corporations and commercial banks have been conveniently erased and transformed into public debt. This process of "debt conversion" is a central feature of the crisis: business and bank losses have been systematically transferred to the state. During the merger boom of the late 1980s, the burden of corporate losses was shifted to the state through the acquisition of bankrupt enterprises. The latter could then be closed down and written off as tax losses. In turn, the "non-performing loans" of the large commercial banks were routinely written off and transformed into pre-tax losses. The "rescue packages" for troubled corporations and commercial banks were based on the principle of shifting the burden of corporate debts onto the State Treasury.

In turn, the many state subsidies – rather than stimulating job creation – were routinely used by large corporations to finance their mega-mergers, introduce labor saving technology and relocate production to the Third World. Not only were the costs associated with corporate restructuring borne by the state, public spending directly contributed to increased concentration of ownership and a significant contraction of the industrial workforce. In turn, the string of bankruptcies of small and medium-sized enterprises and lay-off of workers (who are also tax payers) were also conducive to a significant contraction in tax revenues.

Towards a Narrowing of the Tax Base

The development of a highly regressive tax system had backlashed, contributing to the enlargement of the public debt. While corporate taxes were curtailed, the new tax revenues appropriated from the (lower and middle) salaried population had been recycled towards the servicing of the public debt.[3] While the state was collecting taxes from its citizens, "a tribute" was being paid by the state (in the form of hand-outs and subsidies) to big business.

In turn, spurted by the new banking technologies, the flight of corporate profits to offshore banking havens in the Bahamas, Switzerland, the Channel Islands, Luxembourg, etc., had contributed to further exacerbating the fiscal crisis. The Cayman Islands, a British Crown colony in the Caribbean, for instance, is the fifth largest banking center in the world (i.e. in terms of the size of its deposits, most of which are by dummy or anonymous companies).[4] The enlargement of the budget deficit in the US during the 1980s and 1990s bears a direct relationship to massive tax evasion and the flight of unreported corporate profits. In turn, large amounts of money deposited in the Cayman Islands and the Bahamas (part of which is controlled by criminal organizations) are used to fund business investments in the US.

Under the Political Trusteeship of Finance Capital

A vicious circle had been set in motion. The recipients of government "hand-outs" had become the state's creditors. In turn, the public debt issued by the Treasury to fund big business had been acquired by banks and financial institutions, which were simultaneously the recipients of state subsidies. An absurd situation: the state was "financing its own indebtedness", government "hand-outs" were being recycled towards the purchase of bonds and treasury bills. The government was being squeezed between business groups lobbying for "handouts" on the one hand and its financial creditors on the other hand. And because a large portion of the public debt was held by private banking and financial institutions, the latter were able to pressure governments for an increased command over public resources in the form of more hand-outs and subsidies.

The Illusory "Independence" of the Central Bank

Moreover, the statutes of central banks in most of the OECD countries had been modified to meet the demands of the financial elites. Central banks have become *independent* and *shielded from political influence*.[5] What this means in practice is that the national Treasury is increasingly at the mercy of private commercial creditors. The Central Bank cannot, under its new statutes, be used to provide credit to the state. Under article 104 of the Maastricht Treaty, for instance, "[c]entral bank credit to the government is entirely discretionary, the central bank cannot be forced to provide such credit".[6] These statutes are, therefore, directly conducive to the enlargement of the public debt held by private financial and banking institutions.

In practice, the Central Bank (which is neither accountable to the government nor to the Legislature), operates as an autonomous bureaucracy under the trusteeship of private financial and banking interests. In the US, the Federal Reserve System is dominated by a handful of private banks which are the shareholders of the twelve federal reserve banks. In the European Union, the European central bank, based in Frankfurt, is under the dominion of Germany's banking giants – the Deutsche and Dresdner banks (now merged into a single banking conglomerate), together with a handful of European banks and financial institutions.

What this means is *that monetary policy no longer exists as a means of State intervention; it largely belongs to the realm of private banking*. In contrast to the marked scarcity of state funds and the inability of the State to finance government programmes through monetary policy, "the creation of money" (implying a command over real resources) occurs within the inner web of the international banking system in accordance with the sole pursuit of private wealth. Powerful financial actors not only have the ability of creating and moving money without impediment, but also of manipulating interests rates and precipitating the decline of major currencies as occurred with the spectacular tumble of the pound sterling in 1992. What this signifies, in practice, is that central banks are no longer able to regulate the creation of money in the broad interests of society (e.g. in view of mobilizing production or generating employment).

Crisis of the State

Under neoliberalism, Western social democracy has been steered into a quandary: those elected to high office increasingly act as puppets or bureaucrats acting on behalf of the financial establishment. The State's creditors have become the depositaries of real political power operating discretely behind the scenes. In turn, a uniform economic discourse and ideology has unfolded. A "consensus" on macro-economic reform extends across the entire political spectrum. The fate of public policy is transacted on the US and Eurobond markets, policy options are mechanically presented through the same stylized economic slogans: "we must reduce the deficit, we must combat inflation"; "the economy is overheating: put on the brakes !"

In the United States, Democrats and Republicans have joined hands; in the European Union, "socialist" governments (not to mention the Greens in Germany) have become the protagonists of "strong economic medicine". . . Social Democrats, New Labor and former Communists have become loyal servants of the financial establishment. Their "progressive" rhetoric and their links to organized labor have made them more "effective" in cutting social budgets and laying off workers. The Social Democrats have become more astute and compliant political brokers on behalf of the financial establishment than their Liberal or Conservative counterparts.

The interests of the financial establishment (particularly in the United States) have also permeated the top echelons of the Treasury and the Bretton Woods institutions: the former US Treasury Secretary Mr. Robert Rubin was a senior banking executive at Goldman Sachs, the former President of the World Bank Mr. Lewis Preston was chief executive at J. P. Morgan replaced by James Wolfensohn, a prominent Wall Street investment banker.

While financiers are involved in politics, former politicians and high-ranking officials in international organizations have also acquired a financial stake in the business community. Upon retiring as head of the World Trade Organization (WTO), Peter Sutherland joined Goldman Sachs in Wall Street. Mr. Nicholas Brady – who was a Republican Senator during the Reagan era and a former US Treasury Secretary in the Bush administration – moved into the lucrative business of offshore banking:

> [T]hrough his private US company Darby Overseas is participating in a Cayman islands registered consortium". "[Mr. Brady's company] is to invest in Peru's commercial banking sector, rated a high risk while it awaits a Brady plan to reschedule its debt. (. . .) Darby Overseas was set up a year ago [1993] by Mr. Brady, his chief aide at the Treasury Mr. Hollis McLoughlin, and Mr. Daniel Marx, [former] Argentine finance under-secretary (. . .) The prime mover behind IFH, constituted to bid for Interbanc, is Mr. Carlos Pastor, Peru's economy minister in the early 1980s.[7]

Marred by conflicts of interest, the state system in the West is in crisis as a result of its ambiguous relationship to private economic and financial interests. Under these conditions, the practice of parliamentary democracy has become a ritual. No alternative is offered to the electorate. Neoliberalism is an integral part of the political platform of all major political parties. As in a one party state, the results of the ballot have virtually no impact on the actual conduct of state economic and social policy. . .

Endnotes

1. See Hugh Carnegy, "Moody's Deals Rating Blow to Sweden", *The Financial Times*, London, 6 January 1995, p. 16. see also Hugh Carnegy, "Swedish Cuts Fail to Convince Markets", *The Financial Times*, London, 12 January 1995, p. 2.

2. Figures in Canadian dollars, *La Presse*, (Montreal), 6 May 1995, p. F2.

3. In the US the contribution of corporations to federal revenues declined from 13.8 percent in 1980 (including the taxation of windfall profits) to 8.3 percent in 1992. See *US Statistical Abstract*, 1992.

4. Estimate of Jack A. Blum presented at *Jornadas: Drogas, desarrollo y estado de derecho*, Bilbao, October 1994. See also Jack Blum and Alan Block,"Le blanchiment de l'argent dans les Antilles" in Alain Labrousse and Alain Wallon (editors), *La planète des drogues*, Le Seuil, Paris, 1993.

5. See Carlo Cottarelli, *Limiting Central Bank Credit to the Government*, International Monetary Fund, Washington, 1993, p. 5.

6. *Ibid*, p. 5.

7. Sally Bowen, Brady Investment in Peru, *Financial Times*, London, 22 July 1994.

Chapter 20

Global Financial Meltdown

A new global financial environment has unfolded in several stages since the collapse of the Bretton Woods system of fixed exchange rates in 1971. The debt crisis of the early 1980s (broadly coinciding with the Reagan-Thatcher era) had unleashed a wave of corporate mergers, buy-outs and bankruptcies. These changes have, in turn, paved the way for the consolidation of a new generation of financiers clustered around the merchant banks, the institutional investors, stock brokerage firms, large insurance companies, etc. In this process, commercial banking functions have coalesced with those of the investment banks and stock brokers.[1]

While these "money managers" play a powerful role on financial markets, they are, however, increasingly removed from entrepreneurial functions in the real economy. Their activities (which often escape state regulation) include speculative transactions in commodity futures and derivatives, and the manipulation of currency markets. Major financial actors are routinely involved in "hot money deposits" in "the emerging markets" of Latin America and Southeast Asia, not to mention money laundering and the development of (specialized) "private banks" ("which advise wealthy clients") in the many offshore banking havens. Within this global financial web, money transits at high speed from one banking haven to the next in the intangible form of electronic transfers. "Legal" and "illegal" business activities have become increasingly intertwined, vast amounts of unreported private wealth have been accumulated. Favored by financial deregulation, the criminal mafias have also expanded their role in the spheres of international banking.[2]

The 1987 Wall Street Crash

Black Monday October 19, 1987 was the largest one-day drop in the history of the New York Stock Exchange overshooting the collapse of

October 28, 1929, which prompted the Wall Street crash and the beginning of the Great Depression. In the 1987 meltdown, 22.6 percent of the value of US stocks was wiped out largely during the first hour of trading on Monday morning. The plunge on Wall Street sent a cold shiver through the entire financial system leading to the tumble of the European and Asian stock markets. . .

The Institutional Speculator

The 1987 Wall Street crash served to "clearing the decks" so that only the "fittest" survive. In the wake of crisis, a massive concentration of financial power has taken place. From these transformations, the "institutional speculator" emerged as a powerful actor overshadowing and often undermining bona fide business interests. Using a variety of instruments, these institutional actors appropriate wealth from the real economy. They often dictate the fate of companies listed on the New York Stock Exchange. Totally removed from entrepreneurial functions in the real economy, they have the power of precipitating large industrial corporations into bankruptcy.

In 1993, a report of Germany's Bundesbank had already warned that trade in derivatives could potentially "trigger chain reactions and endanger the financial system as a whole".[3] While committed to financial deregulation, the Chairman of the US Federal Reserve Board Mr. Alan Greenspan had warned that: "Legislation is not enough to prevent a repeat of the Barings crisis in a high tech World where transactions are carried out at the push of the button".[4] According to Greenspan "the efficiency of global financial markets, has the capability of transmitting mistakes at a far faster pace throughout the financial system in ways which were unknown a generation ago. . ."[5] What was not revealed to public opinion was that "these mistakes", resulting from large-scale speculative transactions, were the source of unprecedented accumulation of private wealth.

By 1995, the daily turnover of foreign exchange transactions (US $1300 billion) had exceeded the world's official foreign exchange reserves estimated at US $1202 billion.[6] The command over privately-held foreign exchange reserves in the hands of "institutional speculators" far exceeds the limited capabilities of central banks, – i.e. the latter acting individually or collectively are unable to fight the tide speculative activity.

Table 20.1

New York Stock Exchange: Worst Single-Day Declines

(Dow Jones Industrial Average, percentage change)

Date	Percentage Decline
October 19, 1987	22.6
October 28, 1929	12.8
October 29, 1929	11.7
November 6, 1929	9.9
August 12, 1932	8.4
October 26, 1987	8.0
July 21, 1933	7.8
October 18, 1937	7.6
October 27, 1997	7.2
October 5, 1932	7.2
September 24, 1931	7.1
August 31, 1998	6.4

Source: New York Stock Exchange

The 1997 Financial Meltdown

The 1987 crisis had occurred in October. Almost to the day, ten years later (also in October) on Monday the 27th, 1997, stock markets around the world plummeted in turbulent trading. The Dow Jones average nose-dived by 554 points, a 7.2 percent decline of its value, its 12th-worst one-day fall in the history of the New York Stock Exchange.

Major exchanges around the world are interconnected "around the clock" through instant computer link-up: volatile trading on Wall Street "spilled over" into the European and Asian stock markets thereby rapidly permeating the entire financial system. European stock markets were in disarray with heavy losses recorded on the Frankfurt, Paris and London exchanges. The Hong Kong stock exchange had crashed by 10.41 percent on the previous Thursday ("Black Thursday" October 24th) as mutual fund managers and pension funds swiftly dumped large amounts of Hong Kong blue chip stocks. The slide at Hong Kong's Exchange Square continued unabated at the opening of trade on Monday morning: a 6.7 percent drop on Monday the 27th followed by a 13.7 percent fall on Tuesday (Hong Kong's biggest point loss ever).

The 1997 meltdown of financial markets had been heightened by computerized trading and the absence of state regulation. The NYSE's Superdot electronic order-routing system was able to handle (without queuing) more than 300,000 orders per day (an average of 375 orders per second), representing a daily capacity of more than two billion shares. While its speed and volume had increased tenfold since 1987, the risks of financial instability were significantly greater.

Ten years earlier, in the wake of the 1987 meltdown, the US Treasury was advised by Wall Street not to meddle in financial markets. Free of government encroachment, the New York and Chicago exchanges were invited to establish their own regulatory procedures. The latter largely consisted in freezing computerized programme trading through the use of so-called "circuit-breakers".[7]

In 1997, the circuit breakers proved to be totally ineffective in averting a meltdown. On Monday the 27th of October 1997, a first circuit breaker halted trading for 30 minutes after a 350 point plunge of the Dow Jones. After the 30 minute trading halt, an aura of panic and confusion was installed: brokers started dumping large quantities of stocks which contributed to accelerating the collapse in market values. In the course of the next 25 minutes, the Dow plunged by a further 200 points, triggering a second "circuit breaker" which served to end the trading day on Wall Street.

Box 20.1

Replicating the Policy Failures of the late 1920s

Wall Street was swerving dangerously in volatile trading in the months preceding the Wall Street crash on October 29, 1929. Laissez-faire, under the Coolidge and Hoover administrations, was the order of the day. The possibility of a financial meltdown had never been seriously contemplated. Professor Irving Fisher of Yale University had stated authoritatively in 1928 that "nothing resembling a crash can occur". The illusion of economic prosperity persisted several years after the Wall Street crash of October 1929. In 1930, Irving Fisher stated confidently that "for the immediate future, at least, the perspective is brilliant". According to the prestigious Harvard Economic Society: "manufacturing activity [in 1930] . . . was definitely on the road to recovery" (quoted in John Kenneth Galbraith, *The Great Crash*, 1929, Penguin, London).

Box 20.2

Mainstream Economics Upholds Financial Deregulation

Sounds familiar? In the wake of the 1997 crash, the same complacency prevailed as during the frenzy of the late 1920s. Echoing almost verbatim the economic slogans of Irving Fisher (see box 20.2), today's economics orthodoxy not only refutes the existence of an economic crisis, it denies outright the possibility of a financial meltdown. According to Nobel Laureate Robert Lucas of the University of Chicago, the decisions of economic agents are based on so-called "rational expectations", ruling out the possibility of "systematic errors" which might lead the stock market in the wrong direction. . . It is ironic that precisely at a time when financial markets were in turmoil, the Royal Swedish Academy announced the granting of the 1997 Nobel Prize in Economics to two American economists for their "pioneering formula for the valuation of stock options [and derivatives] used by thousands of traders and investors" (meaning an "algebraic formula" which is routinely used by hedge funds stock market speculators). (See Greg Burns, "Two Americans Share Nobel in Economics", *Chicago Tribune*, October 15, 1997).

The Asian Crisis

When viewed historically, the 1997 financial crisis was far more devastating and destructive than previous financial meltdowns. Both the stock market and currency markets were affected. In the 1987 crisis, national currencies remained relatively stable. In contrast to both the crashes of 1929 and 1987, the 1997-98 financial crisis was marked by the concurrent collapse of currencies and stock markets. An almost symbiotic relationship between the stock exchange and the foreign currency market had unfolded: "institutional speculators" were not only involved in manipulating stock prices, they also had the ability to plunder central banks' foreign exchange reserves, undermining sovereign governments and destabilizing entire national economies.

In the course of 1997, currency speculation in Thailand, Indonesia, Malaysia and the Philippines was conducive to the transfer of billions of dollars of central bank reserves into private financial hands. Several observers have pointed to the deliberate manipulation of equity and currency markets by investment banks and brokerage firms.[8] Ironically, the same Western financial institutions which looted developing countries' central banks, have also offered "to come to the rescue" of Southeast Asia's monetary authorities. ING Baring, for instance, well known for its speculative undertakings, generously offered to underwrite a one-billion dollar loan to the Central Bank of the Philippines (CBP) in July 1997. In the months which followed, most of these borrowed foreign currency reserves were reappropriated by international speculators when the CBP sold large amounts of dollars on the forward market in a desperate attempt to prop up the Peso.

"Economic Contagion"

Business forecasters and academic economists alike had disregarded the dangers of a global financial meltdown alluding to "strong economic fundamentals"; G7 leaders were afraid to say anything or act in a way, which might give the "wrong signals". . . . Wall Street analysts continue to bungle on issues of "market correction" with little understanding of the broader economic picture.

The plunge on the New York Stock Exchange on October 27th 1997 was casually blamed on the "structurally weak economies" of Southeast Asia, until recently heralded as upcoming tigers, now depicted as "lame ducks". The seriousness of the financial crisis was trivialized: Alan

Greenspan, Chairman of the Federal Reserve Board, reassured Wall Street pointing authoritatively to "the contagious character of national economies, spreading weaknesses from country to country". Following Greenspan's verdict (October 28th), the "consensus" among Manhattan brokers and US academics (with debate or analysis) was that "Wall Street had caught the Hong Kong flu".

The 1998 Stock Market Meltdown

In the uncertain wake of Wall Street's recovery from the 1997 "Asian flu" – largely spurred by panic flight out of Japanese stocks – financial markets backslided a few months later to reach a new dramatic turning point in August 1998 with the spectacular nose-dive of the Russian ruble. The Dow Jones plunged by 554 points on August 31, 1998 (its second largest decline in the history of the New York stock exchange) leading, in the course of September, to the dramatic meltdown of stock markets around the World. In a matter of a few weeks, 2300 billion dollars of "paper profits" had evaporated from the US stock market.

The ruble's August 1998 free-fall had spurred Moscow's largest commercial banks into bankruptcy leading to the potential take-over of Russia's financial system by a handful of Western banks and brokerage houses. In turn, the crisis had created the danger of massive debt default to Moscow's Western creditors, including the Deutsche and Dresdner banks. Since the outset of Russia's macro-economic reforms, following the first injection of IMF "shock therapy" in 1992, some 500 billion dollars worth of Russian assets – including plants of the military industrial complex, infrastructure and natural resources – have been confiscated (through the privatization programs and forced bankruptcies) and transferred into the hands of Western capitalists. In the brutal aftermath of the Cold War, an entire economic and social system was being dismantled.

Financial Deregulation

Rather than taming financial markets in the wake of the storm, Washington was busy pushing through the US Senate legislation, which was to significantly increase the powers of the financial services giants and their associated hedge funds. Under the Financial Modernization Act adopted in November 1999 – barely a week before the historic Seattle Millenium Summit of the World Trade Organization (WTO) – US lawmakers had set the stage for a sweeping deregulation of the US banking system.

In the wake of lengthy negotiations, all regulatory restraints on Wall Street's powerful banking conglomerates were revoked "with a stroke of the pen". Under the new rules – ratified by the US Senate and approved by President Clinton – commercial banks, brokerage firms, hedge funds, institutional investors, pension funds and insurance companies can freely invest in each others businesses as well as fully integrate their financial operations.

The legislation had repealed the Glass-Steagall Act of 1933, a pillar of President Roosevelt's "New Deal" which was put in place in response to the climate of corruption, financial manipulation and "insider trading" which led to more than 5,000 bank failures in the years following the 1929 Wall Street crash.[9] Effective control over the entire US financial services industry (including insurance companies, pension funds, securities companies, etc.) had been transferred to a handful of financial conglomerates – which are also the creditors and shareholders of high tech companies, the defense industry, major oil and mining consortia, etc. Moreover, as underwriters of the public debt at federal, state and municipal levels, the financial giants have also reinforced their stranglehold on politicians, as well as their command over the conduct of public policy.

The "global financial supermarket" is to be overseen by the Wall Street giants; competing banking institutions are to be removed from the financial landscape. State level banks across America will be displaced or bought up, leading to a deadly string of bank failures. In turn, the supervisory powers of the Federal Reserve Board (which are increasingly under the direct dominion of Wall Street) have been significantly weakened .

Free from government regulation, the financial giants have the ability to strangle local-level businesses in the US and overshadow the real economy. In fact, due to the lack of competition, the legislation also entitles the financial services giants (bypassing the Federal Reserve Board and acting in tacit collusion with one another) to set interest rates as they please.

The Merger Frenzy

A new era of intense financial rivalry has unfolded. The New World Order – largely under the dominion of American finance capital – was eventually intent on dwarfing rival banking conglomerates in Western Europe and Japan, as well as sealing strategic alliances with a "select club" of German- and British-based banking giants.

Several mammoth bank mergers (including NationsBank with BankAmerica, and Citibank with Travelers Group) had, in fact, already been implemented and rubber-stamped by the Federal Reserve Board (in violation of the pre-existing legislation) prior to the adoption of the 1999 Financial Modernization Act. Citibank, the largest Wall Street bank, and Travelers Group Inc., the financial services and insurance conglomerate (which also owns Solomon Smith Barney, a major brokerage firm) combined their operations in 1998 in a 72 billion dollar merger.[10]

Strategic mergers between American and European banks had also been negotiated bringing into the heart of the US financial landscape some of Europe's key financial players including Deutsche Bank AG (linked up with Banker's Trust) and Credit Suisse (linked up with First Boston). The Hong Kong Shanghai Banking Corporation (HSBC), the UK based banking conglomerate – which had already sealed a partnership with Wells Fargo and Wachovia Corporation – had acquired the late Edmond Safra's Republic New York Bank in a 9 billion dollar deal.[11]

In the meantime, rival European banks excluded from Wall Street's inner circle, were scrambling to compete in an increasingly "unfriendly" global financial environment. Banque Nationale de Paris (BNP) had acquired Société Générale de Banque and Paribas to form one of the World's largest banks. BNP eventually aspires "to move into North America in a bigger way".[12]

Financial Deregulation at a Global Level

While the 1999 US Financial Services Act does not in itself break down remaining barriers to the free movement of capital, in practice, it empowers Wall Street's key players, including Merrill Lynch, Citigroup, J.P. Morgan, Lehman Brothers, etc., to develop a hegemonic position in global banking, overshadowing and ultimately destabilizing financial systems in Asia, Latin America and Eastern Europe. . .

Financial deregulation in the US has created an environment which favors an unprecedented concentration of global financial power. In turn, it has set the pace of global financial and trade reform under the auspices of the IMF and the World Trade Organization (WTO). The provisions of both the WTO General Agreement on Trade in Services (GATS) and of the Financial Services Agreement (FTA) imply the breaking down of remaining impediments to the movement of finance capital meaning that Merrill Lynch, Citigroup or Deutsche-Bankers Trust can go wherever they please, triggering the bankruptcy of national banks and financial institutions.

In practice, this process has already happened in a large number of developing countries under bankruptcy and privatization programs imposed on an hoc basis by the Bretton Woods institutions. The mega-banks have penetrated the financial landscape of developing countries, taking control of banking institutions and financial services. In this process, the financial giants have been granted de facto "national treatment": without recourse to the provisions of the Financial Services Agreement (FTA) of the WTO, Wall Streets banks, for instance, in Korea, Pakistan, Argentina or Brazil have become bona fide "national banks" operating as domestic institutions and governed by domestic laws which are being remolded under IMF-World Bank jurisdiction. (See Chapters 21 and 22.)

In practice the large US and European financial services giants do not require the formal adoption of the GATS to be able to dominate banking institutions worldwide, as well as overshadow national governments. The process of global financial deregulation is, in many regards, a *fait accompli*. Wall Street has routinely invaded country after country. The domestic banking system has been put on the auction block and reorganized under the surveillance of external creditors. National financial institutions are routinely destabilized and driven out of business; mass unemployment and poverty are the invariable results. Assisted by the IMF – which routinely obliges countries to open up their domestic banking sector to foreign investment – retail banking, stock brokerage firms and insurance companies are taken over by foreign capital and reorganized. Citigroup, among other Wall Street majors, has gone on a global shopping spree buying up banks and financial institutions at bargain prices in Asia, Latin America and Eastern Europe. In one fell swoop, Citigroup acquired the 106 branch network of Banco Mayo Cooperativo Ltda., becoming Argentina's second largest bank.

Endnotes

1. In the US, the division between commercial and investment banking is regu-
    lated by the Glass Steagall Act enacted in 1933 during the Great Depression
    to ensure the separation of securities underwriting from lending, to avoid con-
    flicts of interest and prevent the collapse of commercial banks. The Banking
    Association has recently pointed to the importance of amending the Glass
    Steagall act to allow for the full integration of commercial and investment
    banking. See American Banking Association President's Position, "New Ball

Game in Washington", *ABA Banking Journal*, January 1995, p. 17.

2. For detailed analysis on the role of criminal organizations in banking and finance, see Alain Labrousse and Alain Wallon (editors), *"La planète des drogues"*, Editions du Seuil, Paris, 1993 and Observatoire géopolitique des drogues, *La drogue, nouveau désordre mondial*, Hachette, coll. pluriel-Intervention, Paris, 1993.

3. Quoted in Martin Khor, " Baring and the Search for a Rogue Culprit, *Third World Economics*, No. 108, 1-15 March 1995, p. 10.

4. *Ibid.*

5. *Bank for International Settlements Review*, No. 46, 1997.

6. Martin Khor, SEA Currency Turmoil Renews Concern on Financial Speculation, *Third World Resurgence*, No. 86, October 1997, pp. 14-15.

7. "Five Years On, the Crash Still Echoes", *The Financial Times*, October 19, 1992.

8. Philip Wong, member of the Beijing appointed Legislative Assembly accused the Manhattan Brokerage firm Morgan Stanley of *"short-selling the market"*. See "Broker Cleared of Manipulation", *Hong Kong Standard*, 1 November 1997.

9. See Martin McLaughlin, Clinton Republicans agree to Deregulation of US Banking System, World Socialist website, http://www.wsws.org/index.shtml, 1 November 1999.

10. *Ibid.*

11. See *Financial Times*, November 9, 1999, p. 21.

12. Jocelyn Noveck, "Deal would create largest bank", http://sun-sentinel.com/, March 9 1999.

Chapter 21
Economic Warfare

As financial markets tumble and national economies sink deeper into recession, the 1997 East Asian crisis has developed into a global economic crisis. The international money managers – whose speculative assaults have heavily contributed to this development – have been abetted by the IMF with its push for the deregulation of international capital flows. After having whittled away the capacity of national governments to effectively respond to such 'financial warfare', these powerful forces are working behind the scenes to secure even greater control of the Bretton Woods institutions and a more direct role in the shaping of the international financial architecture.

Manipulating the "Free Market"

The worldwide scramble to appropriate wealth through "financial manipulation" is the driving force behind the crisis. It is also the source of economic turmoil and social devastation. This manipulation of market forces by powerful actors constitutes a form of financial and economic warfare. No need to recolonize lost territory or send in invading armies. In the late twentieth century, the outright "conquest of nations" – meaning the control over productive assets, labor, natural resources and institutions can be carried out in an impersonal fashion from the corporate boardroom: commands are dispatched from a computer terminal, or a cell phone. The relevant data are instantly relayed to major financial markets –often resulting in immediate disruptions in the functioning of national economies. "Financial warfare" also applies complex speculative instruments, including the gamut of derivative trade, forward foreign exchange transactions, currency options, hedge funds, index funds, etc. Speculative instruments have been used with the ultimate purpose of capturing financial wealth and acquiring control over productive assets. In the words of Malaysia's Prime

Minister Mahathir Mohamad: "This deliberate devaluation of the currency of a country by currency traders purely for profit is a serious denial of the rights of independent nations".[1]

The appropriation of global wealth, through the manipulation of market forces, is routinely supported by the IMF's lethal macro-economic interventions which, act almost concurrently in ruthlessly disrupting national economies all over the world. "Financial warfare" knows no territorial boundaries; it does not limit its actions to besieging former enemies of the Cold War era. In Korea, Indonesia and Thailand, the vaults of the central banks were pillaged by institutional speculators, while the monetary authorities sought, in vain to prop up their ailing currencies. In 1997, more than 100 billion dollars of Asia's hard currency reserves had been confiscated and transferred (in a matter of months) into private financial hands. In the wake of the currency devaluations, real earnings and employment plummeted virtually overnight leading to mass poverty in countries that had, in the post-War period, registered significant economic and social progress.

The financial scam in the foreign exchange market had destabilized national economies, thereby creating the preconditions for the subsequent plunder of the Asian countries' productive assets by so-called "vulture foreign investors".[2] In Thailand, 56 domestic banks and financial institutions were closed down on orders of the IMF, unemployment virtually doubled overnight.[3] Similarly in Korea, the IMF "rescue operation" has unleashed a lethal chain of bankruptcies leading to the outright liquidation of so-called "troubled merchant banks". (See Chapter 22.)

The Demise of Central Banking

In many regards, this worldwide crisis marks the demise of central banking meaning the derogation of national economic sovereignty and the inability of the national state to control money creation on behalf of society. Privately held money reserves in the hands of "institutional speculators" far exceed the limited capabilities of the world's central banks. The latter, acting individually or collectively, are no longer able to fight the tide of speculative activity. Monetary policy is in the hands of private creditors who have the ability to freeze state budgets, paralyze the payments process, thwart the regular disbursement of wages to millions of workers (as in the former Soviet Union) and precipitate the collapse of production and social programs.

As the crisis deepens, the speculative raids on central bank reserves have been extended into Latin America and the Middle East with devastating economic and social consequences. A new climax was reached in early 1999 with the dramatic collapse of the Sao Paulo stock exchange. (See Chapter 23.)

The pillage of central bank reserves, however, is by no means limited to developing countries. It has also hit several Western countries including Canada and Australia where the monetary authorities were unable to stem the slide of their national currencies. In Canada, billions of dollars were borrowed in 1998 from private financiers to prop up central bank reserves in the wake of speculative assaults. In Japan – where the yen had tumbled to new lows –"the Korean scenario" was viewed (according to economist Michael Hudson), as a "dress rehearsal" for the takeover of Japan's financial sector by a handful of Western investment banks.[4] The big players are Goldman Sachs, Morgan Stanley and Deutsche Morgan Gruenfell, among others who are buying up Japan's bad bank loans at less than ten percent of their face value.

In the immediate wake of the 1997 Asian crisis, Washington had exerted political pressure on Tokyo insisting:

> on nothing less than an immediate disposal of Japan's bad bank loans - preferably to US and other foreign "vulture investors" at distress prices. To achieve their objectives they are even pressuring Japan to rewrite its constitution, restructure its political system and cabinet and redesign its financial system. (. . .) Once foreign investors gain control of Japanese banks, these banks will move to take over Japanese industry.[5]

Creditors and Speculators

In an integrated financial services industry, the world's largest banks and brokerage houses are both creditors and institutional speculators. In context of the Asian crisis, they directly contributed (through their speculative assaults) to destabilizing national currencies thereby boosting the volume of dollar denominated debts. In the wake of the crisis, they reappeared as creditors with a view to collecting the debts which they themselves contributed to creating through the manipulation of currency markets. Finally, they called in "policy advisors" and financial consultants in charge of the World Bank-sponsored "bankruptcy programs", of which they are also the beneficiaries. In Indonesia, for instance, amidst street rioting and in the wake of Suharto's resignation, the privatization of key sectors of the Indonesian economy – ordered by the IMF – was entrusted to eight of the world's largest merchant banks including Lehman Brothers, Credit Suisse-First Boston, Goldman Sachs and UBS/SBC Warburg Dillon Read.[6] The world's largest money managers set countries on fire and are then called in as firemen (under the IMF "rescue plan") to extinguish the blaze. They ultimately decide which enterprises are to be closed down and which are to be auctioned off to foreign investors at bargain prices.

Who Funds the IMF Bailouts ?

Under repeated speculative assaults, Asian central banks in 1997 had entered into multi-billion dollar contracts (in the forward foreign exchange market) in a vain attempt to protect their currency. With the total depletion of their hard currency reserves, the monetary authorities were forced to borrow large amounts of money under the IMF bailout agreement. Following a scheme devised during the Mexican crisis of 1994-95, the bailout money, however, was not intended "to rescue the country". In fact, the money never entered Korea, Thailand or Indonesia. It was earmarked to reimburse the "institutional speculators" to ensure that they would be able to collect their multi-billion dollar loot. In turn, the Asian tigers – tamed by their financial masters – had been transformed into "lame ducks". Korea, Indonesia and Thailand have been locked into servicing these massive dollar denominated debts well into the third millennium.

But "where did the money come from" to finance these multi-billion dollar operations ? Only a small portion of the money was from IMF resources: starting with the Mexican 1995 bail-out, G7 countries, including the US Treasury, were called upon to make large lump-sum contributions to these IMF rescue operations leading to significant hikes in the levels of public debt in G7 countries.[7] In a cruel irony, the issuing of US public debt to finance the Asian bail-outs was underwritten and guaranteed by the same group of Wall Street merchant banks involved in the speculative assaults.

In other words, *those who guarantee the issuing of public debt to finance the bailout* are those who will ultimately appropriate the loot (e.g. as creditors of Korea or Thailand) – i.e. they are the ultimate beneficiaries of the bailout money – which essentially constitutes a "safety net" for the institutional speculator. The vast amounts of money granted under the rescue packages are intended to enable the Asian countries to meet their debt obligations with the financial institutions, which had contributed to destabilizing their national currencies. As a result of this vicious circle, a handful of commercial banks and brokerage houses have enriched themselves beyond bounds; they have also increased their stranglehold over governments and politicians around the world.

Strong Economic Medicine

Since the 1994-95 Mexican crisis, the IMF has played a crucial role in shaping the "financial battlefields" on which the global money managers wage their speculative raids. The global banks are craving for access to inside information. Successful speculative attacks require the concurrent implementation on their behalf of "strong economic medicine" under the IMF bail-out agreements. The "big six" Wall Street commercial banks (including Chase, Bank America, Citigroup and J.P. Morgan) and the "big five" merchant banks (Goldman Sachs, Lehman Brothers, Morgan Stanley and Salomon Smith Barney) were consulted on the clauses to be included in the Asian bail-out agreements. (See Chapter 22.)

While in theory committed to "financial stability", what they really want is to engineer the collapse of national currencies. In the months preceding the Asian crisis, the Institute of International Finance (IIF), a Washington based think-tank representing the interests of some 300 global banks and brokerage houses had "urged authorities in emerging markets to counter upward exchange rate pressures where needed. . ."8 This request was communicated to the IMF. It hinted, in no uncertain terms, that the IMF should encourage national currencies to slide.[9]

Indonesia, in fact, had been ordered by the IMF to unpeg its currency barely three months before the rupiahs dramatic plunge. In the words of American billionaire and presidential candidate Steve Forbes:

Did the IMF help precipitate the crisis ? This agency advocates openness and transparency for national economies, yet it rivals the CIA in cloaking its own operations. Did it, for instance, have secret conversations with Thailand, advocating the devaluation that instantly set off the catastrophic chain of events ? (. . .) Did IMF prescriptions exacerbate the illness ? These countries' moneys were knocked down to absurdly low levels.[10]

Deregulating Capital Movements

The rules regulating the movements of money and capital across international borders contribute to shaping the "financial battlefields" on which banks and speculators wage their deadly assaults. In their worldwide quest to appropriate economic and financial wealth, global banks and multinational corporations have actively pressured for the outright deregulation of international capital flows including the movement of "hot" and "dirty" money.[11] Caving in to these demands (after hasty consultations with G7 finance ministers), a formal verdict to deregulate capital movements was taken by the IMF in 1998. The official communiqué stated that the IMF will proceed with the Amendment of its Articles with a view to "making the liberalization of capital movements one of the purposes of the Fund and extending, as needed, the Fund's jurisdiction for this purpose". [12] The IMF managing director, Mr. Michel Camdessus, nonetheless conceded, in a dispassionate tone, that "a number of developing countries may come under speculative attacks after opening their capital account" while reiterating that this can be avoided by the adoption of "sound macro-economic policies and strong financial systems in member countries". (i.e. the IMF's standard "economic cure for disaster").[13]

Speculators Call the Shots on Crisis Management

As the aggressive scramble for global wealth unfolds, international banks and speculators are anxious to play a more direct role in "policing" country-level economic reforms. Free market conservatives in the United States have demanded greater US control over the IMF. They have also hinted that the IMF should henceforth perform a more placid role (similar to that of the bond rate agencies such as Moody's or Standard and Poor), while consigning the financing of multi-billion dollar bailouts to the private banking sector.[14]

The world's largest banks and investment houses have proposed the creation of a "Financial Watchdog" – a so-called "Private Sector Advisory Council" – with the mandate of "supervising the IMF.[15] The hidden agenda behind this initiative is to transform the IMF – from its present status as an inter-governmental body – into a full-fledged bureaucracy which directly serves the interests of the global banks.

More importantly, the banks and speculators want access to the details of IMF negotiations with member governments which will enable them to effectively wage their speculative assaults. The global banks (pointing to the need for "transparency") have called upon "the IMF to provide valuable insights [on its dealings with national governments] without revealing confidential information. . .".[16] But what they really want is privileged inside information, as well as a direct role in the negotiation of the IMF bailout agreements. In a cruel irony, speculators – rather than elected politicians – are calling the shots on crisis management. In an absurd logic, those who foster financial turbulence have been invited by G7 Finance ministers to identify policies which attenuate financial turbulence.

In turn, the broader structural causes of the economic crisis remain unheralded. Blinded by neoliberal dogma, policy makers are unable to distinguish between "solutions" and "causes." Public opinion is misled. Lost in the barrage of self-serving media reports on the deadly consequences of "economic contagion", the precise "market mechanisms" – which trigger financial instability – are barely mentioned.

The Concentration of Wealth

This restructuring of global financial markets and institutions (alongside the pillage of national economies) has enabled the accumulation of vast amounts of private wealth – a large portion of which has been amassed as a result of strictly speculative transactions. No need to produce commodities: enrichment is increasingly taking place outside the real economy divorced from bona fide productive and commercial activities. According to American billionaire Steven Forbes: *"Successes on the Wall Street stock market [meaning speculative trade] produced most of last year's [1996] surge in billionaires".*[17] In turn, part of the money accumulated from speculative transactions is funnelled towards confidential numbered accounts in the numerous offshore banking havens. This critical drain of billions of dollars in capital flight dramatically reduces state tax revenues, paralyses social programmes, drives up budget deficits and spurs the accumulation of large public debts.

In contrast, the earnings of the direct producers of goods and services are compressed; the standard of living of large sectors of the world population – including the middle classes – has tumbled. Health and education programmes are downsized; wage inequality has risen in the OECD countries. In both the developing and developed countries, poverty has become rampant. The accumulation of financial wealth, resulting from speculative transactions feeds on poverty and low wages.

Endnotes

1. Statement at the Meeting of the Group of 15, Malacca, Malaysia, 3 November 1997, quoted in the *South China Morning Post,* Hong Kong, 3 November 1997.

2. Michael Hudson, *Our World*, Kawasaki, December 23, 1997. See also Michael Hudson and Bill Totten, "Vulture speculators", *Our World*, No. 197, Kawasaki, 12 August 1998.

3. Nicola Bullard, Walden Bello and Kamal Malhotra, "Taming the Tigers: the IMF and the Asian Crisis", Special Issue on the IMF, *Focus on Trade* No. 23, Focus on the Global South, Bangkok, March 1998.

4. Hudson, *op cit.*

5. Michael Hudson, "Big Bang is Culprit behind Yen's Fall", *Our World*, No. 187, Kawasaki, 28 July 1998. See also Secretary of State Madeleine K. Albright and Japanese Foreign Minister Keizo Obuchi, Joint Press Conference, Ikura House, Tokyo, July 4, 1998 contained in Official Press Release, US Department of State, Washington, 7 July, 1998.

6. See Nicola Bullard, Walden Bello and Kamal Malhotra, *op. cit.*

7. On 15 July 1998, the Republican dominated House of Representatives slashed the Clinton Administration request of 18 billion dollars in additional US funding to the IMF to 3.5 billion. Part of the US contribution to the bail-outs would be financed under the Foreign Exchange Stabilization Fund of the Treasury. The US Congress has estimated the increase in the US public debt and the burden on taxpayers of the US contributions to the Asian bail-outs.

8. Institute of International Finance, Report of the Multilateral Agencies Group, IIF *Annual Report,* Washington, 1997.

9. Letter addressed by the Managing Director of the Institute of International Finance Mr. Charles Dallara to Mr. Philip Maystadt, Chairman of the IMF Interim Committee, April 1997, quoted in Institute of International Finance, *1997 Annual Report*, Washington, 1997.

10. Steven Forbes, "Why Reward Bad Behavior, editorial, Forbes Magazine, 4 May 1998.

11. "Hot money" is speculative capital, "dirty money" are the proceeds of organized crime which are routinely laundered in the international financial system.

12. International Monetary Fund, Communiqué of the Interim Committee of the Board of Governors of the International Monetary Fund, Press Release No. 98/14 Washington, April 16, 1998. The controversial proposal to amend its articles on "capital account liberalization" had initially been put forth in April 1997.

13. See Communiqué of the IMF Interim Committee, Hong Kong, 21 September 1997.

14. Institute of International Finance, "East Asian Crises Calls for New

International Measures, Say Financial Leaders", Press Release, 18 April 1998.

15. IMF, Communiqué of the Interim Committee of the Board of Governors, April 16, 1998.

16. The IIF proposes that global banks and brokerage houses could for this purpose "be rotated and selected through a neutral process [to ensure confidentiality], and a regular exchange of views [which] is unlikely to reveal dramatic surprises that turn markets abruptly (. . .). In this era of globalization, both market participants and multilateral institutions have crucial roles to play; the more they understand each other, the greater the prospects for better functioning of markets and financial stability. . .". See Letter of Charles Dallara, Managing Director of the IIF to Mr. Philip Maystadt, Chairman of IMF Interim Committee, IIF, Washington, 8 April 1998.

17. Charles Laurence, "Wall Street Warriors force their way into the Billionaires Club", *Daily Telegraph*, London, 30 September 1997.

Chapter 22

The Recolonization of Korea

In the late days of November 1997 an IMF team of economists led by "trouble-shooter" Hubert Neiss was swiftly rushed to Seoul. Its mandate: negotiate a "Mexican-style bail-out" with a view to rapidly "restoring economic health and stability". An important precedent had been set: the IMF's bitter economic medicine – routinely imposed on the Third World and Eastern Europe – was to be applied for the first time in an advanced industrial economy.

Washington had carefully set the stage in liaison with the US Embassy in Seoul. Barely a week before the arrival of the IMF mission, President Kim Young Sam had sacked Finance Minister Kang Kyong-shik for having allegedly "hindered negotiations" with the IMF. A more "acceptable" individual was appointed on Washington's instructions. Very convenient: the new "negotiator" and Finance Minister Mr. Lim Chang-yuel happened to be a former IMF and World Bank official – dispatched to Washington by Korea's military rulers in the 1980s heyday of Martial Law. (See Box 21.1) Also fired on short notice was presidential economic adviser Kim In-Ho, for having "spurned the IMF option and said Seoul would restore international credibility through its own efforts."[1]

Finance Minister Lim was accustomed to the Washington scene. No sooner had he been appointed, then he was whisked off to Washington for "negotiations" with his former colleague, IMF Deputy Managing Director Stanley Fischer. In fact, the meeting at IMF headquarters had already been scheduled before his appointment as Korea's Finance Minister.

The IMF Mission arrives in Seoul

The government's dealings with the IMF were a closely guarded state secret. On Friday 21st of November, the government officially announced that "it would be seeking an IMF bailout". On the following business day

---

Box 22.1

Korean Finance Minister sacked for "Hindering Negotiations" with the IMF

In 1998, former Finance Minister Kang kyong-shik was jailed without bail for allegedly "hindering negotiations (. . .) with the International Monetary Fund [and for having] failed to tell his successor, Lim Chang-yuel, what had been negotiated before resigning as Finance Minister (. . .) Mr. Kang says he was forced to resign so quickly that he never had a chance to brief Mr. Lim, who signed an agreement for a loan package of nearly $ 60 billion on Dec. 3, [1997]" (Don Kirk, "Vague Charges Accuse Korean Official of Letting Economy Fall", *International Herald Tribune*, Paris, 21 July 1998).

Mr. Lim, upon retiring from his position of Finance Minister, was elected governor of Kyonggi Province and was later arrested on charges of graft and corruption.

– November 24th, "Seoul Black Monday" – the stock market crumbled to a ten year low over feared IMF austerity measures and "expected corporate and bank collapses." In a cruel irony, the IMF intervention was intended to help the country "restore confidence and economic stability". Faithfully obeying orders from Washington, Finance Minister Lim had removed all exchange controls from the currency market with the a view to "wooing back foreign investors", but with the inevitable result of enticing further speculative assaults against the won.[2]

Two days later, November 26th, the IMF mission, headed by Mr. Hubert Neiss, arrived at Seoul's Kimpo airport. And barely four days later on the 30th, the parties had already agreed on a "Preliminary Agreement". According to chief negotiator and Finance Minister Lim, "adjustments [to the agreement] were minor and would not affect the substance of the deal".[3]

In fact, there was nothing to agree upon, the Finance Minister was a former IMF-World Bank official. The draft text had been prepared at IMF headquarters in Washington prior to the arrival of the mission. The "policy solutions" had already been decided in consultation with Wall Street and the US Treasury: no analysis or negotiation was deemed necessary.

IMF Managing Director Michel Camdessus flew into Seoul on the morning of December 3rd to wrap up the deal. A formal "Letter of Intent", drafted in a hurry with the help of IMF officials, was signed by the Governor of the Bank of Korea, Mr. Kyung shik Lee and the Minister of Finance Lim Chang-yuel.[4] Also present at the wrap-up negotiations was David Lipton, US Under-secretary of the Treasury. His timely presence in Seoul was "unofficial" and was not revealed to public opinion until the 57 billion dollar scam had been signed and sealed:

> David Lipton, a senior American Treasury official, was in Seoul during the negotiations last week. Contrary to claims in the Korean press, Mr. Lipton was not actually present in the negotiating room. But Hubert Neiss, the IMF's chief negotiator, several times refined his position after talking to Mr. Lipton. Michel Camdessus, the IMF's managing director, was scheduled to sign a letter agreeing to the loan program on December 3rd. After talking with American officials, he refused to give his approval until all three candidates in Korea's presidential election, which is set for December 18th, assented to the terms.[5]

Shuttling back to Washington

The IMF's mission was briskly wrapped up on December 3; Hubert Neiss shuttled back to Washington. The IMF Executive Board was meeting on the following day (December 4th) to ratify the 57 billion dollar package. Following the Executive Board decision, the IMF Deputy Managing Director Stanley Fischer candidly admitted at wrap up press conference with a sigh of relief:

> There was a new deputy Prime Minister and Finance Minister, Mr. Lim, who fortunately had been an alternate executive director at the Fund and also at the World Bank in the 1980s. So he was familiar with these institutions. But he came in, in less – just over two weeks ago. (…) He was a very tough negotiator; that's only to be expected. And I believe that the agreement that has been reached shows a lot of courage and a lot of wisdom for the future of the Korean economy.[6]

And the same day, back in Seoul, in a prepared televized statement, Finance Minister Lim – visibly perplexed by the course of events apologized to the Nation:

> I apologize on behalf of the staff of the Finance Ministry to the people. (…) The currency crisis in the Southeast Asian countries led to

our own foreign currency crisis. We did not respond wisely [to this crisis]. I apologize for having to take the bailout package from the IMF.[7]

"Arm Twisting" in the wake of the Presidential Race

But the deal was not yet wrapped up. The country was on the eve of a presidential election, and the front-runner opposition center-left candidate Kim Dae-jung remained firmly opposed to the IMF bailout agreement. He warned public opinion and accused the outgoing government of organizing a massive "sell-out" of the Korean economy:

> [F]oreign investors can freely buy our entire financial sector, including 26 banks, 27 securities firms, 12 insurance companies and 21 merchant banks, all of which are listed on the Korean Stock Exchange, for just 5.5 trillion won, that is, $ 3.7 billion.[8]

Political turnaround. Barely two weeks later – upon winning the presidential race – Kim Dae-jung had become an unbending supporter of strong economic medicine:

> I will boldly open the market. I will make it so that foreign investors will invest with confidence"; in a mass rally he confirmed his unbending support for the IMF... Pain is necessary for reform and we should take this risk as opportunity.[9]

Succumbing to political pressure, Kim Dae-jung – a former dissident, political prisoner and starch opponent of the US backed military regimes of Park Chung Hee and Chun Doo Hwan – had caved in to Wall Street and Washington prior to his formal inauguration as the country's democratically elected president. In fact, Washington had demanded – in no uncertain terms – that all three candidates in the presidential race commit themselves to adopting the IMF programme.

Enforcing "Enabling Legislation" through Financial Blackmail

Despite Kim Dae-jung's endorsement, the IMF Agreement was still in a political limbo. Legislation was required to carry out the layoff and firing of workers. No time was lost. US Under-secretary of the Treasury David Lipton shuttled back to Seoul. This time his presence was formally announced. On the 22nd of December Kim Dae-jung – caving in to Washington's demands – agreed in a meeting with Mr. Lipton on the "the need to dismiss workers as part of industrial restructuring to make the economy competitive."[10] Kim Dae-jung had also given a "green light" to the Korean parliament. A special session of the Legislature was held on the following day, December 23. The four main government motions concerning the IMF Agreement were adopted virtually without debate.[11]

Enforced through financial blackmail, legislation had also been approved which stripped the Ministry of Economy and Finance and of its financial regulatory and supervisory functions. South Korea's Parliament had been transformed into a "rubber stamp".

The IMF had also demanded – on behalf of Korea's external creditors – the speedy passage of legislation which would provide for "central bank independence". The latter provision was intended to thwart the ability of the Korean State to finance national economic development "from within" through monetary policy, – i.e. through domestic credit without depending on foreign loans. In one fell swoop, the system of state-supported credit – instrumental in Korea's dynamic industrial development over the last 40 years – was phased out.

Meanwhile, Moody's Investor Service, the Wall Street credit agency – acting on behalf of US banking interests – had rewarded Korea's compliance by "downgrading ratings for Korean government and corporate bonds, including those of 20 banks, to "junk bond" status".[12]

Box 22.2

Negotiating A 57 Billion Dollar Bailout

19 November 1997- 24 December 1997

19 November: Outgoing President Kim Sam-young fires Minister of Finance Kang Kyong-shik for "hindering negotiations" with the IMF. Kang is replaced by Mr. Lim Chang-yuel, a former Executive Director of the IMF.

20 November: Finance Minister Lim is rushed off to Washington for talks with his former colleague, IMF Deputy Managing Director Stanley Fischer.

21 November: The ROK government formally announces that it will be seeking an Agreement with the IMF. The New Finance Minister is put in charge of negotiations with the IMF.

24 November: "Seoul Black Monday". The Seoul stock market crumbles to a ten-year low over feared IMF austerity measures and expected corporate and bank collapses.

26 November: The IMF mission arrives in Seoul headed by Mr. Hubert Neiss.

27 November: Shrouded in secrecy, talks between the IMF mission and ROK government officials commence.

30 November: After four days of negotiations, the IMF and the Government agree on a "Preliminary Agreement".

1 December: The draft agreement is submitted for approval of the ROK Cabinet.

3 December: IMF Managing Director Michel Camdessus arrives in Seoul to wrap up the deal. US Undersecretary of the Treasury David Lipton, in discussions with Camdessus, states that the deal cannot be finalized unless all three presidential candidates give their support to the IMF bailout.

4 December: The final text of the Agreement is ratified by the IMF Executive Board which approves a stand-by arrangement for 21 billion dollars out of a total package of 57 billion.

5 December: Presidential candidate Kim Dae-jung expresses his opposition to the IMF Agreement and warns public opinion on its devastating economic and social impacts.

18 December: Kim Dae-jung wins the Presidential election and immediately declares his unconditional support for the IMF programme.

22 December: US Under-secretary of the Treasury David Lipton arrives in Seoul. Lipton demands Kim Dae-jung to agree to massive layoffs of workers.

23 December: A special session of the Legislature is called. The Legislature rubber stamps four key government motions regarding the IMF programme.

24 December: Wall Street bankers are called to an emergency meeting on Christmas Eve. At midnight, the IMF agrees to rush 10 billion dollars to Seoul to meet an avalanche of maturing short-term debts.

26 December: Boxing Day: President-elect Kim Dae-jung commits himself to tough actions: "Companies must freeze or slash wages. If that proves not enough, layoffs will be inevitable."

Wall Street Bankers meet on Christmas Eve

The Korean Legislature had met in emergency sessions on December 23. The final decision concerning the 57 billion dollar deal took place the following day on Christmas Eve December 24th, after office hours in New York. Wall Street's top financiers from Chase Manhattan, Bank America, Citicorp and J. P. Morgan had been called in for a meeting at the Federal Reserve Bank of New York. Also at the Christmas Eve venue, were representatives of the "big five" New York merchant banks, including Goldman Sachs, Lehman Brothers, Morgan Stanley and Salomon Smith Barney.[13] Almost simultaneously, some 80 European creditor banks – under the chairmanship of Deutsche Bank AG. – were meeting behind closed doors in Frankfurt, while Japan's big ten banks (which hold a significant portion of Korea's short term debt) were involved in high-level discussions in Tokyo together with Mr. Kyong shik Lee, Governor of the Bank of Korea.

And at midnight on Christmas Eve, upon receiving the "green light" from the banks, the IMF was allowed "to rush 10 billion dollars to Seoul to meet the avalanche of maturing short-term debts".[14]

No Capital Inflows under the Bailout

These Christmas Eve meetings were crucial. The banks had insisted that the multibillion dollar bail-out – financed by G7 governments, the IMF, the World Bank and the Asian Development Bank – should, under no circumstances, result in a positive cash inflow into Korea. The coffers of Korea's central Bank had been ransacked. Creditors and speculators were anxiously awaiting to collect the loot. In other words, the bailout money had already been tagged to reimburse Western and Japanese financial institutions, as well as currency traders. The same institutions which had earlier speculated against the Korean won were cashing in on the IMF bailout money. It was a scam. Korea was locked into servicing this multibillion debt until the year 2006.

The Macro-Economic Agenda

The IMF bailout had derogated Korea's economic sovereignty establishing a de facto colonial administration under a democratically elected president. It had plunged the country, virtually overnight, into a deep recession. The social impact was devastating. The standard of living had collapsed the IMF reforms had depressed real wages and triggered massive unemployment.

The Agreement had lifted the ceiling on foreign ownership and had opened up the domestic bond market to foreign investors: "Foreign financial institutions will be allowed to purchase equity in domestic banks without restriction."[15] In turn, the central bank had been crushed. Its foreign exchange reserves ransacked by institutional speculators. In November 1997, the Bank of Korea's reserves had plunged to an all time low of 7.3 billion dollars. The Bank of Korea (BOK) was reorganized, increasingly under the direct supervision of Wall Street and the IMF. Under the bail-out, fiscal and monetary policy was to be dictated by Korea's external creditors. The Agreement marked the demise of central banking in Asia's most vibrant economy.

Dismantling the Chaebols

The devaluation of the won – together with the stock market meltdown – had generated a deadly chain of bankruptcies affecting both financial and industrial enterprises. The devaluation had also contributed to triggering sharp rises in the prices of consumer necessities. A so-called "exit policy" (i.e. bankruptcy programme) had been set in motion: the operations of some nine "troubled" merchant banks were suspended on December 2, 1997 prior to the completion of the IMF mission. In consultation with the IMF, the government was ordered to "prepare a comprehensive action programme to strengthen financial supervision and regulation".[16]

The hidden agenda was to destroy Korean capitalism. The IMF program had contributed to fracturing the chaebols. The latter had been invited to establish "strategic alliances with foreign firms" – meaning their eventual take-over and control by foreign capital. In turn, selected Korean banks were to "be made more attractive" to potential foreign buyers by transferring their non-performing loans to a "public bail-out fund" – the Korea Asset Management Corporation (KAMC). The automotive group KIA, among Korea's largest conglomerates, declared insolvency. A similar fate affected the Halla Group involved in shipbuilding, engineering and auto-parts.

Acting directly on behalf of Wall Street, the IMF had demanded the dismantling of the Daewoo Group including the sell-off of the 12 so-called "troubled" Daewoo affiliate companies. Daewoo Motors was up for grabs, Korea's entire auto parts industry was in crisis leading to mass layoffs and bankruptcies of auto-parts suppliers.[17]

Meanwhile, the creditors of Korea's largest business empire, Hyundai, had demanded the group's break-up. With the so-called "spin off" – meaning the fracture of Hyundai –, foreign capital had been invited in "to pick up the pieces" at a good prices, meaning Hyundai's profitable car and ship building units.

The bankruptcy of the Korean economy was part and parcel of the IMF Agreement. The freeze on credit imposed by the IMF prevented the Central Bank from coming to the rescue of "troubled" enterprises or banks. The agreement stipulated that "such merchant banks that are unable to submit to appropriate restructuring plans within 30 days will have their licences revoked".[18]

The freeze on credit had also contributed to crippling the construction industry and the services economy: "Banks are increasingly reluctant to provide loans to businesses while bracing for the central bank's tighter money supply."[19] According to one report, more than 90 percent of construction companies (with combined debts of $ 20 billion dollars to domestic financial institutions) are in danger of bankruptcy."[20] The contraction of domestic purchasing power (i.e. lower wages and higher unemployment) had also sent "chills through the nations perennially cash-thirsty small businesses". The government had acknowledged that "quite a number of smaller enterprises will go under".[21]

Wall Street on a Shopping Spree

The Merger and Acquisition boom was hitting with a vengeance. Korea's high-tech electronics and manufacturing economy was up for grabs. Western corporations had gone on a shopping spree, buying up industrial assets at rock-bottom prices. The devaluation of the won – combined with the slide of the Seoul stock market – had dramatically depressed the dollar value of Korean assets.

The Hanwha Group was selling its oil refineries to Royal Dutch/Shell after having sold half its chemical joint venture to BASF of Germany."[22] In a matter of a few months, the market value of Samsung Electronics, the world's largest producer of computer memory chips, had tumbled from 6.5 billion to 2.4 billion dollars. "It's now cheaper to buy one of these companies than buy a factory – and you get all the distribution, brand-name recognition and trained labor force free in the bargain."[23]

Taking over Korea's Commercial Banks

Under its "free market" agenda, the IMF had demanded "the nationalization" of the country's "big six" commercial banks, including Korea First Bank (KFB), Seoul Bank, the merged Commercial Bank of Korea with Hanil Bank, the Korea Exchange Bank and Cho Hung Bank.[24] The intention, however, was not to transfer the banks into state hands – the "nationalized banks" had been slated for "re-privatization".

The objective was to transfer a large share of commercial banking into foreign hands: Korea First Bank (KFB) and Seoul Bank were immediately put on the auction block. In charge of the sale was one of Wall Street's largest investment houses: Morgan Stanley Dean Witter.

How did they do it? Only honest "foreign investors" were allowed to participate in the bidding. To ensure transparency, "crony Korean capitalists" were to be held at bay. It was a sell-out. On the advice of Morgan Stanley, the government had also excluded "any consortium of Korean conglomerates and foreign bidders in the privatization of the two banks."[25]

California and Texas Tycoons to the Rescue

America had come to the rescue of Korea's "troubled banks". The auction of commercial bank assets was an obvious fraud. For a meager $ 454 million, a controlling share (51%) of Korea First Bank (KFB) was transferred to Newbridge Capital Ltd, a US outfit specializing in leveraged buyouts. Newbridge was controlled by US financier Richard Blum, husband of California Senator Dianna Feinstein, in partnership with Texas billionaire David "Bondo" Bonderman of the Texas Pacific Group. Bonderman is a close business partner of another prominent Texas tycoon Richard Bass (with ties to George W. Bush, when he was in the Texas oil business), who also has a stake in the KFB buy-out.[26]

In one fell swoop, a California-based investment firm – visibly with no prior experience in commercial banking – had gained control of one of Korea's oldest banking institutions with 5,000 employees and a modern network of branch offices through out the country. And the Western financial media applauds: Newbridge Capital had generously "accepted" to buy Korea First Bank for 500 billion won (454 million dollars). In fact, under the IMF sponsored scam, Blum, Bonderman and associates "had not disbursed a single dollar of their own money. Korea First Bank was handed to them free of charge".[27]

Under the terms of its agreement with Newbridge, the government had granted so-called "put back options" to KFB which entitled the new owners to demand compensation for all losses stemming from non-performing loans made prior to the sale. What this meant, in practice, was a total cash injection by the ROK government (in several installments) into the KFB of 17.3 trillion won, *an amount equivalent to 35 times the price the government received from Newbridge Capital in the first place.*[28] In a modern form of highway robbery, a totally fictitious "investment" of 454 million dollars by Blum, Bonderman and associates – together with General Electric's financial services arm, GE Capital – had enabled the new owners to cash in on a 15.9 billion dollar government hand-out. Not bad ! And behind this lucrative scam, the Wall Street underwriter Morgan Stanley Dean Witter was also cashing in on fat commissions from both the ROK government and the new American owners of KFB.

And how was the government going to finance this multi-billion dollar handout ? Through lower wages, massive layoffs of public employees – including teachers and health workers – and drastic cuts in social programs, as well as billions of dollars of borrowed money.

The government was caught in a vicious circle. *The multibillion dollar handout in favor of Wall Street had been financed by loans from Wall Street, the IMF and the World Bank.* The government was *"financing its own indebtedness"*. In fact, a 2 billion-dollar loan, granted by the World Bank shortly before the KFB sell-off, had already been tagged to help American "investors" acquire a controlling share of the Korean banking sector.

The new American owners of KFB had – from one day to the next – become creditors of Korea's once powerful business conglomerates now down on their knees. The Korean managers were fired; appointed by Newbridge, the new chairman of the KFB board of directors was Robert Barnum, an established financial whiz-kid associated with the Texas scene, closely aligned with Fort Worth billionaire Robert Bass and his Robert Bass Group. Also on the board of directors were Micky Kantor, former US Commerce Secretary and NAFTA-negotiator in the Bush Administration, together with Los Angeles real estate magnate Thomas Barrack, Chairman of Colony Capital, Inc. who used to be Robert Bass's personal money manager.[30]

Financed by the Korean Treasury, the new Texan and Californian owners of KFB had become "domestic creditors" of Korea's "troubled" business conglomerates. *Without investing a single dollar, they had the power to shake up, downsize or close down entire branches of Korean industry "as they see fit"*, including electronics, automobile production, heavy industry, semiconductors, etc. The fate of the workers of the chaebols was also in the hands of the new American owners... In fact, most of the business takeover proposals and "spin-offs" of the chaebols required the direct consent of Western financial interests.

The ROK government had not only lost control over the privatization program, it had allowed the entire financial services industry to be broken into. Chase Manhattan had purchased a majority interest in Good Money Securities. Goldman Sachs had acquired control of Kookmin Bank, while New York Life had taken over its insurance arm Kookmin Life.[31]

The wholesale privatization of major public utilities had also been demanded – including Korea Telecom and Korea Gas. Korea Electric Power Corporation (KEPCO) was to be broken down into several smaller electricity companies prior to being placed on the auction block. Pohang Iron & Steel Corp. (POSCO) was also to become fully privatized. A similar fate awaits Hanjung, the state-owned Korea Heavy Industries and Construction Company, slated to enter into "a strategic alliance" with Westinghouse.

US and German Capitalists share the Spoils

In Korea, American and German business interests have joined hands. As part of the IMF program, the German banking conglomerate – Deutsche Bank AG – was put in charge of the management of Seoul Bank – which had been "nationalized" alongside KFB. Meanwhile, Mr. Hubert Neiss, the man who negotiated the ill-fated December 1997 bailout was no longer with the IMF. He had been appointed President of Deutsche Bank Asia based in Hong Kong. His new mandate includes the management of Seoul Bank, the terms of which are specified in the IMF program, which he himself designed when he was on staff with the IMF in Washington...[32]

In a similar deal, Deutsche Bank's rival Commerzbank AG had been granted "management control" over the Korea Exchange Bank.[33] In other words, the two German banking giants had from one day to the next – without investing a single Deutschmark – become de facto creditors of the chaebols. As "managers" on behalf of the ROK government, Deutsche and Commerzbank were calling the shots on the restructuring of the chaebols bad debts, as well as on the various takeover proposals of Korean industrial assets by foreign capital.

Instating a System of Direct Colonial Rule

In 1945, Japanese colonial rule was displaced by US political and military domination in the Southern part of the Korean peninsula. Syngman Rhee, a Korean expatriate living in the US, was brought in by General MacArthur to form a pro-US puppet government.

Behind the military rulers installed by Washington, South Korea's incipient business groups were largely in control of economic policy. Under this system of "indirect rule", "national capitalism" was allowed to prosper. The military regime was supportive and instrumental in the dynamic development of the Korean chaebols which came to constitute a powerful force on international markets.

The growth of Korean capitalism was short-lived: Already in the 1980s, "economic globalization" had led to shrinking markets and a world economy marked by overproduction. (See Chapter 3) In the 1990s, intense rivalry and competition developed between competing corporate conglomerates. The Korean chaebols were considered as intruders encroaching on the interests of American, European and Japanese corporate power. The IMF 1997 bailout was applied to deliberately weaken Korean capitalism and confiscate the chaebol's industrial assets.

The hidden agenda was "to tame the tigers", dismantle and subdue Korean corporate power. The system of "indirect colonial rule", first instated by the US military under President Sygman Rhee in 1945, had been disbanded. Korea's ruling business elites had been crushed; an entirely new system of government, under President Kim Dae-jung, had been established geared towards the fracture of the chaebols and the dismantling of Korean capitalism. The signing of the IMF bailout Agreement in December 1997, also marks an important and significant transformation in the structure of the Korean State.

Reunification and the "Free Market"

An IMF negotiating mission had been rushed to Seoul in early June 2000, barely a few days before the historic inter-Korean Summit in Pyongyang between President Kim Dae-jung and Democratic People's Republic of Korea (DPRK) Chairman Kim Jong il. Careful timing... The IMF's presence in Seoul was barely noticed by the Korean press. Firmly behind Kim Dae-jung, South Koreans had their eyes riveted on the promise of the coutry's reunification. Other political issues had be shoved to the sidelines.

Meanwhile backstage – removed from the heat of public debate – the IMF team was quietly putting the finishing touches on a Second IMF Agreement including a "Letter of Intent" to be duly signed by Finance Minister Lee Hun-jai, prior to his departure for the Pyongyang Summit.

It was a carefully planned "sell-out": the Second Agreement was more deadly than the first one signed in December 1997. The ROK government had renewed the IMF's stranglehold on the Korean economy until 2003 without any form of public debate or discussion. The Second Agreement (Memorandum of Economic and Financial Policies) had outlined – in significantly more detail than the controversial 1997 bailout – the precise steps to be undertaken. The dismantling and fracturing of South Korean capitalism had been carefully outlined over a three year period (2000-2003).[34]

But the IMF mission had something else up its sleeve. In liaison with the US Embassy, the IMF mission was briefing Finance Minister Lee Hun-jai who was in charge of the Pyongyang Summit's economic cooperation agenda. Lee was a faithful crony of the IMF: prior to assuming the position of Finance Minister, he had been in charge of the infamous Financial Supervisory Commission (FSC) – the powerful IMF sponsored watch dog – responsible for triggering the bankruptcy of the chaebols. Carefully briefed before his departure for Pyongyang, Finance Minister Lee was to uphold American business interests under the disguise of "inter-Korean economic cooperation". Washington's hidden agenda, under the reunification process, is the eventual recolonization of the entire Korean peninsula.

Colonizing North Korea

Under the inter-Korean economic cooperation program signed in Pyongyang, the Seoul government had committed itself to investing in North Korea. In turn, Hyundai – Korea's largest conglomerate – was to invest and build factories in the North.

But the Korean chaebols – including Hyundai – are rapidly being taken over by American companies. In other words, "inter-Korean economic cooperation" may turn out to be a disguised form of "foreign investment" and a new window of opportunity for Wall Street. The new American owners of the chaebols, in consultation with the US State Department, will ultimately be calling the shots on "inter-Korean economic cooperation", including major investments in North Korea:

Kim Dae-jung's strategy is to help Pyongyang with aid and development, *tap its cheap labor* and build goodwill and infrastructure that are also in South Korea's interest... "Everyone has to keep up the pretense that nothing will happen to the North Korean regime, that you can open up and keep your power and we'll help you make deals with the International Monetary Fund and World Bank. (. . .) But ultimately, we hope it does undermine them. It's the Trojan horse."[35]

The government of Nobel Peace Laureate President Kim Dae-jung had "set the stage" on behalf of Washington. With US military might in the background, the promise of reunification – to which all Koreans aspire – could lead to the imposition of so-called "free market" reforms on Communist North Korea, a process which would result in the "recolonization" and impoverishment of the entire Korean peninsula under the dominion of American capital.

Endnotes

1. Agence France Presse, 19 November 1997.

2. Willis Witter , "Economic Chief sacked in South Korean Debt Crisis: Emergency measures are introduced", *Washington Times*, 20 November 1997.

3. Associated Press Worldstream, 30 November 1997.

4. See International Monetary Fund, *Korea, Request for Stand-by Arrangement*, Washington, December 3, 1997. The text of the 1997 IMF Agreement together with "The Memorandum on the Economic Program" was leaked to the Korean press and can be consulted at http://www.chosun.com/feature/imfreport.html.

5. "New Illness, old Medicine", *The Economist*, US Edition, New York, 13 December 1997, p. 65.

6. Transcript of IMF Press Conference, Washington, 5 December 1997, italics added.

7. Rebroadcast with English translation on MacNeil/Lehrer Productions The NewsHour with Jim Lehrer, December 4, 1997, italics added.

8. Michael Hudson, "Draft for Our World", *Our World*, Kyoto, 23 December 1997.

9. National Public Radio, 19 December 1997.

10. John Burton, "Korea Bonds reduced to Junk Status", *Financial Times*, London, 23 December 1997. p. 3.

11. Choe Seung chul, "Assembly Opens to Legislate Key Financial Reforms", *Korea Herald*, 23 December 1997.

12. John Burton, *op cit.*

13. *Financial Times*, 27-28 December 1997, p. 3.

14. Agence France Presse, Paris, 26 December 1997.

15. International Monetary Fund, *Korea: Request for IMF Standby*, includes "Letter of Intent" and "Memorandum on the Economic Program", see para. 32, p. 44. The text can be consulted at http://www.chosun.com/feature/imfreport.html.

16. *Ibid*, para. 25.

17. Autoparts makers step up resistance to Foreign Control of Daewoo Motor, *Korea Herald*, 28, June 2000.

18. Korea, *Request for IMF Standby*, para. 20, p. 8.

19. Sah Dong seok, "Credit Woes Cripple Business Sectors", *Korea Times*, 28 December 1997.

20. Song Jung tae, "Insolvency of Construction Firms rises in 1998", *Korea Herald*, 24 December 1997.

21. *Korean Herald*, 5 December 1997.

22. Michael Hudson, *op cit.*

23. *Ibid.*

24. Catherine Lee, "The Wrong Medicine; Nationalization of Commercial Banks in South Korea", *The Banker*, December 1998.

25. Text of official government statement, quoted in "Korea To Let Only O/S Investors to Buy Two Troubled Banks", *Asia Pulse*, Seoul, 5 November 1998.

26. See Michael Zielenziger, "A rebounding but unreformed South Korea making investors, officials nervous", *Knight Ridder Tribune News Service*, 11 June 1999

27. "More Tax Money for KFB", *Korea Herald,* Seoul, 17 August 2000, p. 1.

28. *Ibid.*

29. *Ibid.*

30. *Asia Pulse*, 21 January 2000.

31. "Struggle to survive will intensify amid M&As", *Business Korea*, Vol 17, No 2, February 2000, p. 30-36.

32. Who What, Where, *The Asian Banker Journal* , 18 May 2000.

33. Commerzbank Pledges Active Role in Cleaning Up Korea Exchange Bank, *Business Korea*, 8 August 2000.

34. Text of "Memorandum of Economic and Financial Policies" and "Letter of Intent", June 14, Ministry of Finance, Seoul, 2000, published in the Republic of Korea Economic Bulletin, June 2000 at http://epic.kdi.re.kr/home/ecobul/indexlist.htm. Also published by the International Monetary Fund (IMF) at http://www.imf.org/external/NP/loi/2000/kor/01/INDEX.HTM. The Memorandum grants management rights to Deutsce Bank over KFB. Los Angeles times, 16 June 2000, italics added.

Chapter 23

The Brazilian Financial Scam

Succumbing to the speculative onslaught, the Sao Paulo stock exchange crumbled on Black Wednesday, 13 January 1999. The vaults of Brazil's central bank had been burst wide open; the Real's "crawling" peg to the dollar was broken.

Central Bank Governor Gustavo Franco was replaced by an economics professor, Francisco Lopes, who was immediately whisked off to Washington together with Finance Minister Pedro Malan for high-level "consultations" with the IMF and the US Treasury. This week-end stint with Washington officials was a preamble to an early morning meeting a few days later at the New York Federal Reserve Bank with Brazil's creditors. On the breakfast list were Quantum Hedge Fund speculator George Soros, Citigroup Vice-President William Rhodes, Jon Corzine from Goldman Sachs and David Komansky of Merrill Lynch.[1] This private meeting, held behind closed doors, was crucial: Rhodes was head of the New York Banking Committee on behalf of Brazil's commercial creditors. He had dealt with president Fernando Henrique Cardoso when he was Finance Minister in 1993-94. The "restructuring" of Brazil's external debt – together with the adoption of the so-called "Real Plan" – had been imposed by the New York Banking Committee. This "economic stabilization" program had contributed to the swelling of Brazil's internal debt from 60 billion dollars in 1994, to more than 350 billion in 1998. . .(See Chapter 13.)

Meanwhile, public opinion had been carefully misled as to the causes of the financial meltdown: the "Asian flu" was said to be spreading. . . The global media had casually laid the blame on Minas Gerais' "rogue governor" Itamar Franco (a former President of Brazil) for declaring a moratorium on debt payments to the federal government.[2] The threat of impending debt default by the state governments was said to have affected Brasilia's "economic credibility".

Brazil's National Congress was also blamed for not having granted a swift and "unconditional rubber-stamp" to the IMF's lethal economic medicine. The latter required budget cuts of the order of 28 billion dollars (including massive lay-offs of civil servants, the dismantling of social programmes, the sale of state assets, the freeze of transfer payments to the state governments and the channelling of state revenues towards debt servicing).[3]

Squeezing Credit

In insisting on tight monetary policy, the Washington-based institutions, in consultation with Wall Street, were also intent on destabilizing Brazil's industrial base, taking over the internal market and speeding up the privatization programme. The government overnight benchmark interest rate was increased on instructions of the IMF to a staggering 39% (per annum), implying commercial bank lending rates between 50% and 90% per annum. Local manufacturing, crippled by insurmountable debts, had been driven into bankruptcy. Purchasing power had crumbled; interests rates on consumer loans were as high as 150% to 250% leading to massive loan default. . .[4]

While "confidence" had been temporarily restored on financial markets, the Real had lost more than 40 percent of its value, leading to an almost immediate surge in the prices of fuel, food and consumer essentials. The demise of the nation's currency had contributed to brutally compressing the standard of living in a country of 160 million people where more than 50 percent of the population are below the poverty line.

In turn, the devaluation had backlashed on Sao Paulo's Southern industrial belt where the (official) rate of unemployment had reached 17 percent. In the days following Black Wednesday January 13th 1999, multinational companies including Ford, General Motors and Volkswagen confirmed work stoppages and the implementation of massive lay-offs of workers.[5]

Background of the IMF Agreement

At first sight, the plight of Brazil appeared to be a standard "re-run" of the 1997 Asian currency crisis. The IMF's lethal "economic medicine" was broadly similar to that imposed in 1997-98 on Korea, Thailand and Indonesia. Yet there was a striking difference in the "timing" (i.e. chronology) of the IMF ploy: in Asia, the IMF "bailouts" had been negotiated on an ad hoc basis "after" rather than "before" the crisis. (See chapters 21 and 22.) The IMF had "come to the rescue" of the "Asian tigers" in the wake of the speculative onslaught, once national currencies had tumbled and the countries were left with insurmountable debts.

In contrast, in the case of Brazil, the IMF financial operation was launched in November 1998 – exactly two months prior to the financial meltdown – as part of a new standing IMF-G7 arrangement. The "economic medicine" was meant to be "preventive" rather than "curative". Officially, it was intended to prevent the occurrence of a financial disaster. In the words of its political architects US Treasury Secretary Robert Rubin and UK Chancellor of the Exchequer Gordon Brown: *"We must do more to (. . .) limit the swings of booms and busts that destroy hope and diminish wealth."*[6]

In practice, the IMF-G7 scheme accomplished exactly the opposite results. Rather than staving off the speculative onslaught, it contributed to accelerating the outflow of money wealth. Twenty billion dollars were taken out of Brazil in the two months following the approval of the IMF "precautionary package" in November: an amount of money equivalent to the massive "up-front" budget cuts required by the IMF.

Marred by capital flight, Brazil's central bank reserves were being plundered at the rate of 400 million dollars a day. From 75 billion dollars in July 1998, central bank reserves dwindled to 27 billion in January 1999. The first tranche of the IMF loan, of more than 9 billion dollars (granted in November 1998), had already been squandered to prop up Brazil's ailing currency; the money was barely sufficient to "finance the flight of capital" in the course of a single month.

Enticing Speculators

The IMF sponsored operation was largely instrumental in enticing speculators to persist in their deadly raids; "The money was there" to be drawn upon and the speculators knew it. If the Central Bank of Brazil were to default on its foreign exchange contracts, the availability of IMF-G7 money "upfront" would enable banks, hedge funds and institutional investors to swiftly collect their multi-billion dollar loot. The IMF programme signed in November 1998 thereby contributed to reducing the risks and "reassuring speculators".

The approximate "timing" of the devaluation was part of the IMF ploy; by ensuring a stable exchange rate in the two-month period following the IMF agreement (13 November 1998), it had allowed speculators to swiftly cash in on an additional 20 billion dollars.

Both Wall Street and the Washington institutions knew that a devaluation was imminent and that the IMF-G7 sponsored "preventive" package was nothing more than a stop gap measure. The IMF programme enabled Wall Street currency speculators "to buy time". The Central Bank had been instructed by the IMF and Wall Street "to hold in" as long as possible. The ploy was to facilitate the plunder of the country's money wealth. The economic team at the Ministry of Finance said that they were "taken by surprise". But they knew all along that the devaluation was coming (. . .) It was a sell out. In January, the IMF agreed to let the currency slide. By that time it was too late, Central Bank reserves had already been ransacked.

"A Marshall Plan for Creditors and Speculators"

From the Davos Economic Summit, Stanley Fischer IMF Senior Deputy Managing Director and main architect of the November "preventive" loan package, headed to Brasilia to negotiate the terms of a new agreement.

Short-term debts had spiralled, "new policy initiatives" were being demanded; the harsh austerity measures, agreed with the IMF a few months earlier, were deemed insufficient to "restore a lasting recovery of confidence". New fiscal targets were established; following the pattern set in the Asian bailouts, Brasilia was "to intensify and broaden the privatization and divestment effort" – laying the basis for the liquidation of federal and state banks, and speeding up the appropriation of Brazil's energy and strategic sectors, public utilities and infrastructure by foreign capital.[7]

In turn, the Central Bank was to be thoroughly revamped under IMF guidance. The monetary authorities had been instructed to uphold the Real under a flexible exchange regime. No exchange controls were allowed. A second tranche of 9 billion dollars (under the 41.5 billion dollar loan) had contributed to replenishing the coffers of the Central Bank (on borrowed money), enticing speculators to continue their deadly raids. Under the new IMF ploy signed in February 1999, capital flight was to continue unabated. Very lucrative: following the financial meltdown of January 13th, capital outflows were running at 200 to 300 million dollars a day.[8]

Wall Street in Charge of Brazil's Central Bank

To ensure the continued success of the speculative onslaught, Professor Francisco Lopes – who had been appointed head of the Central Bank on Black Wednesday January 13 – was sacked two weeks later and replaced by Mr. Arminio Fraga Neto, a former adviser to the Soros Fund in New York. This appointment was made following Finance Malan's meeting with George Soros at the New York Federal Reserve Bank breakfast meeting. Former President Itamar Franco had remarked with a touch of humour: "I am happy to learn that the new Central Bank governor is mega-speculator George Soros".[9]

Wall Street insiders were in command of monetary policy. Brazil's external creditors have the ability to freeze state budgets, paralyse the payments process – including transfers to the state governments – and thwart (as in the former Soviet Union) the regular disbursement of wages to public sector employees, including several million teachers and health workers.

This "programmed bankruptcy" of domestic producers has been instrumented through the credit squeeze, not to mention the threat by Finance Minister Pedro Malan to allow for increased trade liberalization and (import) commodity dumping with a view to obliging domestic enterprises "to be more competitive". Combined with interest rates above 50 percent, the consequence of this policy for many domestic producers is tantamount to bankruptcy, – i.e. pushing domestic prices below costs.

In turn, the dramatic compression of domestic demand (i.e. resulting from increased unemployment and declining real wages) had led to a situation of oversupply and rising stocks of unsold merchandise. . . This ruthless demise of local industry – engineered by macro-economic reform – had created an "enabling environment" which empowered foreign capital to take over the internal market, reinforce its stranglehold over domestic banking and pick up the most profitable productive assets at bargain prices.

The financial crisis has created conditions which favor the rapid recolonization of the Brazilian economy. The depreciation of the Real has depressed the book value (in dollars) of state assets and has contributed to speeding up the privatization programme. The IMF's lethal economic medicine – combined with mounting debt and continued capital flight – spells economic disaster, fragmentation of the federal fiscal structure and social dislocation.

"Dollarization" of Latin America

The Brazilian financial meltdown had also created an environment, which strengthens throughout the Latin American region, the stranglehold of Wall Street creditors over monetary policy. In Argentina, the demise of the central bank was already firmly in place under a colonial style "currency board" arrangement. The Argentinean peso has been replaced by the US dollar, implying not only the complete control over money creation by external creditors. Similarly, the appointment of a Wall Street insider to head the Central Bank of Brazil, is part of the dollarization ploy, leading to the eventual destruction of Brazil's national currency.

Other Latin American countries are slated to follow suit, narrowly viewing the "dollarization" of their currencies as a way of averting a financial disaster. No "soft-landing" is in sight: although dollarization is not formally part of the Free Trade Agreement of the Americas (FTAA) initiative, the hidden agenda is to eventually replace Latin American currencies with the US dollar, initially under a currency board arrangement.

Box 23.1

The Takeover of Brazil's Banking System

ABN AMRO, Lloyds Bank, HSBC and Dresdner are busy acquiring bank assets in Brazil. HSBC acquired close to 1000 branch offices of Banco Amerindus becoming overnight the second largest private retail bank in Brazil.

Wall Street investment banks are often put in charge with the task of selling off state assets in shady insider deals under the IMF privatization and bankruptcy programs.

In Brazil, for instance, Merrill Lynch was put in charge of the privatization of Companhia Vale do Rio Doce (CVRD) one of world's largest mining outfits, on behalf of the Brazilian government. But Merrill Lynch was also representing one of the prospective buyers of CVRD: the Anglo-American mining consortium. In a typical insiders operation, Anglo-American has joined hands with NationsBank (now merged with BankAmerica), alongside an obscure offshore unregistered investment fund "Opportunity Asset Management Fund" which has Citibank and mega-businessman George Soros as investors. (Financial Times, 5 May 1997). Through the acquisition of CVRD, the consortium will control more than 80 percent of Brazil's steel industry. (Geoff Dyer, Soros Consortium set to bid in Brazil Iron Ore Sell-Off, Financial Times, 5 May 1997, p. 1). In turn, the proceeds of the sale of CVRD will be conveniently recycled from the Treasury back towards servicing the external debt of Brazil of which one of new owners of CVRD, namely Citigroup, happens to be Brazil's main creditor and head of the Banking committee responsible for the restructuring of Brazil's multibillion dollar external debt.

Endnotes

1. *Estado De Sao Paulo*, 21 January 1999.
2. A 90 days moratorium was declared. See *Financial Times*, London, January 18, 1999, p. 4.
3. IMF Press Conference by Michel Camdessus and Stanley Fischer, Washington, November 13, 1998. See also "Letter of Intent" and "Brazil: Memorandum of Economic Policies", IMF, Washington, 13 November 1998.
4. See *Estado de Sao Paulo*, 21 January 1999.
5. See Larry Rohter, "Crisis Whipsaws Brazilian Workers", *New York Times*, January 16th, 1998.
6. Quoted in *Financial Times*, London, 31 October-1 November 1998.
7. See Joint Statement of the Ministry of Finance of Brazil and the IMF Team, News Brief no. 99/5, IMF, Washington, 4 February 1999).
8. *Estado de Sao Paulo*, 21 January 1999.
9. "Itamar: Soros presidara o BC", Agencia Estado, *Ultima Noticias*, 2 February 1999.

SELECTED BIBLIOGRAPHY

Amin, Samir, 1990, *Maldevelopment: Anatomy of a Global Failure*, Zed Books Ltd., London, 1990.

African Rights, 1993, *Somalia, Operation Restore Hope: A Preliminary Assessment*, London.

Addison Tony and Demery Lionel, 1987, *"Alleviating* Poverty under Structural Adjustment", *Finance and Development*, Vol. 24, No. 4.

Albanez, T., et al, 1989, *Economic Decline and Child Survival*, UNICEF, Florence.

Altmann, Jorn, 1990, "IMF Conditionality: the Wrong Party Pays the Bill", *Intereconomics*, May-June.

Alvarez, Elena, 1991, *The Illegal Coca Production in Peru: A Preliminary Assessment of its Economic Impact*, Institute of the Americas and University of California at San Diego, February 1991.

Anyiam, Charles and Robert Stock, 1991, *Structural Adjustment Programs and "Reality" of Living Conditions*, CASID annual meetings, Kingston.

Aristide, Jean-Bertrand and Laura Flynn (Editors), 2000, *Eyes of the Heart: Seeking a Path for the Poor in the Age of Globalization*, Common Courage, Monroe, Maine.

Atta Mills, Cadman, 1989, *Structural Adjustment in Sub-Saharan Africa*, Economic Development Institute, World Bank, Washington, DC.

Balassa, B., 1981, *Structural Adjustment Policies in Developing Countries*, World Bank, Washington, DC.

Bamako Initiative Management Unit, 1990, *The Bamako Initiative Strategy in Mauritania*, New York.

Banco Intertamericano de Desarrollo, 1989, Peru: *informe economico*, Washington, DC.

Barratt Brown, M., 1992, *Short-changed, Africa in World Trade*, Pluto Press, London.

Beardsley, Tim, 1993, "Selling to Survive", *Scientific American*, February.

Behrman, Jere and Anil B. Deolalikar, 1991, "The Poor and the Social Sectors during a Period of *Macro-economic Adjustment*: Empirical Evidence from Jamaica", *World Bank Economic Review*, Vol. 5, No. 2.

Bell Michael and R. Sheehy, 1987, "Helping Structural Adjustment in Low Income Countries", *Finance and Development*, 24:4, December.

Bello, Walden and Cunningham, Shea, 1994, *Dark Victory: The US, Structural Adjustment, and Global Poverty*, Food First, London.

Bello, Walden, 2000, "Bringing Financial Crisis to Asia", *The Ecologist*, Vol. 30, No. 6.

Bello, Walden, 2000, "Time to Decide: Radical Reform or Abolition", *The Ecologist*, Vol. 30, No. 6.

Bello, Walden, 2000, "WTO: Serving the Wealthy, Not the Poor", *The Ecologist*, Vol. 30, No. 6.

Beneria, Lourdes and Shelley Feldman, 1992, *Unequal Burden and Persistent Poverty*, Westview Press, Boulder.

Bennett, K., 1991, *Economic Decline and the Growth of the Informal Sector*, CASID Annual Conference, Kingston, Ont.

Bennett, Sara and Manengu Musambo, 1990, *Report on Community Financing and District Management Strengthening in Zambia*, Bamako Initiative Technical Report, UNICEF, New York.

Betz, J., 1990, "The Social Effects of Adjustment Policy in LDCs", *Intereconomics*, May-June.

Berg, Andrew; and Catherine Patillo, 2000, The Challenge of Predicting Economic Crises *Economic Issues* No. 22, International Monetary Fund, Washington.

Bianchi A. (editor), 1985, *La Deuda externa latino americana*, Grupo Editor Latino Americano, Santiago.

Bigelow, Bill and Bob Peterson (Editors), 2002, *Rethinking Globalization:Teaching for Justice in an Unjust World*, Rethinking Schools Press, San Francisco.

Boateng, E. Oti, et al., undated, *A Poverty Profile for Ghana*, 1987-1988, World Bank, Washington, DC.

Bond, Patrick, 1998, *Uneven Zimbabwe, a Study of Finance, Development and Underdevelopment*, Africa World Press, Trenton, New Jersey.

Bourgoignie Georges and Marcelle Genné (Editors), 1990, *Structural Adjustment and Social Realities in Africa*, University of Ottawa, Ottawa.

Brandt, H. et al., 1985, *Structural Distortions and Adjustment Programs in the Poor Countries of Africa*, Deutsches Institut fur Entwicklungs Politik, Berlin.

Brandt Commission, 1983, Common Crisis, North-South Cooperation for World Recovery, Pan Books, New York.

Bruno, Michael (editor), 1991, *Lessons of Economic Stabilisation and its Aftermath*, MIT Press, Cambridge, Mass.

Burkholder, Jim, undated, Humanitarian Intervention ? Veterans For Peace, undated, www.veteransforpeace.org.

Bullard, Nicola, Walden Bello and Kamal Malhotra, 1998, "Taming the Tigers: the IMF and the Asian Crisis", Special Issue on the IMF, *Focus on Trade* No. 23, Focus on the Global South, Bangkok, March 1998.

Calavita, Kitty, et al., 1997, *Big Money Crime: Fraud and Politics in the Savings and Loan Crisis*, University of California Press, San Francisco.

Canadian International Development Agency, 1987, *Sharing our Future*, Hull.

Canadian International Development Agency, 1990, *Working Paper on Poverty Alleviation for the 4As*, Hull.

Camen, Ulrich, 1991, *Country Paper Nepal: Macro-economic Evolution and the Health Sector*, WHO, Geneva.

Cammen, Ulrich and Carrin, Guy, 1991, *Macro-economic Analysis: Guinea, Macro-economic Evolution and the Health Sector*, WHO, Geneva.

Campbell, Bonnie K., 1989, *Political Dimensions of the International Debt Crisis*, Macmillan, London.

Campbell, Bonnie K. and John Loxley (editors) 1990, *Structural Adjustment in Africa*, Macmillan, London.

Campodonico, Humberto, 1989, *"La politica del avestruz"*, in Diego Garcia Sayan (editor), Lima, 1989.

Carrin, Guy and Kodjo, 1991, *The Basic Macro-economics of Government Health Sector Expenditures in Low Income Developing Countries*, WHO, Office of International Cooperation, Geneva.

Cavanagh, John, International Forum on Globalization, and Alternatives Task Force. 2002, *Alternatives to economic globalization: a better world is possible*. Berrett-Koehler, San Francisco CA.

Chauvier, Jean Marie, 1993, "Tourbillon de crises en Russie", *Le Monde diplomatique*, October.

Chossudovsky Michel, 1975, "Hacia el nuevo modelo economico chileno, inflacion y redistribucion del ingreso, 1973-74", *Trimestre Economico*, No. 122.

Chossudovsky, Michel, 1991, "The Globalisation of Poverty and the New World Economic Order", *Economic and Political Weekly*, Vol. 26, No. 44.

Chossudovsky Michel and Pierre Galand, 1997, L'usage de la dette extérieure du Rwanda: la responsabilité des créanciers, United Nations Development Programme (UNDP), Ottawa and Brussels.

Comisión Economica para America Latina y el Caribe, 1990, *Magnitud de la Pobreza en America Latina en los Años Ochenta*, Santiago de Chile.

Commonwealth Secretariat, 1989, *Engendering Adjustment for the 1990s*, Report of a Commonwealth Expert Group on Women and Structural Adjustment, London.

Cornia, Giovanni A., 1989, "Investing in Human Resources: Health, Nutrition and

Development for the 1990s", *Journal of Development Planning*, No. 19.

Cornia, Giovanni and Frances Stewart, *The Fiscal System, Adjustment and the Poor*, UNICEF, Innocenti Occasional Papers No. 11, Florence, 1990.

Cornia, Giovanni A., Richard Jolly and Frances Stewart, 1987, *Adjustment with a Human Face*, Vol. 1, UNICEF, Oxford University Press, New York.

Cornia, Giovanni A. and Richard Strickland, *Rural Differentiation, Poverty and Agricultural Crisis in Sub-Saharan Africa, Towards an Appropriate Policy Response*, UNICEF, Florence.

Corrêa Linhares, Célia Maria and Maristela de Paula Andrade, 1992, "A Açao Oficial e os Conflitos Agrários no Maranhao", *Desenvolvimento e Cidadania*, No. 4, Sao Luis de Maranhao.

Cottarelli, Carlos, 1993, *Limiting Central Bank Credit to the Government*, IMF, Washington, DC.

Cruz Rivero, C., et al., 1991, *The Impact of Economic Crisis and Adjustment on Health Care in Mexico*, WHO, Florence.

Culpeper, Roy, 1987, *Forced Adjustment: The Export Collapse in Sub-Saharan Africa*, North-South Institute, Ottawa.

Culpeper, Roy, 1991, *Growth and Adjustment in Smaller Highly Indebted Countries*, the North-South Institute, Ottawa.

Danaher Kevin, 2001, *Elite Globalization vs People's Globalization*, Global Exchange, San Francisco.

Danaher, Kevin and Burbach, Roger, 2000, *Globalize This: The Battle Against the World Trade Organization*, Community Archives Publications.

Das, Bhagirath Lal, 2002, *The World Trade Organisation, A Guide to the Framework for International Trade*, Third World Network, Penang.

Das, Bhagirath Lal, 2003, WTO: The Doha Agenda, *The New Negotiations on World Trade*,

Zed Books, London and Third World Network, Penang.

Gates, Jeff, 2000, *Democracy at Risk: Rescuing Main Street from Wall Street*, Perseus Press.

Dancourt, Oscar, 1987, "Cuando se abandona las politicas fondomonetaristas", in Herrera, C., Dancourt, O. and G. Alarco, *Reactivación y politica economica heterodoxa*, Fundación Friedrich Ebert, Lima.

Dancourt, Oscar et al., 1990, "Una Propuesta de Reforma Monetaria para Acabar con la Inflacion", Documentos de trabajo No. 90, CISEPA, Pontificia Universidad Catolica del Peru, Lima, July 1990.

Dancourt, Oscar, and Ivory Yong, 1989, "Sobre hyperinflación peruana", *Economía*, XII:23, June 1989.

Denters, Erik M.G., 1996, *Law and Policy of IMF Conditionality*, Kluwer Law International, The Hague.

Devlin, Robert, 1990, "The Menu Approach", *IDS Bulletin*, Vol. 23, No. 2.

Didszun, Klaus, 1990, "On the Problem of Negative Net Transfers to Developing Countries", *Intereconomics,* May-June.

Drewnowski, Jan, 1965, The *Level of Living Index*, UNRISD, Geneva.

Ebel, Beth, 1991, *Patterns of Government Expenditure in Developing Countries during the 1980s*, UNICEF, Florence.

Edwards, S. 1988, *La Crisis de la deuda externa y las politicas de ajuste estructural en America Latina*, Estudios CIEPLAN, Santiago.

Elson, Diane, 1989, "How is Adjustment Affecting Women", *Development*, No. 1.

Faber, Mike and Griffith Jones, S., 1990, "Editorial on Approaches to Third World Debt Reduction", *IDS Bulletin*, Vol. 23, No. 2.

Fabricant, Stephen and Clifford Kamara, 1990, *The Financing of Community Health Service in Sierra Leone*, UNICEF, New York.

Forbes Magazine, International Billionaires, the World's Richest People *Forbes Magazine*, New York, annual. List at http://www.forbes.com/.

Ferroni, Marco and Ravi Kanbur, 1991, *Poverty Conscious Restructuring of Public Expenditure*, SDA Working Paper No. 9, World Bank, Washington, DC.

Figueroa, Adolfo, 1989, "Integración de las politicas de corto y largo plazo", *Economía* XII:23, June.

Food and Agriculture Organization (FAO), 2000, Special Report: FAO/WFP Crop Assessment Mission to Ethiopia, Rome.

Foxley, A., 1987, "Latin American Development after the Debt Crisis", *Journal of Development Economics*, Vol. 27, Nos. 1-2.

French, Hillary, 2000, *Vanishing Borders : Protecting the Planet in the Age of Globalization*, Norton, New York.

Garcia Sayan, Diego (editor), 1989, *Coca, cocaína y narcotrafico*, Comisión Andina de Juristas, Lima.

Gates, Jeff, 2000, *Democracy at Risk: Rescuing Main Street from Wall Street*, Perscus Press. New York.

Gervais, Myriam, 1993, "Etude de la pratique des ajustements au Niger et au Rwanda", *Labor, Capital and Society*, Vol. 26, No. 1.

Gervasi, Sean, 1993, "Germany, US and the Yugoslav Crisis", *Covert Action*, No. 43, Winter 1992-93.

Ghai, Dharam, 1992, *Structural Adjustment, Global Integration and Social Democracy*, UNRISD, Geneva.

Glasberg, Davita Silfen and Skidmore, Dan, 1997, *Corporate Welfare Policy and the Welfare State: Bank Deregulation and the Savings and Loan Bailout (Social Institutions and Social Change)*, Aldine De Gruyter.

Global Outlook, Shanty Bay, Ontario, Quarterly Magazine.

Glover, David, 1991, "A Layman's Guide to Structural Adjustment", *Canadian Journal of Development Studies*, Vol. 12, No. 1.

Goncalves, R. 1986, *Structural Adjustment and Structural Change: In Search of a Solution*, UNCTAD, Geneva.

Griffith-Jones, S. and O. Sunkel, 1986, *Debt and Development Crises*, Oxford, Clarendon Press.

Griffith-Jones, S., 1989, "Debt Reduction with a Human Face", *Development*, No. 1.

Griffith-Jones, S. (editor), 1989, *Debt Management and the Developing Countries*, UNDP, New York.

Grootaert, C. and Marchant T., *The Social Dimensions of Adjustment Survey*, World Bank, Washington, DC.

Guichaoua, André, 1987, *"Les paysans et l'investissement-travail au Burundi et au Rwanda"*, Bureau international du Travail, Geneva,

Guichaoua, André, 1989, *Destins paysans et politiques agraires en Afrique centrale*, L'Harmattan, Paris.

George, Susan, 1999, *The Lugano Report*, Pluto Press, London.

George, Susan and Fabrizio Sabelli, 1994, *Faith and Credit, The World Bank's Secular Empire*, Penguin Books, London.

Haggard, Stephen et al., 1992, *The Politics of Economic Adjustment*, Princeton University Press, Princeton.

Helleiner, G. K., 1987, "Stabilization, Adjustment and the Poor", *World Development*, 15:2 December.

Heller, Peter et al., 1988, *The Implications of Fund-Supported Adjustment for Poverty*, IMF, Washington, DC.

Hicks, R. and O. Per Brekk, 1991, *Assessing the Impact of Structural Adjustment on the Poor, the Case of Malawi*, IMF, Washington, DC.

Hoogfeld, Ankie, 1997, *Globalization and the Postcolonial World, The New Political Economy of Development*, John Hopkins University Press, Baltimore.

Hossein Farzin, 1991, "Food Aid: Positive and Negative Effects in Somalia?", *The Journal of Developing Areas*, January.

Hussein, Mosharaf, A. T. M. Aminul Islam and Sanat Kumar Saha, 1987, *Floods in Bangladesh, Recurrent Disaster and People's Survival*, Universities' Research Centre, Dhaka.

Hudson, Michael, 1998, "Big Bang is Culprit behind Yen's Fall", *Our World*, No. 187, Kawasaki, 28 July 1998.

Hudson, Michael and Bill Totten, 1998, "Vulture speculators", *Our World*, No. 197, Kawasaki, 12 August 1998.

Institute of International Finance, 1997, Report of the Multilateral Agencies

Group, IIF Annual Report, Washington, DC.

Instituto de Pesquisa Economica Aplicada (IPEA), 1993, Mapa da Fome II: *Informaçoes sobre a Indigencia por Municipios da Federaçâo*, Brasilia.

Inter-American Development Bank, 1991, *Economic and Social Progress in Latin America*, 1991 Report, Washington, DC.

International Labour Office, 1992, *Adjustment and Human Resource Development*, Geneva.

International Labour Organization, 1989, *Generating Employment and Incomes in Somalia*, Jobs and Skills Programme for Africa, Addis Ababa.

International Monetary Fund, annual, Annual Report, Washington, DC.

International Monetary Fund, annual, World Economic Outlook, Washington, DC.

International Monetary Fund, 1988, *The Implications of Fund Supported Adjustment Programs for Poverty*, IMF, Washington, DC.

International Monetary Fund, 1991, *Bangladesh: Economic Reform Measures and the Poor*, Washington, DC.

International Monetary Fund, World Bank, Organization for Economic Cooperation and Development and European Bank for Reconstruction and Development, 1991, *A Study of the Soviet Economy*, Paris.

International Monetary Fund and International Development Association, 1996, Heavily Indebted *Poor Countries (HIPC) Initiative: Strengthening the Link Between Debt Relief and Poverty Reduction*, Washington, DC.

International Monetary Fund, 1997, *Korea, Request for Stand-by Arrangement*, Washington, DC, December 3, 997, http://www.chosun.com/feature/imfreport.html.

International Monetary Fund, 1999, *Ethiopia, Recent Economic Developments*, Washington, DC.

Jackson, Karl D. (editor) 1999, *The Asian Contagion: The Causes and Consequences of a Financial Crisis*, Westview Press.

Jamal, V., 1988, "African Crisis, Food Security and Structural Adjustment", *International Labour Review*, 127:6.

Jesperson, Eva, 1991, *External Shocks, Adjustment Policies and Economic and Social Performance*, UNICEF, New York.

Johnson, John H., 1993, *Borrower Ownership of Adjustment Programs and the Political Economy of Reform*, World Bank, Washington, DC.

Jolly, Richard, 1988, "Poverty and Adjustment in the 1990s", in Kallab and Feinberg (eds.), 1988, *Strengthening the Poor: What Have We Learnt*, Overseas Development Council, Transactions Books, New Brunswick, NJ.

Kanbur, Ravi, 1989, *Poverty and the Social Dimensions of Adjustment in Côte d'Ivoire*, World Bank, Washington, DC.

Kapeliouk, Amnon, 1993, "La détresse de la société russe", *Le Monde diploma-

tique, September.

Kaufman, Bruce E., 1989, *The Economics of Labor and Labor Markets*, second edition, Orlando.

Khan, Mohsin, 1990, *"The Macro-economic* Effects of Fund Supported-Adjustment Programs", *IMF Staff Papers*, Vol. 37, No. 2, Washington, DC.

Khor, Martin, 1995, "Baring and the Search for a Rogue Culprit", *Third World Economics*, No. 108, March 1995.

Khor, Martin, 1997, "SEA Currency Turmoil Renews Concern on Financial Speculation", *Third World Resurgence*, No. 86, October 1997.

Khor, Martin, 2000, "The New Frontier", *The Ecologist*, Vol. 30, No. 6.

Khor, Martin, 2000, *Rethinking globalization: critical issues and policy choices*, Zed Books, London, New York.

Khor, Martin, 2000, *Globalisation and the South: Some Critical Issues*, Third World Network, Penang, Malaysia.

Khor, Martin, 2002, *Intellectual Property, Biodiversity and Sustainable Development: Resolving the Difficult Issues*, Zed Books, London, Third World Network, Penang.

Killick, T. (editor), *Adjustment and Financing in the Developing World: the Role of the IMF*, IMF, Washington, DC.

Killick, T., 1993, *The Adaptive Economy, Adjustment Policies in Low Income Countries*, World Bank, Washington, DC.

Kisic, Drago and Veronica Ruiz de Castilla, 1989, "La Economia peruana en el contexto internacional", *CEPEI*, Vol. 2, No. 1, January.

Korten, David, 1999, *The Post Corporate World, Kumarian Press*, West Hartford, Connecticut.

Korten, David, 2001, *When Corporations Rule the World*, Kumarian Press, Inc. West Hartford, Connecticut, and Berrett-Koehler Publishers, Inc., San Francisco.

Krasner, Stephen D., 1985, *Structural Conflict: The Third World against Global Liberalism*, Berkeley, University of California Press.

Krueger, Ann, 1987, "Debt, Capital Flows and LDC Growth", *American Economic Review*, 77:2.

Krueger, Ann, *et al.*, 1990, "Developing Countries' Debt Problems and Efforts at Policy Reform", *Contemporary Policy Issues*, January.

Labour Focus on Eastern Europe , quarterly, Oxford.

Langoni, Carlos, 1987, *The Development Crisis*, International Center for Economic Growth, San Francisco.

Lee, Catherine, 1998, "The Wrong Medicine; Nationalization of Commercial Banks in South Korea", *The Banker*, December, 1998.

Lifschutz, Lawrence, 1979, *Bangladesh, the Unfinished Revolution*, Zed Press,

London.

Lopez Acuña, Daniel, et al., 1991, *Reforma del Estado y Desarrollo Social en America Latina*, PAHO/OPS, Washington, DC.

Lora, G., 1988, *Politica y burguesia narcotraficante*, Mi Kiosco, La Paz.

Loxley, John, 1986, *Debt and Disorder, External Financing for Development*, Westview Press.

Loxley, John, 1991, *Ghana's Recovery: An Assessment of Progress, 1987-1990*, The North-South Institute, Ottawa.

Madrid Declaration of Alternative Forum, 1994, *The Other Voices of the Planet*, Madrid.

Magdoff, Freed, John Bellamy Foster, and Frederick H. Buttel (editors), 2000 *Hungry for Profit, 2000, The Agribusiness Threat to Farmers, Food, and the Environment*, Monthly Review Press, New York.

Malpica, Carlos, 1989, *El poder economico en el Peru*, Vol. I, Mosca Azul Editores, Lima.

Manley, M. and W. Brandt, 1985, *Global Challenge, From Crisis to Cooperation*, Pan Books, London.

Martin, Hans-Peter and Schuman, Harald, 1997, *The Global Trap: Globalization and the Assault on Prosperity and Democracy*, Zed Books.

Martirena Mantel, A. M. (editor), 1987, *External Debt, Savings and Growth in Latin America*, International Monetary Fund-Instituto Torcuato di Tella, Buenos Aires.

Maya, R. S., 1988, *Structural Adjustment in Zimbabwe: Its Impact on Women*, Zimbabwe Institute of Development Studies, Harare.

McAfee, Kathy, 1991, *Storm Signals, Structural Adjustment and Development Alternatives in the Caribbean*, South End Press, Boston, Mass.

McGowan, David, *Derailing Democracy: The America the Media Don't Want You to See*, Common Courage.

McLaughlin, Martin, 1999, "Clinton Republicans agree to Deregulation of US Banking System", World Socialist website, http://www.wsws.org/index.shtml, 1 November 1999.

Mendosa, Teresa, Rebosio Guillermo, and Alvarado, Carmen, 1990, *Canasta optima alimentaria*, Centro de Estudios Nuevaa Economia y Sociedad, Lima.

Miller, M. 1989 *Resolving the Global Debt Crisis*, United Nations Development Programme, New York.

Morales, Juan Antonio, 1987, "Estabilisación y Nueva Politica Economica en Bolivia", *El Trimestre Economico*, Vol. 54.

Morales, Juan Antonio, 1989, *The Costs of the Bolivian Stabilisation Programme*, documento de trabajo, No. 01/89, Universidad Catolica Boliviana, La Paz.

Morales, Juan Antonio, 1990, *The Transition from Stabilisation to Sustained Growth in Bolivia*, paper presented at "Lessons of Economic Stabilisation and Its Aftermath", Bank of Israel and Interamerican Development Bank, Jerusalem, January-February 1990.

Moser, Caroline O. N., 1989, "The Impact of Recession and Structural Adjustment on Women: Ecuador", *Development*, No. 1.

Mosley, 1990, *Increased Aid Flows and Human Resource Development in Africa*, UNICEF, Florence.

Murray, C., 1987, "A Critical Review of International Mortality Data", *Soc. Scie. Med.*, Vol. 25, No. 7.

Nagaraj, K., *et al.*, 1991, "Starvation Deaths in Andhra Pradesh", *Frontline*, 6 December.

Nahimana, Ferdinand, 1993, *Le Rwanda, Emergence d'un État*, L'Harmattan, Paris.

Nelson, Joan M. (editor), 1990, *Economic Crisis and Policy Choice: The Politics of Adjustment in the Third World*, Princeton University Press.

Newbery, David, 1989, "The Debt Crisis", *Development*, No. 1.

North-South Institute, 1988, *Structural Adjustment in Africa: External Financing in Development*, Ottawa, The North-South Institute.

Nuqui, Wilfredo, 1991, *The Health Sector and Social Policy in the Philippines since 1985*, UNICEF, Florence.

Oyejide T. A., 1985, *Nigeria and the IMF*, Heinemann, Ibadan.

Panamerican Health Organization, 1990, *Development and Strengthening of Local Health Systems*, Washington, DC.

Panamerican Health Organization, 1991, *Health Conditions in the Americas*, Vol. 1, Washington, DC.

Pandhe, M. K., 1991, *Surrender of India's Sovereignty and Self-Reliance*, Progressive Printers, New Delhi.

Pastor, Manuel, 1987, "The effects of IMF programs in the Third World", *World Development*, 15:2.

Peet, Richard (editor), 1987, *International Capitalism and Industrial Restructuring*.

Pilger, John, 1998, *Hidden Agendas*, Vintage, London.

Pirages, Dennis C., 1990, *Transformations in the Global Economy*, London, Macmillan.

Polanyi-Levitt, Kari, 1989, *Some Reflections on the LDC Debt Crisis*, Department of Economics, McGill University, Working paper 2/89, Montreal.

Portes, Richard, 1990, "Development Versus Debt: Past and Future", *IDS Bulletin*, Vol. 23, No. 2.

Pronk, Jan, 1989, "Adjustment and Development: Bridging the Gap",

Development, No. 1.

République Rwandaise, Ministère des Finances et de l'Économie, 1987, *L'Économie rwandaise, 25 ans d'efforts* (1962-1987), Kigali.

Raghavan, Chakravarthi, 2000, *The WTO and its Dispute Settlement System: Tilting the Balance against the South*, Third World Network, Penang, Malaysia.

Raghavan, Chakravarthi, 2002, *Developing Countries and Services Trade: Chasing A Black Cat in a Dark Room*, Blindfolded, Third World Network, Penang, Malaysia.

Rhodes, W., 1990, "The Debt Problem at the Crossroads", *IDS Bulletin*, Vol. 23, No. 2.

Ribe, Helen *et al.*, 1989, *How Adjustment Programs can Help the Poor*, World Bank, Washington, DC.

Ritter A. and Pollock, D., 1985, *The Latin American Debt Crisis: Causes, Consequences and Prospects*, North-South Institute, Ottawa.

Rumiya, Jean, 1992 *Le Rwanda sous le régime du mandat belge (1916-1931)*, L'Harmattan, Paris.

Russell, Robert, 1990, "The New Roles and Facilities of the IMF", *IDS Bulletin*, Vol. 23, No. 2.

Sachs, Jeffrey (editor), 1989, *Developing Country Debt and the World Economy*, University of Chicago Press, Chicago.

Sandifor, Peter, et al, 1991, "Why do Child Mortality Rates Fall, An Analysis of the Nicaraguan Experience", *American Journal of Public Health*, Vol. 81, No. 1.

Schadler, Susan, *et al.*, 1993, *Economic Adjustment in Low Income Countries*, IMF, Washington, DC.

Seshamani, V., 1990, Towards Structural Transformation with a Human Focus, The Economic Programs and Policies of Zambia in the 1980s, UNICEF, Florence.

Singh, Kavaljit, 1998, Citizen's Guide to the Globalization of Finance, Madhyam Books, Delhi and Zed Books, London.

Smith, J. W., 2000, *Economic Democracy, the Struggle of the Twenty-first Century*, M. E. Sharpe, New York.

Sobhan, Rehman, 1991, *The Development of the Private Sector in Bangladesh: a Review of the Evolution and Outcome of State Policy*, Research report No. 124, Bangladesh Institute of Development Studies.

Socialist Republic of Vietnam, 1993. *Vietnam: A Development Perspective* (main document prepared for the Paris Donor Conference), Hanoi.

Shiva, Vandana, 2000, "The Threat to Third World Farmers", *The Ecologist*, Vol. 30, No. 6.

Shiva, Vandana, 2000, *Stolen Harvest, the Hijacking of the Global Food Supply*, South End Press, Cambridge Mass.

Shiva, Vandana, 1997, *Biopiracy, the Plunder of Nature and Knowledge*, South End Press, Cambridge, Mass.

David Squire, Lyn, 1991, "Introduction: Poverty and Adjustment in the 1980s", *The World Bank Economic Review*, Vol. 5, No. 2.

Standing Committee on External Affairs, 1990, *Securing Our Global Future: Canada's Unfinished Business of Third World Debt*, Ottawa: House of Commons.

Stiglitz, Joseph, 2002, *Globalization and Its Discontents*, W. W. Norton, New York.

Streeten, P., 1987, "Structural Adjustment: A Survey of the Issues and Options", *World Development*, 15:22, December.

Streeten, Paul, 2001, *Globalisation – Threat or Opportunity*, Copenhagen Business School Press, Copenhagen.

Suarez, Ruben, 1991, *Crisis, Ajuste y Programas de Compensación Social: Experiencias de los Fondos Sociales en Países de America Latina y el Caribe*, Organización Panamericana de la Salud, Washington, DC.

Thomas, Caroline and Peter Wilkin, 1999, Globalization, Human Security and the African Experience, Rienner, London.

Tarp, Finn, 1993, *Stabilisation and Structural Adjustment*, Routledge, London.

Third World Resurgence, monthly, Penang.

Third World Economics, monthly, Penang.

Tomann, H.,1988, "The Debt Crisis and Structural Adjustment in Developing Countries", *Intereconomic* 23:5.

UNICEF, 1989, "Revitalising Primary Health Care/Maternal and Child Health, the Bamako Initiative", report by the Executive Director, New York.

United Nations Conference on the Least Developed Countries, 1990, *Country Presentation by the Government of Rwanda*, Geneva.

United Nations Development Programme, *Human Development Report, annual*, New York.

United Nations Economic Commission for Africa, 1989, *African Alternative Framework to Structural Adjustment Programs for Socio-Economic Recovery and Transformation*, ECA, Addis Ababa.

UNICEF, 1991a, *The State of the World's Children*, 1991, New York.

UNICEF, 1991b, The Bamako Initiative, Progress Report and Recommendation Submitted to Executive Board, 1991 Session, New York.

United States Agency for International Development (USAID), 1993, "Mission to Ethiopia, Concept Paper: Back to The Future", Washington, DC.

Vietnam Ministry of Education, UNDP, UNESCO (National Project Education Sector Review and Human Resources Sector Analysis), 1992, *Vietnam Education and Human Resources Analysis*, Vol. 1, Hanoi.

Wagao, Jumanne H., 1990, *Adjustment Policies in Tanzania, 1981-1989, the Impact on Growth, Structure and Human Welfare*, UNICEF, Florence.

Wallach, Lori, et al., 1999, *Whose Trade Organization?: Corporate Globalization and the Erosion of Democracy*, Public Citizen Inc.

Wallach, Lori, *et al.*, 2000, *The WTO: Five Years of Reasons to Resist Corporate Globalization*, Open Media Pamphlet Series, Seven Stories Press.

Watkins, Kevin, 1997, *Globalisation and Liberalization: Implications for Poverty, Distribution and Inequality*, United Nations Develop Program, Occasional Paper 32.

Weisner, W., "Domestic and External Causes of the Latin American Debt Crisis", *Finance and Development*, 22:1, March 1985.

Williams, Maurice, 1989, "Note on the Structural Adjustment Debate in Africa", and "Options for Relieving Debt of Low Income Countries", *Development*, No. 1.

Williamson, John (editor), 1984, *IMF Conditionality*, Institute for International Economics.

Williamson, John, 1990, "The Debt Crisis at the Turn of the Century", *IDS Bulletin*, Vol. 23, No. 2.

World Bank, *annual, World Debt Tables*, annual, Washington DC.

World Bank, annual, *World Development Report*, Washington DC, Oxford University Press.

World Bank, 1983, Yugoslavia: *Adjustment Policies and Development Perspectives*, Washington, DC.

World Bank, 1989, *Peru, Policies to Stop Hyperinflation and Initiate Economic Recovery*, Washington, DC.

World Bank, 1989, *Adjustment Lending, An Evaluation of Ten Years of Experience*, Washington, DC.

World Bank, 1989, *Sub-Saharan Africa, From Crisis to Sustainable Growth*, Washington, DC.

World Bank and UNDP, 1989, *Africa's Adjustment and Growth in the 1980s*, Washington, DC.

World Bank, 1990, *Social Dimensions of Adjustment Priority Survey*, SDA Working Paper No: 12, Washington, DC.

World Bank, 1990, *Assistance Strategies to Reduce Poverty*, Washington, DC.

World Bank, 1990, *Making Adjustment Work for the Poor*, Washington, DC.

World Bank, 1990, *Analysis Plans for Understanding the Social Dimensions of Adjustment*, Washington DC.

World Bank, 1991, *The Poverty Handbook*, discussion draft, Washington, DC.

World Bank, 1991, *Human Development, A Bank Strategy for the 1990s*, Washington, DC.

World Bank, 1993, *Viet Nam, Transition to Market Economy*, Washington, DC.

World Bank, 1993, *Vietnam, Population, Health and Nutrition Review*, Washington, DC.

World Bank 1994, *Adjustment in Africa*, Washington DC, Oxford University Press.

World Bank, 1995, *Toward Gender Equality: The Role of Public Policy'* , United Nations Fourth Conference on Women, Beijing.

World Bank, 1995 *Advanced Gender Equality: From Concept to Action:* United Nations Fourth Conference on Women, Beijing.

World Bank, 1995 *The Gender Issue as Key to Development*, Washington, DC., Document HCO,95/01.

World Bank, 1995, *Letting Girls Learn*, World Bank Discussion Paper Series, Washington, DC.

World Bank, 2000, Heavily Indebted Poor Countries Initiative, http://www1.worldbank.org/prsp/PRSP_Policy_Papers/prsp_policy_papers.html. Washington, DC.

World Bank, 2000, Poverty Reduction Strategy Papers, http://www1.worldbank.org/prsp/PRSP_Policy_Papers/prsp_policy_papers.html, Washington, DC.

Yoder, R. A., "Are People Willing and Able to Pay for Health Services", *Social Science and Medicine*, Vol. 29.

Zuckerman, Elaine, 1989, *Adjustment Programs and Social Welfare*, World Bank discussion paper No. 44, Washington, DC.

INDEX

Agriculture   24, 43, 46, 49, 53, 56, 90, 95-100, 104, 107, 110, 126, 162, 163, 165,
        175, 183, 188, 203, 213, 222, 224, 226, 231, 233, 244, 250, 280, 288, 289,
        291, 294, 359
African National Congress   125
Agro-Business   126, 128, 139, 141, 168, 180, 202, 289
Andhra Pradesh   153
Angola   125, 128
Anti-export bias   54
Asian Development Bank (ADB)   176
Asian Tigers   2, 324, 359
Assam   115
Australia   97, 323

Bahamas   303
Balance-of-payments   150, 176
Bamako Proposal   51
Bangladesh   7, 81, 82, 84, 159-165, 179
Bank for International Settlements   319
Bank secrecy   233
Banking   7, 11, 43, 54, 56, 57, 82, 150, 154, 161, 171, 182, 190, 207, 211, 219, 222,
        225, 232, 233, 243, 246, 262, 263, 268, 270, 274, 280, 281, 306, 309, 316-
        318, 322, 326, 327, 335, 338, 340-342, 347, 351
Bankreptcy,   2, 6, 8, 9, 26, 42, 53, 70, 75, 108, 129, 150, 152, 162, 167, 171, 173,
        174, 177, 187, 221, 231, 239, 241, 244, 249, 252, 262-265, 267, 268, 282,
        284, 288, 290, 301, 303, 309-311, 318, 322, 323, 338, 339, 344, 348, 351
Banzer, Hugo   234
Barre, Siyad   98
Belaunde Terry, Fernando   210
Bilateral loans   105
Black money   57
Bolivia   20, 58, 222, 223, 229-231, 233, 240
Berisha, Sali   280, 281
Brady, Nicholas   195, 306
Brazil   1, 24, 44, 55, 69, 79, 191-202, 232, 318, 347-352
Bretton Woods agreement   19
Bretton Woods institutions   5, 10, 18, 28, 34, 42-44, 47, 51, 72, 54, 58, 60, 68, 70,
        97, 99, 108, 109, 116, 139, 159, 162, 163, 167-169, 175, 201, 209, 210,

229, 258, 268, 279-281, 283, 287, 290, 294, 295, 296, 305, 318, 321
Budget deficit   45, 47, 51, 54, 97, 175, 193, 196, 302, 303, 327
Bulgaria   2
Bush, George H.W.   224, 261, 340

Cali cartel   223
Calliari, Alcyr   201
Camdessus, Michel   46, 123,157, 193-195, 196, 198, 215, 248, 249, 253, 326, 332,
        333, 336, 354
Canada   31, 33, 74, 76, 77, 113, 302, 323
Capital flight   57, 191, 212, 243, 327, 349-351
Cardoso, Fernando Henrique   197, 200, 203, 346
Caribbean   28, 90, 303, 363, 339
Caste exploitation   154
Cayman Islands   303, 306
Central Intelligence Agency (CIA)   148, 225
Chaebols   338, 342-344
Channel Islands   303
Cheap labour   2, 6, 8, 9, 69, 79, 90, 179, 192, 205, 218, 288, 345
Chiapas region   19
China   2, 10, 12, 21, 23, 29, 69, 73, 23, 79, 80, 113, 168, 178, 227, 259, 328,
Chissano, Joaquim   230
Cholera   2, 17, 62, 216, 291
Civil war   95, 98, 99, 105, 108-118, 120, 132, 138, 168, 257, 267
Climatic conditions   100, 156, 163, 165
Clinton, William   118, 248-250, 316
Coca production/cultivation   223, 224, 233, 357
Coffee production   108, 109
Cold War   1, 17, 23, 24, 38, 139, 239, 242, 315, 322
Colombia   5, 30, 32, 112, 195, 222, 289
Colombian drug cartels   222
Colonialism   20, 4
Commercial banks   56, 131, 191, 193-196, 204, 208, 212, 214, 230, 232, 233, 242,
        243, 246, 251, 254, 263, 302, 303, 315, 316, 318, 325, 340, 346, 362
Conditionalities   24, 35, 42, 43, 47, 58, 66, 105, 106, 114, 157, 224, 225, 250, 285
Congress Party   155
Consumer markets   75, 78
Consumption   18, 23, 70, 75, 77, 78, 96, 98, 100, 101, 107, 137, 138, 150, 154, 184,
        185, 209, 213, 225, 243
Cost Recovery   51, 58, 61-64, 67, 181, 184, 185, 200, 214, 291
Criminal   4, 5, 25, 57, 187, 241, 271, 279, 280, 291, 293-295, 298, 303, 309, 319
Croatia   112, 261, 263, 264, 266-270, 276
Crvenkovski, Branko   268
Currencies   2, 17, 47, 247, 305, 314, 322, 323, 325, 349, 352
Currency markets   309, 310, 323
Czech Republic   75

Dauster, Jorio   193, 194
Dayton agreement   xxiv, 257, 258, 267-271
Debt conversion   302
Debt crisis   1, 26, 42, 51, 59, 77, 107, 144, 159, 209, 345, 357, 359, 363, 364, 365,
      366, 367
Debt rescheduling   42, 99, 267, 268
Debt servicing   37, 42, 45, 51, 56, 57, 99, 107, 110, 141, 150, 177, 192, 193, 195,
      196, 198, 261, 348
Democracy   103, 105, 111, 126, 160, 191, 192, 202, 219, 233, 234, 240, 241, 243,
      251, 259, 271, 280, 281, 305, 306, 358, 359, 363, 365, 367
Devaluation   8, 18, 21, 30, 47-50, 52, 53, 56, 66, 96, 107, 108, 110, 122, 153, 154,
      160, 165, 169, 178, 187, 192, 208, 214, 223, 260, 290, 322, 325, 338, 339,
      348-350
Development Programme   29, 32, 131, 135, 290, 357, 363, 366
Dirty money   6, 11, 57, 225, 232, 233, 273, 280, 281, 285, 291, 293-295, 328
Distribution of income   23, 212
Divestiture   55, 56, 57, 66, 98, 175, 262
Dollarization   23, 48-50, 56, 169, 213, 230, 266, 352
Downsizing   4, 6, 8, 27, 65, 116, 172
Drought   95, 96, 99, 100, 137, 139, 181, 202
Duong, Vanh Minh   168, 172

Eastern Europe   2-4, 6, 9, 17, 22-24, 69-75, 77, 78, 91, 109, 149, 171, 254, 260,
      263, 273, 275, 301, 302, 317, 318, 331, 362
Education   17, 23, 29, 30, 44, 61-63, 66-68, 97, 108, 111, 175, 182-184, 188, 197,
      199, 202, 220, 231, 241, 249, 291, 302, 327, 366
Environment   1, 4, 5, 17, 18, 24, 28, 45, 60, 61, 70, 97, 99, 101, 103, 130, 168, 174,
      192, 227, 271, 272, 280, 283, 295, 329, 351, 352, 363
Ershad, Hussein Mahommed   160, 161
Ethiopia   26, 137-144, 359, 366
Europe   1-4, 6, 7, 10, 17, 22, 23, 24, 30, 31, 33, 37, 53, 69-78, 81, 82, 92, 97, 99,
      109, 110, 113, 126, 131, 141, 258-260, 263, 268, 270, 273-275, 279, 280,
      281, 286, 288, 291, 295-297, 301, 302, 304, 305, 362, 363, 316, 317, 331,
      337, 343, 361, 362
European Community, European Union   97, 110, 243, 259, 279, 253
Exchange rate/s   17, 45, 47, 48, 187, 193, 212-214, 225, 229, 230, 254, 309, 325,
      350

Famines   1, 17, 99, 100, 107, 144, 154, 169, 170, 178, 179, 182
Fajgenbaum, José   194, 195, 197
Farias, P.C.   191
Federal Reserve Board   310, 315-317
Financial markets   7, 11, 302, 309, 310, 312, 315, 321, 327, 348, 313
Food aid   96, 97, 99, 101, 106, 109, 142, 144, 162, 202, 232, 250, 288, 360
Food and Agriculture Organization   138, 144, 359
Franco, Itamar   44, 193, 196, 197, 201, 254, 347, 351, 354

Free trade   10, 11, 13, 31, 69, 70, 74, 76, 77, 133, 352
Free trade zones   70
Fuel   21, 48, 49, 53, 54, 62, 96, 104, 106, 108, 114, 118, 152, 168, 176, 177, 192,
          207, 221, 222, 261, 264, 268, 283, 285, 293, 348, 208
Fujimori, Alberto   21, 207, 215
Fyodorov, Boris   249, 250, 253

G7   20, 27, 33, 194, 248-250, 252, 253, 314, 324, 326, 327, 337, 349, 350
Gaidar, Yegor   247, 253
Gandhi, Mahatma   155
Gandhi, Rajiv   149
Garcia, Alan   207, 210, 212
Garment industry   8, 81, 92, 151, 164, 293
General Agreement on Tariffs and Trade (GATT)   56, 150
General Agreement on Trade in Services (GATS)   317
Gender   28, 65-68
Gerashchenko, V   247, 249
Glass-Stegall   316, 318
Governance   11, 19, 54, 58, 105, 161, 248, 270
Greenspan, Alan   310, 314

Habyarimana, Jouvenal   110, 113-115, 118-120, 124
Haddad, Paulo   196
Haile Mariam, Mengisto   138
Health   xxv, 2, 17, 30, 31, 45, 51, 58, 61, 62, 67, 97, 108, 111, 116, 165, 175, 185,
          186, 197, 216, 231, 241, 291, 341, 251
High technology   79, 239
High-tech economy   245
Hong Kong   71, 92, 173, 176, 180, 311, 312, 315, 318, 319, 328
Hot money   56, 233, 311, 328
Hoxha, Enver   279, 280
Human face   28, 63, 358, 360
Hungary   75, 78

Institutional speculators   310, 314, 322, 324, 338
International Monetary Fund (IMF)   296, 346
India   21, 29, 30, 53, 63, 132, 149, 150, 151, 153-157, 364
Indonesia   2, 314, 322-324, 348
Industrial Delocation   74
Industry - (see also manufacturing)   8, 45, 53, 54, 56, 69, 70, 72-76, 79, 81, 90-92,
          118, 132, 142, 145, 150, 151, 162-164, 172-230, 244-247, 249, 262, 265,
          264, 280, 286, 287, 289, 291, 293, 303, 316, 323, 338, 339, 341, 342, 351,
          353
Infectious diseases   17, 13, 167, 186, 291
Inflation   2, 3, 47, 48, 60, 108, 118, 123, 131, 150, 151, 169, 181, 192, 193, 197,
          199, 207-210, 212-216, 229, 261, 305
Informal sector   8, 21, 53, 356

Inter-american Development Bank   194, 361
International Coffee Agreement (ICA)   103
International Financial Institutions (IFIS)   19, 42, 196, 219
International Labor Organization   6, 13, 25, 101
International Rice Research Institure (IRRI)   181

Japan's Overseas Economic Cooperation Fund   176
Jordan   24, 32
Jute industry   51, 62

Kagame, Paul   111, 115, 117, 119, 120
Kashmir   155
Kim,Dae-jung   334, 335, 336, 343
Korea (South)   2, 69, 79, 92, 176, 318, 322, 324, 331-335, 337, 338-346, 348, 362
Kosovo   112, 264, 270-272, 273, 276, 292, 293
Kosyrev, Andrei   249
Kucan, Milan   267

Labour markets   6, 33, 76, 82, 90, 362
Land   54-57, 100, 101, 106, 108, 111, 125-131, 133, 134, 137, 141-144, 163, 181-
           183, 202, 203, 221, 222, 224, 231, 293
Land tenure   55
Landless farm workers   151, 152, 202
Latin America   1, 4, 28, 31, 37, 62, 69, 73, 74, 78, 149, 207, 218, 210, 254, 309,
           317, 318, 323, 352, 359, 361, 363, 365, 367, 373
Laundering   4, 11, 57, 141, 21, 227, 232, 233, 243, 273, 309
Letter of Intent   44-46, 123, 195, 198, 204, 268, 333, 344, 346, 354
Livestock   95-97, 99, 101
Llosa, Mario Vargas   215, 216
Loan agreements   24, 35, 42-45, 51, 58, 66, 149, 156, 175, 208
London Club/s   20, 43, 54, 249, 251, 261, 253
Long-term debt   37
Losada, Gonzalez Sanchez de   229, 234, 235
Luxembourg   303

Maastricht Treaty   9, 76, 304
Macedonia   264, 267-269, 276, 291-293
Macro-economic policy   9, 20, 35, 44, 47, 62, 72, 99, 160, 165, 167, 187, 200, 209,
           218, 224, 241, 243, 244, 246, 280, 281, 296
Mafias   239, 243, 245, 280, 291-293, 309
Malaria   17, 62, 63, 108, 167, 186, 216
Mandela, Nelson   125, 126, 128
Manufacturing   8, 24, 54, 69-72, 74-76, 78, 79, 85, 90-92, 150, 164, 173, 176, 177,
           200, 230, 231, 233, 294, 339, 348
Maquilas   74
Markovic, Ante   260, 261, 267, 275
Medellin cartel   222, 223

Mello, Fernando Collor de   44, 191, 200, 203
Mello, Zelia Cardoso de   192-195
Mexico   19, 20, 30-32, 69, 73, 76, 77, 79, 90, 358
Miller, Juan Hurtado   207, 363
Military   10-12, 19, 21, 92, 97, 104, 105, 109, 111-114, 116-123, 128, 138, 139,
         159-161, 170, 172, 191, 192, 200, 203, 208, 219-221, 223, 225, 227, 234,
         239, 245, 246, 252, 258, 262, 269-272, 274, 282, 315, 331, 334, 343, 345
Military Professional Resources inc.   112
Milosevic, Llobodan   257, 266
Monetarism   18
Monetary policy   19, 26, 50, 52, 59, 160, 197, 231, 235, 255, 258, 266, 275, 294,
         315, 334, 335, 347, 361
Money, supply of   50, 51
Monopolies   9, 80, 151, 119, 222
Montenegro   276, 291
Morales Bermudez, Francisco   208
Moreira, Marcilio Marques   191, 192, 195, 196, 198, 203
Morocco   19
Mozambique   127, 129-135, 137, 138
Mujib, Sheik   159, 160
Multilateral   10, 26, 44, 46, 54, 110, 115, 121, 176, 183, 197, 201, 218, 293, 295,
         340, 342
Multinational   5, 9, 13, 20, 24-26, 52, 84, 137, 151, 162, 258, 270, 271, 326, 348
Musaveni, Yomeri   111-113

North American Free Trade Agreement (NAFTA)   74, 77, 78, 92, 343
Nagaland   154
Narco-dollars   226, 232, 240, 242, 282
Narco-economy   225, 227, 229, 230, 240, 242
Neoliberal   3, 5, 11, 27, 28, 214, 215, 241, 273, 283, 305, 306, 327
New deal   316
New world order   2, 4, 9, 18, 20, 75, 310, 311
Nguyen, Xian Oanh   177, 196
Nigeria   19, 21, 32

Organisation for Economic Cooperation and Development (OECD)   22, 23, 33, 71,
         79, 80, 154, 214, 331
Offshore bank/banking   7, 11, 57, 212, 244, 254, 281, 304, 309, 312, 331
Organized crime   4, 243, 271, 273, 281, 291, 292

Pakistan   155, 318
Paris Club   56, 98, 120, 132, 140, 145, 176, 184, 204, 263, 264, 267,
Planinc, Milka   260
Paz Estenssoro, Victor   229, 235
Pension plan   195, 199
Perez, Carlos Andres   19
Peru   21, 31, 207, 208, 212, 215, 216, 218, 219, 222, 223, 225, 226, 231, 232, 234,
         310, 312, 358, 362, 368

Philippines   32, 75, 92, 314, 365
Pinochet, Augusto   xxi, 200, 208
Plant closures   4, 75, 76, 79, 246, 271
Pol Pot   135, 171
Poland   76, 77, 79, 221
Policy Framework Paper   46, 47, 141
Price liberalization   47, 159, 240
Privatization   xxii, xxv, 2, 19, 27, 45, 54-57, 61, 96, 107, 110, 114, 139, 140, 193,
            195, 199, 200, 221, 243, 246, 251, 262, 283, 285-287, 293, 302, 315, 318,
            324, 340, 342
Public expenditure   3, 45, 51, 63, 107, 113, 161, 175, 195, 261
Public Expenditure Review (PER)   45, 51, 113
Public utilities   53, 56, 129, 141, 199, 274, 287, 289
Punjab   155, 162

Quick disbursing loans   43, 54, 109, 176, 264, 375

Rahman, Mujibur   160, 166
Rahman, Ziaur   160, 166
Rao, P.V. Narasimha   149, 193
Reagan, Ronald   3, 259, 260, 303, 306, 311
Relocation   6, 69, 72, 74-77, 90, 91, 301
Research and Development   78
Resende, Eliseu   197
Rhodes, William   198, 347, 365
Roosevelt, Franklin   316
Russian Federation   20, 24, 239, 252, 255
Rwandan   103, 105-112, 116-119, 124

Sachs, Jeffrey   240, 305, 306, 323-325, 337, 342, 347, 365
Sahelian belt   99
Saudi Arabia   97
Serbia   358, 264-266, 272, 276, 291, 294
Shock treatment   208, 210, 214, 216, 221, 239, 282, 208, 210
Singapore   69, 92, 187
Singh, Manmohan   152, 157
Singh, V.P.   149
Slovakia   75
Slovenia   261, 263, 265, 266, 267, 276
Social dimensions of adjustment   360, 361, 367
Social safety net   3, 58, 66, 108, 111, 150, 200, 202, 288
Social sectors/programmes   51, 58, 59, 62, 63, 108, 111, 186, 202, 355
Somalia   95, 96-99, 101, 140, 355, 360, 361
Soros, George   268, 272, 273, 347, 351, 353, 354
South-East Asia   183
Soviet Union   1, 2, 9, 17, 21, 23, 24, 78, 242, 245, 246, 254, 263, 273, 322, 355
Souza, Herbert de   201

Speculation 213, 314, 319, 362
Sub-Saharan Africa 1, 8, 9, 21, 22, 26, 30, 31, 48, 53, 61, 62, 67, 73, 97, 99, 101, 102, 106, 121, 137, 144, 240, 250, 254, 355, 358, 367
Subsidies 53, 62, 66, 107, 139, 140, 150, 152, 153, 161, 172, 174, 178, 212, 213, 226, 248, 249, 303, 304
Subsistence agriculture 126, 222
Sweden 272, 302, 306
Switzerland 7, 303
Syria 24

Taiwan 71, 92, 178, 180
Tamil Nadu 149, 152, 157
Targeting 51, 201
Tariffs 54, 222, 229, 230
Tax reform 54, 55, 213
Thailand 2, 30, 34, 75, 81, 314, 322, 324, 348
Tito, B 260
Trade liberalization 19, 24, 54, 66, 107, 139, 150, 193, 230, 351
Transportation 2, 45, 53, 79, 139, 222, 254, 259, 292, 294
Tripura 152
Tudjman, franjo 257, 266, 267
Tunis 19
Tunisia 13, 24

Uganda 108, 111-113, 117, 119, 121, 123, 137
Unemployment 1, 3, 4, 6, 18, 30, 73-75, 179, 192, 252, 264, 268, 279, 282, 302, 318, 322, 337, 348, 351
Uruguay Round 24, 25, 56, 60, 70
United States (US) 3, 5, 13, 18, 28, 30, 31, 33, 81, 113, 117, 127, 144, 159, 169, 183, 194, 201, 223, 225, 227, 244, 267, 288, 305, 326, 366
User fees 20, 53, 61, 62, 66, 67, 96, 111, 185, 186, 241

Velasco, Alvarado 208, 209
Veterinarian services 96, 97
Vietnam 21, 44, 81, 166-180, 182, 183, 185-187, 365, 366, 368
Viljoen, Constand 125, 126, 131, 134
Vo, Van Kiet 170
Vulnerable groups 51, 68, 150

Wagel, Theo 249
Wages xxi, 2, 6, 8, 9, 18, 23, 40, 50-52, 69-84, 90-92, 98, 116, 118, 131, 139, 152, 162, 164, 176, 182, 193, 197, 199, 208, 212, 214, 216, 231, 241, 252, 261, 264, 290, 336, 351
Wall Street 5, 7, 11, 13, 255, 302, 305, 306, 309-318, 324, 325, 327, 329, 332, 334-336, 338-341, 344, 348, 350-353, 358, 359
Washington Consensus 32, 194, 216
Welfare state 3, 11, 18, 241, 260, 301, 302, 359
Wolfensohn, James 305
Women 1, 18, 19, 28, 61, 65-68, 152, 181, 293, 298, 357, 359, 363, 364, 368

Women's rights   65-67
World Bank   xxii, 2, 4, 8, 17, 18, 20, 24, 28-32, 45-47, 51-63, 65, 66, 95, 96, 100,
        103, 107, 110, 113-116, 127, 128, 137, 144, 149, 150, 156, 159-161, 177,
        179, 181, 186, 201, 218, 240, 241, 261, 263, 264, 280, 284
World Trade Organisation (WTO)   10, 11, 24, 70, 126, 306, 315, 317

Yeltsin, Boris   240-243, 248-250, 253
Yugoslav Federation   199
Yugoslavia   17, 257-259, 261, 262, 264, 266-268, 270, 271-276, 282, 367

Zaïr, République du   117
Zia, Khaleda   160, 161, 165
Zimbabwe   32, 100, 140, 287, 356, 363

AGMV Marquis
MEMBER OF SCABRINI MEDIA
Quebec, Canada
2004